I0729662

Transfixed by Prehistory

Transfixed by Prehistory

An Inquiry into Modern Art and Time

Maria Stavrinaki

Translated by Jane Marie Todd

ZONE BOOKS · NEW YORK

2022

© 2022 Urzone, Inc.

ZONE BOOKS

633 Vanderbilt Street

Brooklyn, NY 11218

Printed in the United States of America.

Distributed by Princeton University Press,
Princeton, New Jersey, and Woodstock, United Kingdom

Originally published in France as Maria Stavrinaki, *Saisis par la préhistoire: Enquête sur l'art le temps des modernes* © 2019 by Les presses du réel.

Cet ouvrage a bénéficié du soutien des Programmes d'aide à la publication de l'Institut français.

Library of Congress Cataloging-in-Publication Data
Names: Stavrinaki, Maria, author. | Todd, Jane Marie, translator. |
       Stavrinaki, Maria. Saisis par la préhistoire.
Title: Transfixed by prehistory : An Inquiry into
       Modern Art and Time/ Maria Stavrinaki ; translated by Jane Marie Todd.
Other titles: Saisis par la préhistoire. English
Description: New York : Zone Books, 2022. | Includes bibliographical references
       and index. | Summary: "An examination of how modern art was impacted
       by the concept of prehistory and the prehistoric" — Provided by publisher.
Identifiers: LCCN 2021027385 (print) | LCCN 2021027386 (ebook) |
       ISBN 9781942130659 (hardcover) | ISBN 9781942130666 (ebook)
Subjects: LCSH: Time — Philosophy. | Time and art.
Classification: LCC Q175.32.T56 S7313 2022 (print) | LCC Q175.32.T56 (ebook) |
       DDC 115 — dc23
LC record available at https://lccn.loc.gov/2021027385
LC ebook record available at https://lccn.loc.gov/2021027386

Arrived in the dark. The dark takes us back to the foundation, the origin. The base of deep feelings. From the dark comes the unexplained, the undetailed, the unattached to visible causes, the surprise attack, mystery, the religious, fear . . . and monsters, who emerge from nothingness, not from a mother.

> —Henri Michaux, *Emergences-Ressurgences* (1972)

Contents

Introduction

Prehistory is an invention of the nineteenth century. In a century famous for its technological daring and accelerated pace, three major narratives of Western thought, one after another, delved into a previously unsuspected past. They concerned the age of the earth, the age of the human species, and the age of art. This does not mean that before the nineteenth century, and despite the biblical account attributing only a few thousand years of existence to the earth, no one had had the intuition, if not the certainty, that the earth's age was unfathomable. In modern times, when it had become urgent to extract from nature its every secret, a few curious minds were astonished to discover mineral formations that resembled living things, fossils of totally unknown creatures.[1] Later on, the physics experiments Buffon conducted in his forge led him to believe that the time necessary for metals to condense could not have been prodigiously shorter back when the earth formed within the cosmos. As he commented in his notebooks, "the more we extend time, the more we will approach the truth and reality of the use nature makes of it." But he added that he was determined to "abridge it as much as possible to conform to the limited power of our intelligence."[2] That limited power — which the skeptical philosophers had also encountered — was the result more particularly of a culturally determined transcendental order: eighteenth-century natural history had to accommodate itself to the creation story found in scripture. Granted, this was becoming less of an obstacle, and when it finally disappeared, a remarkable reversal could come about. The nineteenth century not only acknowledged the incalculable age of the earth; surreptitiously, by means of a new metaphysics, it was able to use that idea to fill the place left vacant by God. Henceforth, the "limited power" of human intelligence took on the task of grasping that incalculable age, inventing metaphors and analogies, seeking figures that could make the dissimilar similar and the alien familiar. Our species now took the measure of this new infinity and the endless procession of animal species it revealed.

The abyss opened by the new age attributed to the earth soon opened up in Western man himself. Human beings began to internalize the vastness of long-term natural processes, following three different, but nearly contemporaneous and complementary, paths. First, they undertook a search for human fossils in the geological strata, where fossils of extinct mammals had been found; second, they began to see contemporary man himself as a potential fossil; and finally, in granting the human species a specific and limited place within a larger geological and paleontological narrative, they used figures and concepts from this narrative to understand themselves. Concepts such as strata and fossils, thus metaphorized, would make man intelligible to himself not only within the long biological and cultural evolution of his species, but also as a singular individual, a knowing and sentient being. But the invention of metaphors, which had first served to domesticate the alterity and infiniteness of geology, turned back on its inventor and led to the *ensauvagement*, the "becoming wild," of man himself.

The term "prehistory" (or rather, the adjectival form "prehistoric") was coined by a few Scandinavian archaeologists in the 1830s to describe both the human era before history and the discipline that studied it.[3] The term quickly migrated to the human sciences — linguistics, ethnology, folklore, and psychology — to explain the Indo-European root of a word, the "survival" of a gesture or technique, a dying or vanished race, even the unconscious. Gradually, especially from the 1870s on, as this metaphor acquired the function of a floating signifier, the imaginary of prehistory, accumulating both human and nonhuman representations, also began to inhabit the imaginary of artists, Odilon Redon and Paul Cézanne, for example. The definitive evidence of fossil man was discovered in 1859, but earlier finds had also gradually shifted the ground of knowledge — like any discovery that shakes a belief to its very foundations — abolishing forever the hermetic separation between the earth's history and human history. This was certainly one of the key founding acts of the strange "empirico-transcendental doublet"[4] to which Michel Foucault refers in *The Order of Things*, signifying by that expression the specificity of the modern episteme. The prehistoric traces of human life turned it into an empirical object to be analyzed by a knowing, historically determined subject. But that split between subject and object, that twisting back upon oneself, led to a void and oblivion. When people ceased to look toward the sky and instead looked *into* the earth, what they found there were vestiges of previous human lives that had been totally forgotten. The abyss of time was no longer outside man — it opened up within his own memory. The hypotheses about these forgotten lives, whether they provided material for the fable of endless progress or instead revealed all the doubts and anxiety of the contemporary world, shaped the discourses and works of moderns, who constantly reflected on their own condition.

In 1860, scarcely a year after the discovery that attested to the antiquity of human beings, Édouard Lartet, a geologist who had gone in search of fossils in a few caves, became the "inventor," in spite of himself, of the earliest symbolic artifacts of prehistory. As Kant points out, there is a distinction to be made between a *discovery* and an *invention*. On one hand, in his example, America, unknown to Europeans before Columbus made landfall there, is a discovery. Similarly, prehistory in its actual materiality (its geological strata, its plant, animal, and human fossils and later symbolic artifacts) can said to have been discovered. On the other hand, the "exemplary originality" of invention lies, again according to Kant, in the perfect coincidence between objectivity and subjectivity.[5] Prehistory, as an "idea" that interprets, names, and renames the strata, fossils, and artifacts found, to the point of shaking Western man's ontological and gnoseological foundations, is thus an invention through and through. The invention of engraved Paleolithic works was so stupefying that it has very often gone unnoticed even to our own time. Édouard Lartet barely admitted it to himself: when he published the findings of his excavation, he mentioned these artifacts, but he did so with the same axiomatic neutrality with which he described mandibles.[6] He even provided drawings of the works he found, but only at the very end of his article, after depicting a cross section of the cave, the fossils, and the tools. His colleagues did not highlight his "invention" either, nor have our contemporaries done so. With a few exceptions, they, too, give 1864 as the date of the discovery of Paleolithic mobiliary art.[7] In actuality, 1864 is a "screen memory": it was in that year that Lartet and Henri Christy jointly published a famous article on a similar discovery of engraved objects from the Paleolithic, this time fully acknowledging and interpreting them.[8] What were the reasons for a repression so radical that its effects can still be felt in our own time?

Art, customarily contemplated from a standing position, suddenly extended out horizontally, mixed with the bones of extinct animals and mute minerals. The taxonomy of the world was shattered by that unexpected contiguity of the symbolic and the geological: human fossils mingled with those of vanished animals, thrown together with microscopic objects, often very skillfully engraved. Yet the subjectivity to which these engravings bore witness was not congruent with the normative narratives about art or with prevailing ideas about the earliest human beings. The discovery of "fossil man" drew modern man closer to the animality of natural history, and the axes exhumed from the quarries of Saint-Acheul brought to mind, at best, only the crude gestures of the first creatures. But the discovery of an imitative art more ancient than antiquity pulled in the opposite direction. No existing periodization could accommodate that art, dating to indeterminate eras, marked by the presence of extinct mammals or by an imperceptible evolution in the size and sharpness of "a few pitiful stones."[9] Doctrines about the chronology of art collapsed, as did those about its spatial and racial provenance. It was not the Orient or Egypt, even less Greece, that had given birth to Paleolithic art, then buried and forgotten it. The prehistorian John Lubbock immediately amended the famous expression *ex oriente lux* ("out of the East, light") that had soothed the Romantics, adding this concise sentence: "Suddenly a new light has arisen in the midst of us."[10] The fact that this art was discovered in the very heart of progressive Europe increased the stupor it caused while enhancing the power of its later appropriation.

In fact, if the discovery of parietal art — cave art — had not followed shortly thereafter, Paleolithic mobiliary art, the art present in small artifacts, might have long remained out of sight and outside time, in a sort of Arcadia where art was supposedly practiced as instinctively as hunting. That was, in brief, the interpretation Lartet and Christy gave of these objects, still repressing their stupefying aspect. Ultimately, there was no reason to be surprised by them, since they merely attested to the natural spontaneity of their creators, who expressed automatically what they saw before them. Clearly, stupor was now neutralized not through the rhetoric of description, but through interpretation. But this interpretation could hardly be applied to the decorated Cave of Altamira, discovered near Santander in 1879 by an amateur prehistorian named Marcelino de Sautuola. His publication the next year was met with nothing but incredulity and roused keen opposition among professional prehistorians.[11]

This was not, of course, the first time in the modern era that what was discovered under the earth's soil caused a shock. But it was without a doubt the very first time that such a discovery left people incredulous and at a loss, with no interpretive tools. At the very end of the fifteenth century, when Romans discovered the "grotesques," mural paintings in the underground rooms of Nero's Domus Aurea, they were certainly struck by the hybrid creatures who defied both the laws of physics and those of narrative. Nonetheless, certain canonical texts of antiquity soon provided the keys for identifying these "licentious" paintings, which, as Vitruvius wrote, delighted in representing things that "do not exist, cannot exist, and have never existed."[12] Also, the historian Leonard Barkan wondered why the Renaissance humanists, despite their passion for ancient sculpture, undertook their excavations at random, rather than systematically, even as they set up niches to display objects that had not yet been found. Among the possible reasons, Barkan mentioned the insurmountable gap between a world ardently read and fantasized about and the materially impoverished world of sixteenth-century Rome: "You cannot travel through symbolic space with a shovel."[13] Yet it was the exact opposite situation that for nearly twenty years kept people from exploring the prehistoric caves: even as the mania for archaeology reached its height in the second half of the nineteenth century, no one fantasized about prehistoric art, at least not in the form it had irrupted in the real. Geologists, paleontologists, and amateur prehistorians, equipped with shovels, left in search of bones or a few crude material objects. These items would not disrupt the evolutionist continuum, and they shed light on one another within the regime of empirical equivalence. That regime of drab neutrality was suddenly shattered by the unexpected irruption of the symbolic: engraved objects struck shovels like a thunderclap.

The twenty years that followed the discovery of the decorated Cave of Altamira were marked by silence, scarcely interrupted by a little snickering. In short, it was as if the discoveries of prehistoric art still belonged to what could be called the "thunderstone model." Until the eighteenth century, "ceraunia" and "thunderstone" were the names given to the flints that surfaced in fields or on paths after rainstorms. The carved stones, indicating an intention and possessing the coherence of repeated forms, were literally "thunderous" objects: they had fallen from the sky, piercing the fabric of the known. But the nineteenth century's new order of knowledge was incompatible with such metaphysical apparitions. The objects that turned the "order of things" upside down either had to comply with new narratives, more rational and potentially congruent with the historicization of nature, or be reduced to silence.

Prehistory is through and through a matter of astonishment and stupor. In that respect, it reactivates a long philosophical tradition dating back to classical antiquity and recorded in Plato's *Theaetetus*. This tradition makes *thaumazein* (astonishment) the beginning of philosophy: "When I look steadily . . . [it is] as if darkness were coming over my sight," the young mathematician confesses to Socrates, regarding certain phenomena that unsettle him.[14] This astonishment that *obscures the vision* was literally embodied in those who came face to face with the symbolic figures of prehistory. For a long time, no one even saw the paintings and engravings on the walls of caves. Then, when the problem of "prehistory" was raised, some went so far as quite simply to deny their existence. In the case of symbolic artifacts from the earliest times, they developed hypotheses that made the artifacts compatible with the "known," even giving them names straight out of classical antiquity. Those that were carved in the shape of a woman's nude body were called "Venuses," sometimes described as "immodest," a familiar fantasy that blocked the disconcerting forces of a discovery that lay beyond all fantasizing. Descartes, charting the troubled waters of the soul as it reacts to "rare and extraordinary things," made *admiratio* the most primitive of the soul's primitive passions.[15] "Admiration," which corresponds to "astonishment" in its current sense, was a "sudden surprise" at objects that seem "rare and extraordinary." But that "admiration" was measured. A subject, overcome by stupidity and dullness remained indifferent to the world and incapable of thought; but the "excess of admiration" that Descartes called "astonishment," and that corresponds to what we know as "stupor," was just as negative. "This makes the whole body remain immobile like a statue, and renders one incapable either of perceiving anything of the object but the first face presented or, consequently, of acquiring a more particular knowledge of it. This is what is commonly called 'being astonished.'" And astonishment is an excess of admiration that can never anything but be bad."[16] The two extremes meet: stupor verges on stupidity, and a subject who seeks the extraordinary at all costs finally becomes as insensitive to the world as the dull-witted subject. So it was for the first witnesses to the invention of prehistory: thunderstruck by the excessively new, they turned into statues. The moderns were *transfixed by prehistory*, initially in the sense of being petrified by shock.

In and of itself, parietal art encapsulated the stupor of prehistory by its excesses, its secret locations, and the jumble of its formal compositions. But it was no doubt because the enigma it posed was so opaque that it could eventually be appropriated by moderns at the turn of the twentieth century. Sealed up in caves for millenniums, these images bore witness in the first place to a gaping hole in human memory. When modernity was finally ready to see these paintings, it was because it recognized its own enigma in them: Where did it come from? What was its origin, and what would its posterity be? What art was it capable of "in the age of its technological reproducibility," and to what end?

The monumental paintings in caves also offered modernity the possibility of collective identification. So long as prehistoric art existed only as minuscule objects, it alluded to individual and spontaneous gestures and could be incorporated into the fable of pastoral innocence. It thus remained caught up in the enchanted circle of nature. It was only when modern consciousness took note of the existence of parietal art that prehistory could be seamlessly assimilated to human history, understood as action and as the production of the new. Only then did prehistoric peoples become our fellow creatures. Their collectivities, mere figments to us, were embodied in monumental and serial works suggesting struggles and beliefs that required rites and a minimal social organization. Such speculations fissured the resistance of modernity, which from then on could appropriate the works into the fabric of its historicity. Sometimes modernity came up with evolutionist narratives that conceived of the magic culture of primitive times as a very early stage in the march of progress begun long ago; sometimes it wove more dialectical and more complex narratives, making prehistory less a period that had reached its conclusion than an entirely subjective plastic force that could be linked to the present and thereby produce the possibility of history or, on the contrary, its end.[17]

Prehistory, once it was periodized and objectified, could not escape a historicist reification and reconstitution of the past. But it could just as easily be understood and experienced thanks to its temporal plasticity, for which there was no real equivalent in history. Not circumscribed by a place or a date, prehistory could return anywhere, anytime, and an indeterminate number of times. Universal, global, incomplete, and forever opaque, it lent itself perfectly to the negative or critical side of modernity, as well as to its utopianism. Because prehistory had no chronology, because it was composed of a time that was not clearly delimited, it flouted the orders of time and the natural kingdoms and was always prepared to slip into the present. Finally, because it entailed beginning, change, and end all at once, prehistory in and of itself could encompass common perceptions of history.

In this book, I propose to write the history of a modernity that, in forever reinventing prehistory, constantly invents itself. In its conceptual and artistic ramifications, "prehistoric modernity" has been strangely overlooked. Somewhat like Edgar Allan Poe's "purloined letter," it lies in plain view and is nevertheless invisible, as if, in the end, any reflection on prehistory had to pay tribute to the repression of which it was the object. Any consideration of the conceptual and artistic uses of geological, paleontological, and artistic prehistory by moderns also requires that we understand why historians have misconstrued these practices, whether by overlooking them, or by confusing them with primitivism and archaism, or by focusing on the concepts of progress, tabula rasa, and the future as the exclusive driving forces of modernity. The continuous invention of prehistory is well suited to demonstrate that the way in which "we have never been modern" is not as monolithic and univocal as Bruno Latour suggests.[18]

We have learned to consider modernity through the prism of a few solid and unequivocal dualisms. At a time when the discourse on the Anthropocene receives a great deal of media attention, we are rather too quick to find the foundations of modernity in Bacon's instrumental philosophy and in the Cartesian dualism that separates nature from the human cogito and thus postulates the extension and domestication of the world. In the same spirit, the historian Reinhart Koselleck maintained that Enlightenment notions such as acceleration, progress, and utopia constituted the singularity of the modern historical regime.[19] As for art history, even thirty years ago, we were taught that modernity was the era of the tabula rasa: headed straight for the future, it "shatter[s] against daily life."[20] This narrative allowed for a few exceptions: fin-de-siècle decadentism, primitivism, and the return to order were seen as quasi-mechanical "reactions" against the progressive spirit of modernity. We need to counteract the neutralizing effect of dualist symmetries—action and reaction, avant-garde and rear guard, modern and antimodern, revolutionaries and reactionaries. Such dualism has found a paradoxical, yet all the more striking expression in the disappearance pure and simple of the word "moderns": "we have never been modern." That assertion, of course, implies that we have never been the moderns we believed we were, since we were also fetishists, as much if not more so than the colonized peoples. Granted, but what exactly do we understand by the term "moderns"? Were moderns always monolithic, and are we so even now?

It would be absurd to deny the existence of these oppositions, but the extreme tension between them and the aporias inherent in modernity now have an infinitely greater heuristic value, because they further defamiliarize our view of history and break through the opacity of the present. The "great divide" Latour speaks of has had a necessary critical function, but if we take it simply as our line of sight, we risk allowing it to persist without problematizing it. We must therefore reshape somewhat the identity of moderns, and rather than assign ourselves the role of those who know better than the ancients, rather than impose our critical spirit on the past, rather than see our present as the tail of the comet, we must acquire the means to engage increasingly in the self-critique that every past present has undertaken. Modernity is composed of regression as much as progress, doubt as much as certainty, deceleration as much as acceleration, the *longue durée* as much as change.[21] It is this contradictory historicity that I wish to explore in this book by immersing myself in some of its structuring themes and revelatory moments from the beginning of the nineteenth century to the present. It is my wish to recount the project of *grasping onto everything, in the aim, secret, perhaps, of releasing at least some things from our grasp.*

Prehistory, having broken with the fundaments and codes of the ancient world (both human and nonhuman), forces moderns to place their existence and their historicity over an abyss. As in the Renaissance, nature, continually "reinvented," generates ever more shocks, surprises, and enigmas.[22] "We slip away from ourselves," Edgar Quinet wrote in 1870, in the first wide-ranging reflection on what the long term, in its ramifications, and its tangle of human and nonhuman has done to modern subjectivity.[23] Although evolutionism, positivism, and their present-day cognitivist and genetic incarnations posit that every question has an answer, every enigma its solution, regression in time cannot reconstitute the entire past: the deeper you dig into the past, the thicker its mystery becomes; the farther back you go, the more disturbing the indetermination of types and behaviors. In the "anthropological sleep" Foucault spoke of, there is always the same dream of a *finite* being, both object of knowledge and knowing subject, who bumps up against the unthought, "the inexhaustible double that presents itself to reflection."[24] Man, caught up in the historicity of his physical being, his material activity, and his language, "can be revealed only when bound to a previously existing historicity." He is never contemporary with an origin; he always exists "against a background of the already begun."[25] That is why, in several ways, we imitate the original stupor of the invention of prehistory: we repeat the same lapsus and the same silences; we are astonished at the blindness of the first witnesses; and we can also take that very "stupor" as the object of our reflection. *Transfixed by prehistory, held in its grasp*, moderns themselves *grasped onto it* so as to continue to make art, to write, to think, to live. In this book, I analyze that two-stage process and that reversal.

Beginning in the mid-nineteenth century, the "thunderstone" gradually became an instrument for taking one's distance from everyday life. Prehistory, simultaneously similar and dissimilar to the present, human, nonhuman, and inhuman all at once, turned out to be a formidable machine for producing "defamiliarization." In the end, it remains the only terra incognita on this earth left for moderns to explore. As temporality, it constitutes the human while at the same time exceeding it; as a reservoir of material traces of nature's and man's past, it reveals, now as before, a disconcerting diversity of forms that obscures the divide between words and things. In that sense, the invention of prehistory is a perfect materialization of what Hans Blumenberg, describing the specificity of modern times, has called "the essentialization of the contingent."[26]

But prehistory is also one of the most powerful vectors of the phenomenon Koselleck called the "temporalization" of history, which began in the late eighteenth century. In substance, he was designating the process by which history, as events and as memorable and normative acts, disintegrated in favor of History as a "collective singular" whose meaning is realized in and by time.[27] Koselleck, a historian of semantics, pointed out the decisive role in that process of the utopian thought of the Enlightenment and of the philosophy of history through such concepts as revolution and progress and the sense of acceleration derived from them.[28] All these notions were tied up with the subject's projection into the future and with the idea that his connection to the past and tradition was now broken. Yet the temporalization of history has occurred in both directions, as an absorption in the past and as a projection into the future. Why? In a certain manner, prehistory was invented by an excess of historicism. Modern man, in his desire to draw up a list of everything, to set down in writing the historical narrative of all that exists around him, ran up against the wall of prehistory. Historicist excess ultimately led to the pulverization of history. From the time of its invention, prehistory produced a continuous expansion of time, eroding known historical forms and pulverizing their normative power, blurring the divide between natural kingdoms and the semantic regimes associated with them. In that sense, prehistory put the final nail in the coffin of *historia magistra vitae* — history as life's teacher.

The expansion of time that prehistory produced affects human beings in their very constitution: they lose the distinctive signs and boundaries that separate them from other species and also from their own prosthetic inventions. If we stop thinking about modern acceleration as moving exclusively toward the future and see it as also headed simultaneously toward the most remote past, we will easily grasp a *regressive acceleration* that, even now, leads moderns back to ever more ancient and unexpected paleontological and artistic forms. This ultimately produces a temporal vertigo similar in its intensity to that caused by the feats of science and technology.

The sense of dispossession and rupture is not purely negative, however; it is not purely a privation of the ontological substratum and horizon that human beings need in order to exist. Fundamentally, what characterizes modern subjectivity in its most intimate being is a contradictory dispossession, both destructive power and unsuspected creativity. In this respect, nothing is more revealing than the recurrent prehistoric metaphors in Marcel Proust's *In Search of Lost Time*. From the first pages, he describes the relinquishment of his being whenever he drifts in the limbo of sleep after awakening during the night. Delivered from immediate memory, he then projects himself, in a formidable regressive acceleration, into an ontological state identical to that of the primitive being in the depths of the cave:

> But for me it was enough if, in my own bed, my sleep was so heavy as completely to relax my consciousness; for then I lost all sense of the place in which I had gone to sleep, and when I awoke at midnight, not knowing where I was, I could not be sure at first who I was; I had only the most rudimentary sense of existence, such as may lurk and flicker in the depths of an animal's consciousness; I was more destitute of human qualities than the cave-dweller; but then the memory, not yet of the place in which I was, but of various other places where I had lived, and might now very possibly be, would come like a rope let down from heaven to draw me up out of the abyss of not-being, from which I could never have escaped by myself: in a flash I would traverse and surmount centuries of civilisation, and out of a half-visualised succession of oil-lamps, followed by shirts with turned-down collars, would put together by degrees the component parts of my ego.[29]

Prehistoric time, in breaking with the immediate past — impoverished because so familiar — offers a different past, all the more precious because it must be extracted from oblivion or even reinvented. And that prehistoric past allows one to reconcile the reputedly antithetical notions of end and beginning, rupture and rootedness, novelty and reminiscence, dissimilarity and resemblance, difference and repetition. If the present then retreats into the prehistoric past to "slip away from itself," it does so the better to project onto that past its own anxieties, sometimes warding them off and sometimes pursuing them to their definitive conclusion. Artists, philosophers, and writers can all be found there.

Prehistory extends the mirror of the fossil to reflect the ever-new commodities produced by capitalism (Max Ernst, Walter Benjamin). Rather than the ideal of political engagement, it may provide the model of the very *longue durée* of entropy (Robert Smithson). At the dawn of the atomic age, which created the sense that the geological era *and* the cultural era were changing simultaneously, a simple change of prefix marked prehistory as evidence of a "*post*history" (Arnold Gehlen, Lewis Mumford, Pier Paolo Pasolini, and others). As constant as capitalism itself, that negative use of prehistoric times reminds us that all human history, founded on the subjugation of nature and of human beings, remains within the horizon of natural history and the extinction of species. This critical function, however constant it may be, was marked by three moments of extreme intensity: after the "total mobilization" of World War I, after the atomic bomb and the onset of the "Great Acceleration,"[30] and in the present, with the era that has come to be known as the "Anthropocene." This book, therefore, which opens with the history of the symbolic exploration of nineteenth-century fossils, ends with "posthistory" as artists, writers, and philosophers have conceived it since World War II.

But there is also a positive use of the time of prehistory, the source of many symbols of consolation, creativity, and even utopia. For example, Henri Matisse saw the very recent discovery of parietal art as proof that the only Arcadia possible is that provided by art, now as in prehistoric times. For others, less concerned with preserving the autonomy of art, prehistory exemplifies the contrast between the dearth of material resources and a symbolic surplus. Joan Miró and Georges Bataille took inspiration from the prehistoric in their attempts to remedy a materially abundant, but symbolically impoverished modernity. Clearly, the more one imagines a harsh and dangerous prehistory, the more it confirms the chances for modernity to create its own symbolic universe by bearing witness to the vital role that falls to art. At certain critical moments, when it was a question of denying the obsolescence of painting as a medium or, on the contrary, of inventing as yet unknown artistic objects, prehistoric art offered invaluable suggestions. Far from corroborating the duality of form and function or the antithesis between aesthetics and pragmatism, the earliest art argues for their interdependence.[31] Detached from its material and utilitarian context, the symbolic efficacy attributed to the paintings on the walls of caves was easily transposable to the needs of the present, becoming pure form. It would be wrong, however, to conclude that there was a sharp divide between inert fossils and symbolic processes in the uses that artists, philosophers, and writers made of prehistory. There was no divide between death and life.

It should be pointed out that the indetermination of the natural kingdoms and of semantic regimes is constitutive of the successive inventions of prehistory. End and beginning, inertia and action, renunciation and appropriation of the world, sovereignty of the object that recognizes no master and lyrical affirmation of subjectivity were often combined to express the experience of modern time. Modernity is both belated and premature, hypermnesiac and forgetful. For example, Giorgio de Chirico's "metaphysical" paintings, though they almost never quote prehistoric objects or signs, give the sense of a *second* prehistory, similar in spirit, but not in form, to the first. Just as the earliest human beings lived within a natural world that was incomprehensible to them, moderns live in a world so saturated with history that it has become illegible. Joan Miró, in transforming images of commodities into vaguely ossiform elements floating against a background suggestive of a clay wall, indicates in turn that it is possible to convert fossils into images and to substitute the liberating enchantment of art for the alienating enchantment of capitalism. Claes Oldenburg would also practice a paleontology of the contemporary world by assembling cast-offs somewhat similar to one another in form. These senseless forms bear no likeness to anything, but their juxtaposition in vitrines inspired by those in museums of natural history constructs a mutual resemblance, transforming the most ordinary prose into poetic rhymes.[32] None of these artists claims that his art could save the world or change the direction of history. What they all say, however, is that art, which creates fictions, has a vital role in the long history of human beings, of which their own art is only a moment. Therein lies its force, but also its relativity.

In this book, the idea of "prehistoric modernity" is organized along both a horizontal and a vertical axis. On the horizontal axis, this idea is shaped by constants, that is, by themes that run through the long span of modernity. These include: the dialectic between human history (its end and its beginning) and artistic media; the conjunction between prehistory and the present; the articulation of time scales as the only means available for mastering formless geological time; the formal techniques that artists have borrowed from prehistory and the theories developed over time to interpret them; the magic efficacy of art, as opposed to its reification; the embrace of history or its rejection; the elaboration of questions common to art and the human sciences, such as the *longue durée,* or a "second nature"; the tension between the universality of origins and the urgent need to root art in a soil and a race. On the vertical axis, the idea of prehistory is regularly determined by variables such as historical specificity and the contingency of individuals and events. Precisely because prehistoric art is stupefying in its supposed naturalism and resourcefulness, it did not interest artists — with the notable exception of Matisse — before the 1920s. Then, for various reasons, artists turned to the mineral world, somewhat as they do today, when the stones and places devastated by brutal domestication imperiously appealed to the artist's imagination. To take another example: very early on and then without interruption, caves dominated the imaginary of prehistory, but they were not taken up by artists until the end of World War II and the nuclear cataclysm in Japan. At the same moment, the idea of "posthistory" was articulated as such, though its conceptual apparatus had existed since the invention of prehistory. And though anachronisms are inextricably bound up with prehistory, it was only after 1960 that they were explicitly embraced, affirmed, and defended.

Of course, this array of constants and variables, of long series and disruptive events, is inherent in the way the temporality of prehistory is rooted in the present. As such, "prehistoric modernity" relativizes or even invalidates the legendary rivalry between anthropology and history while clearly differentiating itself from the various forms of primitivism. True, prehistory was enlisted in the merciless indictments of the historical mindset, like those undertaken—at nearly the same time but in different registers—by the artist Jean Dubuffet, the media theorist Marshall McLuhan, and the writer Ernst Jünger. Even so, the invention of prehistory allowed history as a discipline to undergo a metamorphosis. As I have already noted, prehistory is itself a product of the historical mindset, at once its culminating point and its dialectical sublation.[33] But because prehistory is without events, names, and written documents, some could claim that Western man, historical by definition, is finite, while others were able to conceive of a different history that took no heed of the memorable actions of one individual or another whose name might have been preserved in writing. Historicists find prehistory such a faraway land that they exclude it from their domestic domain.

In the twentieth century, history writing moved in the opposite direction, away from written documents. For those who introduced material culture into the study of history, breaking the exclusive connection to texts, the line between prehistory and history became more porous. According to Lucien Febvre, for example, "history is undoubtedly done with written documents. When there are any. But it can also be done, and every attempt must be made to do it, without written documents if none exist. In the absence of known and classified flowers, the historian must make his honey with everything his ingenuity may afford him." In turning all available natural and cultural traces into historical materials, Febvre would speak ironically of the historicist's limits: "Stop pestering him about the masterpieces Father Breuil found in the caves. 'Painting? No. Archaeology! Let's not cavalierly cross the sacred line: History over here, prehistory over there.' ... But ultimately, prehistory is one of the most comical notions imaginable."[34] Febvre's student Fernand Braudel would in fact radicalize that principle, making the geological milieu—the incarnation of the longest *longue durée*—an active factor in human history. But the possibility of a conjunction between prehistory and history is also one of the consequences of the fact that history in its modern form is "doable," as Koselleck argues. Insofar as history is no longer a completed form, but a series of actions unfolding in time, its stupefying encounter with prehistory becomes conceivable. Rather than being "done," that is, consolidated in the past, *prehistory remains to be done* — not in the sense of a "project" to be carried out, a secular teleology to be realized, but as an enigma from the past to be interpreted in terms of the present's needs.

The present appears in this book in two principal forms that in no way exclude a multitude of intermediate positions. In the first place, the present, in the service of the past, "actualizes" it — makes it a contemporary reality — with the greatest possible force, to the point of merging with it and disappearing. Second and conversely, the present is made actual with the assistance of the past, whose material traces establish its present historicity. This opposition between the two forms conceals major differences in the possible uses of prehistory.

Like geology and the discipline of prehistory, art devotes a considerable share of its energy to "actualizing" what was lost. Actualist geology observes the present in order to imagine a past, which, all things considered, is not as irrevocably finite as the catastrophist Cuvier thought. Prehistory is quick to explain cave paintings by analogy, transposing onto them the rites of Stone Age survivors still scraping by in the Australian deserts or the South African forests. In the same way, realist art, now as in the late nineteenth century, attempts to body forth fossils, to reconstitute their daily lives, to give images of them a voice. And because neither science nor history can resuscitate the prehistoric dead, art as "organon," both ideal and perceptible to the senses, readily takes on that task, appealing paradoxically to the tenet of historicism: to tell "what actually happened."[35] Of course, the present cannot avoid projecting its own ideas and affects onto prehistory. Hidden behind František Kupka's anthropoids are males dressed in black, engaged in a struggle of sexual selection; and smoldering in the stricken, wrinkled, emaciated bodies of Fernand Cormon's horde is the artist's obsession with the degeneration of his own era. In both cases, however, the present's interference with the representation of prehistory takes the form of a lapsus. In a rudimentary sacrificial gesture, the present breathes life into the past before expiring.

In contrast to that actualist approach, certain practices point to the artificiality of *both* prehistory *and* its use. Here again, the methods of certain artists coincide with those of a number of prehistorians, anthropologists, and philosophers. Beginning in the 1950s, the prehistorians Annette Laming-Emperaire and André Leroi-Gourhan fought against the direct application of ethnology to prehistoric art and proposed hypotheses based on the internal coherence between series of images and the vestiges found on the ground adjacent to them. Rather than look for answers about the meaning of parietal art in a mimetically reproduced "outside" (in the natural world or among "primitive peoples" living today), they considered the syntactical coherence of the images themselves and the distance between that syntax and life, since the images did not represent realistic scenes.[36] Similarly, artists such as Miró, Picasso, and Dubuffet were as interested in prehistoric forms as in the symbolic procedures used at the time. But when they used identifiable forms, they never did so to "complete" and restore them. Rather, they pointed out their transhistorical or even resolutely contemporary character — in the choice of materials, techniques, and the arrangement of signs. Finally, because the prehistoric world was revealed through a disconcerting multitude of symbols, procedures, and forms, the way these artists used them depended on their own particular needs — they opted sometimes for one, sometimes for another. As a result, prehistory and the present proved to be anthropologically similar, but historically dissimilar, closely related, but forever distinct.

That is also the best way to grasp the difference between primitivism and the modern invention of prehistory: only the reactivation of prehistory allows for a conjunction between anthropological constants and historical variables, because only prehistory could make historical claims within the conceptual world of Western thought. Both phenomena obeyed the modern subject's imperious need to escape a present considered prosaic and a normative past experienced as despotic. In each case, this deliberate disappropriation set in motion a process of projection: primitivism and the use of prehistory were intellectual and psychological constructs of modern man. But what he finds in prehistory is a temporalization, a surplus of historicity, to which primitivism cannot aspire, because it works within a sphere that is at best timeless, at worst governed by the idea of an endless degeneration or a meteoric decline. As I said, the discovery of Paleolithic art in the subsoil of the European continent increased both the stupor of moderns and the intensity of their appropriation of prehistory. Similar finds in colonized territories could not have been attributed to such a remote past: the winds of history had never blown through these regions, considered to be timeless, if not in a state of degeneration. Such images from outside Europe could have been made ten thousand years ago, or they could have been made today: that in fact was the interpretation of the German ethnologist Leo Frobenius in the late nineteenth century.[37] In the West, however, the contrast between the very ancient and the modern was so sharp that it necessarily produced meaning and history. In other words, history lay between prehistory and modernity, and this gap was necessary for the modern dialectization of prehistory, that is, its historicization. At the same time, and this is hardly a contradiction, the awareness of moderns that they walked the same earth as the men and women of prehistory brought a sense of continuity that guaranteed their own identity.

By contrast, primitivism always bore the mark of alterity. After 1912, Picasso discovered conceptual processes in the symbolic world of primitive peoples, rather than the primary drives seen by Emil Nolde and Maurice Vlaminck. Even so, the aestheticization inherent in Picasso's formalist approach effaced any particular or historical sign. He was immediately led to an occasional, temporally circumscribed use of the "primitive," embraced as such, that afterward continued to enrich his practice more discreetly. Nevertheless, references to the "primitive" were not only circumscribed in time, they were also deeply rooted in a place and culture, no less than in a specific race. Because its roots in the particular never totally disappeared, the category of the primitive remains forever marked as anticlassical, anti-European, antimodern. As Frances Connelly demonstrated in her classic study of primitivism, that category was constructed primarily in opposition to Western aesthetic thought.[38]

Compared with primitivism, prehistory is much less likely to serve as a negation of Western aesthetics. Its ambiguity takes a different form: as origin or beginning, it is sometimes universal and sometimes "autochthonous." In other words, when the particularism of prehistory is asserted as a positive fact, it becomes the *proper* identity of one or another *European* people; this particularism must then be constantly proven, reactivated, protected. That is true for the interpretation of the Neolithic by German theorists (Herbert Kühn, Max Verworn, and others), by English artists of the 1930s (Paul Nash, Barbara Hepworth, and others), and by the Dane Asger Jorn. References to prehistory take a completely different form when artists assert its universality, as Picasso and Miró regularly did, appropriating all the formal techniques of prehistory in all its manifestations and inscribing the marks of their own time on them. Finally, Max Raphael and Georges Bataille fought against a primitivism they judged repetitive and sterile, but they did so in the name of a prehistory they understood to be the "indeterminate birth"[39] of history.

In this attempt to interpret the modern experience of time, I had to reactivate the very object of the investigation: the stupor caused by the invention of prehistory. Because prehistory has made the boundaries between disciplines porous and sowed confusion in the classification of knowledge, the guiding ideas in this book come from various types of discourses and forms: works of art, literary writing, the human and social sciences, scientific images, caricatures. Even more important, the *defamiliarization* of the known produced by the invention of prehistory requires a defamiliarization of the history of modernity. Like the artists, I have made use of the forms and procedures bequeathed by "prehistoric modernity," attempting to reveal the blind spots of history and making the discursive and formal objects function as "sources of stupor."

An inquiry into our present condition runs through this book, while the many "ends" announced produce a mesmerizing effect. Scarcely sixty years after the first atomic bombs exploded, the advent of yet another new age, simultaneously geological and cultural, is turning our world upside down. In returning to the foundation of human history over the abyss of the past, we may be better able to think about what is happening to us.

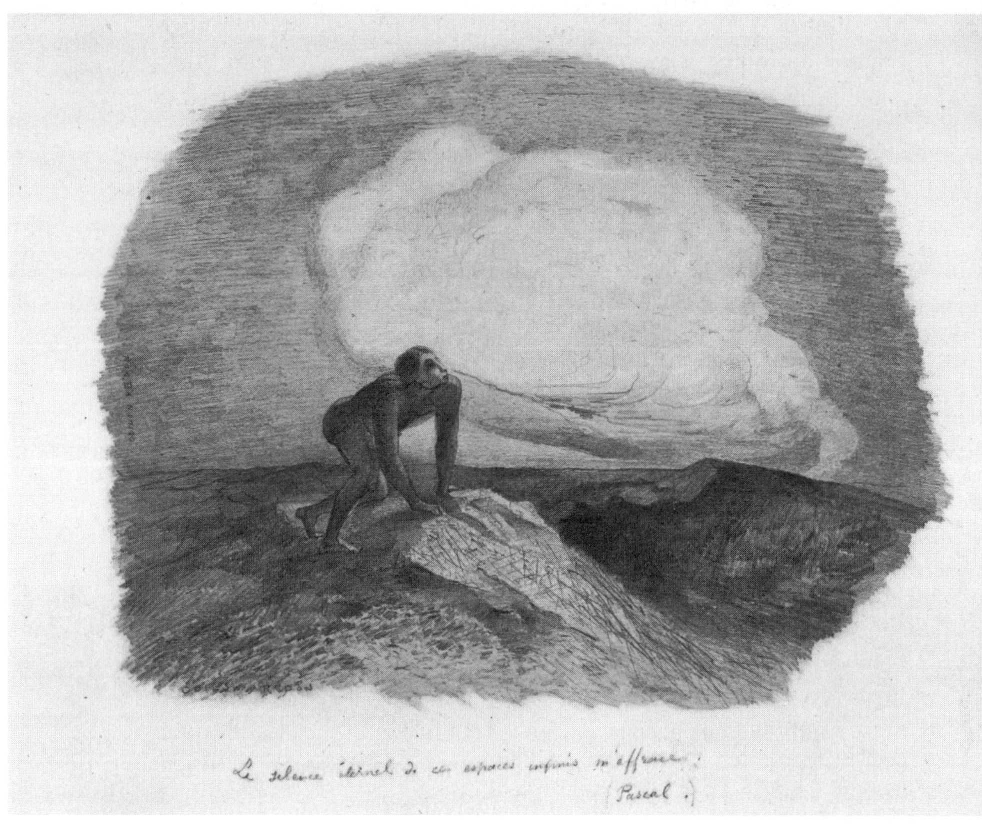

Figure 1.1. Odilon Redon, *The Eternal Silence of These Infinite Spaces Frightens Me*, ca. 1870. Drawing, 8¾ × 10⅝ in. Petit Palais, Paris. © Petit Palais/Roger-Viollet.

"We Slip Away from Ourselves": The Discovery and Internalization of the Earth's Age (Eighteenth to Twentieth Centuries)

A peculiar creature, a sort of anthropoid with the face of an angel, moves between the two immensities of earth and sky (Figure 1.1). Mountain summits extend over the earth as far as the eye can see, while a large cloud crosses the sky. In this drawing by Odilon Redon, which dates to about 1870, the airiness, the rippling effects, and the suppleness of the sky contrast starkly with the rough, sharp, and impenetrable minerality of the mountain massifs. The creature, while forming the visible link between these two spaces, in reality only accentuates their opposition: it is clutching the ground, but its head is raised to the sky, internalizing the contrast within its own body. Its right foot appears firmly planted on the peak it is about to reach, but the creature also extends its long arms to grip the mountaintop like a quadruped. Its body is a much darker shade than the mountain it is climbing and the sky it is contemplating. This anthropoid, in short, is an "intermediate" creature lying between humanity and animality, the infiniteness of earth and that of the heavens. It could be called a creature navigating a "vast middle," in Pascal's expression, between two infinities.

In fact, Redon himself explicitly refers to Pascal, inscribing on the lower edge of the drawing the famous statement about "man's disproportion": "The eternal silence of these infinite spaces frightens me."[2] But where Pascal was describing a *cosmos* of infinite spaces, heliocentric and multiple since Copernicus, Redon's infinity is first and foremost temporal and historically marked. According to Edgar Quinet in 1870, for example, there was no doubt that "the earth's new history will be in our time what the discovery of the earth's movement around the sun was in the Renaissance."[3] The book of nature had long since replaced Holy Scripture. Its pages revealed that the earth's age was not the mere six thousand years assigned to it by the Bible: it was now incommensurable, quite simply eluding human understanding. In fact, the slow pace of geological activity, which Charles Lyell had definitively established in 1830, made any concordance between the biblical account and catastrophist theories — one of the most recent, and certainly the most dazzling, being Cuvier's theory — forever impossible.[4] Unlike the infinite universe of Copernicus, Kepler, and other astronomers in the modern age, the infinite time of the earth was perceptible in geological concretions that human beings walked on, touched with their hands, and could contemplate at any moment. That is no doubt why in his drawing, Redon emphasized the materiality of the mountain, individualizing the features and textures of its ravines and hillsides as so many signs of an erosion that had occurred at different times. But geological time, despite its material self-evidence, was as elusive as the infinite cosmos. The impenetrable minerality remained mute, a muteness interrupted by the subject's terror. "The eternal silence of these infinite spaces frightens me (Pascal)": Redon, concealing himself behind the creature and the quotation from Pascal, inscribed his signature vertically, on the left edge of the picture, like the shadow of the climbing creature.

In about 1870, time, having undergone an infinite expansion, absorbed the history of the human species. It had been accepted for decades that like other species, humans had a paleontological past.[5] Redon's creature was the imaginary expression of a fossil ancestrality that combined humanity and simian animality. Charles Darwin and Thomas Huxley came to resonate with Pascal, who had defined man as "neither angel nor beast."[6] Three moments overlap in the story told by this image: the inaugural and necessarily fantasized moment when the anthropoid creature first encountered the infinite; the historical moment marking the disjunction of time scales, which Redon himself experienced; and, between the two, the Pascalian moment.

Let us first consider the fantasy of origins. Since Giambattista Vico's *Scienza nuova* (1725), early man was thought to have been "terror-stricken" by natural phenomena he was unable to understand.[7] The first astonishment (from the Latin *tonare*, "to thunder"), which was said to have wrested "giants" from their bestial state, was caused by the sky: "At last the sky fearfully rolled with thunder and flashed with lightning. . . . Thereupon a few giants, who must have been the most robust, and who were dispersed through the forests on the mountain heights where the strongest beasts have their dens, were frightened and astonished by the great effect whose cause they did not know, and raised their eyes and became aware of the sky."[8] In 1779, the comte de Buffon published an account of the "seventh epoch" of nature, which had witnessed man's first appearance and was, according to him, still under way. He, too, mentioned the "baleful terror"[9] experienced by witnesses to the latest catastrophes that had given the earth its most recent aspect. And finally, in 1790, Kant argued that only the subject who had crossed the threshold of the supersensible, thanks to his capacity for cognition and his developed aesthetic judgment, could experience the "negative pleasure" of the sublime in the face of the infiniteness of the natural world. According to Kant, what gives rise to the sense of the sublime in the morally autonomous subject elicits only terror in the "uncultivated man" struggling to satisfy his basic needs.[10] Redon's intermediate creature was the very remote ancestor of these "uncultivated" beings, experiencing the first stupor and the first dread when faced with the infinity of the world around him. The creature had no finite object on which to fix his gaze: the world was as naked as the creature itself. In this mutual metaphysical objectification, the creature became human by contemplating transcendence — which existed only by virtue of his experience of it. As for Redon himself, he belonged to an era when it was believed that knowledge could put an end to all forms of primitive terror. Sky and earth were the object of an integral calculus. In 1854, the great scientist Hermann von Helmholtz referred to advances in the discovery of the laws of nature as being the telescope of our mental eye in the night of the past and that of the future.[11] But this telescope revealed a man more "disproportionate" than ever, regressing to a fright that took an especially radical form because it was created by scientific, "objective" knowledge. Odilon Redon invoked Pascal precisely because God had never been so silent. Astronomy first, and then the implacable scale of geology, came to take his place. John Ruskin, both an expert on geology and a fervent believer in God, was heartbroken: "If only the Geologists would let me alone, I could do very well, but those dreadful Hammers! I hear the clink of them at the end of every cadence of the Bible verses."[12]

Earth: The Long Term

The Slow Domestication of Time

The disjunction between the scale of geological time and that of human history was not an experience that struck modern consciousness as swiftly and unexpectedly as a comet. Granted, Redon represented the "fertile moment"[13] when, for the first time, his stupefied creature all of a sudden felt the oppressiveness of two opposing scales, both similarly beyond measure. But the notion of the long term had taken root slowly and discontinuously in Western thought, as many historians of geology and other forms of the *longue durée* have pointed out. When the British geologist Charles Lyell published the first volume of his *Principles of Geology* in 1830, what he believed to be the incalculable age of the earth, which he strove to demonstrate empirically, was a given that a large number of European scholars had already assimilated.[14] But this incommensurability would become an integral part of the common understanding of time only in the course of the nineteenth century.

The principle of superposition, which posits that spatial depth translates into temporal distance — that is, that the deepest layers of rock are also the earliest — gave a coherence to the formless substance of geological time. This principle was articulated at the very end of the seventeenth century by the Danish naturalist Nicolaus Steno, who made his observations in the subsoil of Tuscany.[15] A century later, the British engineer William Smith would join the two parallel threads of earth's time: fossils and strata. Between Steno and Smith, the biblical chronology had at last fallen apart. In linking the typology of fossils to that of strata, Smith made fossils melancholic signs not only of a forgotten past, but also of a history that was potentially legible because carved up into precise eras.[16] These eras became visible *between* the geological strata. They were the "difference" that introduced divisions into formless time. As the philologist and lexicographer Émile Littré formulated it in 1858, "When the eye became skilled at looking, what had seemed uniform was marked by essential differences, and a whole strange and real world appeared within the long perspective of the primordial ages."[17] Buffon had written a century earlier that "to reach back into the different ages of Nature. This is the only way to fix some points in the immensity of space, to place some milestones along the eternal passage of time. Time is like distance: our view would diminish in it, and also even get lost in it, if our history and chronology did not provide lanterns and torches in the darkest places."[18] The act of transposing human periodization — eras and years — to the immensity of time was obviously a way to conceptualize that immensity and domesticate it.

Two documents, one visual, the other literary, express in a striking manner this domestication of the vast and formless time of geology. The frontispiece of W. S. Symonds's *Old Stones* (1884) depicts a ladder leaning against a high cliff (Figure 1.2).[19] Inscribed on the ladder's steps are the names of the geological ages that lie just behind them, stored away in a rock mass. The spacing between the steps becomes wider near the bottom, marring the ladder's flawless precision and regularity. This disproportion is the sign that time is losing its distinctive features, expanding and sinking deeper into the past. Below the ladder is the earth's amorphous bedrock, primordial

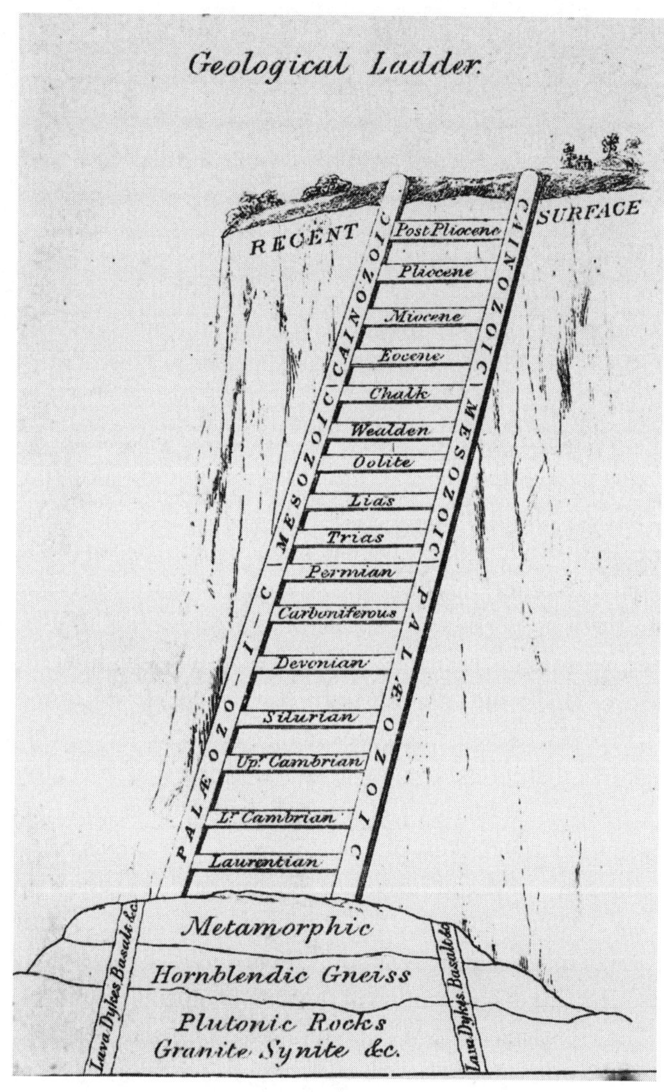

Figure 1.2. Frontispiece, W. S. Symonds, *Old Stones: Notes of Lectures on the Plutonic, Silurian, and Devonian Rocks in the Neighbourhood of Malvern*, new ed. (London, 1884). Bodleian Libraries, University of Oxford, 18855 e. 3. Courtesy Bodleian Libraries, University of Oxford.

matter resistant to all metaphorization. In 1854, these "vast and date-less" rocks were described as "a region older than Death."[20] The ladder on the frontispiece has thus not managed to penetrate this bedrock, but uses it as a solid base. At the other end, the top step provides a glimpse of a landscape with a few minuscule trees and a rock mass. This is the living kingdom, which rises up and breathes on a soil the illustrator calls "recent surface." Like the unfathom-able bedrock of the earth, this surface also eludes metaphorization, but for diametrically opposed reasons: able to sustain and foster human life *directly*, it does not need the mediation of metaphors. It has not yet become a step on the "ladder." The present and the past — recent, remote, and amorphous — constitute geological time in all its density. Transposed from language to the image, the meta-phor of the "ladder of time" — the *échelle du temps*, "time scale" — is raised to the second power, becomes literal and reified, but in a noetic and quasi-metaphysical register that will later be found in de Chirico's paintings, devoid of any human presence. In the trans-position of the everyday human world to impenetrable matter, the ladder's sphere of usefulness is both reversed and broadened. The inaccessible spaces that a ladder ought to bring within reach are also telluric, all the while guaranteeing a return to the starting point: the familiar landscape perfectly adapted to humanity — the present time.

This same process of domesticating a time that is enchanting because impenetrable is described in Herman Melville's "Two Sides to a Tortoise," the second sketch in *The Encantadas* (1854). Looking down over a ship's high side, the narrator sees the boat "deep in the sea with some unwonted weight," transporting "three huge antedi-luvian-looking tortoises," that is, Galapagos tortoises: "These mystic creatures, suddenly translated by night from unutterable solitudes," seemed "newly crawled forth from beneath the foundations of the world." What strikes the narrator above all is the primitive inde-termination of these creatures, which, though alive, are in a fossil state — creatures of "dateless, indefinite endurance." In examining a tortoise shell, with its scars of bruises, "swollen, half obliterate," he felt like "an antiquary of a geologist, studying the bird-tracks and ciphers upon the exhumed slates trod by incredible creatures whose very ghosts are now defunct." Following their "slow weary draggings," he becomes the contemporary of the earliest beings in the history of the world. The tortoises thus spark his dream of the primitive world of volcanoes and inextricable thickets. But the dream does not last. The spell cast by the primitive is only a "first impression": "Strange to say," he concludes, "I sat down with my shipmates, and made a merry repast from tortoise steaks, and tortoise stews; and supper over, out knife, and helped convert the three mighty concave shells into three fanciful soup-tureens, and polished the three flat yellowish calipees into three gorgeous salvers."[21] These are the last words of the story. The "two sides of a tortoise" are thus the enchantment of the encounter with the earth's great age and the neutralization of that enchantment. Like the duality of the tortoise, whose dull-witted movements barely crack the surface of mute minerality, the narrator proceeds in two different ways: he is spellbound by the primitive creature, while at the same time, he overcomes that spell by literally incorporating the organic being and annexing the mineral component through the use of *techne*.

The Need for a Narrative

The domestication of geological time entailed an effort at historicization. The principal method was periodization, which gave a form to the formlessness of time while introducing a plot. Narrativization entailed the invention of events, the description of how they occurred, and the establishment of the order and rhythm of their succession. In a certain manner, that project of historicization would culminate one hundred and fifty years later, in the field of history proper, with Fernand Braudel's theorization of the *longue durée*. Braudel assigned a decisive historical role to a "still-churning geology, whose work time has not yet erased and which continues to rage before our eyes."[22]

But nineteenth-century geologists and paleontologists also adopted tropes that were able to historicize the strangeness of the earth's past. Narrativization required the use of the imagination and its privileged figure, metaphor, as a way to assimilate the unknown.[23] Before the historicization of geological time, the naturalist Robert Hooke and the author Fontenelle, for example, also used metaphors to make intelligible their intuition of a time infinitely more ancient than that of the Egyptian monuments. They portrayed fossils as "medals"[24] or "monuments" of nature.[25] Like any metaphor, according to Aristotle, these two objects enshrined in history were used to show "the similarity in things that are apart"[26] — in this case, to make familiar a thing as stupefying as imprints of collective lives that have vanished forever. But for that very reason, the medal metaphor also pushed the familiar, that is, the human, in the direction of a terra incognita where it became dangerously lost. Indeed, the absoluteness of this type of medal, minted by no one, was beholden to a past so remote it was completely free of the vicissitudes and arbitrariness of human history. That aporia, intrinsic to a metaphor that renders the unfamiliar familiar, but also causes alarm, became acute when geological time was historicized. For Georges Cuvier, geology was a history all the more fascinating for being different from human history: "If you take an interest in following, in the childhood of our species, the nearly obliterated traces of so many vanished nations, how could you not also take some interest in searching, in the shadows of the earth's childhood, for the traces of revolutions predating the existence of all nations?"[27] For Balzac, by contrast, "the earth's childhood" was a monstrous experience that left us "suspended over the boundless abyss of the past." With Cuvier, Balzac continued, "the mind is startled to catch a vista of the milliards of years and millions of peoples which the feeble memory of man and an indestrutible divine tradition have forgotten."[28] On the one hand, the earth's past, by its absolute strangeness, captivated human intelligence and even cast a spell over it. It obliged the intelligence to take leave of itself and unlearn its ordinary ways of understanding time and space. But on the other hand, human intelligence, in spite of everything, fashioned the idea of a "too human" earth, going so far as to attribute to it a "childhood," the intimate time of life that, since Rousseau and the Romantics, had signified an exclusively human experience and interiority. The metaphor of the earth's "childhood" was a way of internalizing the inaccessible.

Two geological narratives predominated in the early nineteenth century: that of sudden, successive, and radical catastrophes and that of a slow, more or less gradual, more or less uniform, more or less repetitive time. Geological catastrophes were modern incarnations of the mythical universal flood, which provided the template for them.[29] Usually they preserved their religious determination, as in the theories of the Reverend William Buckland in England and the minister Edward Hitchcock in North America. Cuvier, by contrast, provided a perfectly secularized version. The Reverend Buckland reconciled geology's long term with that of the Bible, making Noah's flood the last in a long series. Human beings, not having yet been created, could not witness the earlier floods. In 1836, when fossil man was not yet an established reality, Buckland based his compromise between the scriptures and geology on the absence of such fossils in the deepest strata of the earth.[30] As for Hitchcock, the founder of ichnology, the study of tracks and traces, he considered the Bible a moral history that had been revealed to man before he was ready to understand geology — an advanced form of the revelation of the Creation and the Fall. The minister even went so far as to anticipate the promise of a paradisial state: as a religious transhumanist, he painted a picture of a community of glorious bodies living in a united world that had reached its teleological conclusion.

By contrast, there is no trace of God in Cuvier's narrative, which clearly separates human history from natural history. Whereas the constancy of their moral nature allowed human beings to empathize with their own past and thus to gain knowledge of it, nothing gave the observer access to the remote past of the natural world. Geological discontinuity severed all ties between past and present.[31] At the same time, the cyclical connotations of the term "revolution" became less prominent, in favor of its modern sense of "break" or "rupture."[32] In the early nineteenth century, the temporal regime of natural history was no doubt inspired by France's recent political history, but the distinction between human and nonhuman also became blurred as a result.

The paleontologist Stephen Jay Gould has worked hard to deny Charles Lyell the glory of having invented uniformitarianism. Among other things, Gould reminds us that in *Theory of the Earth* (1795), James Hutton had already hypothesized a time that was uniform in its action, but experienced as vertiginous, because it was extraordinarily slow and without "beginning" or "end."[33] But Gould also points out that Hutton's universe was Newtonian, that is, it possessed a strictly mechanical perfection whereby every ruin was automatically offset by a restoration. Lyell really historicized uniform time, stripping away its cyclical automatism in favor of a notion that can be understood as a presentism on the geological scale.[34] Unlike Cuvier — who, along with Buckland, was one of his principal targets — Lyell hypothesized that there was no "interruption in the same uniform order of physical events" and that the same causes could generate an infinite diversity of effects.[35] The earth's history thus became a gradual and imperturbable accumulation of effects whose mode of formation was always observable. According to Cuvier, all that remained visible of the past were fossils. History existed in a state of petrification: the gigantic petrification of the earth itself, which had once been shaken by a succession of spasms, and the petrification of organisms within the earth that, one by one, had gone extinct. For Lyell, on the contrary, geological processes could be observed in real time, though only with extreme difficulty, because they are so slow as to be imperceptible. For Cuvier, the earth's past was forever lost, its processes inaccessible. But for Lyell, this past did not pass away: it formed a time that was always present, but nevertheless historical, since its changing effects gradually accumulated. He hypothesized that the earth's elusive past was observable in the pure present.

Clearly, the aim of Lyell's epistemological project was to rescue the past from permanent oblivion by guaranteeing the geologist a sort of temporal ubiquity. In a somewhat similar vein, Gustave Le Bon would later say that the evolutionist historian regards with "impassivity" "things flowing into the eternal abyss," since "time does not annihilate anything." The historian, Le Bon also wrote, "holds the magic wand that makes vanished forms emerge from the womb of time. At his call the entire series of things is reborn."[36] The geologist's omnipotence, however, was caught up in the spiral of the inaccessible, because the present ultimately proved as elusive as its absolute opposite, the very long term. That tension, unavowable, but real and intractable, would ceaselessly obsess Lyell's thinking. His account, though more monotonous and "realistic" than Cuvier's, was no less beholden to the need to invent metaphors.

Many of the artists who took an interest in the earth's very long term seized on that tension, as well. From Paul Cézanne to On Kawara, that is, from a phenomenological pictorial approach to a disincarnate, conceptual, and linguistic approach, these artists sought to conceive of and even to experience the earth's antiquity by engaging with the temporality most opposed to it a priori: the present. Their present is different from the geologist's, however. It accumulates nothing, appropriates nothing; it disrupts the equilibrium and even opens up the abyss of time. It is a time deliberately beyond reach. How are we to understand this antithesis? Surely not by radically separating the field of scientific objectivity from that of fictional subjectivity nor by separating knowledge, presumed to be useful and profitable, from a supposedly gratuitous and extravagant fiction. On the contrary, we must focus on the uses — equally contradictory, but different from one another — that both artists and scientists have made of fiction and its different methodologies in their aim to unite the "I" with the infinite and the present with geological time.

Fiction, Both Poison and Remedy

Lyell's epistemological project was to constitute a "diurnal" geology. The Enlightenment, in asserting the experimental and positive nature of geology, had ultimately gained the upper hand, even over the opacity of the subterranean world. Lyell pointed out that if one "firmly believes in the resemblance or identity of the ancient and present system of terrestrial changes," "every fact collected respecting the causes in diurnal action" will afford "a key to the interpretation of some mystery in the past." It is undeniable, he added, that "all the existing continents and submarine abysses may have originated in movements of this kind, continued throughout incalculable periods of time."[37] There was thus no longer a hidden agent, as God had been in his time. There were no pasts lost forever, as Cuvier had believed, no inexplicable causes personified, as in the notion of wonders or in primitive animism: everything of the sort faded away in the dazzling light of Reason. God, catastrophism, and mythic and literary fictions became indiscriminately embedded in the strata of human memory.[38] As I mentioned, however, diurnal geology did not remain untouched by fictionality. Not only did it have the capacity to generate fictions of enormous legendary power, above all, it was also full of, even structured by, tropes considered to be constitutive of fictional discourses.

Thirty years after painting *The Garden of the Hesperides* (1806), J. M. W. Turner replaced the dragon from the famous myth with a dinosaur.[39] Was this a realist rectification, a historicist gesture? It was much rather a strictly fabulous realism: the past, whose geological and paleontological ramifications had been discovered, turned out to be even more prodigious than the dragons and other wonders the human imagination had spawned over time.[40] The forms and sizes of previously unknown creatures came to fulfill this need for fiction, which had populated primitive times and the edges of the earth with chimerical and mysterious beings. Camille Flammarion, for example, would admire the "colossal" iguanodons: "What prodigious masses! What animals and plants, compared to our world today! These fantastic beings are truly the equal of those the human imagination invented: the centaurs, the fauna, the griffins, the hamadryads, the chimera, the ghouls, the vampires, the hydras, the dragons, the Cerberuses. And they are real: they lived."[41] Émile Littré also compared the resources of science to those of poetry: "Primitive poetry dreamed of entering subterranean spaces by one of the yawning caverns, there to invoke strange and monstrous forms that, along with the dead, would inhabit the darkness of the abysses. Science made poetry's dream a reality; it carried out that descent *toward things sunk in the deep earth and dark shadow (res alta terra et caligine mersas)*."[42] Edgar Quinet would soon claim that paradoxically, the moderns were superior to the ancients thanks to history itself—but a history infinitely more remote than the classical past and even alien to the human past: "Among the ancients and the moderns, sculpture and painting expanded the real world by inventing beings that could never have existed.... The artist ... would have the advantage of finding close at hand forms already fashioned in nature's workshop; he could thus be a realist even while exceeding the bounds of the contemporary world, which seems to be the supreme aim of art."[43]

Clearly, science now ranked alongside fiction, because it proved the reality of the impossible. The vastness of time and the implausible creatures that had inhabited it surpassed all the familiar facts about the present. For that very reason, science resorted to the stylistic and methodological techniques of fiction, both consciously and unconsciously. Geological discourse, dethroning the other established narratives, usurped their narrative methods and forms of intelligibility. The literary theorist Gillian Beer was the first to show that though *Principles of Geology* teems with negative references to fiction—in the name of the rational truth of uniformitarian geology—Lyell nevertheless availed himself of the resources of fiction to make the stupefying truth more easily assimilable.[44]

Lyell's writings fall within a classic Platonic logic. He differentiates three types of illusions: an evolutionary illusion, justifiable in his view; an epistemological illusion, which he judged unforgivable; and a literary illusion he believed pointless, albeit harmless. According to Lyell (as Redon's creature, stunned by the two infinities, also showed), "In an early state of advancement, when a great number of natural appearances are unintelligible, an eclipse, an earthquake, a flood, or the approach of a comet ... are regarded as prodigies."[45] But what the gradualist and soon-to-be evolutionist found justifiable in the hypertrophied mythopoetic faculty of primitive peoples turned out to be unforgivable in a scientific discourse. Lyell considered the "fanciful conjectures" of the catastrophists to be the consequence of their unavowed dependence on the Bible. Their use of acceleration, revolution, and other notions to describe the condensation of time were the only means they had to reconcile geology with the brief duration of the earth as the theological narrative construed it. Yet these notions were fictional in the strict sense, having their origin in novels or even fairy-tales. What the fairy-tale did with space, the catastrophists did with time:[46] they obliterated distances and gaps. In short, Lyell might very well have subscribed to this statement later made by Fernand Braudel: "Fortunately or unfortunately, our profession does not have the admirable suppleness of the novel."[47] Lyell fought metaphor with metaphor. Turning first against his scientific opponents, he remarked that to posit the acceleration of geological time was to act *as if* historians were condensing a span of two thousand years into a century, and he added that "armies and fleets would appear to be assembled only to be destroyed, and cities built merely to fall in ruins."[48] Like Cuvier, the British geologist thus appealed to human history, ontologically familiar and culturally assimilated, to make the earth's history comprehensible *by analogy*.[49] The darkness of geological prehistory was that of human thought, and the only torch that could illuminate it was metaphor, whose semantic plasticity translated into temporal plasticity. Metaphor and analogy magically brought about a prodigious acceleration of time and finally a humanization of the nonhuman.

Nevertheless, the theorist of geological actualism did not confine himself to using analogy as a figure of discourse; he also employed it as a method of scientific induction. Lyell's methodological analogy consists of actualism itself: "Every fact collected respecting the causes in diurnal action . . . [affords] a key to the interpretation of some mystery in the past."[50] Fiction, a Trojan horse of sorts, thus came to occupy the very center of diurnal empiricism. The actualist analogy made up for "man's disproportion." Thanks to it, man could compensate for his limited existence in time and earthly space, the largest part of which — the ocean — still remained unknown. Significantly, Braudel, too, would emphasize the actualizing force of geology. The enormously long past of the Mediterranean basin, he writes in *Memory and the Mediterranean*, was still present: "Everything seems to come back to life," provided you look into it, forgetting structures and events the better to grasp the incredible constraining force of the environment — the longest of *longues durées*.[51]

The web of metaphors that formed around geological time might have constituted a perfect paradigm for Hans Blumenberg's metaphorological analysis of Western thought. The metaphors of the ladder and of childhood, of revolutions and fairy tales, supplemented the concept of indeterminate time and attempted to approach "a totality inaccessible" to any scientific approach, "yet still given to experience as a task."[52] Metaphor, far from being limited to an intellectual exercise, has a vital function, according to Blumenberg, since it is supposed to set aside and contradict the "absolutism of reality."[53] And what sort of absolutism could prove more implacable than that of a reality surpassing the resources of thought and implying, as we will see, the disappearance of the species? Among the paradigms Blumenberg studied was that of the "terra incognita," which responded to the urgency of conceptualizing infinite space after the Copernican revolution.[54] And it is not by chance that the "terra incognita" that stretched out to the stars and beyond became a gnoseological precedent for the discovery of a time extending so far into the past that it became unknown. Frédérique Aït-Touati has shown how fiction was used systematically both by astronomers and by poets to make the invisibility and inaccessibility of outer space visible.[55] For Kepler, Fontenelle, and Cyrano, fiction was a "prolongation of the telescope,"[56] placing before all eyes what permanently eluded them. Its utility was twofold and contradictory: it both projected earthly practices onto interplanetary space and shook up these practices by bringing them face to face with worlds even newer than America. A comparison between the disciplines of astronomy and geology would soon become one of the guiding threads of the scientific and fictional discourse about earthly time. It was this comparison, both gnoseological and psychological, that Redon also reactivated in his drawing of the first creature confronting infinity.

Lyell himself used an analogy with outer space to justify what was a heresy in his geological system: the absence of a "beginning." "The system which does not find traces of a beginning, like the physical astronomer, whose finest telescope only discovers myriads of other worlds, is the most sublime."[57] Like Cuvier, he saw astronomy as a transcendental precedent: because it was possible to conceive of the sublimity of the universe, it would ultimately also be possible to conceive of the sublimity of earthly time. In the end, however, nothing would attest more powerfully to the mind's "superiority" than the expansion of "our dominion over time," which contains "all the ages, even though they be myriads of years, over which science may enable us to extend our thoughts, and whence we may derive . . . fresh ideas — power — and delight."[58] In spite of everything, space remained an exteriority jealously holding onto its share of transcendence, whereas geological time was twofold in nature, combining the flexibility of the immaterial and the concreteness of the sensible. Like any sort of time, it was analogical, metaphorizable, combinable, endowed with the inner flexibility that is superior to the ultimate exteriority of extension. But geological time is nonetheless spatialized, objectified, sensible, eminently material, and a priori tangible. That dual nature of geology, immaterial and sensible, eminently plastic and cruelly permanent, was reflected in the twofold function of geology as a discipline, which produced a temporal vertigo even as it offered the means to end it.

It would be difficult to find a more striking expression of geology's *pharmakon* quality than Edgar Quinet's *The Creation*. This astonishing text begins with Quinet's experience of stupor the first time he went to Hautes-Alpes. "I thought I was on another planet. That horizon seemed to me beyond the human faculties."[59] What challenged his faculties, almost ejecting him from his usual world, was first and foremost his experience of time as a sort of a spiral, a bottomless abyss:

> Antiquity retreats from us on all sides: Iron Age, Bronze Age, Stone Age. Beyond that threshold, the geological eras open like a tangible infinity. What will become of us in the midst of these centuries that fall in line around us? We have been playing with eternity in the smallest pebble; what, then, will we make of man? Just yesterday, he was astonished that he passed so quickly on earth; how much shorter his life has now become in comparison with the incalculable age that presses on him and oppresses him on all sides! He was

only a point in the span of time; that point is being erased and disappears in the immensity. *We slip away from ourselves.*[60]

His experience of slipping away from himself on the summits of the Alps was a form of vertigo, but a vertigo more temporal than spatial and for which there was a remedy: "When . . . I felt I was losing my footing, vertigo taking hold of me, I had one method that always allowed me to avoid it. I asked myself a very precise question about geology: What rock is that? From what era? How was it formed?" It was thus the science of geology that put an end to vertigo. In its latest incarnation, the conquest of Reason was transmuted into the experience of the Kantian sublime. As Quinet said, "The imagination was pushed aside, and it regained its balance; reason awakened, and one faculty came to the assistance of another."[61]

In short, uniformitarianism inflicted the pain, but immediately provided the remedy. Thanks to this theory, time retreated indefinitely, even as it was imprisoned in the capsule of the present. As Lyell wrote to a geologist friend: "Probably, there was a beginning — it is a metaphysical question, worthy a theologian — probably there will be an end. . . . It is not the beginning I look for, but proofs of a *progressive* state of existence in the globe."[62] Furthermore, nothing really prevented the specter of metaphysics from returning in more or less unexpected forms. As Louis Simond, an author of travel narratives, noted: "From metaphysics, which is now somewhat neglected, the Scottish scholars moved on to geology, from the mind to stones, subjects that are almost equally impenetrable." Referring to James Hutton's theory, he immediately noted that "the extremely slow pace of that natural process . . . only marks the imperceptibility of our own timespan."[63] The perspicacious observer understood that Lyell's infinitesimal present was as imperceptible as the long term. That is why metaphors and fictions had to be enlisted to show and prove what experience ultimately did not allow one to observe. The present, as Lyell conceived it, identical to the past, could easily lead to metaphysics; expanding and stretching back to the mists of time, it thereby lost its domesticated and reassuring character. The ladder of time fell apart.

Humankind: The Long Term

The Past

MAN IS A THINKING MOUNTAIN

The contradiction between the long term, under the control of the present, and a present that slipped away from itself and sank into the abyss of time grew and intensified in the second half of the nineteenth century. It was transposed from geology and paleontology to the discourses and practices that had man as their object — especially linguistics, ethnology, psychology, art, and literature. This immeasurably long term, from which both the species and the individual felt excluded a priori, was increasingly internalized, even becoming a constitutive trait of humanity itself. It was as if the corollary of the historicization of nature was the *ensavaugement* of man in his most intimate being. Many sought to internalize the incommensurable in order to constitute a reassuring chain flawlessly linking earth and man, time and history, geology and biography, but this internalization ended up opening the abyss of time in the depths of man himself. Metaphysical anxiety, heretofore perpetuated primarily by the idea of God, was soon converted into historical fact, which became even harder to escape. Therefore, now that we have followed the metaphors that were used to conceive of and become familiar with the earth's long term, we need to move in the opposite direction and follow the metaphorization of that long term as a specifically human quality. It is helpful once more to recall Blumenberg, who explained the "potentially metaphorical constitution" of man by the fact that he "grasps himself only by taking a detour through what he is not."[64]

Let us note from the outset that the long term functioned both as a constraint and as the possibility of openness and freedom. On the one hand, a certain unconsciousness was attributed to it and assumed the inevitability of fate: all of us, whether we wish it or not, would be led back to the forgotten past — our own, that of our species, and that of the earth as a whole. On the other hand, that same unconsciousness opened onto the future, delivering human beings from the narrow confines of a tired, stereotypical history and revealing the potential of what Marcel Proust would call an "involuntary" memory, that is, a dormant memory, but one capable of reawakening. The long term thus threatened to crush at any moment Pascal's "disproportionate man," but it also functioned as an escape route: being unknown, it fostered the imagination. Dinosaurs could replace the dragons in Turner's history painting because both had the spark of the fantastic and the patina of truth, just like human memory. First and foremost, the remote past was *brand new, never before seen,* so much so that it caused stupor. Raymond Schwab, in a now-forgotten article titled "The Renaissance of the Archaic," interpreted the regressive tendency of modern art as merely a symptom of the frenetic quest for astonishment and shock. In pursuit of an ever-retreating past, art finally slipped over the slopes of "Les Ezyies," "Frobenius," and "the prehistoric of Boucher de Perthes." "It must be added," he wrote with a good dose of irony, "that when someone is dead for as long as the primitives have been dead, he becomes an incredible being and thereby reintroduces us to mystery."[65] Apart from the strangeness of the remote past, it was also its continuing expansion and indetermination, making it cross through periods and ages, but also the natural kingdoms, that disrupted history in its known form. The internalization of the long term was thus a profoundly contradictory process, wavering constantly between past and present, constraint and freedom.

The republican Quinet, exiled from France by Louis Napoléon Bonaparte, discovered in the Alps a span of time long enough to protect him from his "bewilderment" in the human present.[66] Temporal vertigo led him to understand that the "contemporary world," composed of loss and conflicts, was not the only world.[67] What was Napoléon le Petit's authoritarian regime, compared with the immensity of the ages? Nothing, but also and simultaneously everything. Later, in fact, Quinet would refer to that political regime as to a past that belonged to him all the more, inasmuch as he had buried it within himself: "The thoughts we dismiss obey us only in appearance. Pushed away, they take refuge farther off, in the depths of our being. If we track them down there, they retreat even farther, into fibers of one sort or another, where they rule over us, in spite of us, unbeknown to us."[68] He described these repressed thoughts as "mysteries that still envelop us, not, I would say, in the sky or on earth, but in the marrow of our bones, in our fibers, in our nerves." Thus, the infinite, which had formerly been projected into the stars, was in reality only within our memory: "Here, right next to us, within us, is what lies beyond reach."[69] The stupefying geology Quinet had discovered in the Alps was carved into his own psyche: man is "like a continent, a world in which only the shores, the cliffs, a few coastal landscapes, and the steep promontories have been identified. But the interior of that world and, within that interior, the successive formations, the age-old deposit, the accumulated work of the imperceptible agents" is a "terra incognita."[70] Recall the prehistorian John Lubbock, remembering the Orientalizing dreams of an entire century: "While we have been straining our eyes to the East, and eagerly watching excavations in Egypt and Assyria, suddenly a new light has arisen in the midst of us."[71] The most ancient past of all resided in the supposedly most familiar sediment, that of Europe and of man himself.

When the analogy between man and geology ultimately became part of the field of biology via the laws of heredity, all its performative potential was realized, even literalized. Hence, an individual's history could become interlinked with that of the species, and all the links in the chain of time could be calmly laid out. This process occurred through the use of all sorts of theories of regression, which hypothesized survivals, "engrams," atavisms, even the law of recapitulation,[72] all nomadic and interrelated concepts to which I will return in Chapter 2. For the time being, I note that all these concepts circulating between the natural and the human sciences shared two fundamental premises: first, that the past is never really past, and second, that natural time and human time are similarly inclined to reverse direction, and *there is thus no real ontological break between nature and man*, contrary to what Vico in his time, or later, Cuvier, had thought. For Flammarion, regressions are always possible, but time tends to accumulate, in nature and in man, in accord with an endless evolutionary process: "Yes," he wrote, "we have our roots in the past, we still have mineral in our bones, we inherited the best patrimony from our ancestors in the zoological series, and we are still somewhat plantlike in certain respects."[73] The psychologist Théodule Ribot, demonstrating his "law of regression" in the pathologies of memory, warned against the assumption that "memories are deposited in the brain in the form of strata, arranged chronologically, like geological stratifications."[74] Yet Friedrich Nietzsche, though an attentive reader of Ribot, did conceive of the human brain as a geology, stratified and furrowed in the course of its long evolution. It seemed to him that "cruel" men are "surviving specimens of earlier civilizations. The mountain height of humanity here reveals its lower formations, which might otherwise remain hidden from view." Living fossils of the human past, these specimens "appal us," though they are a wholly mineral unconscious and "as little responsible on this account as is a piece of granite for being granite."[75] The brains of civilized beings still retained the traces of that primitive and unconscious minerality, "but these courses and windings are no longer the bed in which flows the stream of our feeling."[76] As Quinet had also said, what truly marked the difference between human beings and the other species was the transcendental nature of history: only man is conscious of the strata that compose his being. Historical man is a thinking mountain, and no other being sums up "in himself, in a visible way, the annals sunken under the layers of the globe, nor that power of change, of renewal, that links one epoch to another." Quinet added that it was possible to "rediscover in man his diverse, Silurian, Permian, Jurassic, Cretaceous, Eocene epochs, that is, his times of stagnation, storms, explosion, upheavals and falls, centuries-long dormant periods, then his sudden eruptions, his giants and his infinitely small things."[77]

That geological metaphorization of human thought and of the human psyche was correlated with an epistemological turn that began in the mid-nineteenth century. According to the historian Claude Blanckaert,[78] who has reconstituted that turn, William Whewell's *History of the Inductive Sciences from the Earliest Times to the Present* (1837) was fundamental in this respect in that it was the first to place the cosmos, the earth, and man within the same cognitive field. They could all be studied using the "paletiological" method, which consisted of identifying the ancient causes that lay at the origin of phenomena.[79] Comparative linguistics, in its fantasy of reconstituting the protolanguage, established an enduring equivalence between the fossils of the antediluvian world and those discovered in the roots of words from different languages and in the interrelationships among these words. In 1859, pointing out the uncertainty of an Indo-European language spoken at the dawn of time, Adolphe Pictet compared his project of "reviving the past in tableaux animated by the spirit of ancient times" to "earthly paleontology," which "sought to retrace for us a few scenes of the antediluvian world."[80] But Pictet was convinced that "words endure just as much as bones."[81] F. Max Müller agreed, affirming in turn that the monosyllabic period "was the beginning of language, just as surely as granite rocks formed the first layer of earth," and that philology is the science allowing us to "study more closely the various layers of which our language is composed and to analyze the elements with which the granite of our thoughts is formed."[82] In *The Future of Science* (1848), Ernest Renan readily conceded that it was impossible to reach "the trace of the primeval world . . . beneath the numerous layers of peoples and idioms which have absolutely been piled upon on one another in certain countries." But he consoled himself with the thought that there were languages "less worked up by successive revolutions, that are less variable in their forms, and spoken by peoples doomed to remain stationary."[83]

We will have occasion to return at great length to that presumed equivalence between some living peoples and geological fossils. For the moment, I simply note that the two principal disciplines engaged in internalizing the long term were ethnology and psychology. Lubbock clearly stated that prehistoric archaeology was modeled on geology: "Deprived, therefore, as regards this period, of any assistance from history, but relieved at the same time from the embarrassing interference of tradition, the archaeologist is free to follow the methods which have been successfully pursued in geology — the rude bones and stone implements of bygone ages being to the one what the remains of extinct animals are to the other." And what was true for the artifacts was also true for human beings: "In fact, the Van

Diemaner and South American are to the antiquary what the opossum and the sloth are to the geologist."[84] The evolutionary ladder, in short, was applicable to all the supports and objects of knowledge: strata, artifacts, human beings. James Frazer transposed that ladder to civilized societies. Analyzing the universal belief in magic, he presented it as a "solid stratum of intellectual agreement among the dull, the weak, the ignorant, and the superstitious, who constitute, unfortunately, the vast majority of mankind." And just as the globe had been formed from a common core, "one of the great achievements of the nineteenth century" was to "run shafts down into this low mental stratum" (he meant magic) "and thus to discover its substantial identity everywhere. It is beneath our feet — and not very far beneath them — here in Europe at the present day, and it crops up on the surface in the heart of the Australian wilderness and wherever the advent of a higher civilisation has not crushed it under ground."[85] What for certain European populations remained buried was on display in Australia, spread out across the horizontality of the desert, where the Aborigines led their rudimentary and repetitive lives.

In the early twentieth century, at a time when the theory of recapitulation had not yet been challenged (it even provided Freud with the coherence and universality necessary for his theory of the unconscious), the long term contained even that prehistory from which human beings were excluded, the geological and the paleontological.[86] For the psychoanalyst Sándor Ferenczi, every birth was a repetition of the human species emerging from the sea, "a recapitulation on the part of the individual of the great catastrophe which at the time of the recession of the ocean forced so many animals, and certainly our own animal ancestors, to adapt themselves to a land existence, above all to renounce gill-breathing and provide themselves with organs for the respiration of air."[87] The universal catastrophe was thus translated into an original personal trauma, an "engram,"[88] Ferenczi also said, engraved forever in the constitution of each individual, past and future. It could only be repressed, not erased. Was it possible to return to the time before the catastrophe? In a certain manner, yes: sexual pleasure and hypnosis were two forms of the "thalassal regressive trend," that is, "the striving toward the aquatic mode of existence abandoned in primeval times."[89] Freud himself sought the sources of neurotic survivals in a past even more remote than the prehistory of human beings he had described in *Totem and Taboo* and *Moses and Monotheism*. In a fragment from 1915, he saw infantile anxiety as the phylogenetic heritage of the "anxiety from the beginning of the Ice Age,"[90] and, in another fragment, written toward the end of his life, he projected himself back into "a prehistoric landscape — for instance, in the Jurassic," where "the great saurians are still running about; the horsetails grow as high as palms."[91] The use of the present tense in this passage expresses all the force of the survival from the past.

The aging heroine of Virginia Woolf's last novel, *Between the Acts* (1941), combined pell-mell snatches of memory from her youth and readings about the earth before human beings existed, "before there was a channel, when the earth, upon which the Windsor chair was planted, was a riot of rhododendrons, and humming birds quivered at the mouths of scarlet trumpets, as she had read that morning in her Outline of History." In Woolf's subjective or "mind" time, the past irrupts into the present with such intensity that it replaces perception: "It took her five seconds in actual time, in mind time ever so much longer, to separate Grace herself, with blue china on a tray, from the leather-covered grunting monster who was about, as the door opened, to demolish a whole tree in the green steaming undergrowth of the primeval forest."[92]

There was only one way to proceed when faced with the aporia and strangeness of the long term as the history books and manuals taught it: namely, to internalize it at the risk of losing contact with the present — to sew it in the colorful fabric of "mind time," which, however, had neither a coherent weft nor a pattern. The past became available through snatches of memory and momentary lapses — what the Land Art artist Robert Smithson would later call "monumental vacancies,"[93] which he would attempt to signify in works rooted in the earth and composed of mineral materials. And when he analyzed his approach in the 1960s, he would often describe his own brain as "in a constant

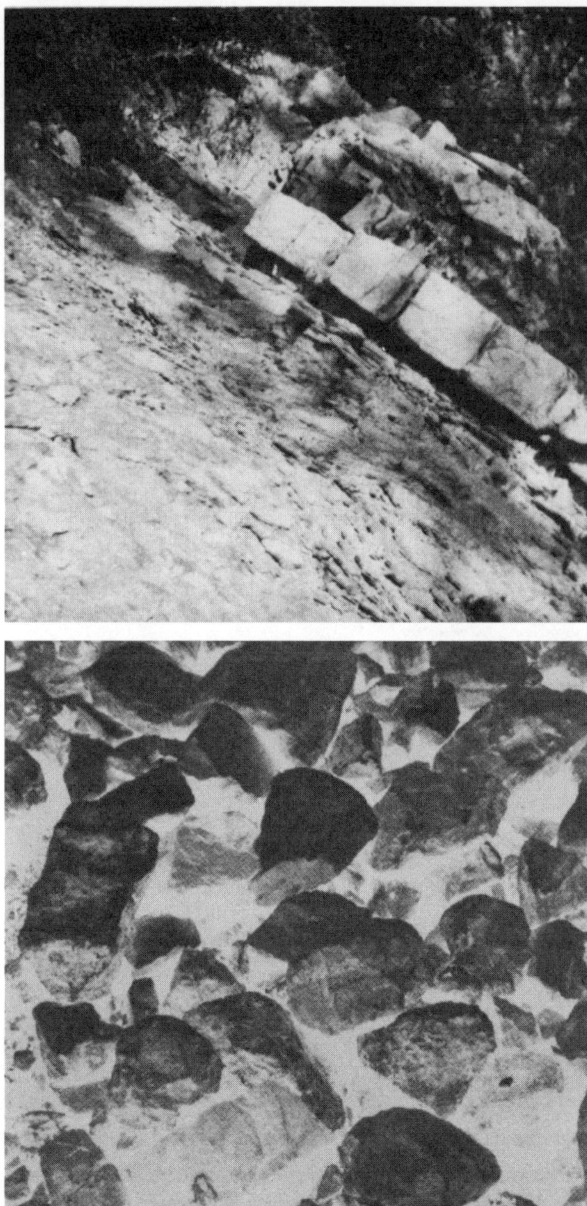

Figure 1.3. *Strata, a Geophotographic Fiction*, 1970. Archives of American Art, Washington, DC, Robert Smithson and Nancy Holt papers, 1905–87, bulk 1952–87. Photo: © 2021 Holt/Smithson Foundation/VAGA at ARS, NY.

state of erosion," where "mental rivers wear away abstract banks, brain waves undermine cliffs of thought, ideas decompose into stones of unknowing, and conceptual crystallizations break apart into deposits of gritty reason"[94] (Figure 1.3). In the end, for what other fissure could geological erosion be the metaphor, if not that of human mortality itself? In *Man in the Holocene* (1979), Max Frisch would compare the stroke suffered by an old man living in a remote corner of Ticino to a cataclysm, a landslide. Frisch makes the reader a witness to the experience of total spatial and temporal disorientation that leads the old man increasingly to wall himself off from the world. The loss of memory takes the form of countless memos, primarily on geology and paleontology, a deposit scattered across the walls, fossils of a former encyclopedic knowledge. The old man constantly projects his collapse onto the geological scale, where saurians are vanishing, mountains crumble in torrential rain, and mute and nameless species are alive.[95] Soon, the earth will exist without him: a man annexes the earth's past and that of the species to experience his own end as both the subject and the only witness to his death. In all these texts, the geological metaphor causes a maximal and irremediable disappropriation, the very same that the early geological metaphors attempted to obscure.

CÉZANNE'S GEOLOGY

Paul Cézanne was without a doubt the first painter to have worked methodically and somewhat obstinately on the analogy between the abyss of time and the abyss of the self. Beginning in the 1890s and for the last fifteen years of his life, the buried past of his youth made a resurgence. After leaving Paris and landing "back in the Midi,"[96] Cézanne began to paint Mont Sainte-Victoire, as well as other landscapes near Aix-en-Provence, his native city. He did so day after day, every year for the rest of his life, until his death in 1906. Memories emerged of his happy adolescence, transfigured in his compositions of bathers. But the work of memory itself, its conflictual relationship with the perception of the present, primarily took the form of geological landscapes from which — with a single exception — every human figure is banished.

Whereas the Sainte-Victoire massif rises up, impenetrable and sovereign, through the compact accumulation of its strata and its quasi-pyramidal form, the rocky landscapes of Fontainebleau, for example, have an almost cataclysmic appearance — forbidding, chaotic, jagged. Even when these landscapes bear the traces of human labor, Cézanne returns them to the natural kingdom and the earth's long term. *Bibémus Quarries* (1895) (Figure 1.4) depicts a limestone site exploited since Roman times and abandoned toward the end of the nineteenth century, around the time Cézanne painted it. The masses of ocher limestone, hewn by successive generations, are like giant bones, paleontological remains of some unknown antediluvian species, eaten away by the natural elements. These smoothly polished and flattened masses, depicted frontally and occupying most of the painting, barely allow the blue zone of the sky to peek through above the green trees growing here and there in thick clumps. Cézanne also painted the debris of old mills at the Château-Noir, as in *The Millstone* (1892–1894), where blocks of hewn stone are scattered amid the rocks and leafy tree trunks. In these works, man has not been absent from the beginning; he has disappeared and been forgotten. And just as the walls of *Bibémus Quarries* form an impenetrable surface that blocks the gaze, allowing it at the very most to glide along the fissures, intersections, angles, and holes, Cézanne's indistinct and chaotic landscapes obstruct the viewer's sight with the diagonal line of the trunks, the teetering masses of rock, and the thick vegetation — all obstacles to visual perception and corporeal projection. Cézanne wrote that we must "seek to express the confused sensations we bring with us when we are born."[97] He thought he had found them in these landscapes molded by time, but largely out of reach and resistant to the actions and appropriation of the present. Having fallen outside the realm of the familiar and the useful, these landscapes were overtaken by what Henri Bergson called the "powerless" past, different in nature from the "sensori-motor" present, which propels the body to action.[98] This past, which is without immediate utility, emerges from consciousness and forms the matter of time, Bergsonian "duration": prepared to return, but only capriciously and contingently, it looks for a fissure

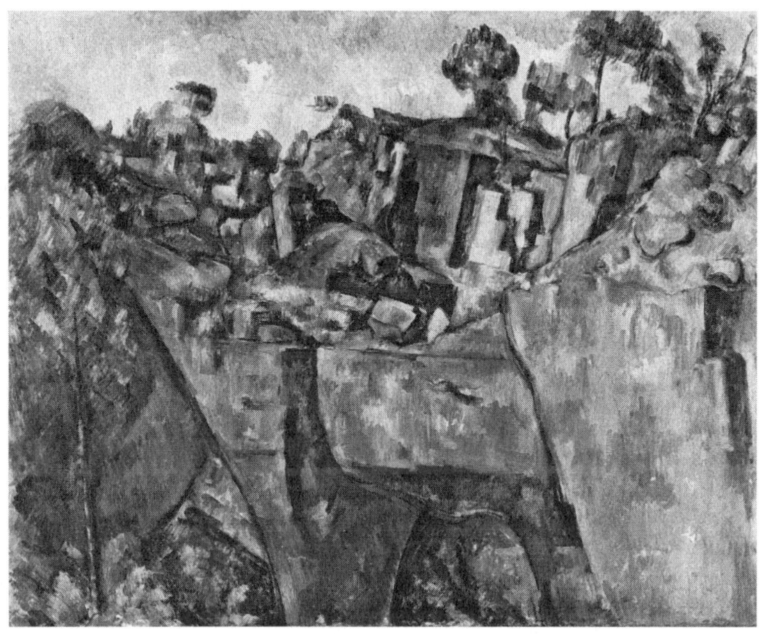

Figure 1.4. Paul Cézanne, *Bibémus Quarries*,
ca. 1895. Oil on canvas, 25½ × 31⅞ in.
Museum Folkwang, Essen. © Museum Folkwang Essen/ARTOTHEK.

in the present. It is no different for Cézanne, who chose the landscapes marked by geological time because he could also inscribe in
them the fissures of his own subjective time.

As we are often reminded, Meyer Schapiro demonstrated that the
young Cézanne's sexuality, finding expression in a few hallucinations
of orgies and violence, was suppressed and repressed through the act
of painting his still lifes with apples.[99] Less well known is Schapiro's
hypothesis that these hallucinations burst forth again in the landscapes of Cézanne's final years, marked by the violence of nature: "He
recreates on his canvases a space, still detached, but even farther from
humanity, in which his old aggressive impulses have been transposed

to nature itself. For the early scenes of murder and rape and gloomy introspection, he substitutes an abandoned catastrophic landscape."[100] Nude women, murders, and scenes of cannibalism are now stripped of their human elements and transferred to inert matter, which protects the painter from the "grapnel" of the living thing, even while giving free rein to the fantasies of the past. Jean-Claude Lebensztejn has also pointed out "the persistence of memory" in Cézanne, especially "the memorable return of the young Cézanne in the elderly man" and the way this "affected the paintings of his last years."[101]

It was the young Cézanne, in fact, who examined the sediment in the soil of Aix with his friend Antoine-Fortuné Marion, who would later become a renowned paleontologist and the director of the Aix museum.[102] Nina Athanassoglou-Kallmyer was the first art historian to work the geological vein in Cézanne, taking a particular interest in his early years as a way to understand the landscapes from the end of his life.[103] A sketchbook dating to about 1858, according to the catalogue raisonné of his drawings (the painter would have been nineteen) includes four successive pages of geological sketches. On four of these pages, Cézanne had previously done a few hasty sketches and studies inspired by history paintings. Marion had drawn schematic stacks of geological strata on the first two pages, adding the names of the corresponding geological eras (Figures 1.5 and 1.6). On the two following pages, the drawings are noticeably different; Marion's neutral horizontality is replaced by a more pronounced and tormented verticality. These more iconic drawings are no doubt by Cézanne himself. The masses of stone are once again drawn over preexisting sketches, including one of a pastoral concert, which contrasts sharply with the tormented masses in the superimposed drawing. Finally, on the edge of the drawing, Cézanne drew a male figure, elegantly dressed and sporting a top hat, visibly planted after the fact on an actual geological base composed of several concentric sedimentary layers filled with stones and carved with incisions. On these pages, the tradition of European painting merges with the ephemeral present, both of them engulfed in the very long term. A soldier in an eighteenth-century uniform becomes the substratum for Marion's geological diagrams; a calm pastoral concert is transplanted to a menacing landscape; one of Cézanne's contemporaries is immobilized on a pile of sediment. The painter deliberately plays with human scale. But the disjunction will come to occupy the center of the landscapes of his final years: between a man's fleeting perception of nature and the permanence of the latter; between a painter who wants to "realize the landscape" and a world already perfectly "realized" in and of itself; and finally, between modernity, which passes away, and the long term, which endures.

When Cézanne proved critical of an impressionism that, it seemed to him, pulverized vision, he found a natural ally in geology, its solidity and permanence. The geological *longue durée* came to predominate both as motif and as the expression of time. The artist Robert Smithson, with his customary perspicacity, remarked in the 1960s that Cézanne chose a site for its "physicality" and the impact of that physicality on perception to create the sense of "being on the ground, thrown back on to a kind of soil."[104] He was not mistaken: whereas the impressionists applied the contingency of their subjective perception to the most evanescent motifs in nature and in the social world of modernity, Cézanne applied that contingency to motifs as enduring and persistent as Mont Sainte-Victoire.

The Sainte-Victoire massif contained in concentrated form what Cézanne was looking for: of an indeterminate age, it was solid and above all *sovereign*—like the "Pater Omnipotens Aeterne Deus," whom the painter humbly recognized as his only master.[105] Mont Sainte-Victoire was not merely a motif. It represented the painter's "geological"[106] perception because it inextricably linked present sensations and memories. Cézanne's compositions knit together superimposed and contiguous, increasingly unstable layers. He sought to erase all the memories that intervened between his motif and himself, often repeating that it was necessary to "see nature as if no one had seen it before you."[107] The "realization" of his "little sensations of color" was therefore supposed to allow the present to grasp hold of the world. But Cézanne also tried to give his little sensations the solidity of the mountain and of his own past, which was increasingly

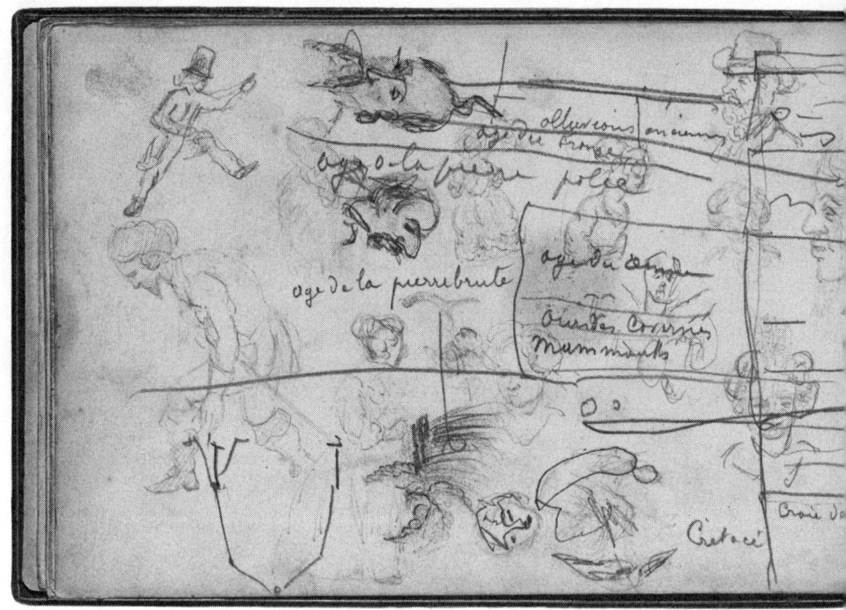

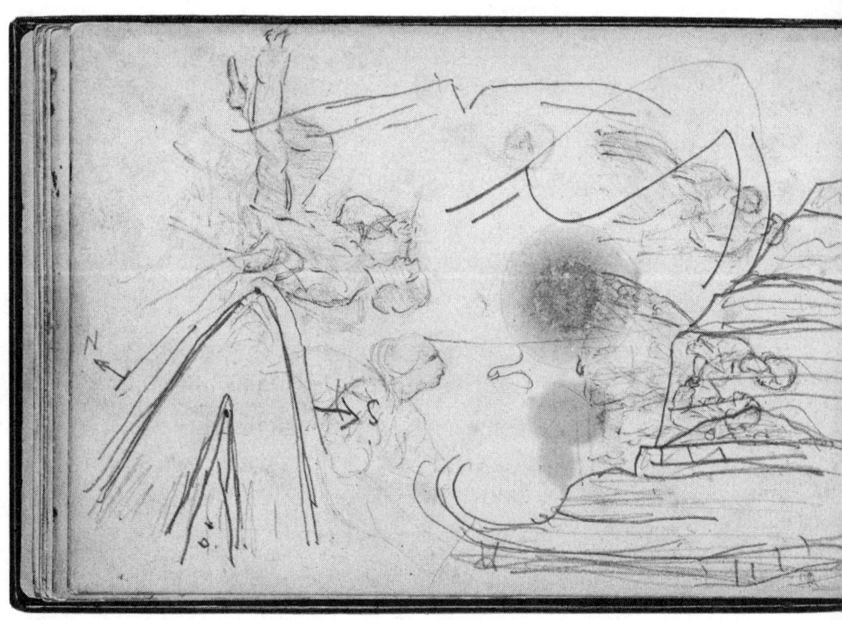

Figures 1.5. and 1.6. Paul Cézanne, *Sketchbook*, ca. 1858–60, 5⅞ × 9¼ in. Musée d'Orsay, Paris, held at the Louvre, RF19949-15-folio 7 and RF19949-16-folio 8; RF19949-19-folio 9 and RF19949-20-folio 10. © RMN-Grand Palais (Musée d'Orsay)/Michel Urtado.

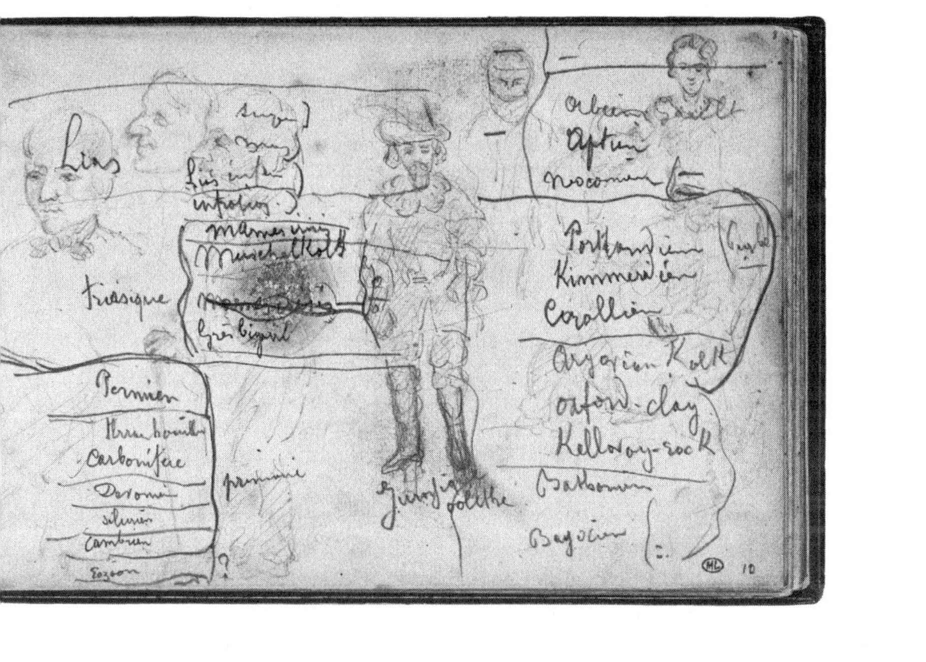

Lias
Lias inf.
infralias
triasique
marnes irisées
Muschelkalk
Grès bigarré
Permien
Houille
Carbonifère
Devonien
silurien
Cambrien
Eozoon
primaire
Albien
Aptien
Neocomien
Portlandien
Kimmeridien
Corallien
Argovien Kalk
oxford-clay
Kelloway-rock
Bathonien
Bajocien
10

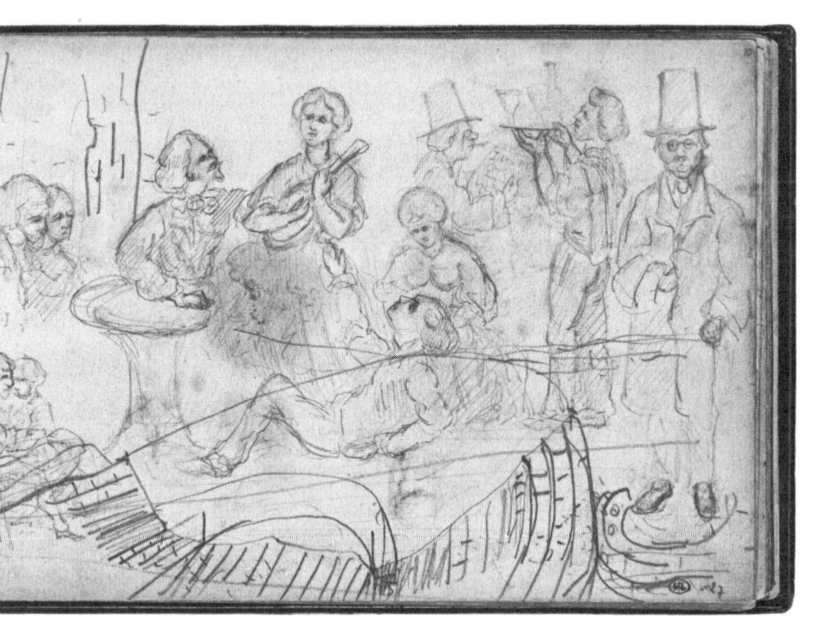

indistinguishable from his object: "It's impossible," he wrote to Gasquet, "to be unmoved when we recall those bygone days, and that atmosphere we breathed awares, which is no doubt the source of our outlook today."[108] A newborn and an old man at the same time, Cézanne knew that the past was engraved on his body against his will, that it could therefore burst forth at any moment in "the realization of his sensations."

It was no doubt for these reasons that the painter banished human figures from his landscape: the frontal and unmediated relationship with his motif that he ordinarily chose delineated a world as sovereign as it was dependent on man. It was through an "I" that the world lived: "if I die, it will all be over, but no matter."[109] Only once did Cézanne place a figure in a geological landscape: *In the Bibémus Quarries* (1895) (Figure 1.7) shows a tiny male figure seated on a rock in the middle of the ocher-colored landscape of the quarries. The vertical walls almost totally cover the surface of the painting, literally burying the figure in the bowels of the earth. He is caught between two large folds that converge to form the apex of an enormous triangle. The man's face, barely outlined, almost merges with this geological environment, while his body stands out somewhat more by its contour and the white of his shirt. This man is an "intermediate" figure, but in a different way than Redon's creature. There is no longer any transcendence that could exert an opposing force on his body; moreover, the body itself deposits part of its expressiveness in the surrounding world. In formal terms, Redon's "intermediate" being is at odds with both earth and sky. For Cézanne, on the contrary, man is simultaneously absorbed and crushed by his geological environment. Here, the dramatic tension is played out within formal immanence, because that tension is the expression of human desire: the triangle in which the man is seated is clearly sexual; he appears to be almost sucked up by this giant vagina dug into the quarries. But at the same time, the lower part of his body remains suspended, as if furtively or awkwardly placed there by the hand of God — or the artist. One half of the man's body is in a relation of erotic fusion with the landscape, assimilated to such an extent that the man loses his individuality; but

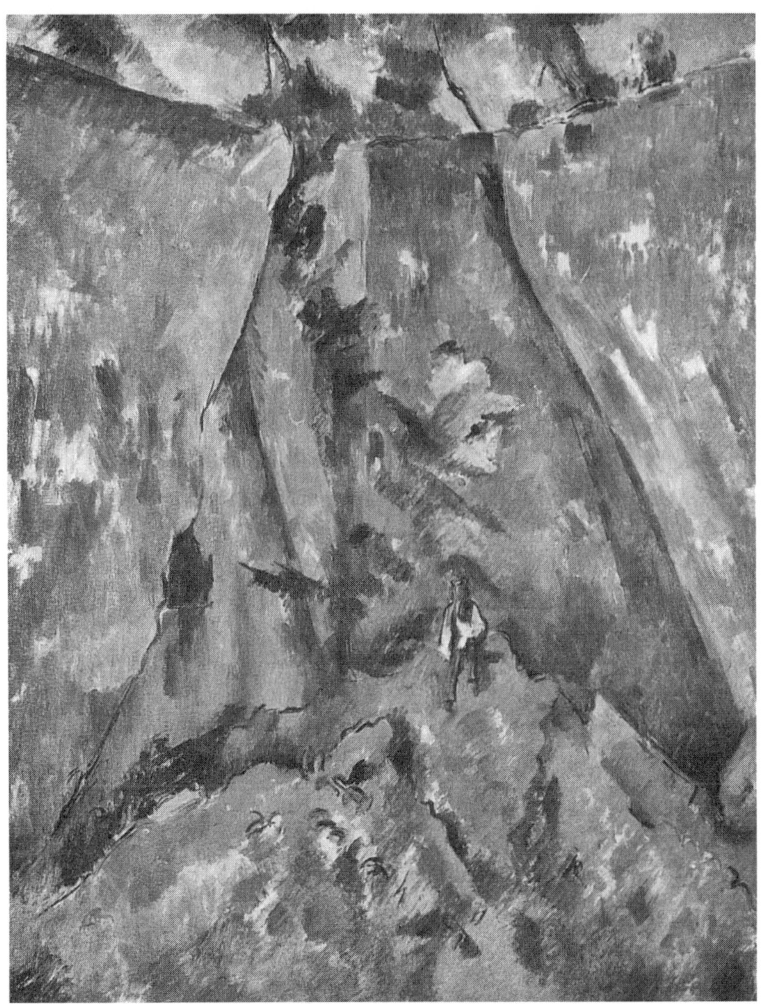

Figure 1.7. Paul Cézanne, *In the Bibémus Quarries*, ca. 1895. Oil on canvas, 31 × 25 in. Private collection, Paris.

the other half seems ill adapted to the landscape or crushed by geology. Through that duality, a constant tension is once again played out in Cézanne's painting, a result of his effort to find a balance between the sovereignty of nature and his subjective appropriation of it. But *In the Bibémus Quarries* is also the return of a specter: like so many other triangular structures with a sexual charge that haunt Cézanne's paintings, the geological vagina is a memory of *The Eternal Feminine* (1877), henceforth engraved in stone. Finally, this vagina is a recollection of modern painting, the paintings of Courbet, for example, whose caves and springs were all geological metaphors for woman.

This, then, is how the unconscious past — Cézanne's own, that of painting, and that of the earth — survived in his present. Like Lyell, Cézanne could do no more than attempt to live and understand geological time through his present. But the painter took the reverse tack from the geologist: rather than seek to make the unknown past familiar, he allowed himself to be invaded by it, to make what was most familiar strange. The past, because of its untamed state, could protect him from an excessively domesticated present and the lightning speed of progress, toward which, as is widely known, he harbored mistrust. It was that junction between the known and the unknown, between past and present, that he called "realization." His paintings were both solid entities and perceptual processes. Once again, Cézanne, unlike Lyell, did not aspire to imprison geological time in the capsule of the present: he was content to see his paintings as the result of a brief encounter between subject and world — a cross section of time.

In September 1939, when the artist Robert Morris was still a child, he discovered *Mont Sainte-Victoire Seen from Les Lauves* (1902–1906) at the Nelson-Atkins Museum of Art in Kansas City. He devoted an elegiac and joyful text titled "Cézanne's Mountains" (1998) to it a few decades later.[110] Amazed by the later Cézanne he had discovered in proletarian Kansas City, Morris projected himself onto the painter, interpreting the landscapes of Cézanne's final years as a melancholic "recalling" of his own childhood. According to Morris, the sedimentation of dabs of paint that made the sky so indistinguishable from the mountain — the lower part so quick to rise up and the distant to draw nearer than the near — created a "nausea of consciousness" that expressed the irresolvable tension between the expansion of vision and the limitations of the hand, between the organic body and sovereign minerality. But by way of compensation, there was a full and carnal affection by means of a past that was disintegrating, turning out to be hardly different in the end from modernity.

The Future

THE LONG TERM AND ACCELERATION: THE TWO ASPECTS
OF THE TEMPORALIZATION OF HISTORY

In the nineteenth century, time not only became more embedded in the past, it also stretched out toward an indefinite future. A history of the long term that confined itself to connecting it to the present and did not engage the future would be incomplete. It is therefore necessary to examine how, beginning in the nineteenth century, connections were established between the diverging temporalities of the remote past and the boundless future. In 1865, Lubbock, one of the first to propose the term "prehistory," was filled with hope: "We are in reality but on the threshold of civilization. Far from showing any indication of having come to an end, the tendency to improvement seems latterly to have proceeded with augmented impetus and accelerated rapidity." He concluded that it was "surely unreasonable to suppose that a process which has been going on for so many thousand years should have now suddenly ceased."[111] Assurances about the future were thus to be found, quite simply, in the past: time formed an uninterrupted line. Lubbock naturally endorsed the conclusion of Alfred Wallace, the coinventor (with Darwin) of the principle of "natural selection": "We can anticipate the time when the earth will produce only cultivated plants and domestic animals; when man's selection shall have supplanted 'natural selection'; and when the ocean will be the only domain in which that power can be exerted, which for countless cycles of ages ruled supreme over the earth."[112] After domesticating the elusive past, nothing could prevent nineteenth-century man from domesticating a future that was by definition unknown. Nevertheless, Lubbock and Wallace, in displacing

Eden from the past to the future, in so joyfully prefiguring mono-culture, which Claude Lévi-Strauss would deplore in *Tristes Tropiques* (1955), were in reality only fending off the specter of the extinction of our species. Extinction had in fact been a very important lever of natural evolution. Lubbock warded off the anxiety of extinction by invoking an acceleration of technology, but technology was far from a reliable and unqualified solution.

Among the first documents to attest to the anxiety roused in modern consciousness by the revelation of the earth's immeasurable age is a curious cartoon that the British geologist Thomas de la Beche sent to the Reverend Buckland in 1857 (Figure 1.8). It depicts an ichthyosaur wearing a morning coat, delivering a lecture to his young congeners in the middle of a lush forest. Appearing in the center of the image is a human skull crushed by a paving stone, an ironic vestige of a geological age when man's sovereignty was indisputable. It has been interpreted as an extreme commentary on Lyell's theses regarding the slowness of geological processes and the cyclical activity of the climate, which, according to him, lay behind the formation and extinction of species.[113] De la Beche exaggerated to the point of absurdity that eternal return of geology by positing human culture — and in particular the professorial techniques of the body — as the quasi-ethnological *survival* of a vanished age. Every fossil became a sign of an immeasurably long term precisely by bearing witness to the finitude of its species. The myriad extinctions potentially revealed by the earth's depths anticipated the imminent extinction of the human species, just as the fall of God led mechanically to that of his creature. The link by analogy between human history and the geological scale was projected onto the earth not only *before* human beings but also *after* them.

In the late nineteenth century, H. G. Wells, author of *The Time Machine*, whose debt to Darwin's theory of evolution is well known, speculated on the possible modes of human extinction, which he believed to be inevitable.[114] The Enlightenment narrative, then, was coming to an end, having achieved its apotheosis. Had not Condorcet said that "no bounds have been fixed to the improvement of the human faculties; that the perfectibility of man is absolutely

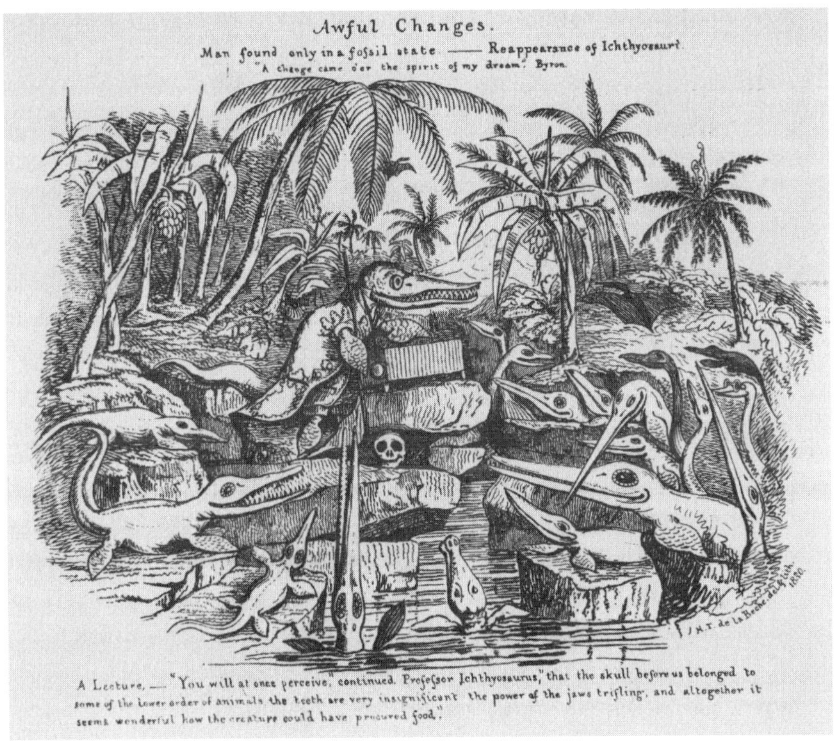

Figure 1.8. Thomas de la Beche, caricature of Charles Lyell sent to the Reverend Buckland and published by him as the frontispiece to his *Curiosities of Natural History* (London: Richard Bentley, 1857).

indefinite; that the progress of this perfectibility, henceforth above the control of every power that would impede it, has no other limit than the duration of the globe on which nature has placed us"?[115] Scarcely a century later, Quinet seemed to be responding directly to Condorcet when he clearly disassociated the end of man and that of the earth: "Man knew, in fact, that he is not immortal; but until now, he had persuaded himself that if he had to perish, everything living would perish with him. He imagined that he had taken possession of the earth such that it could not fail to belong to him. The idea of having successors had never entered his mind."[116]

It can never be stressed enough that prehistory, since its constitution as a body of knowledge and as an object of time consciousness, has been inextricably linked to the idea of the "end" and remains so in our own time. From the start, prehistory was associated with a theme that, after World War II, would be called "posthistory." Like De la Beche's caricature of Lyell, the geologist Gideon A. Mantell's *The Medals of Creation* (1844) looked forward to a distant future. An undetermined, still-unknown subject was studying the vestiges of what was called simply "the human epoch" and not yet the "Anthropocene."

> Their most striking features would be the remains of Man, and the productions of human art — the domes of his temples, the columns of his palaces, the arches of his stupendous bridges of iron and stone, the ruins of his towns and cities, and the durable remains of his earthly tenement imbedded in the rocks and strata — these would be the "Medals of Creation: of the *Human Epoch*, and transmit to the remotest periods of time, a faithful record of the present condition of the surface of the earth, and of its inhabitants.[117]

What remains to be understood, however, is the particular historical charge that the notion of extinction carried in the mid-nineteenth century. Through what specific filters was it understood and felt? Lubbock placed the emphasis on the unprecedented acceleration his century was witnessing: the achievements that had piled up within a few years were equivalent to those that had required centuries of human activity. Yet that productivist acceleration also possessed a proportional force of fossilization. Charles Lyell himself, who put the last nail in the coffin of Cuvier's geological catastrophism, wondered whether man, the only species that combined "physical *evolution*" and "moral *revolution*," would one day manage to change the evolutionary regime of *physis* by triggering the first revolution.[118] Although carefully refraining from giving a clear answer, he made it understood that the agents of the catastrophe had changed: the cause would no longer be divine transcendence or geological immensity, but the minuscule human factor. The process was thus circular: man was domesticating nature, but that domestication in turn played a role in the fossilization characteristic of natural evolution.

Many said they were convinced that humanity would one day or another be replaced by a superior species, in accordance with Darwin's principle of natural selection: "Judging from the past, we may safely infer that not one living species will transmit its unaltered likeness to a distant futurity. And of the species now living very few will transmit progeny of any kind to a far distant futurity."[119] In an increasingly domesticated world, it was not absurd to envision a human being self-formed with the assistance of technology as that future progeny. Some went so far as to imagine a natural selection occurring at man's expense. As an organism, man was potentially obsolete because incapable of responding to the demands of the mechanical environment he himself had created. Prehistory had revealed giant organisms long since vanished, and Samuel Butler saw the machines of his time as the extinct organisms of the future, calling them "the antediluvian prototypes of the race."[120] In opposition to an evolution that would allow machines, always improving and always impassive, to become "the successor in the supremacy of the earth," the people in Butler's utopian novel *Erewhon* (1872), living in complete anonymity on the far side of the New Zealand glaciers, waged a revolution against the machines.[121] The novel describes the people of Erewhon as an inverted image of the machine. They were a new organism, but one created by a moral revolution that diverted a natural evolution occurring over billions of years, beginning with an earth without life and ending in human civilizations. Since nothing could guarantee that a higher form of consciousness would develop in the machine, or even that machines would manage to reproduce themselves without human intervention, the residents of Erewhon took their own evolution in hand, confining themselves to the early Neolithic world.

But fossilizing acceleration also generated very pessimistic visions of an ultimately inanimate and empty world. Even as human beings became accustomed to observing the petrified remains and imprints of extinct species, they realized that their own creations were disappearing at an increasingly rapid pace under the capitalist regime of novelty. Twentieth-century artists repeatedly seized on that analogy. The materials they produced—both images and discourses—will help us understand why, since the mid-nineteenth century, *the more deeply embedded one becomes in prehistory, the more one accelerates toward the end; and the more one accelerates, the more one becomes embedded in prehistory.*

Gideon A. Mantell gives a striking formulation of this alliance, a priori paradoxical, between acceleration and the expansion of time.

> That splendid railway, the Great Western, by which the geologist may be transported in five or six hours, from the *Tertiary* strata of the metropolis, to the magnificent cliffs of Mountain limestone at Clifton, exposes in its course several fine sections, and passes within a moderate distance of some interesting localities of organic remains. This railroad traverses the *Tertiary* strata by Ealing, Hanwell, and Slough, entering the *Chalk* near Maidenhead, and pursuing rather a circuitous route to Wallingford.[122]

The nineteenth-century railroad, an agent and a symbol of the acceleration of time and the shrinking of space, moved so fast that it passed through different geological ages.[123]

Since the nineteenth century, the remote past, like the future, had been sucked up into the vortex of time. Acceleration and expansion were two sides of the same coin, namely, "temporalization," as Reinhart Koselleck called this experience of history.[124] We are beginning to understand why humanity's universal past, which was dissolving for lack of names and in the uncertainty of its places, times, and forms, was just as active in that temporalization of history. The push to learn about an extraordinarily remote archaeological past acted as a regressive acceleration, causing a form of vertigo that did not differ much in the end from that produced by physical speed. Together, a regressive acceleration and a technical acceleration erased the outlines of history, invalidating norms and pulverizing forms. As Quinet had suggested, the past straddled different periods and ages, but also natural kingdoms. That is why even as history seemed to be "positively" approaching its origin, it also felt definitively orphaned by it. The political implications of the privilege given to geological knowledge by the Industrial Revolution and the rise of capitalism, in their search for raw materials, have already been pointed out.[125] The mines offered an extraordinary field of exploration for the new discipline. But it is important to note, as well, that this discipline in return provided the coal industry with an extremely ambivalent political, ontological, and metaphysical experience. In the last third of the nineteenth century, the mathematician and philosopher Antoine Augustin Cournot had a few dazzling intuitions about the strange path that "the progress" theorized by the Enlightenment was taking. He described the transition from an aristocratic political model linked to the Christian conception of man as "king of Creation," to a political model of capitalist activity that made (European) man "the concessioner of the planet." The first model, in its characteristic stasis, was indifferent to questions of time, but the tension between millennial accumulation and voracious acceleration was central to the second:

> Man ascended or descended (as you choose to understand it) from the king of Creation he had been — or believed he had been — to the role of concessioner of a planet. In surveying the extension and thickness of these fossil layers, which required thousands of years to accumulate, which experienced the upheaval of so many revolutions before man appeared on earth, and which his industrious activity is so rapidly devouring today, he was able to push back to an indefinite past the first signs of his providential destinies and feel that the future is measured not only in terms of individuals, but also in terms of nations, in a different sense than was formerly believed. He had to develop a property, he had a mine to exploit.[126]

Nothing is more revealing of the double bind caused by the discovery of the long term than the preparations made in Sydenham Park in 1854 to accommodate the Crystal Palace, initially built for the Great Exhibition in London in 1851. This iron-and-glass edifice, the fabulous origin of heroic modernism,[127] though at first intended to be short-lived, would for a long time yet attest to the feats of British industry. But the most remote parts of the park were reserved for two reconstitutions of the distant past: first, an ideal-typical geological cross

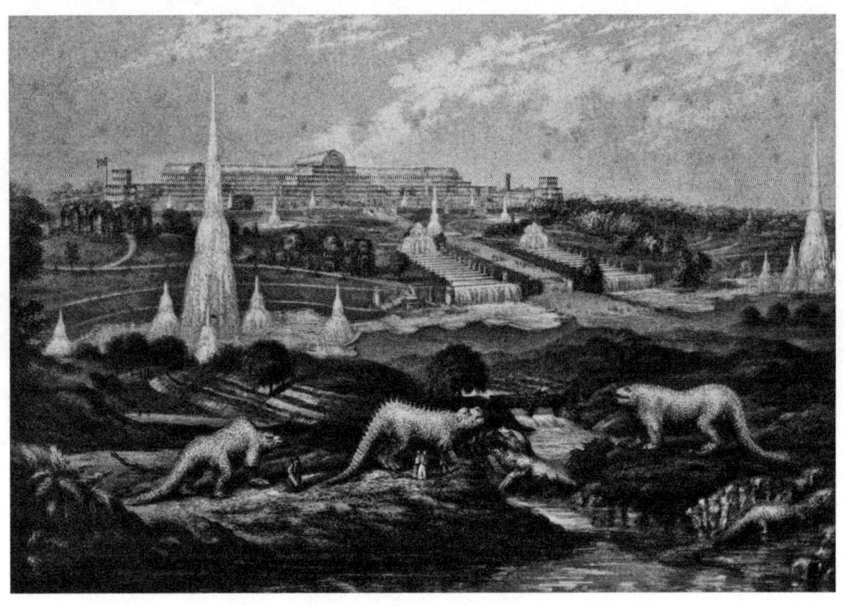

Figure 1.9. George Baxter, *The Crystal Palace and Gardens*, 1854. Chromolithograph, 4¼×6¼ in. The British Museum, London.

section, and second, the exhibition on an artificial island of a few life-size dinosaurs (Figure 1.9).[128] Tours of the site were meant to reassure crowds about how far humanity had traveled since its origins and how it had taken possession of the earth that had fallen to it — British capitalism being, of course, only its most recent achievement. The promenade in Sydenham Park was both propaganda in the interest of progress and a mode of enchantment for the masses in an age when progress was rationalizing relations of production, living conditions, and objects. But a few years before Bergson's critique of the "spatialization of duration," it also offered the experience of various domesticated timescales, as if gently to acclimatize the masses to the sense of their own insignificance.

The itinerary was so well designed that it seemed to have seized

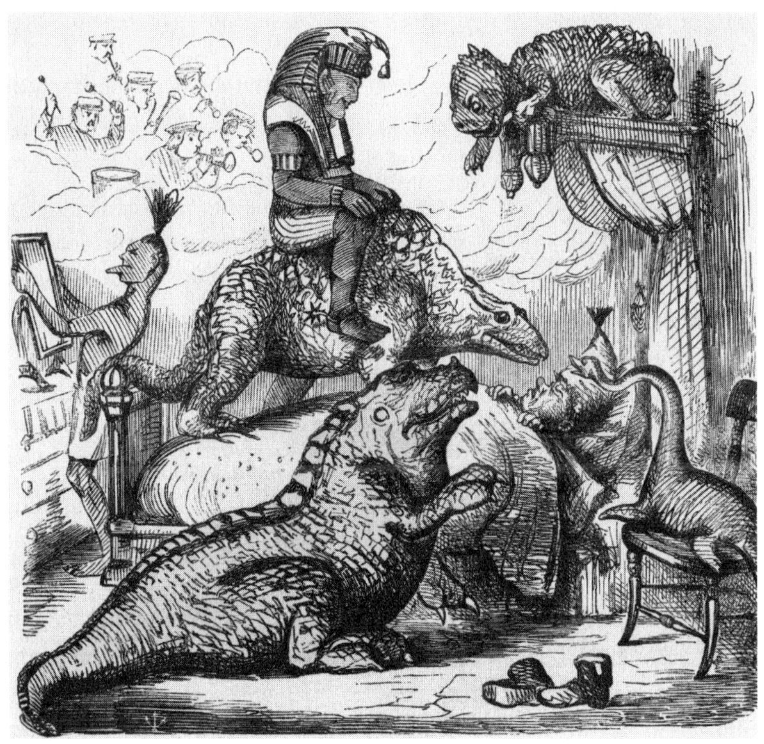

Figure 1.10. "The Effects of a Hearty Dinner after Visiting the Antediluvian Department at the Crystal Palace," *Punch* 28, January–June 1855, Punch Cartoon Library / TopFoto.

control of the dazzling speed of time. But it did so at the cost of participating, through the reification and accumulation of human and natural history, in the process Marx had only recently called the "nightmare" of the past.[129] It took a caricature to show, with striking acuity, the nightmarish implications of the display of the long term within the enclosure of Sydenham Park. "The Effects of a Hearty Dinner after Visiting the Antediluvian Department at the Crystal Palace" (*Punch*, 1855) (Figure 1.10) shows a sleeping man whose dream

is invaded by representatives of a remote past. But far from some ata-
vistic return of prehistory, the dream is an anxious response to the
very recent discovery, in the very heart of London, of an unsuspected
past: dinosaurs of different species surround the dreamer's motionless body; one of them, which is almost stepping on him, is ridden
by an ancient Egyptian, who regards the sleeping bourgeois with a
mocking expression. The plush bedroom, with its sheets and volumi-
nous, billowing curtains, is besieged by these representatives of the
remote past. Meanwhile, an orchestra, seated on clouds stacked up to
the ceiling, plays the notes of the Apocalypse on drums and trumpets.
Yet it is no longer God who brings on that apocalypse, but rather the
overabundance of history — modern man being the latest innovation.
Like all the novelties that preceded him, this man is being dragged
toward his own extinction. And if the troop of old dinosaurs mocks
the sleeper, it does so to remind him of the sad metaphysical truth of
the return of the same. That is why they form a circle with modern
man at its center, a circle symbolizing the repressed content of an
indeterminate evolutionary history. An isolated figure remains apart
from the mocking circle, however: a Native American, who forms
a circle in and of himself. Turning his back to the others, he sticks
his tongue out at himself in a mirror. This "native" is thus the only
one to live outside history. By that very fact, he is also the inverted
image of the sleeping man: his naïveté intact, he is making fun of
himself as spontaneously as a child might have done, whereas only
the mediation of a pitiless history has allowed the modern evolved
being to realize its insignificance — though only momentarily and
in his dream.

Past and Future: Man as Spectator
PREHISTORY AND THE MACHINE: THE PHOTOGRAPH AS FOSSIL
Fossils and Shells is one of the very first daguerreotypes (1839) (Figure
1.11). Some of the mineralized remains it depicts, some immensely
old, others more recent, are displayed on three stacked shelves. In
the center of the image, an ammonite draws our eye to the bottom of
its spiral. What other body than a fossil could have better complied

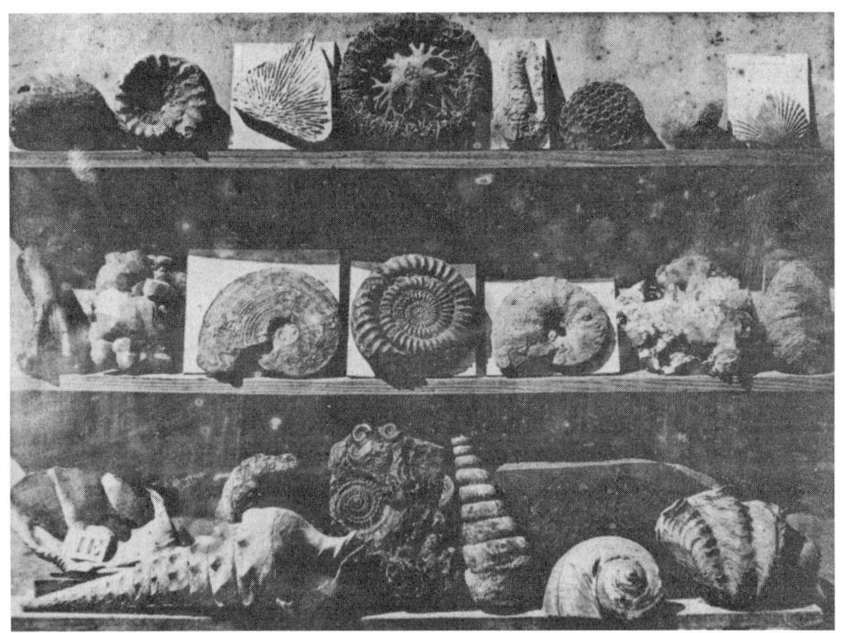

Figure 1.11. Louis Jacques Mandé Daguerre,
Fossils and Shells, 1839. Daguerreotype,
6⅜ × 8¼ in. (plate); 8⅝ × 10⅝ in. (frame).
© Musée des arts et métiers–CNAM, Paris.
Photo: Studio CNAM, inv. 08745-0002.

with the constraint of the long posing time needed for early photographs? Above all, however, this fossil is a mise en abyme for the photographic process itself. In 1839, many described photographs as drawings done by the sun,[130] often making reference as well to "nature painting itself,"[131] a way to emphasize the immediacy of the photographic signifier and the supposed absence of any human intervention. Daguerre added a tactile model to this optical, solar model of mimetic immediacy: the fossils here are presented as self-created, petrified masses and as imprints left on the stone by extinct organisms in the darkness of the earth.[132]

These fossils, then, are the first "photographs" of the world without man, depicted in turn in one of the earliest photographs in human history. It should be understood that the photograph draws its legitimacy from an original reproducibility, with human beings defying the immeasurability of the long term by appropriating its processes and logic. Our eyes, plunging into the vortex of the ammonite, realize (both perform and understand) the identity between the present instant and the immemorial past. Time, at its beginning and at its end, is literally *fixed* by the photograph, as if possessed by it. Daguerre showed that nature and photography operate in the same haptic manner to fix time and create memory. But the fossilizing process of nature also revealed the fact that mechanical automatism was its faithful, but paradoxical avatar: "We live in a remarkable time," wrote Jules Jamin shortly after the invention of photography was made official. "We no longer dream of producing anything by ourselves: rather, we seek with unparalleled perseverance the means to have things reproduced for us and in our place."[133]

The relation between machines and nature worked in both directions: the machine created fossils, and nature fossilized automatically. For Daguerre, that chiasmus had an emancipatory significance. But the artists who would take an interest in prehistory around World War I, and then after the atomic bomb was dropped, would grasp its nightmarish potential, as in the cartoon of the sleeping man. Giorgio de Chirico and Max Ernst, the first representatives of the expanded avant-garde milieu to have paid particular attention to the temporal world of prehistory, were utterly indifferent to the human artifacts of the Paleolithic period, though their stupefying authenticity had recently been recognized. The interest of these two men was directed exclusively at fossils. For artists seeking to break with imitation, the supposed naturalism of the parietal compositions and of Paleolithic mobiliary art had no utility. Conversely, they could project a number of their aspirations onto fossils. Because fossils were created automatically, they complied with the laws of the modern mechanical world. At the same time, the mutism of fossils corresponded to formalist hermeticism, the idea of an autonomous structure closed on itself, independent of all context and all biography. More generally, the impersonal character of the formation of fossils, which Fontenelle had already mentioned in the eighteenth century, perfectly suited the artists' growing rejection of all psychology. Indeed, fossils attested to a world that knew absolutely nothing of man, and this was not insignificant for a generation of artists who, in Apollinaire's words, sought to "inhuman."[134] Finally—and it is not immaterial that de Chirico and Ernst turned to prehistory around the time of World War I—fossils corresponded to their vision of a history lived as a "nightmare." We need to examine this entire tangle of threads.

Three Artists:
Giorgio de Chirico, Max Ernst, Robert Smithson

Second Prehistory: De Chirico

For most artists, what changed after Cézanne was that the "first man" also became the "last man." De Chirico's world, as devoid of human presence as Cézanne's landscapes, is compact and suffocating, rigid and disincarnated, a world that aspires to "metaphysics." His *pittura metafisica*, however, is mediated by "things." In these paintings, the rare surfaces of sky are heavy and impenetrable, as if they, too, are reified. Nature is replaced by an obsessive, but incoherent geometry. Transformed into an enormous internal space, the natural world appears simultaneously full and empty. Although utterly domesticated, the space no longer appears to be so, not only because of the sense of disorder and visual confusion emanating from it, but also because the many objects found in this space have lost their use value, becoming spectral entities—at once present and absent. All these objects, in fact, belong to the noetic order of representation: rulers, set squares, plates bearing drawings or cryptic writing, geographical maps and star charts, paintings, and a large number of frames (Figure 1.12). Even the edible items such as candy and cookies are transfigured into quasi-Platonic entities to be contemplated. All of this corresponds perfectly with the convictions the painter expressed about the role of the art of his time: "Confronted with the

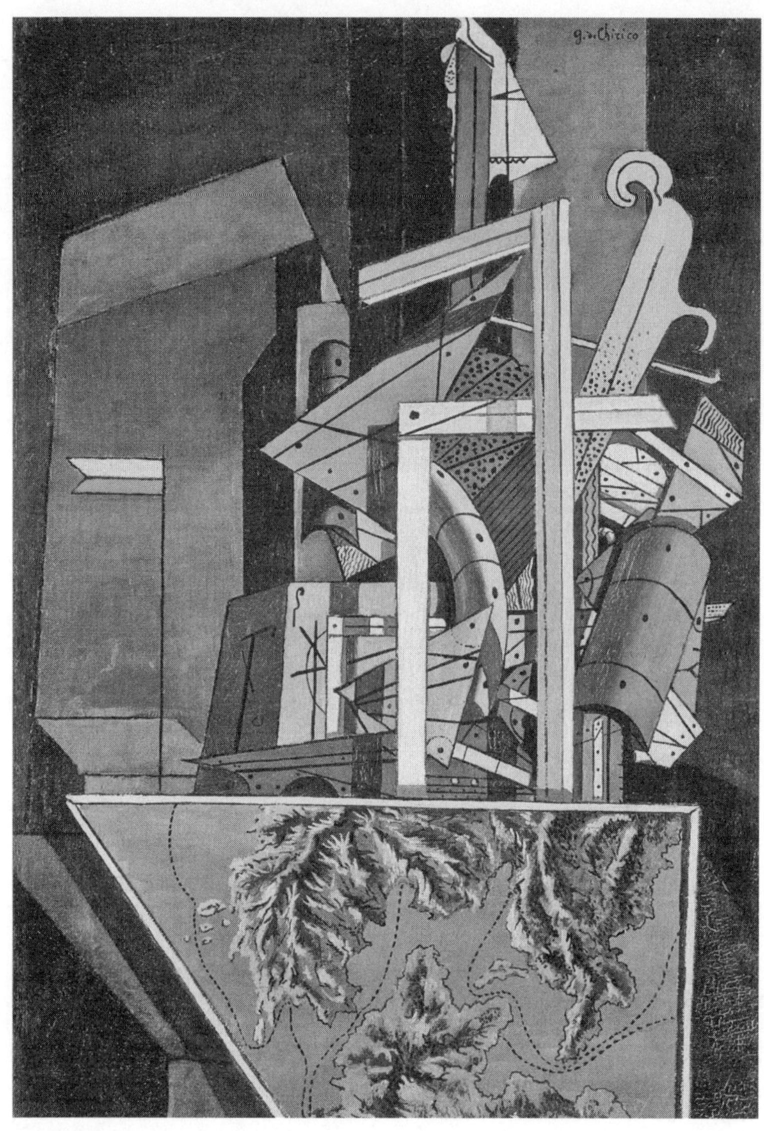

Figure 1.12. Giorgio de Chirico, *The Melancholy of Departure*, 1916. Oil on canvas, 20⅜ × 14 in. © Tate Gallery, London.

inexorable reality, art, like a beautiful prophetic dream dreamt open-eyed and at noonday, continually precedes and counsels us, today more than ever, to frame the universe and completely mineralize it."[135] Without once making use of minerality as such, de Chirico believed he was using mineralization as a process of pictorial composition. This process was supposedly introduced by others before him — Cézanne, of course, but even more Picasso, who had fathomed Cézanne's works better than anyone.[136]

De Chirico would transform Picasso's sylvan world of 1908–1909, where mythological figures proliferated and natural kingdoms overlapped without distinction, into an artificial natural world where human creations entirely replaced natural formations, even appropriating their wildness.[137] In 1913–1914, these artificial creations were historical signs: sculptures and arcades signified a history that returned again and again, ad infinitum. Antiquity, the Renaissance, and modernity became specters of one another: the analogies that de Chirico established between them and the way he mixed the different forms created a historical and ultimately atemporal world of equivalences. The public squares so important in the paintings of these years expressed this atemporality with their wide, empty expanses. But in 1914, these expanses coiled up on themselves, so to speak, folding back to form interiors. Even as the objects lost their thickness, the projection planes — drawings, fossil imprints, unknown writing systems — proliferated (*The Fatal Temple*, 1914; *Portrait of Guillaume Apollinaire*, 1914) (Figure 1.13). De Chirico constructed an artificial natural world composed of projections of the human mind, but these projections seemed to have escaped all control. He banished every living creature, focusing his compositions exclusively on things. And finally, he transformed the fierce mutism of Picasso's compositions into symbolic oracles whose meaning the viewer had to decipher indefinitely.[138] The viewer thus became an indispensable part of de Chirico's picture, the living part that was to breathe new life into its minerality.

De Chirico's symbolization of cubism brought about a sort of improbable synthesis of Cézanne and Redon. The Italian painter wrote: "The earth itself, hard and firm, that we feel under the soles

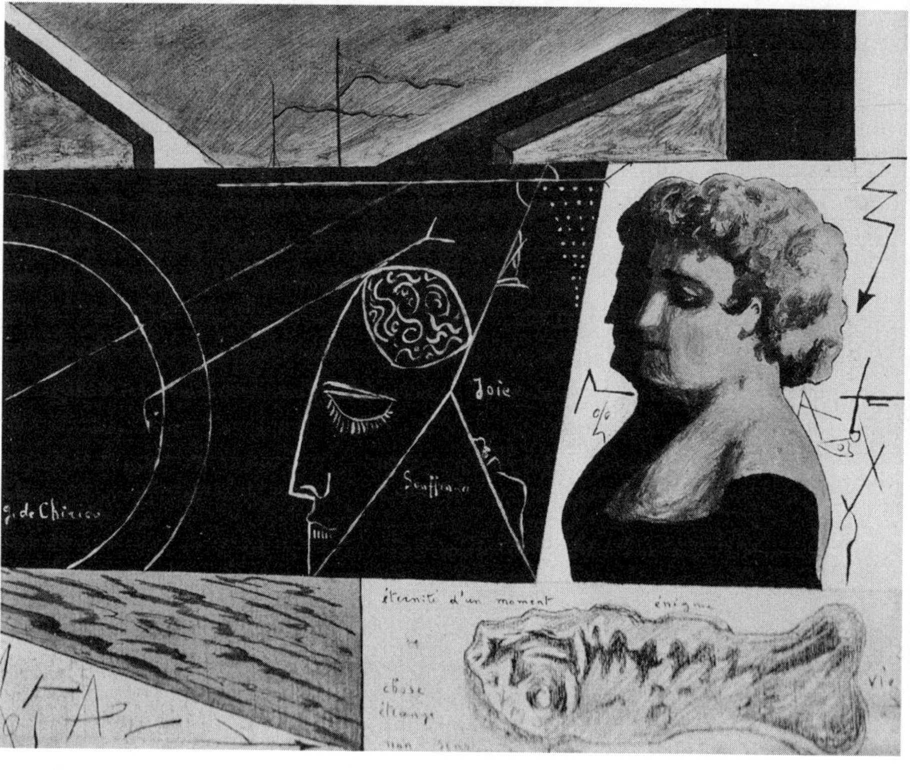

Figure 1.13. Giorgio de Chirico, *The Fatal Temple*, 1914. Oil and pencil on canvas, 13 × 16 in. Philadelphia Museum of Art: A. E. Gallatin Collection, 1947, 1947-88-14. © ARS, New York / SIAE, Rome.

of our boots is now outclassed by the metaphysical dimensions of human constructions."[139] Formerly, Redon's creature felt dread at a temporally and spatially vast world, but one as metaphysically naked and brand-new as the creature itself. Now the mineral soil of de Chirico's compositions was itself metaphysical, because saturated with human history. Unlike in Wallace's and Lubbock's prophesies, domesticated nature was certainly not a new Eden. On the contrary, the coexistence of objects in de Chirico's compositions is incoherent in every respect; their contiguity is arbitrary, forming an inextricable tangle; their different scales are at odds, some objects being disproportionately large, as if seen by a child or distorted by memory; the objects are presented from various forced and contradictory perspectives, and finally, they are systematically stripped of all utility. But for all these reasons, de Chirico's world is "metaphysical": any *grasp* of things is barred, they can only be *scrutinized* at length in an attempt to discover their meaning. This world is not designed to be touched, even less used, only indefinitely contemplated.

How can anyone pronounce a first word in the twentieth century? Unlike Cézanne, de Chirico believed it impossible. De Chirico accentuated the world's saturation, pushing it to the point of fossilization. Furthermore, apart from a few rare instances of fish fossils in his paintings, this fossilization was only metaphorical, finding its way into the qualities of rigidity, confinement, and the pileup of forms. The stratification of these forms can be called contradictory, because they are arranged not vertically, but horizontally, and are rendered in perspective. In fact, de Chirico never displayed vertical strata of objects in his paintings: his "geological" layers tend to be spread out over a horizontal expanse in accord with a system of multiple forced perspectives. That is because evolutionary time, as it acquires concrete form as stratifications, has little place in his system of representation: the multiple perspectives imply a history without telos, a cyclical history that happens, passes away, then returns.

De Chirico distinguished the prehistoric artist, who naïvely resorted to an "impressionistic" representation of nature, from the "metaphysician" artist living in a later era: in no case could they share the same systems of representation. But it was as if prehistoric man lived in the pure present, whereas modern man, a latecomer, had to unite the past with the future — since the beginning and the end form a circle in de Chirico's painting:

> The extreme complexity of our psyche resembles the ultrasimplicity of theirs. . . . The troglodyte does not know how to draw; his mind, smothered

under strata of terrifying darkness, sees the world in the dim dusk of a night-mare; his soul, bristling with disturbing questions, is obsessed by fear. As for the new metaphysical painter, he knows too many things. On his skull, in his heart, too many impressions, reminiscences, memories, and prophecies have left their stamp, as on soft wax disks: writings, deities. . . . Then he turns back to contemplate the ceiling and the walls of his bedroom, the objects around him, and the men passing in the street, and he observes that they no longer conform to the logic of yesterday, today, and tomorrow. He receives impressions no longer, but discovers, endlessly discovers, new aspects and new specters.[140]

Like Redon's creature, the primitive man of prehistory was in the grip of terrors caused by his ignorance. Impressed by a natural world he barely understood, he laboriously transposed his impressions to his drawings. The metaphysical artist's brain, by contrast, is exactly like the one described by Nietzsche and Quinet: like a geological formation, it is marked with many folds and furrows, molded by the long succession of centuries. Once the explorations of remote time and space were at an end, modern man could only return to his environment, his immediate surroundings — and prehistory was there, within reach, as it had always been since its invention. Around him and deep within him, it was ready to reveal its painful truths and offer its promises. Like Cézanne, de Chirico banished all human figures from his paintings, and the paintings, asserting their thing-ness, concentrated their plastic force to address the viewer directly and powerfully. Aspiring to make his art "an antianthropic remedy," de Chirico noted that "the aim of the painting of the future will be to suppress man as a point of reference," to "see everything, even man, as a thing."[141] He reinforced the thingness of the world, including the sky. His aim was to give the viewer the sense of being witness to a world from which his species was absent — that is, of being both the last and the first man. Standing on a threshold, the viewer would feel the metaphysical ambivalence of being simultaneously guest and intruder, rejected and welcomed. In extracting his objects from their ordinary relationships, de Chirico distanced them from what Bergson called the "psychomotor" present. These objects, forming incoherent relationships resulting from a fortuitous contiguity, produced the sense of a strangeness that was negative and positive at the same time. They were signs of a dysfunction and an *ensauvagement*, specters of the past and oracles of the future. Carl Einstein, theorist of the avant-garde and its first historian, formulated very precisely the temporal bifurcation peculiar to modernity and activated by the art of his time: "In the end, the development of an increasingly differentiated civilization, the constant increase in the volume of experiences, were to burden the human mind. The volume of experiences had grown so much that it was no longer possible to be in control of them. Any excessive increase in mnemonic material produces automatic forgetting in the long run. That is, any growth of civilization entails a regression."[142] De Chirico, among the first artists to interpret modern hypermnesia as a regression to prehistory, combined two meanings of the term: geological and nonhuman prehistory was transmuted in his paintings into an artistic prehistory. But this had nothing to do with the Paleolithic and Neolithic art, because artistic prehistory was made up entirely of fossils.[143] De Chirico said he experienced his own time as a second prehistory whose artifacts therefore took on the spectral quality of petrified organisms:

> The sense of prehistory, the feelings of the primitive artist, are reborn in me.... Thought must detach itself from everything called logic and meaning, must take its distance from all human impediments, to such a degree that *things* appear to it in a new light, as if illuminated by a constellation shining for the first time ... The birth of the day will come. It is the hour of the enigma. It is also the hour of prehistory. One of the strangest and most profound sensations that prehistory has left with us is the sensation of the omen. It will always exist. It is, at it were, an eternal preview of the meaninglessness of the universe. The first man must have seen omens everywhere, he must have shuddered with every step he took.[144]

When objects were removed from the context of their reified relationships and hackneyed meanings, they became as strange as the world must have been for the "first" human beings. The result was a sublimation of the loss of meaning. It was also a sublimation into an original founding mystery of the actual incomprehension of rational and historical man in the face of the artifacts he unearthed from the remote past.[145]

Prehistory, never literally present in de Chirico's paintings, was instead a metaphor, the conceptual equivalent of the artistic process of *defamiliarization*. The absence of literalness is by no means a "gap," but a highly significant choice: *second* prehistory has *no object* in common with the first; the two share only the cognitive *relationships* they maintain with their respective objects. It is characteristic of prehistory to reveal the unknown, which unsettles the known; the incommensurate, which extends beyond established parameters; and the ambiguous, which pulverizes the univocal. That is undoubtedly why the formalist Viktor Shklovsky, in a famous text of 1917, also made use of the mineral metaphor. In it, he articulated for the first time the notion of defamiliarization (*ostranenie*), largely inspired by his observation of cubism and its transpositions to the plastic arts and poetry in Russia. The aim of defamiliarization, he wrote, is to "to make forms difficult, to increase the difficulty and length of perception." "Art exists that one may recover the sensation of life; it exists to make one feel things, to make the stone stony."[146] The stone exemplifies the object furthest from life, the most closed on itself, the most mute, the most alien to the human, and hence the least likely to spark an automatic identification. But this also means that it falls to compositions as closed and inextricable as stone itself to make the viewer feel the stoniness of stone. That is no doubt what Picasso was trying to do when he appealed to the indetermination of the natural kingdoms and the semantic regimes in a few of his 1908 paintings (the most important of them were purchased and exhibited in Russia).[147] In de Chirico's case, the symbolization of cubism led to a different type of defamiliarization, more *deferred* and mediated because applied to human artifacts. His assertion that the aim of his painting was dehumanization ultimately followed from that practice: to learn to experience the world, man first had to unlearn what he was. This latecomer would reconstitute himself as a subject by contemplating the unknown world of art. Art complies with the regime of slow time, and its task is to interrupt automatism. In extracting objects from their useful relationships, these pictures transmit not communicative speech, but sovereign oracles destined to be interpreted again and again in exactly the same way that artifacts revealed by the remote past, especially those of earliest prehistory, are and always will be interpreted.

"Second Nature": War and Capitalism in Max Ernst (1920–1921)
The use of prehistory as metaphor would enter a new phase after World War I. A German artist back from the front, where he had been mobilized for four years, decrypted the mineral metaphor in de Chirico's compositions so skillfully that he made it literal in his own works. Max Ernst, repetitively appealing to the imaginary of geology and paleontology in 1920–1921, produced landscapes of antediluvian catastrophes that could have been caused either by the "state of exception" known as war or by the slow and ordinary corrosion produced by industrial capitalism. Like de Chirico, whose paintings he was fascinated to discover in 1919, Max Ernst was indifferent to the human artifacts of prehistory, preferring petrified formations from the most remote past.[148] But Ernst, unlike de Chirico, abandoned the classic medium of painting for new pictorial techniques, in particular, the reproducibility of typography and photography. For him, the materiality of prehistory, literal and no longer metaphorical, was available by means of reproducibility, that of the images from a school atlas he was using at the time, for example.[149]

In the case of Max Ernst, vast prehistory came to stand side by side with the presentist world of Dada and more generally that of modernity as a whole. But while the Berlin Dadaists were arranging photographs of events and actions from their terrible contemporary political history (the end of World War I and the Sparticist uprising in November 1918), Max Ernst abandoned any allusion to the political history of his time and even any reference to human action as such. His presentism was inanimate and immobile, verging on the eternal present of geology, where the most recent human artifacts were deposited as sediment. In projecting himself onto the very long term, he petrified actions, pulverized their agents, and obscured the volatile diversity of human historicity. This ontological projection onto the *longue durée* was expressed through two complementary forms of visual projection: the bird's-eye view, by means of aerial photography, and geological stratification, which Ernst imitated in an important series of works dating to 1920–1921. In the end, both views, one horizontal, the other vertical, were macroscopic, generating impersonal, flat forms hardened to the point of petrification. Viewing the present from a distance, these works were profoundly melancholic, detached, and inactive. In short, Max Ernst's approach had nothing in common with the activism of some members of Berlin Dada.[150] Without ever commenting on an event or official figure in the young Weimar Republic, he exiled himself to a future when everything would have assumed a definitive mineral form.

The Cormorants is a minuscule collage composed primarily of two large photographic reproductions. Max Ernst took to the extreme de Chirico's bewildering process of combining several contradictory perspectives in the same space (Figure 1.14). Most of the collage is occupied by an aerial photograph of three harbor structures, while the foreground shows a frontal, closeup image of flamingoes walking elegantly along the water's edge. This transition from an aerial to a frontal view and from distance to proximity is also signified by a change of color, from gray to yellow. The water is also different in the two views: motionless and smooth as a polished stone in the aerial photograph, in the closeup, it displays ripplets dappled with light. The aerial view petrifies: it schematizes, hardens, condenses, and flattens the forms in the extreme. Despite the abstraction of the details, however, it does not produce a clear and unambiguous image. On the contrary, the optical distance and uniformly gray tones of the harbor structures make them strange and difficult to identify, especially since all three are obscured by forms partially superimposed on them: from left to right, a drawing of a cross section of a human brain, a photograph of a rose window from Reims Cathedral — a symbol of German "barbarism," because it was bombed[151] — and a photograph of a round stone. All these additions

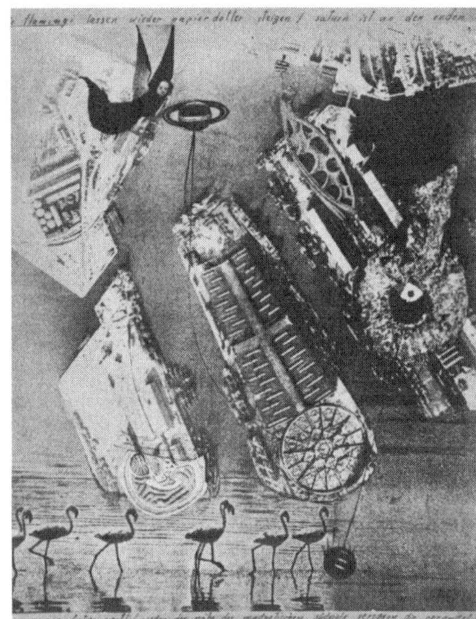

Figure 1.14. Max Ernst, *The Cormorants*, 1920. Collage, 6 × 5 in. Simone Collinet Collection, Paris. Photo: © 2021 ARS, NY / ADAGP, Paris.

are disproportionately large for such a small composition. But the ambiguity of the structures seen from above is attributable primarily to their regularity, which could be that of machines or of the skeletons of prehistoric organisms. Since World War I, the formal analogy between machines and the extinct organisms of prehistory had continually surfaced in texts and images. Even as Ernst was elaborating his mechanical geologies, Frans Masereel was drawing illustrations for a screenplay by Romain Rolland titled *The Revolt of the Machines; or, Invention Run Wild* (1921). The screenplay begins with a celebration of modern man, who, relieved of all toil thanks to the latest mechanical inventions, thinks he has left far behind the "poor creatures that have as yet barely emerged from the primordial ooze."[152] But history comes full circle: a sudden revolt by the machines causes an apocalypse, borrowed as much from biblical descriptions as from Buffon's natural history. The survivors, pursued by the machines to the mountain summits, perceive "the long neck of a machine resembling a plesiosaurus, which, reaching over the defenders' barrier, snatches up one of them."[153] As if echoing Samuel Butler's erroneous predictions, Masereel's engraving depicts the bucket of an excavator, similar to a dinosaur's maw equipped with sharp teeth, opening in front of several humans, who cling to one another in fear (Figure 1.15). Masereel's return to prehistory is not identical to Ernst's, however. Masereel chooses the moment of battle, that is, an action of maximum intensity, though directed against human beings. Modern man's defeat by machines is the very condition for the advent of a new Neolithic age, the return of an original pastoral state (just as Butler had suggested in *Erewhon*). Ernst, by contrast, positions himself in the aftermath: after the fact, after the apocalypse, after life. His forms, viewed from above, are inert because conceived and produced under the sign of Saturn. The transition from the world of inertia to that of life is neither gentle nor gradual; it occurs by successive jolts and shocks. *The Cormorants* is an image of acedia on a geological scale. Its heavy and motionless forms belong to the literary, medical, and philosophical tradition of melancholy, as Jean Starobinski describes it: "To be sure, it is a means of warding off the passage of time and images of destruction, but it does so by arresting life as a whole, casting the gaze of the Medusa over oneself and the world."[154]

In this case, the gaze of the Medusa is the camera's gaze. Aerial photography was one of the fundamental technical processes invented during World War I. Max Ernst, assigned to read maps and charts at the front, had firsthand experience of war imagery. We know he found the photograph of the harbor structures in the city of Dünkirchen in a 1917 atlas that reproduced aviation photographs taken during the war.[155] We also know that one of the principal responses of the belligerents to the danger of being identified "from above" was to camouflage military installations by imitating the formations and colors of the natural environment.[156] The structures seen from above in Ernst's work are similarly camouflaged and indeterminate, recalling both human constructions and the mineral formations of the natural world.[157] The artist, dissolving the individuality of things and, like camouflage, blurring the physical separation between their forms, meant to keep the viewer's gaze in a constant state of defamiliarization, shifting back and forth between near and far, the

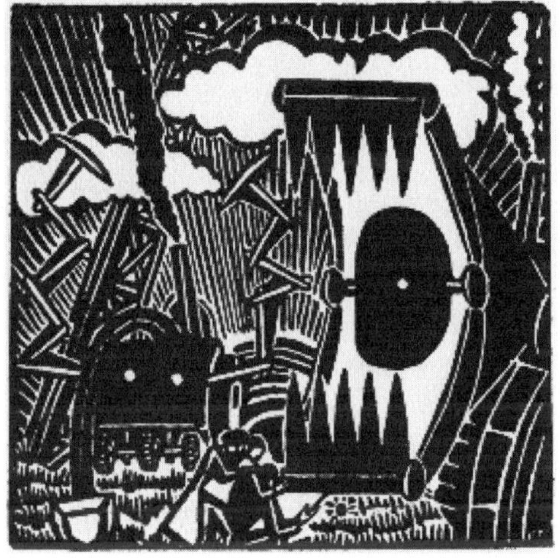

Figure 1.15. Franz Masereel, *The Revolt of the Machines*, 1921. Wood engraving. Photo: © 2021 ARS, NY / ADAGP, Paris.

undifferentiated mineral grisaille and the abstract forms that stand out from it. Although Ernst eliminated details and events — which, as Braudel would write in 1958, constitute "the most capricious, the most deceptive of *durées*" — he obtained a clearer image of their structures, "a reality that time wears down only slowly and carries along for a very long time."[158] One aspect is clear, however: the posthistorical minerality of these structures, their fabricated character, which makes them slip back into the undiscerning regime of nature.

In 1920, Sigmund Freud, speculating on psychic impulses independent of and perhaps more primitive than the "pleasure principle," came up with the theory of the "death drive." The same year, Max Ernst took reality as a whole back to "*an earlier state of things* which the living entity has been obliged to abandon," and which "an urge inherent in organic life" seeks to restore, namely, the inorganic state, death.[159] The only trace of a human body in his collage is a lifeless brain; the bones and arteries are depicted as elements of an ordinary mechanical assemblage. From an iconic standpoint, the human species is reduced to a brain, the mutilated and thus utterly ineffective seat of the organism's sensorimotor reflexes. The only trace of life offered the viewer, therefore, would come from what he is not, namely, the water and the fowl. The minute, delicate movements of the flamingoes contrast utterly with the massive immobility of the structures photographed from above. They also allow the viewer a minimal sense of motion. Clearly, Ernst's viewer does not have the sovereign and irreplaceable role that de Chirico's paintings confer on her by entrusting her with the task of deciphering the oracles. Ernst's viewer has only a tiny margin: she seizes the slightest movement and simply identifies with the multitude embodied in the water, a metaphor for the masses that history has ceaselessly galvanized and that it has revealed to be its true subject. After all, the liquid and mineral forms of Ernst's image share the qualities of anonymity and impersonality. *The Cormorants* is an image of mass warfare—a fossil of the "total mobilization" Ernst Jünger would later hail as part of his Fascistic vitalism.[160]

Ernst's fragments are neutral, indifferent assemblages of a disenchanted immanence that does not even suffer Cézanne's torments. No less than Cézanne or Quinet, however, he finds in the petrification of affects a certain protection that reduces a painful history to a fissure on the colossal body of the centuries.[161] That relativizing and apotropaic function of the *longue durée* will become more prominent in his series of collages called "Übermalungen," from which the living thing is radically banished. In these "overpaintings," brilliantly studied by Ralph Ubl, Ernst uses reproductions, in particular from a sales catalogue of teaching aids (*Lehrmittel*) for use in schools. With its twenty-four-hundred illustrations, it covers every field of knowledge, from geology and zoology to art history.[162] The *Bibliotheka Paedagogica*, first published in Cologne in 1890, went through fourteen editions. The artist would choose a plate—a botanical or zoological classification table, equine anatomy chart, or geological stratification—that he then transformed by partially covering it with paint, drawings, or other media. Many of these images, generally in minuscule formats, use geological and paleontological imagery. The accumulation of images covering knowledge in its totality has the self-assurance of a taxonomy, yet the different images are essentially equivalent to one another. Nothing is really established or acquired, no experience gained. The artist hijacks the images and returns them to their prehistoricity, that is, to their status as documents of a past whose meaning is altogether unknown. In combining reproducibility and prehistoricity in these images, Ernst expresses the same sudden estrangement from tradition and the past that Benjamin would identify in the early 1930s. There is a "hiatus" between past and present: "The prehistoric moment in the past is no longer masked, as it used to be, by the tradition of church and family," the philosopher wrote.

> The old prehistoric dread already envelops the world of our parents because we ourselves are no longer bound to this world by tradition. The material worlds break up more rapidly; what they contain of the mythic comes more quickly and more brutally to the fore; and a wholly different familiar world must be speedily set up to oppose it. This is how the accelerated tempo of technology appears in light of the prehistoric history of the present.[163]

Sometimes, the vertical accumulation of the earth's strata covers almost the entire image. *Frau Wirtin an der Lahn* (1920), though an impenetrably dense composition, is completely flat, like a stage backdrop. Most of the compositions show geological strata composed of several materials — real or imitated — in the foreground: a heterogeneous, mismatched collection of large machine skeletons rise up from the ground, looming over minuscule mountain chains and glaciers. The rarefied atmosphere, impenetrable, is mineral white and covered in a layer of hoarfrost. The mountain ranges, even more deeply embedded in the past than the extinct organisms of modernity, seem small and flat by comparison. The interplay between different scales, which the artist had introduced in *The Cormorants* through the use of aerial photography, is here transposed to the relative dimensions of the tremendously old mountains and the most recent fossils of human history. As for Max Ernst's subterranean world, it is invariably filled with mechanical debris. Circular motifs are omnipresent, as if to signify by their virtual repetition the tautological status of the fossils. All these compositions are planted, as it were, in the eternal present of a prehistory without a human presence.

Ernst's geology, however, does not stand in absolute opposition to the political engagement of the Berlin Dadaists. Without ever directly confronting political problems, his use of geology neverthe-less constitutes an eminently critical analysis, converging with some of the fundamental philosophical inquiries of Marxism at the time. In projecting himself onto a land without human beings, Max Ernst was conducting an artistic reflection on the reification of humans by capitalism similar in that respect to Georg Lukács's analyses in *History and Class Consciousness* (1922).[164] It is as if Ernst were maximizing man's relation to his labor and the production of objects by extending these relations to the geological scale. In the first place, the reduction by Taylorization of the worker's freedom to act is projected onto that scale. The viewer adopts a contemplative point of view, which is paradoxically comparable to that of the worker vis-à-vis production, occurring, as Lukács wrote, "independently of man's consciousness and impervious to human intervention."[165] Behind the frenetic pace of machines, Ernst captured man's essential inaction, signified in his works by the total absence of human agents—a technique pio-neered by de Chirico's thingly metaphysics. The mechanical fossils of Ernst's compositions are similar to the carcasses of time to which Marx referred in his critique of the radical quantification of life by capitalism: "Time is everything, man is nothing; he is, at the most, time's carcase [*sic*]."[166] But Ernst eliminated the carcasses of men and exhibits only what stand in for them: the carcasses of their products. Once again, he showed in an exaggerated manner the mechanism behind the fetishism of commodities, which, as Marx demonstrated, had gained the upper hand in the heyday of joyful capitalism.[167] Max Ernst's eternal geographical present thus metaphorizes the contin-uum of a time identical to itself, fixed and spatialized—a specter of reified time that reigned when the factories were still in opera-tion. It was also Lukács, in *Theory of the Novel* (1916), who first used the expression "second nature" to describe a historical reality that, though entirely man-made, rejected and expelled human beings: "This second nature," he explained, "is not dumb, sensuous and yet senseless like the first: it is a complex of senses—meanings—which has become rigid and strange, and which no longer awakens inte-riority; it is a charnel house of long-dead interiorities."[168] Unlike the essentially living matter of first nature, the matter of second nature is composed exclusively of man's exoskeleton: his protheses, his machines, his artifacts, his cities, his networks — in sum, all the products of long human history whose debris fills Max Ernst's over-paintings and that appear to be truly finite. In the end, many others after him would explore that obtuse and sterile minerality of "second nature."

Time against History and against Itself: Robert Smithson (1960s–1970s)
In the mid-1960s, when Smithson turned directly to geology and anchored his artistic practice in it (it would soon be known as "Land Art"), "second nature" was seemingly even more fossilized than it had been for Max Ernst. All the same, the American artist only rarely and selectively used objects to signify that fossilization. There are several reasons for this. Above all, Smithson projected himself into a future time when all fossils of the human world would be assimilated to a "dedifferentiated" posthistorical matter.[169] After World War II, the progress of technology and globalized capitalism through the myriad products consumed in everyday life gave rise to the sense of an unprecedented acceleration of time that has recently come to be known as "the great acceleration."[170] In a flash, or rather two, the atomic bombs the United States dropped on Japan also demonstrated that the domestication of nature by human beings could end in the fossilization of both. Smithson, a voracious reader of books on cybernetics, geology, and anthropology, had discovered the nomadic concept of "entropy": having resurfaced in the nineteenth century, this concept contradicted the postulate of the physical conservation of energy, instead positing the possibility of its dissipation. The historical consciousness of the time could easily project its fears onto that virtual disintegration of the natural and artificial worlds — assuming this distinction still had any meaning. Like Claude Lévi-Strauss, Smithson was convinced that "the world began without man and will end without him."[171] The anthropologist did not detect in human beings any Promethean posture aimed at "vainly opposing a universal decline"; on the contrary, he saw man as a mere cog in the

world's machine, working in his own way — that is, through his institutions and creations — "towards the disintegration of the original order of things and precipitating a highly organized matter towards a greater inertia, an inertia which will one day will be final."[172] The growing complexity and sophistication of human institutions and information, far from leading indefinitely to improvements, as nineteenth-century evolutionism had predicted, instead produced entropy. Smithson's *Spiral Jetty* (Figure 1.16), though belonging to a remarkably diverse and very sophisticated intellectual heritage, was an artistic configuration of inert matter, and its ultimate purpose was to disappear by merging with that matter. The anthropology of the time was disintegrating its object through the analysis of cultural invariants shared by different human societies. Art, Smithson believed, ought to follow the same path. According to him, to take ourselves for the measure of art is to deprive ourselves of the minute resources at our disposal for living in a world that treats us with sovereign disregard.

Jennifer Roberts has brilliantly shown Smithson's complicated relationship to Christianity.[173] Torn between faith and a raging skepticism, the American artist devoted himself to an art that ridiculed the doloristic thematics of Christ's anthropomorphism. He was also preoccupied with the contradictions inherent in the doctrines of the Incarnation (which he traced even in abstract expressionist painting) and the end of time, when deserving human beings would return to Paradise. The problem for Smithson was Christianity's dual concession to the human scale, that of a deity who had taken on a human image and a human life and that of a time not only perfectly scaled to human intelligence, but also affording man a teleological destiny. "If only the Geologists would let me alone, I could do very well, but those dreadful Hammers! I hear the clink of them at the end of every cadence of the Bible verses" — Ruskin's statement[174] did not escape Smithson's notice, and he added: "Prior to the coming of geology, the worldview was essentially dominated by Judeo-Christian values, right up to, I'd say, the eighteenth century. Geology upset all that. Our sense of time became much greater. We're no longer dealing

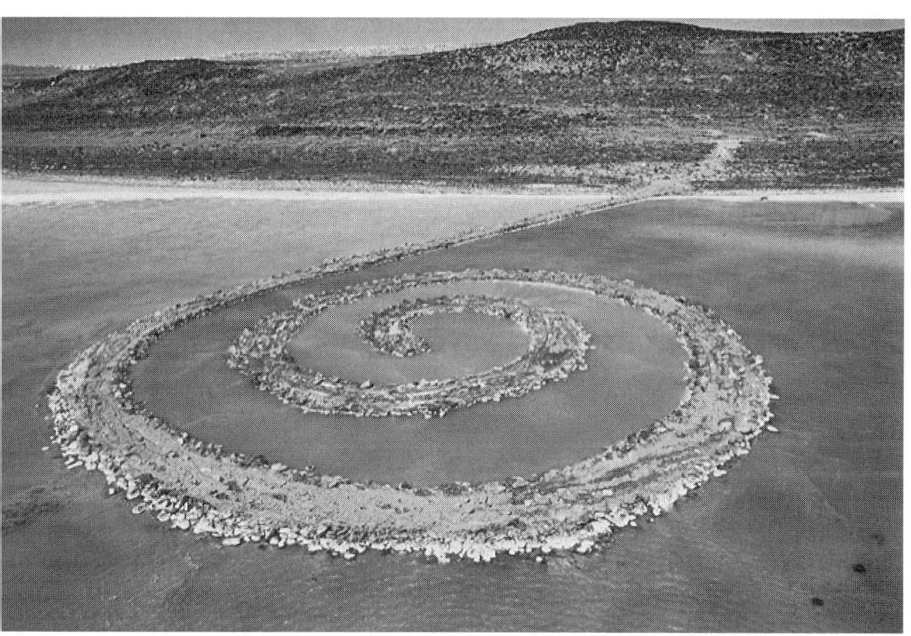

Figure 1.16. Robert Smithson, *Spiral Jetty*, 1970. Great Salt Lake, Utah. Salt crystals, stones, water. 1,401 ft., 6⅞ in. × 15 ft. Collection Dia Art Foundation, New York. Photo: Gianfranco Gorgoni. © Holt/Smithson Foundation and Dia Art Foundation/VAGA at ARS, NY.

with Classical civilization."[175] In prodigiously lengthening humanity's "sense of time," geology reduced human history and a fortiori "classicism" to an insignificant entity. That is why Smithson carefully distinguished between the notion of history and that of time: in every case, when history makes an appearance in his discourse, it is strictly human, whereas time is what allows man to escape the narrow place assigned him — and therefore also his history. In other words, history has contours, whereas time is a plastic force: "History is representational, while time is abstract."[176] Smithson arrived at these statements through geology, which thus allowed him to liberate himself from history, Christianity, and the reifying effects of capitalism on objects, including works of art.

In his writings, "history" designates everything that was done and will be done by man, in two general senses. For him, history is the reification of formations and artifacts, both symbolic and common, that have accumulated over the course of millenniums, and it is action, which Jean-Paul Sartre's existentialism had just defined as the only nature imputable to man—a nature that is never complete, but always to be constructed.[177] For Smithson, as for many artists of his generation, action, despite being a process, no more escaped the power of reification wielded by capitalism and history than did objects. History is "a facsimile of events held together by flimsy biographical information."[178]

Initially, then, Smithson attempted to leave history behind by availing himself of the resources of Christianity. In that respect, he was following a tradition dating back to Romanticism and therefore as old as modernity itself. Adopting one of the orientations of twentieth-century conservative thought, he indulged in a critique of the "-isms" that had followed one after another in the first half of the century, seeing them as successive incarnations of Renaissance individualism and aestheticism. After the war—and henceforth on the American continent—these "-isms" were further diluted into actions and happenings. What until cubism, futurism, and Dadaism had borne proper names was now dissolved into universal concepts, which were nothing less than signs of the complete secularization of art. Hence the autonomy of art culminated in its opposite, the most radical heteronomy: mere fragments found on the sidewalk were now identified as art; art quite simply "happened" at the same time as life and by the same gestures in a present that was, so to speak, tautological. "Sometimes," concluded Smithson, "I wish somebody would free us from freedom."[179]

To deliver oneself from one's freedom is to submit voluntarily to transcendent and absolute forms that reduce human crisis, decision, and action to mere vanities. Where Sartrian existentialism had allowed some artists to understand action painting as a symbolic affirmation of freedom, Smithson, inspired by reactionary modernism in Great Britain between 1910 and 1940, found in the religious tradition constraining forms that could relieve him of his freedom by acquainting him with the existential resources of passivity and the contemplation of an inaccessible eternity. Like the British philosopher T. E. Hulme, who abhorred the Renaissance because it had ushered in humanist eudaemonism and materialism, Smithson was at the time inspired by the Byzantine Empire, where believers shattered icons because of an immoderate faith, and not out of aestheticism.[180] For Hulme, history was of interest only if by its relativism and pluralism it bore witness to its own falseness.[181] What Smithson found in all these representatives of British reactionary modernism was a pessimism about the value of man — a Sorelian pessimism that contained within itself a certain sense of the tragic. But how could he both relativize man's value and appeal to a religion whose central doctrine was the Incarnation? How could Smithson leave behind the "nightmare of history"[182] while appealing to one of its monsters?

Smithson abandoned the "gardens of history" in favor of the "sites of time."[183] The garden, the quintessence of domesticated nature and the archetype (in the form of Eden) of Judeo-Christian eschatology, was in his case subsumed by the geological site. Ancient mines, quarries, geological cross sections, and urban fringes, where nature reasserted its rights over ephemeral human constructions, were the places where he would engage in the dialectic between human history and the erosive power of time. Feeling that "Europe had exhausted its culture," and later abandoning the idea of reestablishing the "traditional art work in terms of the Eliot-Pound-Wydham-Lewis situation," he began to take an interest in the "construct of physical matter." He added: "Also the entire history of the West was swallowed up in a preoccupation with notions of pre-history and the great pre-historic epics starting with the age of rocks. . . . The Triassic and Jurassic and all those different periods sort of subsumed all the efforts of these civilizations that had interested me."[184] Smithson made good use of these two aspects of geology: the sovereign and transcendent timescale, but also physical matter. Like Christ, geology was incarnated in the sensible world, but it did not conform to the human scale. Henceforth, that transcendence, buried and in great part inaccessible, would supply the artist with the absolute he needed:

> I think most of us are very aware of time on a geological scale, of the great extent of time which has gone into the sculpting of matter. Take an Anthony Caro: that expresses a certain nostalgia for a Garden of Eden view of the world, whereas I think in terms of millions of years, including times when humans weren't around. Anthony Caro never thought about the ground his work stands on. In fact, I see his work as anthropocentric cubism. He has yet to discover the dreadful object. And then to leave it. He has a long way to go.[185]

"The dreadful object": geology was of the same nature as the *pharmakon*, both remedy and poison. Obviously, the American artist's *pharmakon* was quite different from that of Lyell and Quinet, for whom the discipline of geology, even as it opened the chasm of time, was able to put an end to vertigo, domesticating the formless and the boundless. Hence, geology used metaphors to keep terror at bay. Such an optimistic rationalism was neither credible nor desirable for Smithson, who was seeking only one thing: to remain on the edge of the abyss. His imagination, which, in his own words, was not illogical, but "alogical,"[186] perfectly grasped the contradictory nature of the "dreadful object." Geology, indifferent to the human scale, assigns human beings clear limits; but by the same token, it procures them the tragic matter they need to power their fictions and avoid succumbing to vertigo. "Surd" is the name for that fictional chasm. Smithson borrowed it from a literary work, Samuel Beckett's novel *The Unnamable*. Once you entered the "surd" zone, the categories of reason — proportions, grids, standards and measurements of all kinds — proved useless, ready to sink into the chasm of time, like all products of history.

Spiral Jetty was a "surd" zone by virtue of its isolated location, so remote and uncertain that visitors were sometimes obliged to turn back after long searching for it in the desert along paths that led to dead ends.[187] It was also "surd" by virtue of its intermediate position between the earth and the lake water that submerged its helical structure for several years. Not only was this work not "abstract" — unlike Caro's sculptures, immutable entities independent of any context — *Spiral Jetty* was made from the same material as the ground supporting it. It even allowed itself to be swallowed up like a prehistoric continent or an archaic construction. Finally and above all, *Spiral Jetty* was a "surd" zone in terms of its formal layout, requiring those who found themselves in its presence or who watched the eponymous film Smithson had made about it to project themselves into it and then move away:

> After a point, measurable steps ("Scale skal n. it. or L; it. *Scala;* L *scala* usually *scalae* pl., I.a. originally a ladder; a flight of stairs; hence b. a means of ascent") descend from logic to the "surd state." The rationality of a grid on a map sinks into what it is supposed to define. Logical purity suddenly finds itself in a bog, and welcomes the unexpected event. . . . In the Spiral Jetty the surd takes over and leads one into a world that cannot be expressed by number or rationality. Ambiguities are admitted rather than rejected, contradictions are increased rather than decreased — the *alogos* undermines the *logos.*[188]

Recall the straight ladder on the frontispiece of *Old Stones* (see Figure 1.2), a book from the second half of the nineteenth century. Sinking into the earth, that ladder struck the primeval bedrock, the only zone that resisted the ladder's rationalizing process. But Smithson inverted that logic. Extremely rational in its mechanisms and stages, his logic was converted into *"alogon."* It was as if, for him, the primeval bedrock were overtaking the present. Reason allowed itself to be invaded by the geological unconscious, which allowed Smithson to see himself as a distant descendant of Cézanne.[189] As a result, the "recent surface" in the nineteenth-century frontispiece, which was supposed to support and sustain the present, was now becoming as indistinct as the deepest geological strata. At the same time, the law of conservation that the present obeyed was being converted into the law of entropy. Spreading out across the earth's horizontality, having appropriated its matter to the point of submersion, *Spiral Jetty* confirmed all these reversals triggered by upward thrust. In that way, the "surd" metaphor took the place of the ladder, with its precisely cut steps and the regular intervals between them. In any case, no single object could have contained "surd" in and of itself, not even the spiral.

That is because "surd" required an execution, a procedure, even a drama. Rather than a single straight and solid ladder, the "surd" zone called for what Smithson called a "relationship" or a "dialectic" of scales: "The scale of the Spiral Jetty tends to fluctuate depending where the viewer happens to be. Size determines an object, but scale determines art. A crack in the wall if viewed in terms of scale, not size, could be called the Grand Canyon. A room could be made to take on the immensity of the solar system. . . . For me scale operates by uncertainty."[190] Objects had a definite size in two worlds: Newton's old physical world and the human world of commodities. But art has to be an *uncertain* world, where the most dreadful and the most innocuous objects lose their fixed values and through analogies and inversions can be converted into their opposite and establish new relationships. Geology constitutes the ineluctable human horizon, but in their fictions, human beings can render it as a flexible and manageable scale. That was the minimal action Smithson allowed himself: to disconnect and assemble timescales to produce meaning intentionally—not blindly, like nature. He called that minimal action a "dialectic," as well: "You have to have this dialectic, otherwise you have the tragic view where everything is sort of fatalistic, but with this [dialectic] you can somehow go back and forth, and there tends to be a rather impersonal view."[191]

According to Smithson, the first dialectician was Pascal. Rather than bow to the Cartesian idea of a mechanistic universe, Pascal had chosen to confront the "infinite spaces" that frightened him.[192] Pascalian man, a "middle" between the nothing and the all, naturally found his place in Smithson's fictional space. Every time Smithson projected himself into the future, he discovered it was "lost somewhere in the dumps of the non-historical past"[193] and that "always going backwards,"[194] it revealed "the sameness of pre- and post-history."[195] What does that sameness of prehistory and posthistory signify? For his experience of time, it signifies three things.

In the first place, for Smithson, as for Cézanne, de Chirico, and Max Ernst, prehistory is an exercise of thought, a metaphorical projection, an interplay of scales that makes the world, presumed to be fixed, and the present, presumed to be objective, strange and provisional. Prehistory is "surd": it corresponds to rational systems that appear illogical to those still living within history. It interferes in the present, weakening its sclerotic body and substituting the phenomenological actuality of perception. Smithson recounted that finding himself in the Great Salt Lake for the first time, and noticing abandoned oil rigs and a hut mounted on pilings (which could have been belonged to the "missing link"), a "great pleasure" came over him "from seeing also those incoherent structures." "This site gave evidence of a succession of man-made systems mired in abandoned hopes."[196] In short, he noted the very Pascalian equivalence of the cognitive systems invented over the centuries: none of them was fixed, and all were probable. The same thesis, formulated in negative terms, essentially meant that all systems created by human thought since prehistory had collapsed, one after another.

Second, Smithson's anachronistic use of prehistory was based on Pascalian probability. The clear choice of anachronism as such became more prevalent among various thinkers and artists beginning in the 1950s. One reason was that the communication and dissemination of mass culture were making historical eras ever more interchangeable and history as a totality ever more simultaneous. If the past and the future were equivalent, nothing prevented them from substituting for each other. In its optimistic version, that interchangeability produced André Malraux's "Imaginary Museum," which inspired many artists, and Marshall McLuhan's belief that humanity was entering a new era of nomadism and orality: "Electric speed mingles the culture of prehistory with the dregs of industrial marketers, the nonliterate with the semiliterate and the postliterate."[197] Fundamentally optimistic, McLuhan's vision spawned the idea of a *human* posthistory that combined emancipation and brotherhood. Smithson contrasted his own disenchanted view with that return to a supposedly postindustrial golden age: "This sense of extreme past and future has its partial origin with the Museum of Natural History; there the 'cave-man' and the 'space-man' may be seen under one roof. In this museum all 'nature' is stuffed and interchangeable."[198] In contrast to McLuhan's irenic and humanistic anachronisms, Smith proposed his own anachronisms, sarcastic and reifying.

Third and finally, Smithson's pessimism gave a prophetic value to prehistory consistent with Lévi-Strauss's "the world began without man and will end without him."[199] In conclusion, Smithson's prehistory is as much a cognitive force as an objectified and spatialized image of the future, driving out — far out — the "Garden of Eden" of the nineteenth-century evolutionists.

An avid reader of J. G. Ballard's and Brian Aldiss's science fiction, Smithson was perfectly well aware that the acceleration of time had ultimately overtaken its absolute opposite, the slow pace of geology. Mantell's "railway," having traveled through the sediments of the past, hurtled straight toward the sediments of the future. In J. G. Ballard's *The Terminal Beach*, a novel set on an island used for nuclear tests, the hero prefigures the last man, maintaining relationships only with his own memory, a corpse, and the surrounding space:

> The series of weapons tests had fused the sand in layers, and the pseudogeological strata condensed the brief epochs, microseconds in duration, of thermonuclear time. Typically the island inverted the geologist's maxim, "The key to the past lies in the present." Here, the key to the present lay in the future. This island was a fossil of time future, its bunkers and blockhouses illustrating the principle that the fossil record of life was one of armour and the exoskeleton.[200]

For Smithson, this regime of a specifically geological acceleration had reached the ordinary zones of human activity. Although without the lightning speed of Ballard's utopian island, geological acceleration spread methodically over the continent of the present, seizing hold of objects and their configurations in space.

In his fictional documentary *A Tour of the Monuments of Passaic, New Jersey*, Smithson decided to take on the role of "geologic agent,"[201] but only to explore the strata of the present in the suburb where he had grown up. He photographed places where old and new construction fused "into a unitary chaos."[202] He also appropriated the so-called documentary and realist quality of photography to present objects as "fossils of the future": "Since it was Saturday, many machines were not working, and this caused them to resemble prehistoric creatures trapped in the mud, or, better, extinct machines — mechanical dinosaurs stripped of their skin."[203] When human activity stopped, the objects it had used were overtaken by inertia, whose prototype, once again, was fossil prehistory. The same need for inertia had led Smithson to choose Salt Lake, Utah, whose salt-saturated water made human navigation impracticable. Under the rule of inertia, the inactive machines became formations as abstract as the spiral. They were "simulacra," "structural objects" that, as Roland Barthes said, relinquish their functionality in favor of their intelligibility and metaphorical profundity.[204] Like de Chirico before him, Smithson believed that "objects are phantoms of the mind, as false as angels."[205] This became obvious when they were at rest: in Passaic, every object was "a dead metaphor."[206] Seen from above, *Spiral Jetty* became a flower: its ornamental inutility prefigured its future inertia, even while exhibiting the heroic gesture of its gratuitousness.

With Smithson, the minute space falling to tragic man in an entropic universe was strictly fictional and hardly extends beyond the field of action narrowly defined. Since Schelling and Hegel, the notion of tragedy had legitimized history as an affirmation of human freedom against necessity, even constituting the conceptual matrix of dialectics. Smithson, however, disengaged that dialectic from any political action. As a matter of fact, he did not establish any relationships with his peers.[207] The slow action of the earth was sufficient for him,[208] he said, and whereas a number of artists were interested in what was "happening," he himself was interested in what "was not happening."[209] Convinced that action is "the source of all misery,"[210] he concluded that "the artist should be an actor who refuses to act."[211] Like Lévi-Strauss, the artist thought in terms of impersonal and archetypal structures that varied very little by place and century. That is also why Smithson identified completely with the first and last sentences of Borges's text called "Pascal's Sphere": "Perhaps universal history is the history of a few metaphors," and, "perhaps universal history is the history of the various intonations of a few metaphors."[212] In other words, human freedom could be summed up as the almost imperceptible variation of "various intonations." And just as Borges made his text a mirror of Pascal's sphere, condensing in three pages the *longue durée* of a metaphor, Smithson made *Spiral Jetty* the mirror of man's relationship — not only transhistorical but also atemporal — with the world.

After the End: Francis Ponge as Read by Jean-Paul Sartre
In 1944, Sartre did a captivating analysis of a collection of poems titled *Partisan of Things*, which Francis Ponge had published in 1942. In "Man and Things," Sartre describes the poet's dual objectivist approach. Because Ponge believed that it was possible to strip objects of their human meanings, he attempted to make his own words into absolutes, hermetically sealed and independent of their author. In Ponge's world, where realism held sway as a guiding premise, the power of the spoken word was measured by its capacity to restore the strangeness that objects contain when they are not attached to any project. The "human mollusk," wrote Ponge, has at his disposal "the thing most proportioned and suited to his body, yet as utterly different from his form as can be imagined: I mean WORDS."[213] Although emphasizing the difference between language and the natural world that creates it, the poet immediately naturalized language. He did so by projecting himself forward to a time after the extinction of the human race, when some ape or other animal, as yet unknown, would find, among others fossils, those of the "Louvre of the written word." Even later, "at the end of the whole animal kingdom, air and tiny grains of sand slowly seep into it, while on the ground it goes on sparkling and eroding, and disintegrates brilliantly," until "AT LAST! — *one* is no longer there, and cannot refashion the sand, not even into glass, IT IS THE END!"[214] The fossilization of human language would thus bear witness to a final leap of human consciousness, which would survive its own death as a "one" and, contemplating the ultimate disintegration of the world, would "AT LAST!" set

itself free. Sartre did not refrain from pointing out the contradiction at work in that universe, which, though closed, "demands, precisely, a human witness."[215] He viewed "that effort to see oneself in the eyes of an alien species, to seek repose, finally, from the painful obligation to be a subject," as one "of the consequences of the Death of God. So long as God was alive, man was at peace: he knew he was being watched. Now that he alone is God, and his gaze makes every thing flourish, he strains his neck trying to get a look at himself."[216]

The three artistic moments I have identified — represented by de Chirico, Ernst, and Smithson — attest to that straining of the neck to get a look at oneself from above, beyond one's own death, the death of man as both individual and species. In different ways and to varying degrees, all three artists were, like Ponge, "partisans of things." All their approaches have the same critical value, since in condemning their objects to inertia, they attempt to extract them from the reifying activity of man, the "concessioner" of the whole planet. But this inertia also immediately entails the devalorization of any action, including political action, it, too, suspected of instrumentalizing the world. Worse, despite their declared antihumanism, the three artists assume there is a transcendent consciousness, a "one" that, having survived its own extinction, would be content to contemplate its objects from above. The geological metaphor — virtual in de Chirico, literal in Ernst, and material in Smithson — ceaselessly produces familiarity with the dread of a world without a human presence. But that leads each of these artists to project himself forward, to a time "after the end," in an ultimate attempt to familiarize himself with the inconceivable and perhaps as well to make himself immortal.

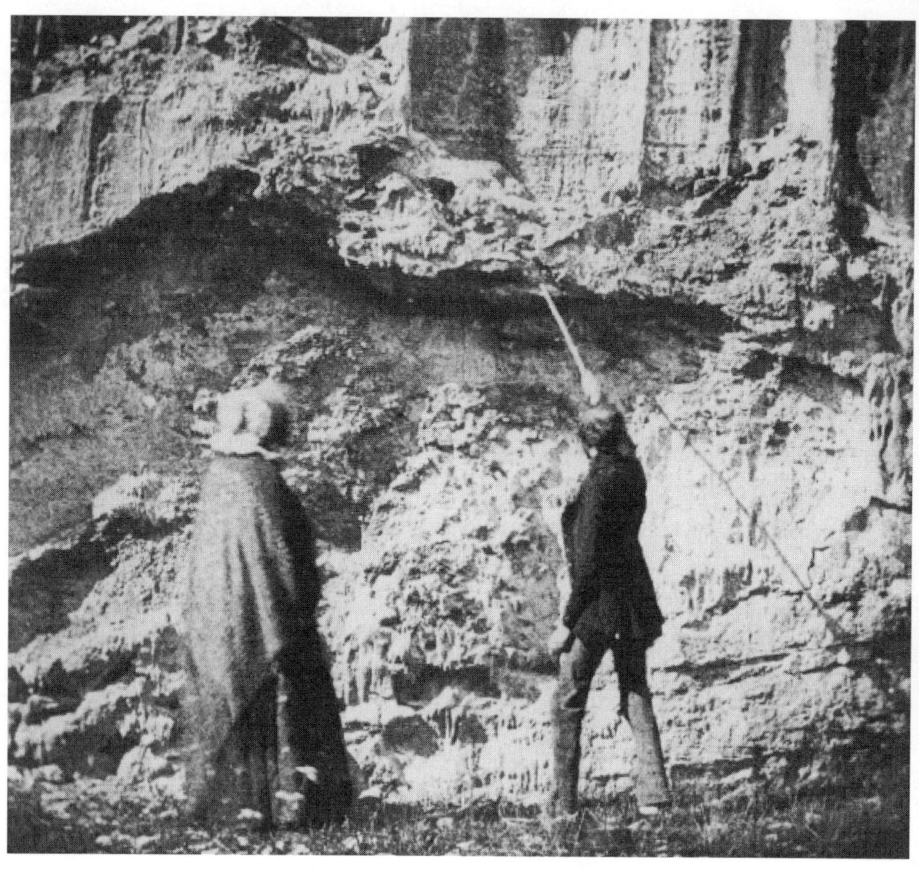

Figure 2.1. W. H. F. Talbot, *The Geologists*, ca. 1843. National Media Museum, Bradford, England. © National Science & Media Museum/ Science & Society Picture Library.

Reconstituting the Antiquity

of Humankind and of Art

The Age of Man

Two photographs taken sixteen years apart indicate how geology was slipping toward prehistory—from the discovery of the earth's antiquity to the much shorter duration of humanity. The first photograph, by William Henry Fox Talbot, was taken in 1843. Titled *The Geologists*, it depicts a bourgeois man and woman seen from the back, examining the wall of a particularly rugged cliff (Figure 2.1).[1] Raising a stick, whose shadow is projected onto the bright, sunlit wall, the man shows his companion something that our eyes cannot really make out in the undifferentiated matter of the rock. This thing, pointed out twice—by the stick and by its shadow—thus remains doubly invisible to us. We may suppose it is a fossil, like those existing in the English county of Dorset, where the semicloseup photograph was taken. Its frontality is in fact very marked: Talbot set up his camera near the two figures, and they stand even closer to the rock. The woman, wrapped completely in a long coat and shawl, seems inactive and monolithic, as if she were looking at the cliff with her whole body. By contrast, the man's legs are spread, conveying an energy consistent with the deictic gesture, which is about to make a thing surge up from the undifferentiated matter. This thing he will erect into a sign. The two postures are complementary in their very opposition: they repeat the dialectic that prevailed when the earth's antiquity was recognized, when it was necessary to observe the formless at length in order to identify the differences that would make it legible.

This same dialectic also unfolds in the second photograph: it provides indirect proof of the existence of not just any fossil, but that of a man who breathed the same air and walked the same earth as the extinct animals whose countless fossils had recently been found in the strata of the Lower Quaternary in Europe. This photograph was taken on April 27, 1859, in the quarry of Saint-Acheul, near Amiens, by the British geologist Joseph Prestwich, accompanied by the archaeologist John Evans (Figure 2.2). Evans, a specialist in Celtic coins, developed the theory of "alteration," a process of formal regression he discerned in the history of human artifacts.[2] In an overhead shot, the photograph shows the deep hole of the quarry. At the bottom are two men dressed in work clothes. The wheelbarrow ordinarily used to transport cleared mounds of dirt is immobile, having been converted into a seat for one of the two workers. We see only his profile; all his attention is focused on the index finger of the second worker, who, standing against the high wall opposite, is looking at the camera while showing something "drowned [sic] in the pile."[3] This thing is an "ax," whose geological location indicates that its creator, endowed with sufficient intelligence to design and carve a tool, was the contemporary of the extinct animal species whose remains filled these geological layers.

This photograph, claiming to offer proof of a find in situ of an "antediluvian" object (the term used at the time for the era preceding the biblical flood), fixed forever the precise moment when modern man became aware of his abyssal past.[4] Since at least the eighteenth century, the idea had spread that the earth had a longer past than the Bible claimed, but there was still a considerable gap between human history and the earth's history. Indeed, the narrative of human origins was still confused in Europe, with frequent references to the Bible, and was also the object of so-called conjectural or rational histories.[5] The canonical forms of these narratives were developed by the philosophers Locke, Rousseau, and Condorcet — well after

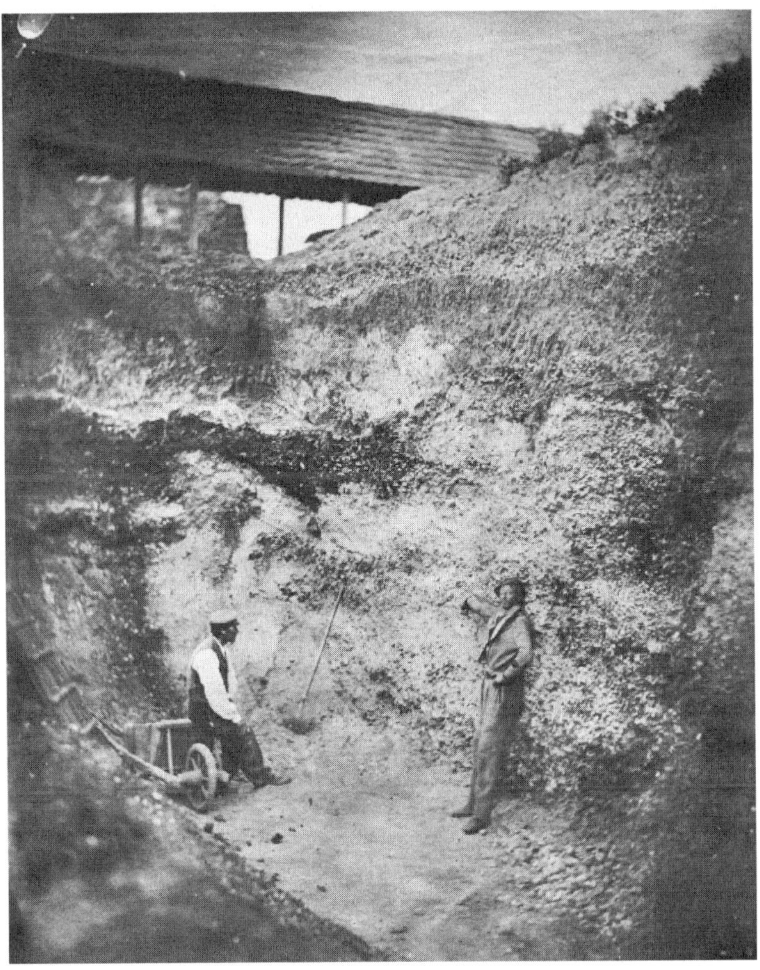

Figure 2.2. "The worker points to the ax embedded in the mass of stones. Saint-Acheul. First authentic ax found in the quarry 1859." Snapshot taken for Joseph Prestwich, April 27, 1859. Bibliothèque Centrale Louis Aragon, Amiens, Ms 1370 E.

Lucretius's descriptions of primitive human beings living naked in the forests with no knowledge of fire or metals.[6] "How many centuries may have elapsed before men were in a position to see a fire other than the one in the sky?" wondered Rousseau in the *Discourse on Inequality* (1754).[7] In the absence of documents, one could only presume an indeterminate and very long term, the conditions of the species' primitive life being situated in the uncertain sphere of the origin, by definition without chronology.

Now the discovery of artifacts adjacent to the fossils of extinct organisms would ascribe a place to the human species, not in a precise historical chronology, but within the existing paleontological and geological periodization. Man was thus a creature of the Reindeer Age or the Quaternary. He thereby stepped out of written and oral history, becoming a paleontological specimen. "Human paleontology," the anthropologist Ernest-Théodore Hamy wrote, corresponds to "the history of human races whose remains or debris belong to deposits predating the present period."[8] In short, there had been an epoch — the longest epoch — when man existed, but about which he had in the meantime forgotten everything. The hiatus that had formerly separated geology from history now became anthropological. Opening up within man himself, this hiatus, as well as the means to fill it, would come to be called "prehistory." The adjectival form of the word was used for the first time by Danish archaeologists in 1834, was transposed to French by the linguist Adolphe Pictet in 1837,[9] and was disseminated in the European languages in the mid-1860s, though it coexisted until the turn of the century with a legion of antagonistic terms, most of them now forgotten. The term "prehistory" and its derivatives came to signify both the period and the discipline that would study it.[10]

Of the tens of millenniums that human beings had already spent on earth (Lyell was thinking in terms of a thousand centuries, while his Scottish counterpart, Hugh Falconer, was more cautious, imagining only two hundred centuries), almost nothing was known except that they had for a long time used carved stone tools. Evidence of these had been provided by the primitive societies of the

Americas and Australia since the seventeenth century and by the flints scattered in the fields of Europe.[11] "Know thyself": the injunction engraved on the Temple of Delphi was quoted again and again in books published after the discovery of humankind's antiquity.[12] This axiom conformed to a tradition inaugurated by Linnaeus, who had argued that man is distinguished from the apes not by biological differences, but by his capacity to think about himself.[13]

It was as if the hole in the quarry of Saint-Acheul gave material form to the "thickness" of the past and simultaneously to its emptiness.[14] As Evans noted in his diary shortly before going to the Somme with Prestwich: "Think of their finding flint axes and arrowheads at Abbeville in conjunction with bones of Elephants and Rhinoceroses 40 ft below the surface in a bed of drift.... I can hardly believe it. It will make my ancient Britons quite modern if man is carried back in England to the days when Elephants, Rhinoceroses, Hippopotamuses and Tigers were also inhabitants of the country."[15] If Greek models became increasingly unrecognizable with every copy the barbarians made of them, why should it not be the same, but in reverse, for a human genealogy dating back to a past that had previously been imagined to be "without men"? Evans knew many things about the barbarians, but nothing at all about fossil man.

In the photograph, the deposits in the Somme constitute the foundations, literal and metaphorical, physical and metaphysical, of human existence. Whereas Talbot's two British geologists were *facing* the wall to examine its composition, the two anonymous workers posed *in* the quarry to demonstrate that man belonged to the geological past. Abandoning his purely *theoretical* position in front of the wall of rock, man not only stripped off his elegant costume, he aligned himself with the rock itself — but only to detach himself from it immediately, to seek an understanding of the past's meaning. The worker's deictic gesture truly expresses this contortion: man both belongs to the material world and maintains a theoretical distance from it.

Ever since Daguerre's 1839 photograph of an ammonite and other fossils, photography as a medium had placed its indexical and instantaneous nature in the service of an encounter between modern man, the inventor of prodigious machines, and a past that seemed to retreat indefinitely, a past of which only fragile traces, buried and previously unnoticed, remains. The two workers in the photograph, remunerated by Jacques Boucher de Crèvecoeur de Perthes (1788–1868) to excavate these alluvial terraces in the Somme in search of irrefutable proof of man dating back to before the "Flood," replay the moment of a revelation: the "discovery of fossil man" was truly symbolizable within the economy of an image. But the two men, inactive, like their tools, are posed less as the "agents" of that discovery than as its first "witnesses." Moreover, it is by virtue of their *anonymity* as ordinary and nameless representatives of the human species that they themselves are part of the "proof." They stand in a direct line of descent — but which one? — from the faceless and nameless creature that, at the dawn of time, had fashioned the ax now sticking out of the deep rock.

Before Boucher de Perthes and before the ax of Saint-Acheul, many flints and organic remains of fossil man had been found in France, both in the Somme and elsewhere (especially the Midi), and also in England, Belgium, and Germany. Each discovery gave rise to new questions about human identity. Wiktor Stoczkowski has pointed out the importance of Paul Tournal, a pharmacist and amateur paleontologist who very early on had disconnected the antiquity of man from mythical narratives about the flood, narratives on which Boucher de Perthes still relied to a great extent. In 1829, in bone caves near Bize (in Aude), Tournal had in fact discovered remains of an extinct animal next to human bones, which led him to "raise the question of the existence of man in his fossil state."[16] The same year, theorizing his find, he construed geology as the sole source of the "antehistorical" human past, that is, the past that took place *before* history: "Geology, providing a supplement to our short years, will come to reawaken human pride by showing the antiquity of the race; for only geology can now give us a few notions about the age of man's first appearance on earth."[17] A few years later, the anthropologist and paleontologist Philippe-Charles Schmerling found two skulls in the early Quaternary layers of a cave near Liège. They were not the first of their type, and they would be identified as Neanderthal fossils well after the discovery of similar fossilized debris in the Neander Valley, near Düsseldorf, in 1856. In the 1840s, the paleontologist Édouard Lartet discovered his first fossil apes in Garonne. And since even the most illustrious fixists (Linnaeus, Blumenbach, and Cuvier) considered the ape the mammal closest to man, Lartet dispassionately deduced that man could have existed during the same period and in the same environment.[18] Boucher de Perthes had begun his research in the alluvial terraces near Abbeville in 1837 to prove that human beings had truly existed at the time of the biblical flood and quite certainly in a lower form than that of "Adamic" man as he now existed.[19] The excavations done under his direction had allowed him to identify two different types of industry, which he attributed to two civilizations separated by the last great cataclysm: in the "deepest layers," well below the polished stone tools he attributed to the Celts, Boucher de Perthes had found axes made of carved stones that he ascribed to the "most ancient populations."[20] Finally, in 1858, the most respected British geologists excavated Brixham Cave, which, having never been explored, had a very pure geological composition. There, Lyell, Prestwich, and Falconer found the same juxtaposition of fauna and carved artifacts that Boucher de Perthes had identified years before on the other side of the channel.[21]

The carved human artifact in the layers of Saint-Acheul, a true metonym for fossil man, was still in its original context, having been left almost undisturbed and unchanged across the centuries: "Here there is no longer any doubt possible," Boucher de Perthes wrote in 1847, "because, unlike the bogs, these diluvian deposits do not have an elastic and permeable mass; and unlike the bone caves, they do not have a gaping chasm open to all comers. . . . How would it be possible to characterize the epochs in that hodgepodge of all ages, that neutral terrain, a sort of caravanserai of past generations?"[22] The impermeability and thus legibility of the diluvian beds stood in contrast to the "hodgepodge" of ages and the "caravanserai of generations": "Each period is clear-cut. These horizontally stacked layers, these beds of different shades and materials, show us in capital letters the history of the past."[23] Although the site had a very clear stratified composition, the signs had for a long time remained ambiguous. The recognition of man's antiquity had in fact run up against two opposing forces of time. On the one hand, the intervening time had compressed the traces of the distant past to an incredible degree, if it had not crushed them altogether. On the other, primitive man himself had detached himself from nature only with great difficulty, so that the indistinction between man and nature at the origin could also be found in the gnoseological present. How, then, to discern the differences that would extricate man and his works from the indistinction of nature? The threshold between nature and culture played a key role in the constitution of prehistory's imaginary. In the first place, the discipline had from the start installed itself between geology and history. At the same time, the periods that corresponded to the evolution of the natural world, of extinct and still-living organisms, and of human industry were superposed and overlapping. Geological time (the Tertiary and Quaternary) was divided into ages (Stone, Bronze, Iron), which were divided into periods (Paleolithic, Neolithic, and so on), which were divided into epochs (the typology of geological terrains).[24] In the second place, it had to be proven that fossil man's objects were different from mere stones that the water had tossed about and that the earth had abraded for hundreds of centuries. In the third place, the narrative accounts depicted fossil man himself — as a perceiving and feeling being, as an economic agent, and as an artist — detaching himself only slowly and painfully from animality and nature, the backdrop for his actions. Finally, for all these reasons at once, the intentional marks of his artistic works were intractably indistinguishable from those that the forces of nature or the claws of animals had accidentally inflicted on stone during its long history.

In short, it was as if the dynamic of acknowledging man's antiquity was exactly the opposite of what had prevailed in the recognition of the earth's age. The metaphors of medal and monument had familiarized researchers with the radical strangeness of fossils; now the literalness, the source, and the humanity of these metaphors had to be restored.

The Indistinction between Man and Nature

The chapter that opens Élie Faure's *Art History* (1909), titled "Before History," is a *parergon* in the formal and conceptual sense of the term. Its very first lines describe the regime of indistinction that reigned well before history. The evolution of the earth, that of the organisms living there since the dawn of time, and that of human culture were all bound up together during this period. Nothing belonged to a stable kingdom within the telluric metamorphosis:

> The earth is the womb and the killer, the diffuse matter that imbibes death in order to foster life. Living things dissolve in the earth, dead things move in it. The earth wears away stone and gives it the golden pallor of bone and ivory. In contact with the earth, bone and ivory, before being devoured, become rough as stone. Carved flints look like large triangular teeth, and the teeth of swallowed-up monsters are like pulpy tubers ready to germinate. Skulls, vertebrae, and carapaces have the dark and soft patina of old perfect sculptures. Primitive engravings resemble these fossil imprints, which revealed to us the nature of shells, plants, extinct insects, spirals, arborescences, ferns, elytrons, and veined leaves. A prehistoric museum is a petrified garden where the slow action of earth and water on buried matter unites the work of humans and that of the elements.[25]

What Élie Faure describes in his telluric nostalgia as both a "prehistoric museum" and a "petrified garden," fashioned by the combined activity of man and earth, was the reality that the discipline of prehistory struck up against. That reality constituted the discipline in the mid-nineteenth century and continues to shape it today. The inextricability of nature and culture is a constitutive aporia of prehistory, the source of the most contradictory narratives and practices, which vigorously seize hold of an enigmatic and lacunary origin, but often only to find the means to feed evolutionist fantasies.

"A Few Pitiful Stones": From Indistinction to Evolution

For a long time, the flints found in the fields after a storm were called "cerauniae," because they were believed to have fallen from the sky with the thunderbolts.[26] "Thunderous" objects because they appeared in a sudden, irregular, and essentially inexplicable manner, the flints were inserted into a first interpretive framework after the travels and discoveries that confirmed the dazzling thesis John Locke had developed in 1689: "in the beginning, all the world was America."[27] America represented what Europe had once been from a technological standpoint; now the flints extended that past to the world as a whole. Antoine de Jussieu, inverting Locke's famous remark, would say shortly thereafter that these "thunderstones" found in Europe were "instruments" carved by "the first inhabitants" of the continent.[28] Even so, the analogy between the flints and the remote past had to be situated chronologically. The nineteenth century, the century of history, took on the task. Boucher de Perthes said: "When the ground one explores is without other symptoms of intelligent life, when it is a question of a people whose very existence is in doubt, every vestige becomes history."[29] In his eyes, the many stone fragments he found in the deepest layers of the earth were too similar to be simply the product of chance. The marquis de Nadaillac, in his epigraph to his book on the "first men," published in 1881, cited the principle of the seventeenth-century antiquarians: *facta, non verba* — deeds, not words. "The starting point for prehistoric science is truly curious," he added. "It was a few pitiful stones, often barely rough-hewn, a few fragile instruments made of bone, a few formless monuments, that allowed for . . . the reconstitution of an entire past well before written history, a past that left no trace in the memories of men and where, by all appearances, our globe itself displayed none of its present conditions."[30] At nearly the same moment, General Augustus Lane-Fox Pitt Rivers brushed aside the oxymoron of a revolutionary discovery attributable to a few "pitiful stones." In his writings, the aporia of the indistinction between nature and culture was metamorphosed, magnified, and elevated to the rank of law: the law of evolution and progress. Pitt Rivers's evolutionism thus repressed all "curiosity," sealed the fissure, and finally filled the original void by positing a positive and limitless continuity between nature and culture: "The principles of variation and natural selection," he wrote in 1875, have established a bond of union between the physical and culture sciences which can never be broken. History is but another term for evolution. . . . But our position with regard to culture has always been one which has forced on our comprehension the reality of progress, whilst with respect to the slow progress of external nature, it has been concealed from us, owing to the brief span of human existence and our imperfect records of the past.[31]

Human beings, failing to attain the scale of natural evolution because of their all-too-brief time on earth, projected onto nature the idea of evolution and progress attested by their own history as it appeared in their memories and in documents. Their present, continuously accelerating, illuminated the past and demonstrated their unstoppable ascent: "The age in which we live is not more remarkable for its rapid onward movement than for its intelligent retrospect of the past. It is reconstructive as well as progressive. The light which is kindled by the practical discoveries of modern science, throws back its rays, and enables us to distinguish objects of interest, which have been unnoticed in the gloom of bygone ages, or passed over with contempt."[32]

For the museum that Pitt Rivers founded at Oxford in 1884, courtesy of his impressive collection of archaeological and ethnological objects, he arranged weapons, bows, pottery, and so forth into series organized typologically and sequentially, supposedly beginning with the earliest in the evolutionary process, that is, with the form he found the most "simple." His notion of primitive simplicity can be encapsulated in the equivalence he established between the "most simple," the "lowest," and the "slowest."[33] But what might that original form lying in the depths of the earth have been? Confounding in its simplicity, it was marked by a pace of evolution so slow that it was barely distinguishable from mineral inertia. Clearly, the simplest form was nowhere to be found, totally indiscernible among all the stones and fragments on which no hand had bestowed intentionality.

Pitt Rivers, pursuing the speculative methods of the eighteenth century while conferring on them the authority of positive truths, imagined a "creature" similar to a higher animal, one capable of grasping a stone to break nuts, but incapable of carving it into a form more appropriate to its purpose. The "creature," tirelessly repeating the same gesture to perform the most diverse tasks, must have seen the stone break more than once. It must have observed the fragments, and after a great deal of time had elapsed, must have begun to gather them up to make use of them. The fragments, lighter and thinner than their nucleus, ultimately proved more manageable. Later, the creature Pitt Rivers ventured to call "primaeval man" must have observed natural forms that already suited one need or another: a branch, for example, could be used as a bow. These were, so to speak, the ready-mades of prehistory. During these long early stages, nature supplied human intelligence with forms, and nature also reabsorbed these forms after their use. In this regime of absolute organicity, where man was still not detached from his environment or his animal origins, what came from nature could only return to it.

Animal Ancestry: The Chasm within Ourselves
Lyell, a geologist and the author of the first authoritative work (published in 1863) on the age of human beings, remained somewhat cautious about the evolution of the species. He kept his distance from transformist and evolutionist theories alike — from those who saw man as descending from the apes, whether directly or not, and those (represented especially by the anthropologist Armand de Quatrefages) who defended man's specificity, the result of his perfectibility.[34] Man's animal ancestry — a question Darwin himself had left hanging in *On the Origin of Species* — was first theorized by the Darwinist Thomas H. Huxley. Using the now-familiar metaphor of the abyss, he evoked the obscure and terrifying ancestry of human beings. Buffon and Quinet had speculated about the abyss of time that separated ideas about man from the duration of the earth's existence, but it was now within man himself that the abyss opened up.

In 1868, in the preface to the French translation of his *Evidence as to Man's Place in Nature* (1863), Huxley recalled the day when, from the mountain heights of the Grands Mulets in the Alps, he anxiously contemplated Chamonix: it seemed to him that the village lay "at the bottom of a prodigious *abyss* or *chasm*." That enormous chasm, the Bossons glacier, with its frightening crevasses, which he would have to cross to reach Chamonix, was unfamiliar to him, but Huxley was well aware that it "had been crossed hundreds of times by those who knew the way and had special assistance." The same feeling of anxiety, as it happens, seized hold of him when he considered "a man and an ape side by side": "There may be or may have been a path from one to the other, I'm sure of it. But now the distance between the two is plainly abysmal, and I would rather acknowledge that fact and my ignorance of the path than let myself fall into one of the open crevasses."[35] The theory of evolution promised the possibility that he would not fall prey to vertigo if he cautiously traced the path of knowledge capable of abolishing the dreadful fear of the "abyss."

Scarcely a year later, the naturalist Alfred Wallace advanced the hypothesis, reasonable in his view, of a being whose body, like the rest of the organic world, had remained subject to the vagaries of the environment so long as his brain had not evolved sufficiently to adapt to using his tools, his language, and his social skills. The intransigent materialist and evolutionist Gabriel de Mortillet, a dominant figure in the institutionalization of prehistory in France from 1860 on, was firmly convinced of the existence of what was called "Tertiary man," the "precursor" of present-day man. He speculated about an "Eolithic period" prior to the Paleolithic and the Neolithic, in the famous distinction introduced by John Lubbock and still in use.[36] The Eoliths, scattered widely in the Tertiary strata, remained permanently unidentifiable as such, but at least Mortillet could indicate the "first tool" carved by Tertiary man. The notches, cuts, and incisions that human beings had made in stones and bones over the ages could be easily mistaken for the tooth and claw prints of animals or for "geological impressions" left on the stones. By contrast, crude flints, generally triangular in shape and found in multiple places, exhibited formal analogies indicating they had been "sought out, desired, and intentionally executed."[37] Granted, the being intelligent enough "to start a fire and carve flints and quartzites" was not a "man" in the true sense of the term. He was rather his "precursor," the missing link between man and ape. As its composite name indicates, "anthropopithecus" was situated between the anthropos and the pithecus. Haeckel would later reverse the terms, yielding "pithecanthropus," to which he added the adjective "alalus" to indicate that the being did not have the power of speech.[38]

Encountering the First Paleolithic Artworks:
Atemporality and Natural Adaptation

A year after the paleontologists Lartet and Christy published the carved and engraved Paleolithic objects they had discovered in many caves in the Midi of France, Adrien de Longpérier, curator of antiquities at the Musée du Louvre, expressed his complete incredulity that these artworks were authentic. Replying in a letter of July 8, 1865, to the superintendent of the Beaux-Arts regarding a few engraved objects collected by Louis Marie de Lastic Saint-Jal in the Cavern of Bruniquel (commonly called Courbet Cave), de Longpérier based his misgivings on multiple factors (Figure 2.3). These objects were therefore acquired not by the Louvre, but by the British Museum, where they remain.

"If the reindeer bone engraved on two of its faces . . . is authentic, this is a document so new and unexpected for art history that all possible efforts should be made to ensure that the museum comes into possession of it," the French archaeologist Longpérier wrote. But there was a great deal of evidence for the object's inauthenticity:

> This is no longer just a crude image in which the representation of a living thing is more or less recognizable, but an outline drawing with internal details, executed with a confidence and skill that explains the existence of artists as practiced as those who engraved Greek vases from the seventh century B.C.E. And yet the reindeer of Bruniquel belong to an age so remote that it eludes historians and falls into the field of geologists. It is extraordinary that though nothing similar has yet been discovered in Egypt, Phoenicia, or Greece, all countries in which art was practiced at an early date, artists contemporaneous with fauna now unknown on our soil are said to have existed in Gaul, artists who, in an incalculably remote time, had done drawings the like of which the Gauls never did in historical times![39]

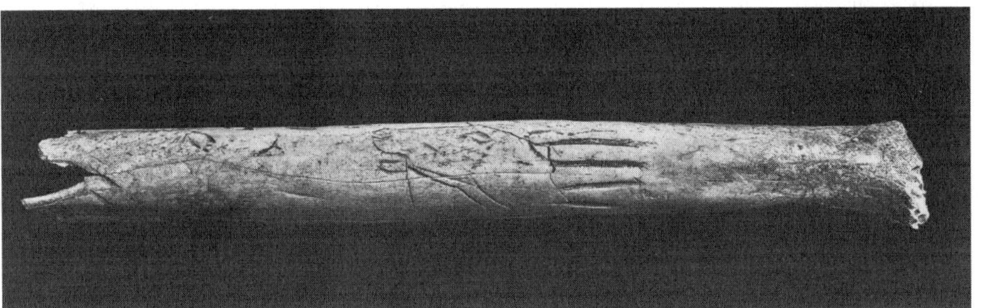

Figure 2.3. Engraved antler, refitted from two pieces, with three reindeer heads and an ibex head, all facing left. Found by Vicomte Louis Marie de Lastic Saint-Jal. Bone, 4⅜ × ⅛ × ⅞ in. Courbet Cave, Tarn, France, Midi Pyrénées, Late Magdalenian. © The Trustees of the British Museum.

The reasoning was admirable. The Greek norm surfaced precisely when de Longpérier expressed his astonishment that prehistoric men drew as well as seventh-century Greeks. The classical canon certainly remained intact, but an archaic Greece — suddenly projected back some hundreds of centuries — was an anachronism that neither the century's evolutionism nor the timeless ideal could support. Prehistoric finds inordinately expanded the time of art history, thereby rendering any congruence with the scale of universal history impossible. De Longpérier was thus frightened to see the symbolic realm of human beings suddenly overlap with the mineral mutism of geological times. Simultaneously, the time-honored fields of the discipline — especially Greece and Egypt — lost their value as templates. Unable to conceive of the idea that the human species was universally a creator of symbolic artifacts, de Longpérier sought to identify these artifacts in terms of a race or a people, attributing the creation of the engraved bones to the remote ancestors of the Gauls (though he knew nothing about them) and expressing astonishment that the "historical Gauls" had been unable to hold onto their gift. In short, the genetic transmission of art was seriously disrupted.[40]

Clearly, the discovery of Paleolithic art gave rise to a disorientation both spatial and temporal, scrambling the genealogical narrative of art history. The first prehistoric artifacts constituted not simply a "huge fact," but a cataclysm: "On the day one of these engraved bones has been authentically extracted from an intact bloc, the history of art within humanity will have acquired a huge piece of information. But so long as the bones have been examined only in isolation and by geologists who do not know how forgers of antiquities proceed, the question will remain in doubt."[41] And that cataclysm turned upside down not only the art history *of* humanity, but also and especially the value of art *within* humanity. This was less the concern of the discipline and more an anthropological question, as de Longpérier had clearly sensed. It was as if art history had overstepped its historiographical boundaries and turned toward anthropology.[42] That anthropological turn of art, inaugurated by Gottfried Semper, would find increasing confirmation. De Longpérier no doubt wondered what the function of art had been in the life and evolution of prehistoric man. Why create artistic objects in such remote times, which were still imagined to have been difficult? The cataclysm of history engulfed all the little facts (documents and events) that art history had learned to collect to explain the works of the past, using history as its model. But these discoveries, given their deep stratigraphy and material density, also upended to an equal degree the idealistic speculations of the philosophy of art. Throughout the nineteenth century, art history, torn between atemporal ideal and historicist imperative, speculations and facts, the philosophy of art and history, had had trouble finding its bearings. The discovery of the "first human artifacts" in the layers of the Quaternary hardly helped matters, since it weakened all the assumptions on which the new discipline was attempting to establish its foundations. Even more radically, it intensified the anxiety about the antiquity of humankind.

Notes to Serve the History of Primitive Art, compiled by the prehistorian Édouard Piette some thirty years after the first discovery of

Paleolithic art objects, shows clearly how the second shock wave to reach historical consciousness at the time was experienced:

> We were still debating the simultaneous existence of man and the major extinct species... when Lartet and Christy began their excavations in the caves. The result of their explorations astonished even them. That man of the olden days, the Quaternary, whom some did not want to believe in, whom others regarded as a savage having only just emerged from his animality, had elevated himself to an understanding of the plastic arts and had taken an avid interest in them.... He had represented, not without a remarkable talent for imitation, the animals among whom he lived: the mammoth, the reindeer, the Equidae, and others. This revelation produced feelings of admiration or skepticism in the scientific world and a great enthusiasm among the explorers of caves.[43]

It was necessary, first, to unlearn the belief that the contemporaneous existence of men and extinct animal species was an anachronism, then immediately attempt to think of that contemporary of primitive animals as an artist. At a time when the discussions of paleontologists about what distinguished man from animal (tools, language, art, perfectibility, ontological and historical self-reflexivity, metaphysical meaning, or all of them combined?)[44] were at their height, the discovery of prehistoric art only further muddled that great divide. It forced them to restructure categories, to question their limits, and to rethink the "specificity" of man and his art.

The paleontologist Lartet came across the first artifacts unexpectedly, while looking in caves for fossilized bones of animals and human beings, as was his habit. On the ground of the cave, where bones mingled with bewilderingly delicate pebbles and artifacts, the disciplines blurred and redefined themselves to adapt to their new objects. Ordinarily, 1864 is taken to be the year of the discovery of Paleolithic "mobiliary art." But as I said in the Introduction, this was really a screen memory that concealed Lartet's petrified astonishment when he discovered the first symbolic artifacts of the Paleolithic in 1861. His "New Research on the Coexistence of Man and the Large Fossil Mammals" even referred three times to the "artist" who

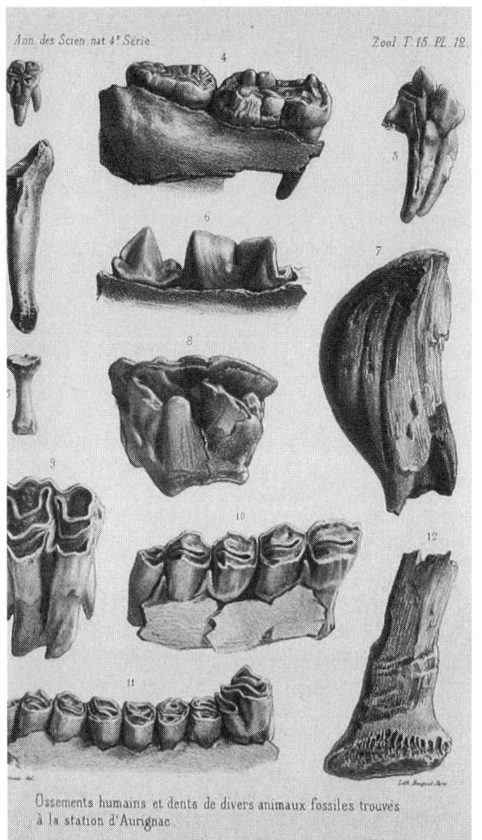

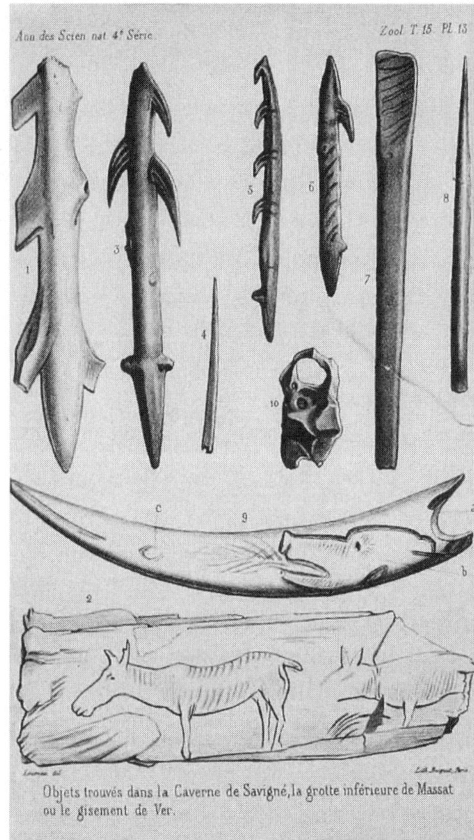

Figures 2.4 and 2.5. Édouard Lartet, "Nouvelles recherches sur la coexistence de l'homme et des grands mammifères fossiles," *Annales des sciences naturelles*, 4th series, 15, *Zoology* (Paris: Victor Masson et Fils, 1861), pp. 210–11.

had carved and engraved animal figures on a canine tooth and on stag antlers.[45] Nevertheless, Lartet did not point out the originality of his find, nor did he lay claim to the discovery: he simply called these objects "curious," as if everyone already knew that Quaternary man was an artist. One hundred and fifty years later, 1864 is still given as the year of the discovery of Paleolithic art, and Lartet's stunned silence in 1861 is unknowingly reproduced.

His language was purely descriptive, using the neutral tone that befits what is commonplace — or, on the contrary, unassimilable in the strict sense:

> The most curious piece I obtained from the excavations of the lower cave of Massat is represented on plate 13, fig. 9: it is a stag antler, broken at point *a*, where someone made a round hole, intended no doubt to allow it to be easily suspended as an ornament or other treasured object. Ahead of the break, toward the left of the figure, the profile of the animal's head, the maw half-open, can be easily distinguished. The lines of the profile, the position of the eye, and the direction of the short ears leave no doubt that the artist who executed this fairly accurate drawing meant to represent a bear's head.[46]

Lartet identified the engraved figure, called it "accurate," and attributed a decorative function to it (Figures 2.4 and 2.5). In that respect, he proceeded like an archaeologist or even a paleontologist, seeking to document the geological eras and their fauna. This is clear in what immediately follows: "The relative flatness of the brow would indicate that this is not the great bear from the caves, but rather the present-day bear of the Pyrenees. As we have just seen, a jaw fragment from such a bear was found in the same cave."[47] Halfway between the work of art and the scientific *document*, this object was astonishing for the delicacy of the drawing, done with a barely rough-hewn flint, but it proved just as surely that the Cantabrian brown bear had existed during the Paleolithic period.

It took three years for Lartet, this time with his excavation partner Henry Christy, to lay claim to the originality of a similar discovery by including it in the subtitle of an article they published in the *Revue archéologique* in 1864. Yet they did so only quietly. Their

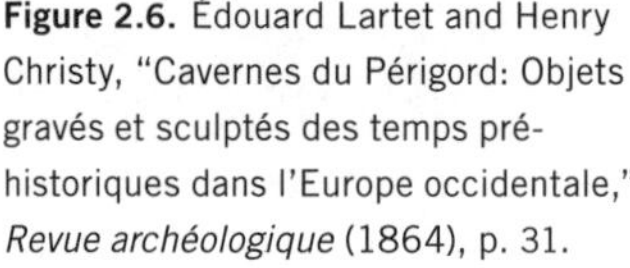

Figure 2.6. Édouard Lartet and Henry Christy, "Cavernes du Périgord: Objets gravés et sculptés des temps préhistoriques dans l'Europe occidentale," *Revue archéologique* (1864), p. 31.

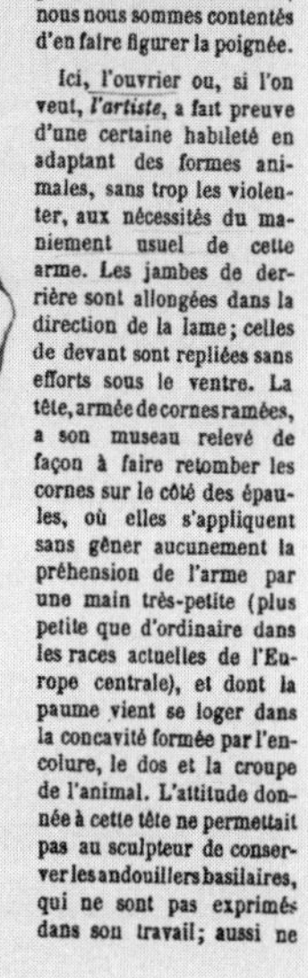

une autre figure gravée simplement au trait, et que l'on pourrait accepter comme une forme intentionnelle de poisson.

Le morceau capital de notre collection d'objets sculptés de Laugerie-Basse est un poignard ou sorte d'épée détachée tout d'une pièce du merrain d'un bois de renne. La longueur de cette arme ne nous permettant pas non plus de la représenter dans son entier, nous nous sommes contentés d'en faire figurer la poignée.

Ici, l'ouvrier ou, si l'on veut, *l'artiste*, a fait preuve d'une certaine habileté en adaptant des formes animales, sans trop les violenter, aux nécessités du maniement usuel de cette arme. Les jambes de derrière sont allongées dans la direction de la lame; celles de devant sont repliées sans efforts sous le ventre. La tête, armée de cornes ramées, a son museau relevé de façon à faire retomber les cornes sur le côté des épaules, où elles s'appliquent sans gêner aucunement la préhension de l'arme par une main très-petite (plus petite que d'ordinaire dans les races actuelles de l'Europe centrale), et dont la paume vient se loger dans la concavité formée par l'encolure, le dos et la croupe de l'animal. L'attitude donnée à cette tête ne permettait pas au sculpteur de conserver les andouillers basilaires, qui ne sont pas exprimés dans son travail; aussi ne

discovery, never mentioned on its own, was submerged in a more general "demonstration" and in supposedly "direct" and "rigorous" "evidence."[48] References to the engraved objects (slabs of shale found in the cave of Les Eyzies, tools and reindeer-wood ornaments discovered at La Madeleine metro station in Paris) were combined with descriptions of fragments of cervids, felines, and fish. Nevertheless, the two authors emphasized the extraordinary quality of the artifacts buried at La Madeleine, thereby conferring a real importance on the site. These artifacts attested to an extreme refinement, and the drawings on them, done "with vigor and without hesitation," were evidence of a "sure and practiced hand."[49] One tool especially, which they called a "dagger," showed that "the worker or, if you like, the artist, displayed a certain skill in adapting animal forms, without doing too much violence to them, to the way the weapon was usually handled" (Figure 2.6).[50] This was an acknowledgment that the prehistoric artist had enough intelligence and technical experience to adapt form to function. The two paleontologists concluded that the "aborigines" of the past lived by hunting and fishing, sewed together hides for clothing, and as yet had no knowledge of polished stone and also no domesticated animals.

What about art in all that? What was its place in this first reconstitution of the material lives of the aborigines from the past? In that remote time, did these people cultivate art as *naturally* as they hunted and fished? Lartet and Christy attributed an ornamental function to these objects: "Their ornaments, their decorated utensils . . . attest to their instincts for luxury and a certain degree of artistic culture."[51] The two paleontologists saw ornament as a form of "surplus" and "excess," the formal excess literally translating the *surplus* of time at the disposal of their creators and the *excretion* of a sensible world in which they were supposedly *saturated*. Lartet and Christy noted:

> hunting and fishing provided amply for the needs of these aborigines and thus left them the leisure time for a relatively untroubled existence. And if necessity is the mother of invention, it can also be said that the leisure time afforded by an easy life gives birth to the arts. Why should we be surprised that hunters of reindeer, aurochs, and ibex successfully represented these animal forms so familiar to their sight, when, in our own time, we see the simplest shepherds of the Swiss Oberland, with no resources other than the tips of their knives, reproduce the animals in their mountains, the chamois among others, with more truth and animated movement in their attitudes than the best workers in our cities could do?[52]

This was a groundbreaking text both for aesthetics and for political ideology. It argued, first, that the engraved designs and carved works were simply prehistoric people's sensory reactions to nature. Sensitive recorders of their environment, they transcribed its stimuli onto the materials they had at hand. Being themselves an integral part of nature, they traced the natural world as they breathed, with perceptual, spatiotemporal, and formal immediacy. As we will see, it was this idea that would allow many artists and theorists to construe prehistoric artists as the first "impressionists" of human history. In addition, Lartet and Christy disengaged prehistoric man from animality, situating him in an Arcadia to which the objects discovered finally bore witness. Compatible with the fable of Paradise, this Arcadia and the finds related to it would be dispassionately included in the creationist Louis Figuier's *Earth before the Flood*, in which primitive man is depicted as a handsome Adam with his nuclear family.[53] Suspended in a state of grace, that of a perpetual present oblivious by definition to the torments of history, prehistoric Arcadia fed many fantasies over the course of long modernity. Its advantage, when compared with past Arcadias, was that it was proven "historically." At the very end of the nineteenth century, certain anarchists considered it material proof of the "state of nature." An image published in the review *L'État naturel* depicts a brutally anachronistic encounter on the outskirts of Paris between a prehistoric man, robust and half naked, and scrawny proletarians in rags, "dilapidated and grotesque," according to the caption. The nocturnal silhouettes of the tower designed by the engineer Eiffel and of a few monuments commemorating triumphs from French history can be made out in the distant background, as if they already belonged to the past.[54]

Lartet and Christy's naturalistic and naturalizing interpretation of prehistoric art was an attempt to *normalize* the abnormal. It was necessary to present these artifacts as the products of an activity that was in no way extraordinary for the human beings of that time, even while exempting them from the obligation to bear witness to the evolution of art history. The only way to escape that aporia was quite simply to remove the artifacts from history by invoking the idea of their "gratuitousness." In 1889, Salomon Reinach wrote that this was "art in the strict sense, because it is a luxury, and this luxury is expressed by the decoration of objects whose decoration does not augment their utility."[55] Art thus manifested itself in its natural and eternal purity, independent of any particular conditions, including technical conditions. Aloïs Riegl also considered these symbolic artifacts of Paleolithic prehistory to be unhoped-for allies in his struggle against the materialism of the Semperian school: "We are confronted here with an art that covers cultural periods of humankind whose temporal boundaries completely escape us. These documents, though rare, are present, whereas materialist theories are based on nothing."[56] On the one hand, the naturalism of that art, according to Riegl, clearly attested to its independence from any technique, which, had it prevailed, would have culminated in more schematic and abstract forms. On the other hand, it proved that art existed as "an instinct that becomes an act,"[57] natural at first, then adaptable to evolutionary change.

Prehistory was commonly understood at the time to be a "wild" state, an Arcadia that was sylvan rather than pastoral. For the prehistorian Émile Cartailhac, the "Reindeer Age" (corresponding more or less to the Paleolithic in Lartet's periodization) was the "artistic period par excellence of all prehistoric eras,"[58] because art had been able to develop gratuitously and naïvely, obeying no social imperatives. The absence of artificial constructs, including social institutions, guaranteed that an art as pure and "native" as nature itself would thrive. In his essays on language and on inequality, Rousseau had outlined that original state of primitive humanity, which for a long time lacked any horizontal or vertical social structures, any organized bonds among contemporaries, and any concern about transmission from one generation to the next.[59] Condorcet in turn portrayed these peoples as being dependent on "chance and the seasons," confining themselves to "improving their personal skills and address."[60] Cartailhac also spoke of the isolation of Paleolithic artists: "They truly had a passion for art, and at every opportunity, they would do drawings, which they abandoned or destroyed without regret, having achieved their aim of personal satisfaction. In societies of a very high order, the majority enjoys the works produced by the minority, an artistic elite. In the Reindeer Age, every individual was isolated, each having a share of artistic creativity."[61] The fact that every individual was a potential artist by virtue of his very isolation thus argued in favor of the naturalness of his art. And for the same reasons, that art was in turn described as being "isolated" within human evolution, that is, unique and without influence. In the first place, Paleolithic art, since it was pure origin, could not have had any precedent: "Here, it's something completely different, it's an unexpected, unprecedented efflorescence. For the first time, man draws, engraves, sculpts, represents the living things around him with an astonishing aesthetic, and he does not overlook his own image."[62] Second, that "unexpected efflorescence" ended abruptly with the disappearance of Paleolithic art, which, a long time later, would be followed by a Neolithic art that differed from it in every way. Mortillet had used the term "hiatus" to designate the break between the culture of the Paleolithic period and that of the Neolithic; Cartailhac took the geological metaphor even further, claiming there was much more than a "hiatus," namely, a true "abyss."[63] In 1889, Salomon Reinach memorably formulated the genealogical aporia of a sudden efflorescence and disappearance of Paleolithic art, quoting a famous line from Ovid's *Metamorphoses*: "We see no tradition more ancient from which it is derived and no more recent tradition that owes its origin to it. *Proles sine matre creata.*" And Reinach immediately added: *"Mater sine prole defuncta.* This is one of the facts that becomes obvious upon observation, but which is still impossible to explain."[64] Prehistory, "a child born without a mother" and "a mother who died without a child," is simultaneously self-formed and sterile: the naturalization of Paleolithic art came in response to that unthinkable genealogical aporia.[65] And that is how the fictionality of myth, Ovidian, in this case, was once more surpassed by the discoveries of prehistory.

Lartet, Cartailhac, and Pitt Rivers, all in denial, argued that it was no more paradoxical that exquisite drawings could be exhumed next to the remains of extinct animal species than that these works should have no progeny in the evolution of art; it was in fact perfectly *natural*. This idea of "nature," fashioned at great length by explorers of the New World and Enlightenment philosophers, still had to be adapted to the new data. The Jesuit Joseph-François Laffitau had described American savages as "men who lack everything, who have no literature, no science, no apparent laws, no temple for the most part, no organized religion," as if they "had simply arisen from the earth's ooze."[66] Cartailhac said the same thing about prehistoric peoples: they existed within and at the behest of nature without ever developing real social structures. They were spontaneous and anarchical individualities, and their acts of creation were consistent with their being. He called their art an "event,"[67] the better to underscore how extraordinary it was. As for its stupefying naturalism, it was after all faithful to the sensualism of the eighteenth century. Maine de Biran had wanted to show that "man is not distinguished at first glance from the objects of his representations; he exists entirely outside himself; nature is man, man is nature."[68] And Ernest Renan went even further in *The Origin of Language* (1848): "Primitive man did not live by himself; he was spread out all over the world, from which he barely distinguished himself."[69] It was only a short step to recognize that natural man was a being capable not only of experiencing sensations, but also of *reproducing* them. All in all, this was hardly surprising at a time when mechanical reproduction was making great strides and photography posed a challenge to the impressionist painters.

In 1865, Lubbock was astonished at the astonishment elicited by the engraved animals of Bruniquel and elsewhere. Even while conceding that it was "natural to feel some surprise at finding these works of art," he immediately noted that "there are instances among recent savages of a certain skill in drawing and sculpture."[70] From the earliest discoveries of prehistoric art, the equivalence between childhood, prehistoric peoples, and savages served to seal the breach and restore the broken genealogy of evolution. Henry Balfour, curator of the Pitt Rivers Museum at Oxford, thus posited the "adaptive" stage as the first in the evolution of art: "Man simply accepted and adapted effects that were accidentally suggested to him."[71] In short, art was originally a *natural adaptation*: like animals who adapted to their environment, prehistoric man had adapted his sensations to stone. As for moderns, they had only to adapt slowly and gradually to the stupor caused by prehistory.

From the Ground to the Walls of Caves: First Fissures, First Modern Appropriations of Prehistoric Art

Enigma, Filiation, History

The last great discovery from prehistory's long past was that of parietal painting, which had been sealed up for millenniums in a few caves in France and Spain. Some had been known and visited for a long time, but their paintings had never attracted any attention. Even as the caves of Niaux and Gargas began to be systematically excavated, the eyes of specialists remained, as it were, riveted to the ground, never looking up at the walls. In an important article, Béatrice Fraenkel has pointed out this persistent "blindness" and the tropes that structured the "revelation" of parietal art at the turn of the twentieth century.[72] Félix Garrigou, she recalls, had perceived the drawings in the Cave of Niaux in 1866: "Secondary corridor to the left and, to the right, large corridor ending in a rotunda. Wall with odd drawings cattle and horses???" Another time, Garrigou noted: "A large round room bearing odd drawings. What is that? Amateur artists having drawn animals. Why so? Already seen before."[73] Garrigou's question marks indicate precisely the insurmountable aporia caused by the sight of paintings in the "Salon Noir" of Niaux. These "odd" drawings made no sense: their paradoxical location suggested "amateur artists," similar to Lartet's "shepherds of the Swiss Oberland," but did not manage to explain "why" the artists would have chosen caves, in particular. Above all, these "amateurs" were not situated chronologically, as if their "naïveté" — and Garrigou with them — exempted them from the chronologizing imperatives of modern thought. The difference in scale between the engraved objects of prehistory and these wall frescoes was too great to be conceivable. For years, the commune had leased the Cave of Niaux to a guide, and the tourists he led into it had "too often inscribed their names and dates even in regions far from the entrance." None of these modern engravers had stopped to look at the paintings of bison, even though they were so "fresh" that, in 1906, their discoverers "believed that some visitor had at the very least gone over them in black."[74]

Three decades after Garrigou's perplexed notes, François Daleau discovered in turn the Grotte de Pair-non-Pair in Gironde. After several visits, he wrote in his notebook on July 21, 1896 (Figure 2.7):

> Upon arriving in the cave, my eyes fell by chance on the engravings on the east wall (I noticed these drawings for the first time on December 29, 1883 . . .). I see, or believe I see, a quadruped, its badly drawn head sporting a brace? I take the pencil and transfer the drawing shown below onto my notepad. Then, to see better, I pass the tip of my finger over the engraved lines and follow their contours by touch; the muddy ground settles in the groove, which I am convinced I did not damage. I have often tried to draw and understand these engravings. I have never seen them so clearly as today. Is it a question of light or of vision? It's a bit like the riddle from a few years ago: "Where is the cat?"[75]

Although he had seen the engravings of Pair-non-Pair several times already, it was only this time that Daleau's *sight* and *touch* truly opened up to them. In his description, characterized by archaeological neutrality and meticulousness, the engravings gradually began to emerge as phenomenological entities: indisputable, but indecipherable presences. Ultimately, the enigma eclipsed the neutrality and exactitude of science. Garrigou *looked*, but barely saw the drawings, while Daleau ultimately *saw* the drawings, but found only riddles or enigmas. The revelation of these paintings openned onto a chasm, like the quarries of Saint-Acheul.

What happened between Niaux and Pair-non-Pair, Garrigou and Daleau? In 1879, Marcelino Sanz de Sautuola, a lawyer with a passion for prehistory, discovered the paintings of Altamira. It was the second time he had visited the cave, located at the top of a hill and discovered shortly before by a peasant. (Its entrance had been blocked thirteen thousand years earlier after a collapse.) Accompanied by his eight-year-old daughter, Sautuola was examining the ground for prehistoric debris when she, lifting her eyes toward the cave's extremely low ceiling, made out figures of animals she took for "bulls" (Figure 2.8). Large figures in red and black ocher were spread out and juxtaposed along the ceiling and lateral walls of other parts of the

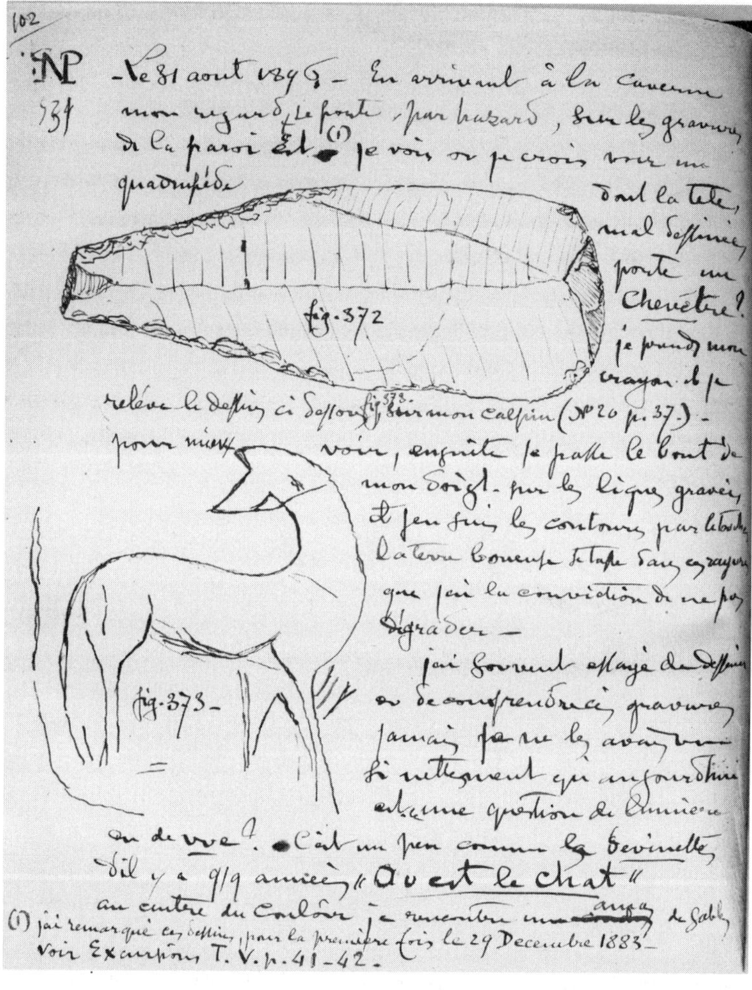

Figure 2.7. François Daleau, notebook of the excavation of the Grotte de Pair-non-Pair (Prignac-et-Marcamps, Gironde, December 27, 1883), July 21, 1896. Handwritten notebook. Musée d'Aquitaine, Bordeaux: Daleau Collection, acq. 1927. © Mairie de Bordeaux, reproduction Lysiane Gauthier.

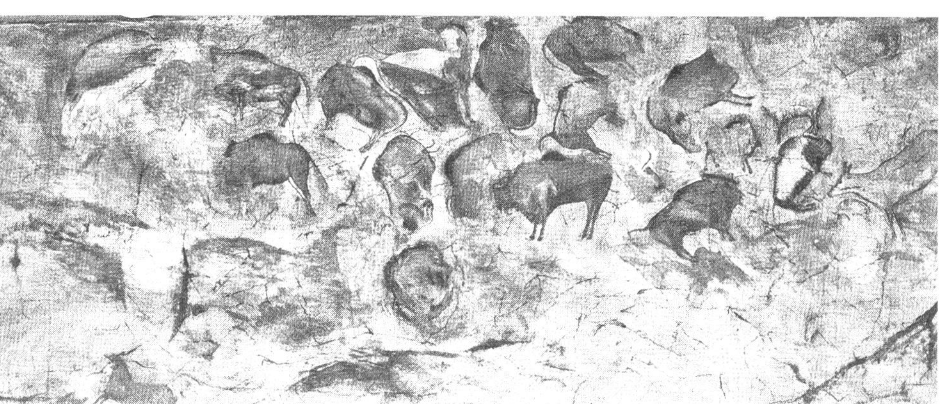

Figure 2.8. Paul Rattier y Josse, *The Ceiling of Bisons in Altamira (Santillana Del Mar, Cantabria)*, ca. 1880. Drawing on tracing paper, 46 × 115¼ in. Museo Nacional y Centro de Investigación, Altamira. © MAS | Museo de Arte Moderno y Contemporáneo de Santander y Cantabria.

cave. Like Garrigou, Sautuola had noticed dark drawings on the walls on his first visit, but without paying them any attention. Soon after observing them, he would become convinced that the creators of these images were Paleolithic peoples and that he himself had just discovered the mural art of prehistory. The hypothesis was publicly defended by a respected Spanish prehistorian, Juan de Vilanova.

Sautuola's *Brief Notes on Some Prehistoric Objects from the Province of Santander* (1880) is a work of about forty pages, the first to be published on parietal painting.[76] Its title refers to "some prehistoric objects," and not to large paintings from the dawn of time that had heretofore been totally unknown. It attests to the same mute astonishment and appeals to the same "axiomatic neutrality" that Lartet and Christy used in describing prehistoric mobiliary art. After some fifteen pages devoted to his underground finds, Sautuola wrote:

> The visitor is surprised upon contemplating, on the vault of the cave, a large quantity of animals, painted … it seems, with black and red ocher, and large in size, representing for the most part animals that, given their humps, bear some resemblance to bison. Two of them are complete and in profile, others have no head, some are in incomprehensible positions, and only a few traces of others remain, the colors used to paint them having more or less disappeared.[77]

Continuing with the description of paintings of animals more than six feet tall, he noted that "the artist was very experienced in making them, since we may observe that his hand was firm and not hesitant, for every line is done in a single stroke, as clean as possible." The self-assurance of the gesture, in contrast to the poverty of the tools, was a structuring theme in the interpretation of prehistoric mobiliary art, but the "strangeness"[78] of such accomplished parietal paintings was multiplied by other factors: the cramped space would have required that the artist adopt a painful posture; the darkness of the cave would have called for surface lighting; and the bosselated irregularity of the walls would surely have demanded especially skillful and deft gestures.[79]

The Paleolithic origin of the paintings was virulently disputed by French positivistic and secular prehistorians, who reproached the Spanish Catholics for wanting to prove the existence of God via parietal painting. Why, otherwise, would they portray such boorish primitive men as beings with lofty metaphysical needs? The major difference between the two revelations of prehistoric art — mobiliary and parietal — in fact rested on that point, which was simply a question of scale. The minuscule objects could be construed as a *pastime* for isolated individuals, while the monumentality of the caves presupposed a collective investment, a social organization, metaphysical aspirations, in short, an intentionality that was hard to square with the rudimentary character and naturalness generally attributed to prehistory. At issue was a change of scale, a change of social model, and a change of ontological and metaphysical paradigm, as well. Mobiliary art, being small in scale, could be assimilated to imperceptible events, spontaneous gestures, and ordinary individuals, while the monumental art of the caves involved the *longue durée* of institutions and rites. Cartailhac and Breuil, the first two prehistorians to study Altamira, to which they devoted a monograph in 1906, wrote: "May our efforts illuminate somewhat the dark night that, for so many thousands of years, has shrouded the very existence of these peoples; and if, admiring their works, we may have an inkling of what fulfilled their existence and served as a symbol to their aspirations, it will seem to us that we can learn to respect them, to recognize them as our ancestors."[80] The recognition of parietal art raised the question of *filiation*, really for the first time. So long as the prehistoric art known to exist took the form of minuscule objects, its creators could remain within a mythic and timeless sphere, "untouched" and "sterile" by definition and therefore incapable of founding a genealogy. Parietal art, by contrast, inevitably raised the question of the origin. Necessarily collective and social, that art called for a narrativization capable of inspiring "respect" for these cave dweller painters, making them "forebears" worthy of their progeny. That acknowledgment of paternity (in reverse, as it were), which basically consisted of assimilating stupor, came about in two stages: that of archaeology and that of interpretation and fantasy.

FIRST STAGE IN THE MECHANISM FOR ASSIMILATING STUPOR:
THE ARCHAEOLOGICAL AUTHENTICATION
OF THE DECORATED CAVES

Between 1895 and 1900, decorated caves—painted, engraved, or both—were discovered one after another, first in France and then in Spain. In 1896, eighteen years after Léopold Chiron, Paul Raymond discovered engravings in the Magdalenian Chabot Cave. Chiron had encountered nothing but incredulity,[81] and though Raymond noticed "curious strokes," he found it pretentious to call them "drawings."[82] In 1897, Émile Rivière delivered the first major paper on a decorated cave, the Grotte de la Mouthe, to the Société d'Anthropologie, exhibiting photographs of the cave for the first time. These pictures removed the animals from the spatial and optical confusion of their context, essentially making them "portraits." They provided proof of authenticity and also conformed to the aesthetic habitus of optical unity, which for a long time yet would prevent the "confused" aspect of the painted walls from being assimilated. Rivière's discoveries began to "awaken memories," for example, of the walls of the cave of Marsala. In 1901, Louis Capitan and Denis Peyrony, assisted by the young priest Henri Breuil, a very gifted painter, discovered the cave of Les Combarelles[83] and later that of Font-de-Gaume (Figures 2.9a, 2.9b, 2.10), where they transferred onto paper dozens of the engravings found there. Capitan and Breuil affirmed that "these figurations, whose antiquity cannot be denied, could have been executed only by artists who were reproducing the animals they saw. They therefore date back to the era when the mammoth and the reindeer lived in France, and so are Paleolithic and very likely Magdalenian."[84] Acknowledging a certain subjectivism, they adopted a stance somewhere between aesthetic appreciation — noting the very convincing naturalism of these images "reproducing the animals" seen — and the positivism of cited evidence.[85]

THE SECOND STAGE: THE INTERPRETATION OF PARIETAL ART
After the first question — "Is it real?" — came a second: "Why?" In early 1902, the popular science review *La Nature* published an essay by Capitan and Breuil titled "Origins of Art" in which reproductions of drawings of mammoths, Cervidae, Equidae, and ibex were often superimposed, as in the original drawings (Figure 2.11). With this publication, parietal art was becoming a public affair. The two specialists put forward the first hypotheses on this art, art deemed "improbable."[86] Indeed, if mobiliary art was still "curious," "immobiliary" art was much more so:

> What was the meaning of these figures? Why draw them so far underground, at points where it was probably necessary to light one's way with a hollow stone . . . filled with fat and a moss wick? What idea guided these primitive peoples when they produced such multiple and complicated drawings? Why draw them in this gallery, which was probably always uninhabitable? Was there some idea related to fetishism, or ordinary religion, or totemism? All questions we can do no more than raise.[87]

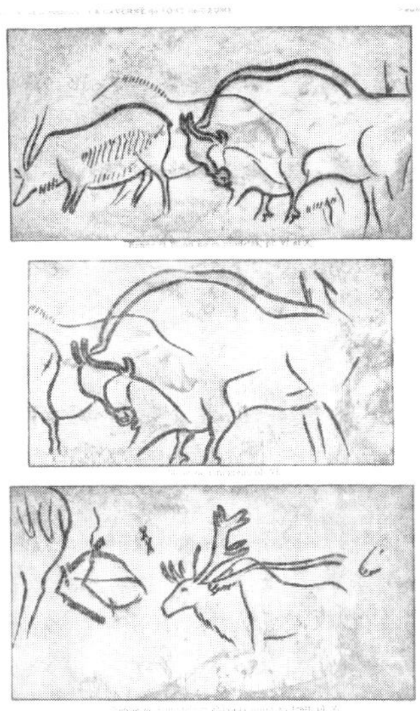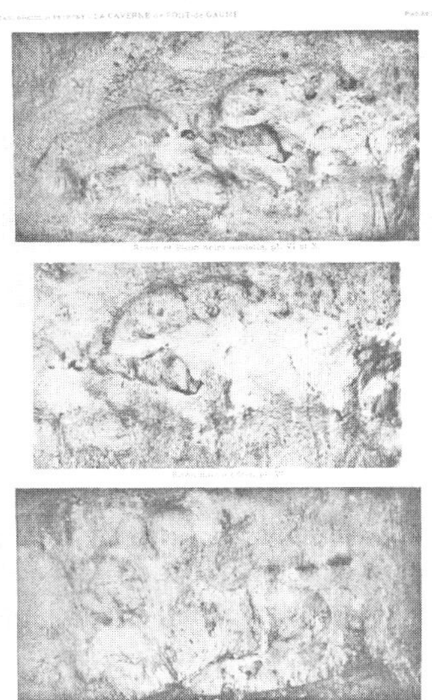

Figures 2.9a and b. Drawings of frescoes and engravings on tracing paper and photographs of the same frescoes and engravings, Font-de-Gaume, Les Eyzies-de-Tayac, Dordogne. Magdalenian period, 17,000–10,000 BCE. Discovered by Denis Peyrony, Louis Capitan, and Henri Breuil, September 12, 1901. In Louis Capitan and Abbé Henri Breuil, *La Caverne de Font-de-Gaume aux Eyzies Dordogne* (Monaco: Imprimerie de Monaco, 1910), plate L1.

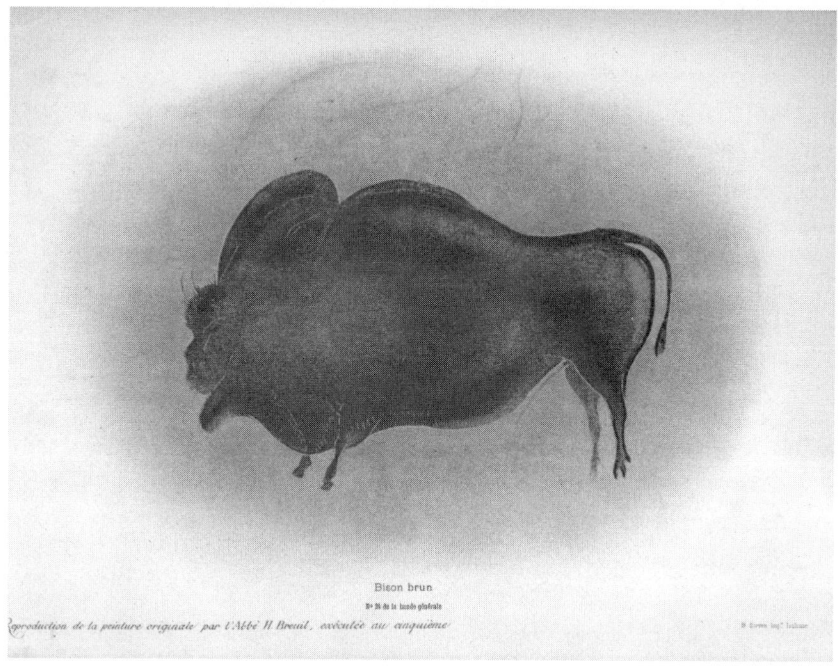

Figure 2.10. Brown bison, copied by Abbé Henri Breuil, *La Caverne de Font-de-Gaume aux Eyzies Dordogne* (Monaco: Imprimerie de Monaco, 1910).

The solution to all these enigmas lay solely in the realm of magic or even religion and totemism. But from a formal standpoint, astonishment at these figures was even more powerful than that caused by minuscule prehistoric artifacts: though analogous to the engravings done by "recent Bushmen on the walls of certain caves," those "of our country are far more artistic."[88] When the prehistorians made transfers of the drawings of dozens of animals, they repeated the corporeal experience of creation, the gesture itself. That tactile experience allowed them to attest that "nothing has been left to fancy or to interpretation,"[89] which in fact was confirmed by the optical experience

Quelle était l'idée directrice de ces primitifs dans la confection de ces dessins si multiples et si compliqués? Pourquoi les avoir tracés dans ce boyau qui fut probablement toujours inhabitable? Y avait-il là une idée fétichique ou religieuse quelconque ou totemiste? Autant de questions que nous ne pouvons que soulever.

Il en est de même de la question d'art pur, plus étrange encore. Ce sont là, en

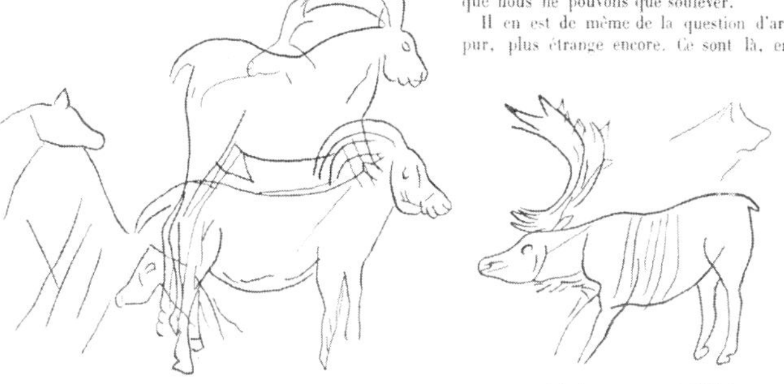

Fig. 4. — Reproduction d'un point de la paroi de la grotte. (Dimensions : bouquetin, 0m,65 de largeur; renne, 0m,59 de largeur.)

effet, œuvres sincères, vivantes, reproduction exacte de la nature et par suite nécessitant un dressage de la vue et une éducation de la main manquant ordinairement chez les primitifs et qui nécessairement

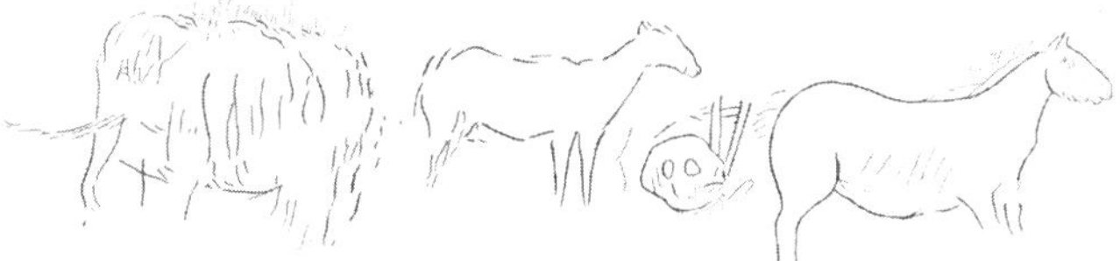

Fig. 5. — Reproduction d'un point de la paroi de la grotte. (Dimensions : tête, 0m,18 de largeur; cheval de droite, 0m,36 de largeur.)

avaient dû être acquis par les hommes qui ont tracé ces figures. Et pourtant, on les voit apparaître tout d'un coup vers le commencement de l'époque glyptique, déjà arrivées à leur apogée. Elles persistent

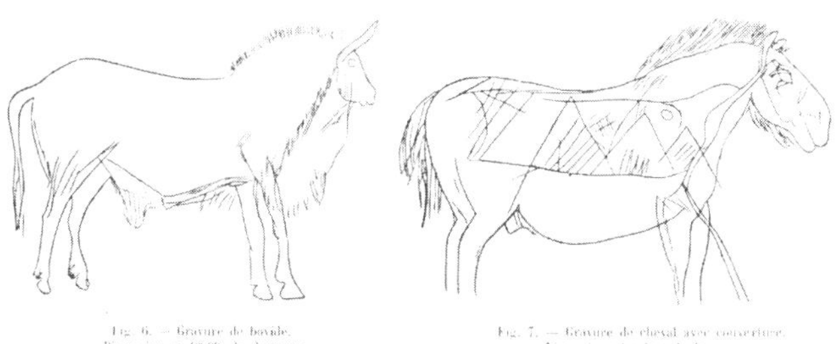

Fig. 6. — Gravure de bovidé. (Dimension : 0m,90 de largeur.)

Fig. 7. — Gravure de cheval avec couverture. (Dimension : 1 mètre de largeur.)

ainsi durant toute cette période, puis disparaissent avec elle — or cette disparition est définitive. De l'art paléolithique, il ne reste plus, en effet, dès le début du néolithique, que les manifestations conven-

Figure 2.11. Louis Capitan and Abbé Henri Breuil, "Origines de l'art: Les gravures sur les parois des grottes préhistoriques anciennes," *La Nature* 30.1503 (March 1902), p. 229.

of these "sincere, living works, an exact reproduction of nature that consequently requires training one's sight, educating one's hand, skills ordinarily lacking in the primitive peoples and which were necessarily acquired by the men who drew these figures."[90] The origin of art proved not only enigmatic, but more definitively, aporetic: in their conclusion, the two authors evoked the sudden disappearance of Paleolithic art, whose figures "never again reappeared."

Mobiliary art found a place in the imaginary of a utopian prehistory that lacked a well-defined social structure and was exempt from any political implications. By contrast, parietal painting, in its failure to conform — in its physical, conceptual, and stylistic features — to the aesthetic and ideological norms of those years, introduced the first shadows of "society" into the realm of prehistory. In France, society was one of the objects of the all-powerful Durkheimian school of sociology, which at the time was becoming the model for the human sciences in general. Magic, considered the first stage in the symbolic representation of the world, and totemism, understood as an "elementary" social structure of humanity, were able to provide an explanation for that mute art from the dawn of time. Magic and totemism necessarily conferred a new status on art. It was no longer possible to impute an absolute "purity" to it or to imagine that it had been practiced by just anyone. In a letter Breuil sent to Reinach after spending some time in the sumptuous Cave of Altamira, where, "without an order intelligible for us," drawings proliferated, graffiti and scrawls intertwined, and abstract signs repeated themselves, he wondered: "But what rationale presided over the systematic and comprehensive ornamentation of the walls and ceilings across vast regions? What rationale presided over the uniform characteristics of this art, so unified that it is as if a single man, or a single group of men, produced it?" "It's all strange," he continued. "I am often haunted by the idea I once expressed to you about a caste of artists, perhaps more or less sacerdotal, presiding over an artistic development whose aim may have been religious. Their training, moreover, maintained a uniform tradition over relatively long periods of time and across a vast region."[91]

Clearly, parietal art required new hermeneutic tools. Even though they did not entirely succeed in undermining the presuppositions of the discipline, they transformed Paleolithic prehistory into an object that lent itself to appropriation by moderns. To repeat: a wholly ahistorical prehistory, elaborated on the basis of the engraved artifacts, remained a naïve prehistory; as such, it was definitively obsolete, irrecuperable, and in any case inappropriate for the constitution of the "origin" of moderns. It is when the flaws and contradictions between sacred and profane, between hermetic language and instrumental language, between artists and others, came to light in the interpretations of parietal compositions that modernity began to project itself onto that prehistory. Moderns knew almost nothing about it, but they believed it was the beginning of their desires and their sorrows. With parietal art, a certain *critical* historicity of modernity could finally come into play. Whereas atemporal pastorality in particular had provided the codes for understanding mobiliary art, "contemporary primitivity," that of "savages," supplied the codes for parietal art. But that situation immediately generated a profound and persistent contradiction: parietal painting, having become familiar enough to be able to constitute the imaginary of our direct origin, nevertheless suffered from the same stigmas as those inflicted on "savages" by Western thought.

Homeopathic Magic: The Beginning of the Sacred
In 1882, Andrew Lang, the British founder of folklore studies, argued that the interpretation of art as an "expression of the imitative faculty" of human beings was largely invalidated by "art's beginnings."[92] This interpretation was merely a projection on the part of moderns, for whom "no doubt the desire to imitate nature, by painting or sculpture, has become almost an innate impulse, an in-born instinct." Accustomed to detecting in every realm of culture folkloric "survivals" of a remote past that had become unconscious, Lang saw that "imitation" as the mental and social fossil, as it were, of a prehistoric art whose mimetic form served practical aims: "We inherit the love, the disinterested love, of imitative art from very remote ancestors,

whose habits of imitation had a direct, interested and practical purpose."[93] Lang did not specify the nature of this "direct" purpose that the imitative art of our remote ancestors supposedly served, but he situated it vaguely in the relations they maintained with animals. A few years later, Salomon Reinach described more precisely the role art played in such relations. Now that parietal art had finally been "recognized," the question of its purpose inevitably arose. In a 1903 essay titled "Art and Magic," Reinach rightly observed that animals were by far the most frequent motifs in Quaternary art, but he was mistaken when he added that all these animals were "those on which a people of hunters and fishermen feeds itself."[94] This error, however, allowed him to conclude that cave dwellers had "not only sought to occupy their leisure time or record their visual memories," but also "knew what they were doing and why they were doing it."[95] Looking to ethnography, which took an interest in the magic techniques of "contemporary primitives," Reinach opted to explain prehistoric art in terms of "homeopathic magic": "the image of a being or object allows one to seize that object or that being; the maker or owner of an image can *influence* what it represents." In that way, it promoted "the proliferation of game on which the existence of the clan or tribe depended."[96] Inspired by Walter Baldwin Spencer and Francis James Gillen, who had studied Australian totemism, Reinach construed the dark caves as the site for the secret ceremonies of aborigines from the past organized into totemic societies. Reinach's interpretation was very effective: it made these men the first potentially historical beings, even though their names and precise place in history were forever unknown. The theory of magic, despite its many lacunae, offered an all-encompassing and rational interpretation of the Paleolithic period. Cartailhac himself adhered to it without delay, and after his visit to the Salon Noir of Niaux, took to imagining "the magic incantation of some great sorcerer working in front of the groups of images, while around him, on the inclines of the vast amphitheater, illuminated by a number of portable lanterns, the tribe built its self-confidence and counted on the sureness of its blows and the profusion of game."[97] On the eve of World War II, comte Henri Begouën, a well-known prehistorian whose sons had discovered the Cave of the Trois-Frères, also described without a second thought the ceremonies of prehistoric times. Granted, "the echo of the songs" had not come down to us, but "the ground has preserved a few imprints that we may consider, without too much temerity, to have transmitted to us the memory of a few ritual dances."[98] The footprints in the Tuc d'Audoubert cave showed him "something deliberate," and "since these heel marks clearly trace out five different paths," he deduced "that these steps were directed, commanded, which would indicate a sort of ritual dance. And these were the heels of young people between thirteen and fourteen years old."[99] The initiation rite was obvious, even after thousands of years!

The hypothesis of the magic function of parietal painting was the second factor that made it an origin worthy of the moderns. Curiously, for the time being, it did not encourage materialist interpretations, which tended to arise later on, with Marxist interpretations of prehistory. Although inspired by "contemporary" primitive societies, which were considered inferior, the theory of magic painting also appropriated typical characteristics of the two paradigmatic forms of sacred art in the West: Greek tragedy and the Christian mass. It was not by chance that Cartailhac spoke of the Niaux "amphitheater," not fortuitous that Reinach compared the caves to "catacombs," not innocent that Altamira would be called a "temple of art"[100] and even the Cappella Sistina of prehistory — a designation Lascaux would later vie for. Nor was it without reason that a few human figures with animal heads and with their hands raised would be interpreted as signs of "piety" and "devotion."[101] In short, a common thread connected the sacred spaces of the caves, Greek amphitheaters, and churches before snapping in our disenchanted modernity, which regarded itself in the mirror of art. In writing simultaneously about Édouard Manet and about Lascaux, Georges Bataille would clearly grasp how, when prehistoric art was first discovered, the sacred was converted into the aesthetic of modern art. The first prehistorians for their part, though they were secular, undoubtedly sought to link the caves to the cathedrals because they felt the modern absence of the sacred. Hence, Reinach could say of the "magic" forms of prehistory:

> They show us humanity's first steps on the path to the worship of animals (as in Egypt), then to the worship of idols in human form (as in Greece), and finally to that of a god conceived as pure spirit. The study of the birth of religion merges to a certain extent with that of the beginnings of art. Art and religion, born together, have remained closely bound for many long centuries; their affinity is still perceptible for thinking people today.[102]

Fleshing Out Fossils, Objects, and Images

Living Fossils

Just as for a long time the name "Venus" concealed the enigma of the strange female figures in stone and ivory exhumed from caves, "contemporary primitives," by their supposed analogy to prehistoric peoples, predominated in a lasting way in interpretations of parietal frescoes and engravings. These two associations — the first with ancient Greece, the second with the racialized world of primitive peoples — conferred a certain self-evidence on an otherwise unintelligible prehistory. Through the intervention of ethnologists, the primitive peoples of Africa and Australia — "living fossils," of a sort — offered up the coherent narrative so sorely lacking among prehistorians. They literally *fleshed out* prehistory: their orality provided a supplement to prehistoric mutism, their bodies enveloped the bones and set the images in motion, while their societies, despite being at a rudimentary stage, lent their institutional structure to the giant frescoes painted in dark spaces. Reinach, the originator of the magic interpretation of parietal art, thus referred to "a few points of the distant objects we have been able to focus on, with the assistance of the image we have almost before our eyes."[103] If even the earth's age could be internalized as a metaphor for human memory (both emotional and organic) throughout the nineteenth century, how could one fail to seek in living fossils *survivals* of these ancient human beings who had left no representations of themselves, whether written or figurative? The notion of "survival," whose evolutionist origin is often too quickly forgotten, appeared in 1871 in Edward Tylor's book *Primitive Culture*.[104] Positing the progress of the Western world and its value as a standard for humanity as a whole, the ethnologist united under the term "survival" "processes, customs, opinions," and even "gestures" of an "older condition of culture" carried by force of habit into a "new" state of society and leading us "back to the habits of hundreds and even thousands of years ago."[105] Tylor posited the existence of collective "savage" survivals, both in certain remote regions and within modern societies. But a survival has no intrinsic meaning; it exists only against and in spite of a certain temporality: progress or the glorious present. Opposing interpretations that made savages the incarnation of the "Fall"—the ruin of a historical dynamic and therefore a refutation of any evolutionist optimism—Tylor viewed them as the "rudiments" of human history. He established an opposition between the threat of a time that could only fall into the abyss of nothingness and a time that perpetually survived, if only through stagnation and fossilization. Did not this fossil provide proof of the positive—albeit uneven—evolution of the species?[106]

The first interpretations of prehistory obsessively made use of the notion of a distant survival, preserved in the colonies and at the same time presumed to be radically alien to Western man. Later, interpretations of modern man as a "regressive" being emerged, as we saw in the previous chapter. Reinach, who had an answer for everything, because he had done so much work on archaic ethnology and archaeology, both Greek and "barbarian," formulated concisely the analogy between mineral stratification and the historical position of "savages":

> Soon you manage to convince yourself that the savage of today resembles a limestone shoal that could have surfaced in a region of alluvial deposits; in digging under the sands to a sufficient depth, you will find that same limestone. Likewise, in excavating the depths of the history of civilized peoples, you will find, in 3000, 4000, or 5000 BCE, our savage's way of thinking. Hence a savage in our time allows us a glimpse, I will even say a knowledge, of the opinions of our most remote ancestors, who belonged to nations that matured

and became civilized more quickly, but who went through the same phase in which the savage we are studying still finds himself.[107]

What in the 1930s Ernst Bloch would call "the contemporaneity of the noncontemporaneous"[108] gradually came to light during the nineteenth century, when the universal time of progress made it possible to situate on the evolutionary ladder and with ever greater accuracy each of the societies discovered around the globe. Evolution finally made human history intelligible, as it had previously done for the history of earth and its organisms. In 1848, it was *as a historian* that Renan reformulated Laffitau's theory about savages arising from "the earth's ooze": "Such is the infinite variety of the movement [driving humanity] that it would be possible at any given moment to find in the different regions inhabited by man all the diverse ages we see spread out across his history. The races and climates produce simultaneously the same differences in humanity that time has shown to occur in succession over the course of its development."[109] The different stages of history were literally spatialized, unfolding in a simultaneity that had previously been the exclusive preserve of God.

One of the first to use the adjective "prehistoric" was the Scotsman Daniel Wilson, who in 1853 employed the term to designate the American Indians. The ethnology he practiced established a link between geology and archaeology:[110] a discipline of the present and of the living thing, ethnology ensured the transition from natural minerality to man-made objects. It therefore *gave life* to objects by attributing a subject and a meaning to them. It extricated them from the kingdom of the dead, from geology and archaeology or history. Most ethnologists and prehistorians would adopt and consistently apply the analogy between prehistoric man and the savage — from Lubbock, who spoke of "non-metallic savages,"[111] that is, Stone Age men, to Tylor and Leo Frobenius, who explored the length and breadth of Africa and Australia. For some, Tylor and Quatrefages, for example, it was in fact less caution than analogical excess that led them to decree that the last "survivals" of Stone Age men had died out in 1877 with the last Tasmanian, final representative of a race "with wooly hair," that had, as it were, melted away in contact with the Europeans.[112] Quatrefages seemed to be echoing Pitt Rivers when he said that the Tasmanians left "absolutely empty the box" they occupied "in the ethnological table of humanity."[113] Just as the first human artifact had vanished into the indistinction of nature, the first human specimen had disappeared into the indistinction of the past under the weight of colonial culture.

In the following stage, the Aborigines of Australia, the Bushmen, and the Pygmies provided "living proof" of "savage" artists and hunters. The striking example of paintings by Pygmies was widely cited by Leo Frobenius and after him by many prehistorians and other thinkers confronting the mysteries of the origin.[114] Let us recall the principal elements of the narrative. Frobenius asked a group of Pygmies to go on an antelope hunt. But that request could not be granted immediately, because such a causality — immediate desire followed by satisfaction — was unknown to the Pygmies, belonging, rather to the rational world that Frobenius had left behind. The group wished to give him satisfaction, however, while following their own rules. They engaged in a preliminary rite that included a dance and then drew an antelope on the ground, in complete secrecy, far from the ethnologist's gaze — except that he was observing from a hiding place. Frobenius suddenly intruded to photograph the drawing. He was caught at it, however, and was therefore unsuccessful. The next day, the men left for the hunt. They returned with the prey and repeated the rite, with the real antelope this time. The entire rite sequence was made known to Frobenius after the fact — by a woman, of course, who revealed the secret. This narrative, whose dubious accuracy does not compromise its interest, served to legitimize all the interpretations of scenes that Frobenius had identified for his gigantic archival project on the rock paintings of Africa, Australia, and Europe.[115] Each time, Frobenius and his collaborators sought analogies between myths and images, pursuing an essentially iconological approach, except that the text in question was not written, but oral. Frobenius's narrative, elevated to the rank of a paradigm or *architext*, would be referenced by many authors. Herbert Read, for example, argued that prehistoric art, the first stage in the general evolution of the image, possessed a literally "vital" meaning.[116] And Frobenius provided Henri Begouën with evidence — important because it was living proof — for his theory of magic art. The same anecdote would also be found during and after World War II in the avant-garde reviews fighting against the reification of images and seeking to lay the foundations for a new culture and also in Theodor Adorno's *Aesthetic Theory*, which established a parallel between modernism's struggle against alienation and reification, on the one hand, and theories on the magic origin of art, on the other.[117]

Nevertheless, though magic in fact provided a coherent explanation for parietal images deemed "improbable," it had the disadvantage of pulling art and its origin down to the "bottom" of the human ladder. Cartailhac, for example, contested the ethnological method applied to prehistory, believing that "it is not possible to assimilate at random modern savages to our primitive ancestors. One group bore within it the hopes for humanity, while the genius of the other may be on the decline."[118] As for Tylor, he noted that none of the modern-day tribes were an authentic survival of prehistoric men, because their present condition was the "complex result of not only a long but also an eventful history," marked by the "degradation caused by war, disease, oppression, and other mishaps."[119] It was their encounter with Westerners that had introduced history and its events into the *longue durée* of savages, and that history, which had been inflicted on them, could only be negative. It was precisely this negativity that distinguished savages from the prehistoric peoples.

Naturalism, an Ontology of Immediacy

The naturalism of animal representations, the expression of a full life and a full presence, seemed to symbolize prehistoric man generally. The efforts to make these "improbable" images intelligible by means of homeopathic magic made it possible to account for their naturalism in two ways: they were not merely *similia*, fellow creatures capable of killing their own; they also generated metamorphoses and rites whereby men came to inhabit the skins of animals. In the 1920s, Father Breuil put a great deal of emphasis on the plurality of causes that had given rise to art. In two texts devoted to "the origin of art," he mentioned dramatic mimetism, in particular, which itself originated in camouflage practices used in hunting comparable to those made famous by George Catlin, a painter of Amerindians.[120] The naturalism of animal forms was thus also an imprint of the bodies of hunters engaged in rites that imitated animals.

Furthermore, magic took into account the physical practice of the "hunt," since hunters had been obliged to develop physical aptitudes that influenced their way of painting. Speculations were advanced about their eyesight, which must have been sharp enough to identify game and its tracks in the darkness: all the French prehistorians said so. Some, like Bégouën, imagined that because the hunters had "lain in wait for the prey for many long hours," its image was "in some sense photographed on their retinas and could afterward be faithfully reproduced."[121] In 1919, the art historian Henri Focillon would in turn praise the naturalism of the "audacious race" that "grew up" in the caves:

> By the power of images, they fended off the menacing witnesses to their isolation. A sharp, incisive, and pure stroke chose and fixed the essential form, which the hunter's keen eye was able to discern: the delicacy of the sinewy hock, the fullness of the musculature, the heaviness of the monstrous steps that make the earth tremble, the tracery of antlers that spreads out on the reindeer's skull like some wild ornamental jewelry.[122]

The same discourse developed in Germany, where in 1912, the prehistorian Friedrich Behn published a short text titled "The Animal in the Art of Diluvian Man": "These first artists in the world, whose names are now buried in the chaos of past millenniums, engraved, painted, and modeled what they saw. And they saw animals with the eyes of a hunter, as they really were, free from all imagination and all ornamental form, in a perfect objectivity, an authentic naturalism."[123] In a more "positivistic" manner, the Marxist ethnologist Ernst

Grosse, a proponent of the theory of natural selection, saw realism as the artistic expression of the survival instinct among those forced to develop keen perception.[124] The physician Max Verworn's *On the Psychology of Primitive Art* (1907) had a lasting influence in Germany. Verworn argued that the *physioplastic* figures of the Paleolithic, which he distinguished from the *ideoplastic* figures of the Neolithic, were mere motor reactions on the part of hunters, who asked no questions about the causes of things and were "perfectly unacquainted" with "any theorization and speculation." They spent their entire lives spotting, hunting, and exchanging game in a flow without beginning or end — thus experiencing the eternal present.[125] The prehistorian Herbert Kühn, the author of many books and the founder in 1925 of the annual international review *Ipek: Jahrbuch für Prähistorische und Ethnographische Kunst*, was beholden to that interpretation when he described Paleolithic art as a "sensory, naturalistic submission to the 'here,' attention to motion, freedom, struggle, life itself. That art is the present, it is the instant, which is completely at odds with everything that is past and everything that is future."[126] Two years later, he transposed his theory into a materialism that virulently contested Riegl's metaphysics of *Kunstwollen* (the will to art): it was the material conditions of life that made art a destiny. Paleolithic art expressed the "parasitical economy" of hunters, which stood opposed to the "symbiotic economy" of Neolithic farmers. The parasitical economy drew directly from nature what it needed, plants or animals; the same was true of art, which found models in the material surroundings, and not in the subject's ideational resources. Hunting was thus an "economic naturalism," impelling men to live "without care" (*Sorglos*), to focus on the "present" in an "anarchical" manner and "without a state structure."[127]

It was truly this extreme presentism that led prehistorians to see the images in caves as individual and isolated representations, independent of any syntax. These prehistoric artists, riveted to the present and with no awareness of the past or future, could represent only the precipitates of their sensations, individual and fleeting impressions. What was true for images was also true for words. Had not

Rousseau (yes, again) assumed that "the words, first made use of by men, had in their mind a much more extensive signification" and that "every word" had "the meaning of an entire proposition"?[128] Closer to our own time, had not Wilhelm Wundt assumed in his Herculean project for a *Völkerpsychologie* that when language succeeded gestures, it took the form of "monosyllabic words"?[129] Wundt's theories formed the basis for what the prehistorian Moritz Hoernes declared to be the "monosyllabism" of these images.[130] One of his sources was the writings of Karl von den Steinen, an explorer of central Brazil, who reported in particular that the Xingu customarily spoke while making signs in the sand; he concluded that art originally had a "communicative" function.[131] Wundt called this first art *Augenblickskunst* (art of the instant). It had no roots in the past and did not project itself into the future, serving only the imperatives of the present.[132] All in all, though the Paleolithic peoples had revealed themselves to be more "social" than what the small artifacts buried in caves suggested, there was no justification for seeing the paintings on the walls as unified "compositions." (That is the reason Reinach's totemist hypothesis ultimately remained vague and allusive.) Furthermore, these aspects tallied perfectly with the hunt's magic character, since every image was understood as the accidental imprint of a single, independent rite.

Beginning in the 1940s, the art historian Max Raphaël would contest that narrative, as would Annette Laming-Emperaire and André Leroi-Gourhan in the 1950s, when they identified the frequency of certain invariable relationships in the caves. Max Raphaël's Marxism and the nascent structuralism of the two prehistorians allowed them to understand that the absence of an "order intelligible for us," in Breuil's words, actually contained a meaning. But whereas Raphaël saw totemic clans fighting for power,[133] Laming-Emperaire and Leroi-Gourhan refrained from giving these structures a precise content, simply conducting a statistical analysis of the figures and their syntax. They argued that this was a first *writing* of collective "narratives," narratives whose social and sexual meaning would forever elude us.[134]

The Realism of Moderns: Reconstituting Loss

The realist premise deeply marked the first encounter between the moderns and prehistory. Not only was naturalism discerned in each of the relations prehistoric men maintained with the world, but above all, moderns themselves became realists—a higher form of naturalist—both by their scientific methods, through which they sought to define "prehistory," and by the artistic representations given of them. Prehistory now gave rise to the same quest for truth and the same need to reconstitute reality as had existed since the mid-nineteenth century, both in the field of art and in many fields of knowledge. The normalization of the abnormal gained ground: epistemologically, realism took the specific form of racial and historicist notions combined (an especially telling oxymoron in the case of prehistory); aesthetically, the first artists to take an interest in the representation of prehistory were primarily, though not exclusively, academic painters (*artistes pompiers*).[135] Precisely because knowledge about it was lacunary, prehistory called more urgently than any other object for a realist response. It was taken for granted that what had been destroyed over the centuries could be *reconstituted* through the realism of moderns. The sparser the evidence, the more realism proposed to consolidate it; the deeper the abyss between prehistory and the present time, the more realism rushed to fill it.

Felicitously, the first bust of a Paleolithic woman, which Édouard Piette found at Le Mas-d'Azil in 1887–1888, provided unexpected information "about the character of the Quaternary human races."[136] Other busts had also been found in France, and Piette noted the formal dissimilarities among them, concluding that the races that had produced them were also dissimilar. Was it not well established that prehistoric peoples depicted only what they saw? "To acquire a more perfect knowledge of these races, we must examine the statuettes and engravings by means of which they represented themselves."[137] The stupefying *Lady with the Hood*, whose delicate features seemed so unlike the other known Venuses, was meticulously measured: the cranial, facial, and nasal data proved there was no relation of kinship between her and the present-day populations (Figure 2.12). Piette would thus distinguish two, and later four, Paleolithic races, plus the races that resulted from their interbreeding. The Le Mas-d'Azil figurine, with its "enormous fatty gibbosity," belonged to a group of the "steatogenic" type (obviously, skeletons could offer no clues about it), while more delicate and slender figurines attested to a "sarcogynic" group (Figure 2.13). Not only had the two races been contemporaneous, they had without a doubt coexisted in the caves, since their "photographic" archives had been found on the same sites. The sculptures "with sagging bellies and pendular breasts, with folds of fat along their sides," and with "distinctive" features such as a "flat and receding" chin also made him think of a different "hairy" race, similar to the present-day "Bushmen." By contrast, *Lady with the Hood*, according to him, belonged to the Mongolian race. In conclusion, Piette offered a striking example of the principle of "automimesis," which, as Éric Michaud has argued, established in a lasting manner the fantastical genealogy of art history.[138] According to Winckelmann's groundbreaking theory about the Egyptians and the Greeks, peoples and races made their symbolic artifacts in their own image. The artifacts thus served as biological identification, charged with guaranteeing the purity of the race in the future. In that way, Piette treated the artifacts as natural fossilized specimens, practicing a sort of literal naturalism. But the Le Mas-d'Azil prehistorian ventured even further, to a cultural reconstitution of prehistory: still treating the figures as if they were photographs, he identified the habits of dress of two races, the more slender customarily wearing clothes and the plumper one only ornaments. Who said that prehistoric women had vanished forever? In interpreting the statuettes literally, disregarding the gap between art and nature, Piette removed from them any fictional dimension, which was sacrificed to the insatiable need to *reconstitute* the bodies of these strangers, prehistoric men and women. "Can we reconstitute the man, the actual first artist whose venerable works have come down to us over such a long succession of centuries?" asked the physician and artist Paul Richer.[139] He replied with a sculpture called *First Artist* (1890) (Figure 2.14), which presented "the truly astonishing spectacle of fossil man, a sort of powerful-looking athlete."[140] Beginning

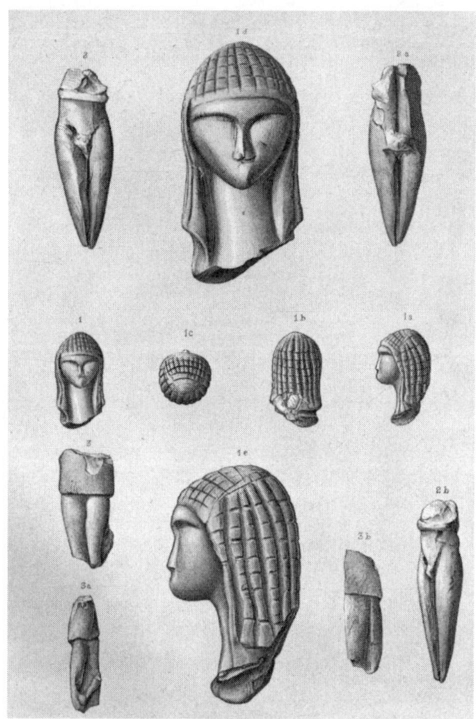

Figure 2.12. Drawing of *Lady with the Hood*, in Édouard Piette, *L'art pendant l'âge du renne* (Paris: Masson, 1907), plate 70.

Figure 2.13. Édouard Piette, fragment of a female statuette in ivory found in the base of the sculpture in the round in the Grotte du Pape in Brassempouy. In Édouard Piette, *L'art pendant l'âge du renne* (Paris: Masson, 1907), plate 72.

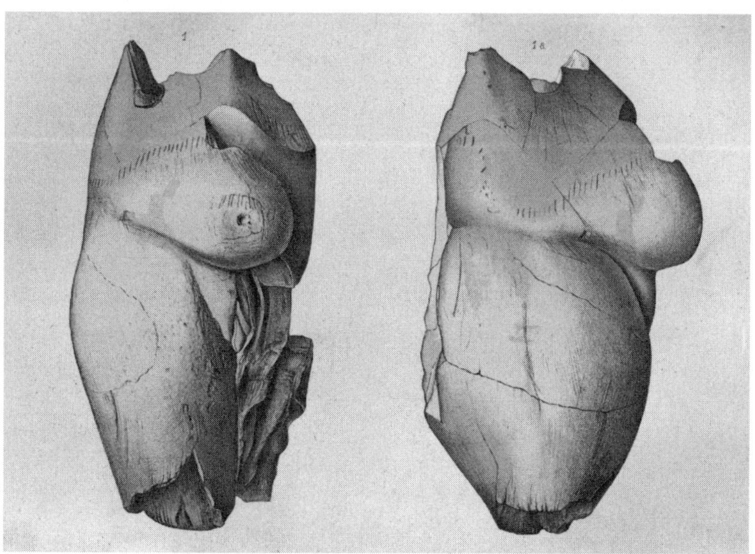

in the 1880s, the realism of artists fascinated by prehistory was based on two principles. First, it sought to turn fossils into bodies full of life, and second, in order to give an artistic representation of prehistory, it followed the *actualist* method of prehistorians, who found in "savages" the explanation for mute prehistoric artifacts.

In a long text of 1891 that rigorously detailed the process of creating *First Artist*, Paul Richer accorded an important place to anthropology and archaeology. In keeping with the epistemological turn, the shift from history to anthropology and archaeology, art no longer would represent individuals or events, not even the most important, but rather *types* — in this case the Cro-Magnon racial type and the "first artist" behavioral type.[141] Paradoxically, these *types* were fashioned in a historicist spirit through the reconstitution of supposedly authentic models. Anonymous bones, reconstituted into skeletons, readily created the image of a universal type. Hence the body of *First Artist* was *modeled*, literally and metaphorically, on Cro-Magnon man, whom anthropologists such as Quatrefages had previously reconstituted. The head was cast from the skull discovered at the eponymous rock shelter (wide brow, large, hooked nose, probably small eyes), and like the skeleton itself, his body was exactly six feet tall. Any truth not provided by the bones was supplied by (ethnological) analogy and by the figures engraved on various artifacts. It was deductive reasoning, however, that persuaded Paul Richer to give his hunter artist the body of an "athlete" and a "broad and powerful" chest, "like individuals trained for running and physical exertion."[142] He eliminated any "excess fat, which would have been an obstacle to his agility."[143] *First Artist* thus represented a man worthy of being our ancestor — a man like us, or even better than us. Richer concluded by quoting Cartailhac: "They come from our soil and from our forefathers; they are family souvenirs and therefore worthy of sharper attention."[144]

Richer's *First Artist*, seated on a rock, is easily and joyfully carving a little mammoth, which Richer did not copy from any precise artifact. At the sculptor's feet, however, are various "authentic" engraved and sculpted objects: a "rod of command," a carved reindeer, an engraving of a mammoth. Significantly, the text Richer published in *L'Artiste*

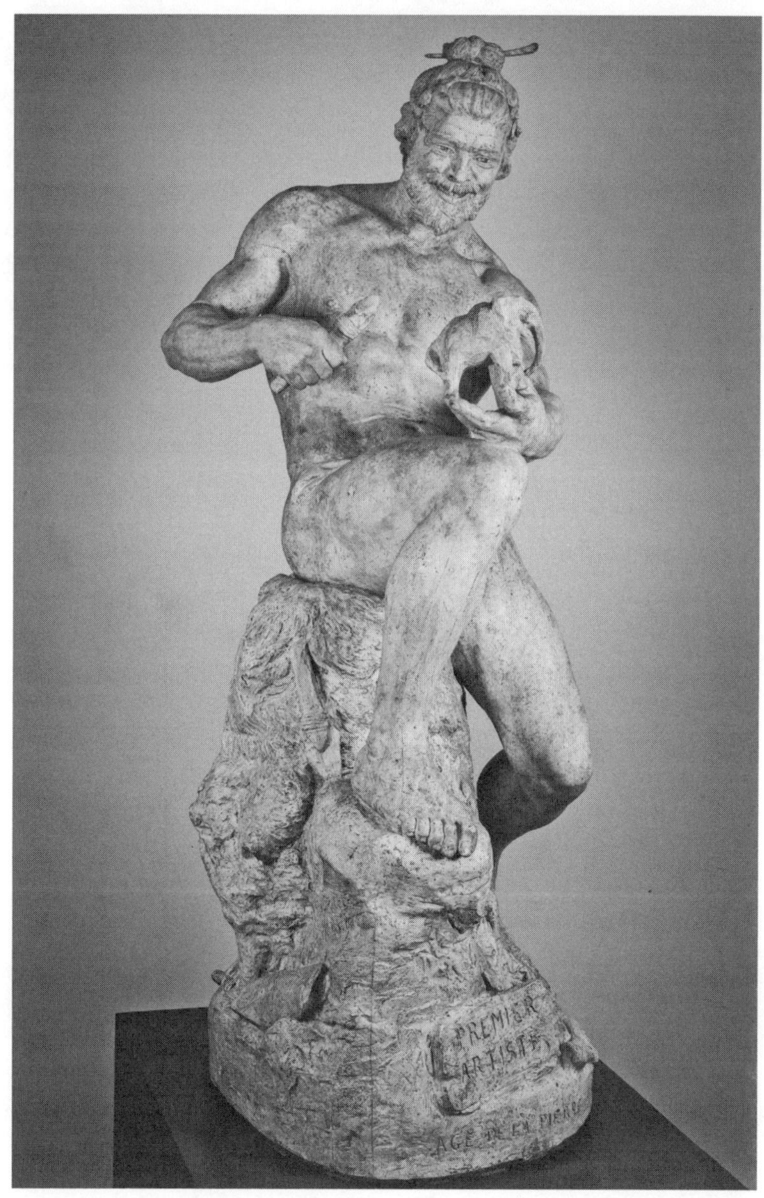

Figure 2.14. Paul Richer, *First Artist*, ca. 1890.
Plaster, 70⅜ × 26¼ × 31⅜ in. Musée Crozatier,
Le Puy-en-Velay. © Luc Olivier.

was titled "Prehistoric Art," deliberately blurring the line between the art of prehistory itself and its representation by the modern artist. The accuracy of the representation would have almost eliminated the gap between the referent and the sign if the modern artist, calling on his greater knowledge, had not elevated contingency to typology and naturalism to realism. Indeed, what he placed *before the eyes* was prehistoric man and prehistoric art extricated from any naturalist contingency and erected into realist types through the synthetic mediation of modern thought. The racial and behavioral type of the "first man" originated in precise and objective — punctilious, if you like — documentation. In that respect, Richer followed the method of any *artiste pompier*: he was maniacally exhaustive in citing the evidence, whether his works were prehistoric, Orientalist, or classical in their inspiration. The smooth, even form shared by all these subgenres and all these different eras was the automatized expression of a single way of proceeding. Also notable was the migration of motifs, gestures, and postures from one historical universe to another: *Portrait of the Aurochs* (1903), by Paul Jamin, another great realist of prehistory, depicts half-naked women — similar to the odalisques of an imaginary Orient — who admire the painter executing the famous portrait on the rock wall.

Realist painters, utterly impervious to the formal features of prehistoric artifacts, whether mobiliary art or parietal art, were primarily interested in reconstituting situations and scenes from life. Freed from all ontological and epistemological indetermination, prehistory was thereby *reified* and clarified *in everyone's eyes*. The prehistorian Louis Capitan, paying tribute to Paul Jamin, who died in 1903, acknowledged that his friend had "rendered a great and real service to prehistoric anthropology by pointing the way toward a curious method of restoration that we can usefully adopt while supporting and corroborating it with positive observations. We can then do trial reconstitutions of prehistoric life."[145]

The paintings tended to represent hunting scenes and chance encounters with dangerous animals. Because the imaginary of prehistory was complex, split between Arcadia and savagery, the viewer

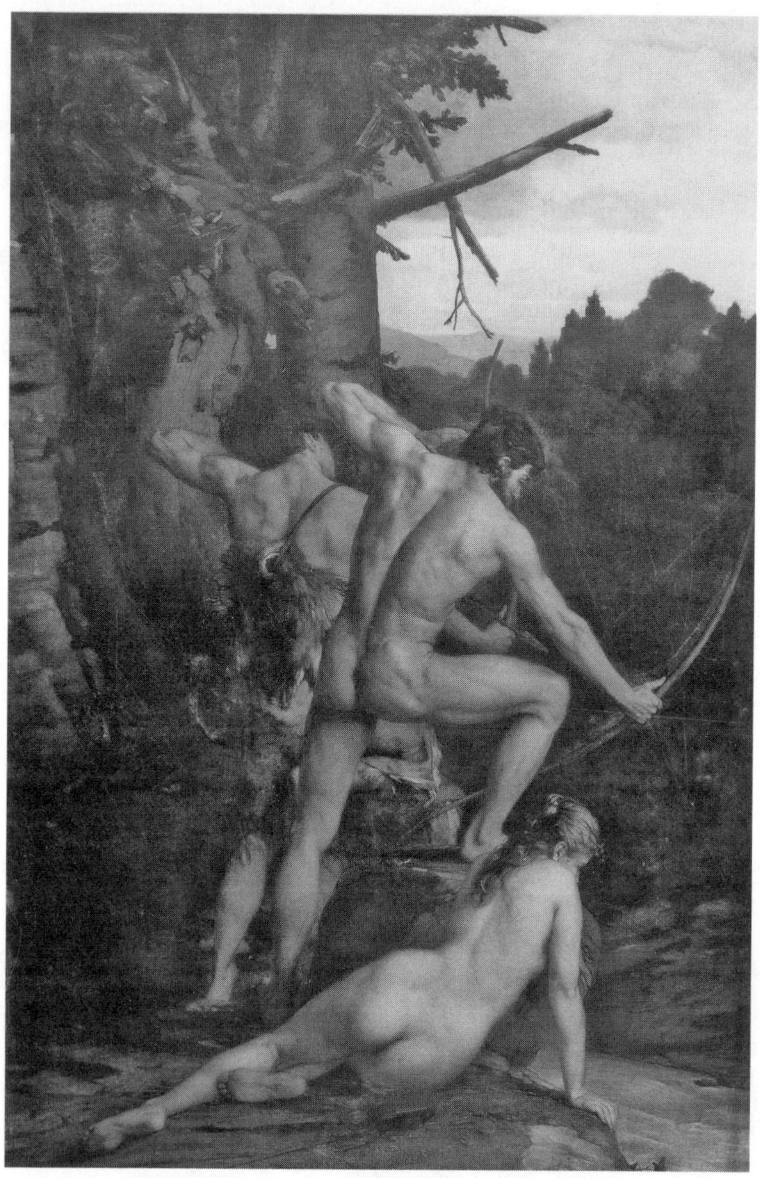

Figure 2.15. Emmanuel Benner, *Hunters in Wait*, 1879. Oil on canvas, 94⅜ × 57¾ in. Musée Petiet, Limoux. Photo: Philippe Benoist, Images Bleu-sud.

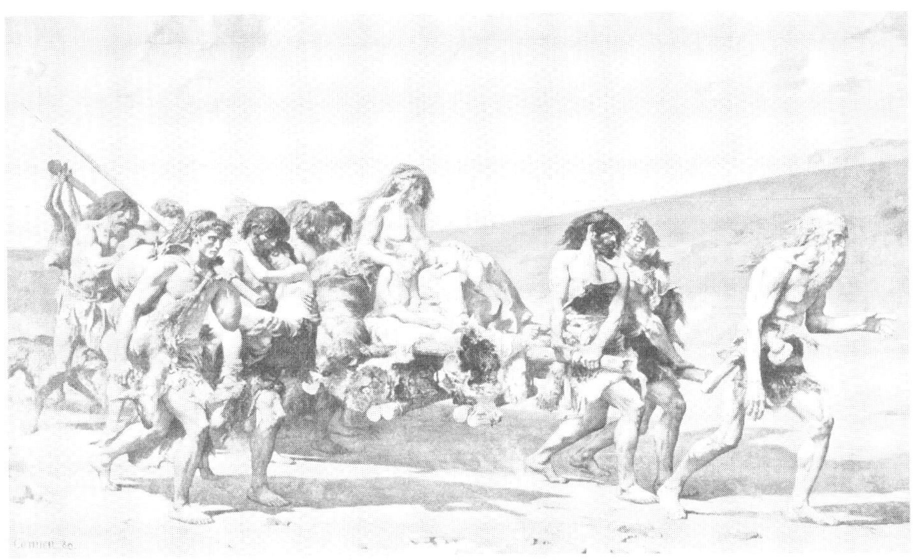

Figure 2.16. Fernand Cormon, *Cain*, 1880. Oil
on canvas, 157⅜ × 275½ in. Musée d'Orsay,
Paris, acquired from the artist by the state at
the Salon in 1880. Photo: Hervé Lewandowski.
© RMN-Grand Palais / Art Resource, NY.

was treated both to landscapes of dense scrub, abounding in resources
predestined for humans beings, and mineral landscapes so inhospitable they did not offer the slightest assistance to nomadic tribes. The
painter Emmanuel Benner focused on hunting scenes where bodies
"lying in wait" were themselves stretched like bows (Figure 2.15).
Conversely, at the Salon of 1880, Fernand Cormon exhibited an enormous *grande machine* (a large historical painting) depicting Cain with
his descendants, wretched creatures exhausted from wandering in
an unforgiving landscape.[146] While Benner depicted bodies as vigor-
ous and robust as the dense, unspoiled nature that surrounded them,
Cormon's bodies were as dry as the desert in which they wandered
like the damned (Figure 2.16). Sharp and swift as arrows in Benner's

work, in Corman's they were bowed, stocky, even in a state of collapse, pulled down by the force of gravity and time. Critics described Cormon's painting as "repulsive": animalistic regression, entrenching man "so close to his origin," was superimposed on signs of degeneration. In a cyclical scheme, the imaginary of geological extinction was reproduced in moderns' fear of their own extinction generated by human prehistory.[147]

Whether it was conceived as a golden age or as the beginning of the Fall, prehistory required a mimetic continuity between man and his environment. The mimetic relationship that modern man maintained with prehistoric bodies was portrayed as multiple from the start. The robust bodies of prehistoric men were exhibited as ancestors just as worthy as the nudes of antiquity; as for the bodies of beasts, they also played on the impulse toward identification in moderns, leading them to "regress" atavistically.

CHAPTER THREE

The Artificiality of Prehistory: A Disjunctive Genealogy of Art

At a Distance

As the realist obsession with "reconstitution" was reaching its peak and penetrating every representation of prehistory, the first dissonant voices could be heard among the proponents of "art for art's sake," articulating a very different narrative regarding the genesis, function, and legacy of prehistoric art. In 1888, the English painter Whistler wrote "Ten o'Clock,"[1] in which he sought to refute the reign of utility in the modern era and the supremacy of moral values in art by projecting himself back to "the beginning":

> Man went forth every day — some to do battle, some to the chase . . . all that they might gain and live, or lose and die. Until there was found among them one, differing from the rest, whose pursuits attracted him not, and so he staid by the tents with the women, and traced strange devices with a burnt stick upon a gourd. This man, who took no joy in the ways of his brethren — who cared not for conquest, and fretted in the field-this designer of quaint patterns — this deviser of the beautiful — who perceived in Nature about him curious carvings, as faces are seen in the fire — this dreamer apart, was the first artist.[2]

Whistler could not even conceive that the first creator could have been a collective subject — disembodied humanity or a people of any sort. He imagined the first artist only as a singular individual, the exact opposite of Richer's synthetic realist "type." Since the beginning of time, only *subjectivities* had existed, irreducible to any racial or behavioral type. The individual portrayed by Whistler loathed hunting and fighting and preferred to remain behind with the women; averse to *action*, he spent his time dreaming, trying his hand at many a useless thing. A "domestic" and therefore profoundly "antinaturalistic" being, he maintained a great *distance* from immediate reality. He stayed away from those of his own sex, from action, and from the outdoors. The forms created by that first artist did not come from experience; they were *suggested* to him by his imagination, like images seen in a fire. In that way, Whistler's Japanese-style interiors were the remote descendants of that first distance in prehistory.

Barely three years later, Oscar Wilde speculated about "who he was who first, *without ever having gone out to the rude chase*, told the wandering cavemen at sunset how he had dragged the Megatherium from the purple darkness of its jasper cave, or slain the Mammoth in single combat and brought back its gilded tusks."[3] The origin of art, then, lay with a "liar," and our "modern anthropologists," obsessed with truth, had not informed us of that fact: "Whatever his name or race, he certainly was the true founder of social intercourse. For the aim of the liar is simply to charm, to delight, to give pleasure."[4] For Wilde, lies were the origin not only of art, but also of "social intercourse," which in no way hinged on some need for solidarity, as Leo Tolstoy and Roger Marx would soon claim, but rather on the simple desire to boast and "charm."[5] Wilde and Whistler deliberately placed themselves within the lineage of that "first artist," except that the aesthetes' line of descent had no genetic continuity, being composed solely of individuals, differences, and gaps. It was in imagining the first man and "embroidering" on him for his own benefit that Wilde pursued fiction, which he believed to be the origin of art.

This notion in no way made prehistoric art the first stage in an incremental process. On the contrary, consistent with the artificiality and sterility characteristic of aestheticism in general, it condemned the entire history of the species to the status of a "childless mother" and a "motherless child." It was that disjunctive genealogy of prehistory that interested some of the greatest artists of the twentieth century. It is important to distinguish here between the "art for art's sake" embraced by ethnologists and prehistorians and the "art for art's sake" of aestheticism. For the aesthetes, who considered the "first artist" a fierce adversary of both truth and nature, art for art's sake was not to be confused with the idea of a naïve art.

A few decades after Whistler and Wilde, another aesthete, Barnett Newman, would take an ironic stance toward the "Truth" of paleontologists who studied early man. In the wake of Rousseau, he argued instead that "the human in language is literature, not communication" and that "just as man's first speech was poetic before it became utilitarian, so man first built an idol of mud before he fashioned an ax."[6] The first gesture was thus not dictated by physical needs, but by metaphysical urgency: art, the big lie, "an act of defiance against man's fall,"[7] would exist so long as man was searching for "real life."

Parallel to naturalism and realism, *artificiality* also wove together various narratives about prehistory—those of the discipline itself, but also of philosophy, anthropology, and art. In these discourses and works, artificiality was neither an epiphenomenon nor, as Piette would have said, a complement to the body, like an ornament or clothing. Artificiality was an ontological component of the body, said to be necessary for human survival and evolution. All these narratives and all these theories converged in the definition of man as a premature, lacunary, or indeterminate being. Less mature upon birth than the other animals and for that reason requiring a long period of protection before becoming autonomous, man is also less specialized and more indeterminate in his abilities and defenses. He appears to be a being who, while proceeding from a common animal stock, is *naturally artificial*, forming objects and himself with the assistance of necessary *supplements* such as technology, culture, art, or writing—all mutually complementary notions that exist side by side and must therefore be understood in a broad sense.[8] For that reason, it was certainly not by chance that the first artists to seize on the hypothesis of artificiality were "aesthetes" who broke with the growing predominance of realism and nature, but also with the nine-teenth-century "crowd." Indeed, for Whistler, even more than for Wilde, the first artist must have been an aristocrat avant la lettre, one who kept his distance from the majority and from common sense. Conversely, the human sciences grounded prehistoric artificiality in the collectivity or, at least—as in the case of Leroi-Gourhan, in par-ticular—located it at the intersection of society and the individual, social constraint and individual freedom, repetition and difference.

In 1932, Henri Bergson coined the expression "myth-making func-tion" or "myth-making faculty" to explain this strange specificity of *Homo sapiens*: "the only being endowed with reason," man was also the only one "to pin its existence to unreasonable things."[9] His "hallu-cinations"—spirits, gods, even literary and artistic fictions—allowed him to "guard against certain dangers posed by the intelligence."[10] For him, fiction was an "accumulated force," formed over the long history of evolution and compensating for the absence of an instinct as immediate as an animal's.[11] Bergson radically separated man from the beasts he must have hunted and from which he had to protect himself—and it was precisely because he was *dissimilar* to them that man needed to represent them. Arnold Gehlen, one of the principal representatives of philosophical anthropology in Germany, would define man—based on Bergson, as well as on the discoveries of pale-ontology and fetal biology—as a "deficient (*Mängelwesen*) being" who, over the course of his long evolution, was able to compensate for that lacuna and "relieve" himself of his troubles by means of the "institu-tions" he invented.[12] Gehlen's "deficient" being was also very indebted to Herder, who in 1772 had characterized man as an "indeterminate" being, the only one of all the animals not to be attached to a precise "environment." But while Herder had seen language as a remedy for that indetermination, Gehlen transferred the remedy function to the disciplinary and hierarchical forms of social institutions. After Nazism, Hans Blumenberg, an attentive reader of Gehlen, would convert the authoritarian dimension of his thought into a philosophy of "care" (*Sorge*) for the other, which man was said to have developed in the face of "the absolutism of reality." And "care" had come into being, according to Blumenberg, when man had sought refuge in "the cave."

Blumenberg followed up on Whistler's and Wilde's metaphors, seeing the cave as a feminine place. The members of our species, after wandering in the savanna and then in the forest, which required a diffuse and continuous attention, arrived in the cave, where they were able to give themselves over to dreams — a "cultural sleep" — and concentrate on the inventions of the imagination. It was then that man began to invent "metaphors," that is, to grasp who he is "only through the detour of what he is not."[13] Mural paintings made present what was absent for those who remained behind: women, old people, and children, who for lack of an experience based in action were less inclined toward realism. Their actions were performed "from a distance, in absentia," opening the gap (between them and reality) where the origin of speech resided. Hence art became a "conspiracy" against the strongest man and a "compensation" for the one "excluded from the hunt," who would become a "dreamer" and a "storyteller." Like Epimetheus, the forgetful Titan who assigned qualities to every living creature except man (who therefore had no qualities), and like the late nineteenth-century artists and aesthetes speculating on the "first artist," the theorist of metaphorology fictionalized the prehistoric cave.[14] How could man have survived in spite of his biological destitution? Blumenberg called on anthropology to free itself from the grip of naturalism and finally to reflect on the role of "artificiality" in human evolution. It was this perspective that anthropologists such as Clifford Geertz and more recently Tim Ingold pursued, especially in their deconstruction of a strictly typological or culturalist, naturalist, or functionalist anthropology in favor of a vision of the constant and unbounded interaction between nature and culture over the long history of the human species.[15]

These anthropologists were greatly indebted to Leroi-Gourhan's analyses: he had resolved the conflict between prehistoric art's utility and its gratuitousness by grounding the condition of art — that is, "the operational sequence" of gestures and words — in man's long body memory.[16] Prehistoric man's figurative activities had not only preserved the body memory of the rhythm adopted in executing various tasks, it was also the depository of a social memory, transferred from individuals to objects or the walls of caves. Leroi-Gourhan did not rule out connections between art and rites. But rather than seek an "origin" of art in religion or hunting, rather than separate out religious ceremony, aesthetic representation, and technical activity, he envisioned artistic practices on a "continuum" with technology and religious manifestations—knowledge of which always remained inaccessible to us. In all these different activities, man displayed a faculty for "symbolization," that is, a "distance taking" from "the environment both internal and external in which he is immersed," carried out by the operational sequence of gestures and words.[17]

For Leroi-Gourhan, prehistoric man, far from being "monosyllabic," was an agent autoaffected by continuous articulations, relationships, and syntax, that is, by linguistic constructs. Furthermore, despite the work of detaching himself from nature that symbolization required, his slightest gesture remained rooted in nature through body memory and social memory. Seeking how one "code of emotions" or another is constituted to ensure the individual a place within the collectivity, he postulated that art is biologically and even paleontologically fixed: "The purest art," he wrote, "always plunges deepest; only the uppermost tip emerges from the plinth of flesh and bone, without which it would not exist." At the same time, he emphasized the social utility of art: "It is tied to the biological foundations and rests on a pragmatic, social significance, for speech and figurative representation are the cement that binds the constituent elements of the ethnic cell."[18] And though Leroi-Gourhan wrote that "all art . . . is utilitarian," he immediately added: "The gratuitousness of art does not lie in its motivation but in the flowering of the language of forms."[19] Indeed, "in an exclusively human way," art "offers the individual artist or spectator a liberating escape while holding them safe within the collective mentality or the nonconformist dream." This "twofold nature of art—collective and personal—makes it impossible to separate the functional completely from the gratuitous, to separate art for something's sake from art for art's sake."[20]

Few works encapsulate that vision of art's duality — collective and personal, unified and disjunctive, reassuring and troubling — better than Matisse's *The Joy of Life*, in which a quotation of parietal art appears for the first time (Figure 3.1). This picture, painted in 1905–1906, is of interest for two reasons: it is a good demonstration of the anthropological function of art Leroi-Gourhan set out, and it succeeds at that task in great part thanks to its aesthetic use of prehistory. *Joy of Life* is the first twentieth-century work of art to constitute what I will call "the disjunctive genealogy of prehistory." For a long time, therefore, it was the only work to incorporate prehistoric art into its formal and narrative system, since it was not until the mid-1920s that Miró and Picasso took an interest in the symbolic expressions of prehistoric peoples. From about 1915 to 1925, even as de Chirico and Max Ernst were painting a mineral prehistory, more or less excluding man from its space and time, Matisse sought to express a prehistory of interiority. He was the first artist to take an interest in the symbolic artifacts of prehistory not as documents to be reconstituted, as Richer or Jamin had done, but as fictive and singular forms created by human beings at a precise moment in their long history.

In its intransigent aestheticism, including the role played by the representation of the "origin of painting," *The Joy of Life* reveals its open and eminently anthropological character. A modern painting may have no usefulness apart from the greatest one: to provide *joy* or *happiness*, to help man live, and not just survive. Prehistory, out of step with the references, frameworks, and discursive habitus of art history, allowed Matisse to place himself within a temporality extending far beyond the polemics of modernism (*The Joy of Life*, in fact, was received with strong reservations, if not outright hostility, at the Salon d'Automne in 1906) and to ground his work in the very *longue durée*. For him, as for de Chirico and Smithson, prehistory functioned above all as a conceptual and formal procedure of estrangement — the same that Whistler's or Wilde's "first artist" implemented in representing what he did not have before his eyes. When modernity discovered prehistory, it acquired a means to place itself at a distance and as a result to symbolize itself and thus demonstrate its legitimacy. At the same time, modernity would claim that despite temporal distance and differences, nothing had fundamentally changed since the beginnings of time.

The Joy of Life

Attention has long focused on the eclecticism and disjunctive aesthetic of *The Joy of Life*, a programmatic painting by means of which Matisse sought to place himself within the great tradition of painting.[21] Although depicting an Arcadia probably called forth by Mallarmé's *Afternoon of a Faun*, the painting was no more linked to that work than to any other narrative. In the middle of a wood and near a riverbank, several figures, most of them female, are engaged in all sorts of activities having nothing whatever to do with labor: love, music, dance, self-adornment, flower gathering, hiking, or idleness pure and simple. It is a closed painting, as heterogeneous as a dream. On either side of the composition, tree foliage forms large patches of warm colors in the manner of Gauguin's cloisonnism, suggesting the swaying curtains of a theater set. These *cloisons* deploy from top to bottom and in depth, moving ever closer to the middle of the composition, where, for the first time in Matisse's oeuvre, a ring of dancers is depicted. In the background, the sea appears motionless, a layer of color between the color of the sky and that of the earth. The billowing, theatrical structure of the trees encloses the figures and keeps the outside world at a distance. These figures adopt postures and perform disparate and antitheatrical gestures. Each also seems to be painted in a different way, to be hermetic and self-absorbed; none establishes a relationship with the others, none makes a single gesture or addresses a single glance toward the viewer. It might be said of the figures in *The Joy of Life* what the symbolist Gustave Moreau, Matisse's master, wrote about Michelangelo's figures: they "seemed to be fixed in a gesture of ideal somnambulism," in "an attitude resembling sleep," absorbed in a "revery so deep as to make them appear fast asleep or carried off toward worlds other than the one we inhabit."[22] Although the painting abounds in gestures and expressive movements, the discordance among them destroys any

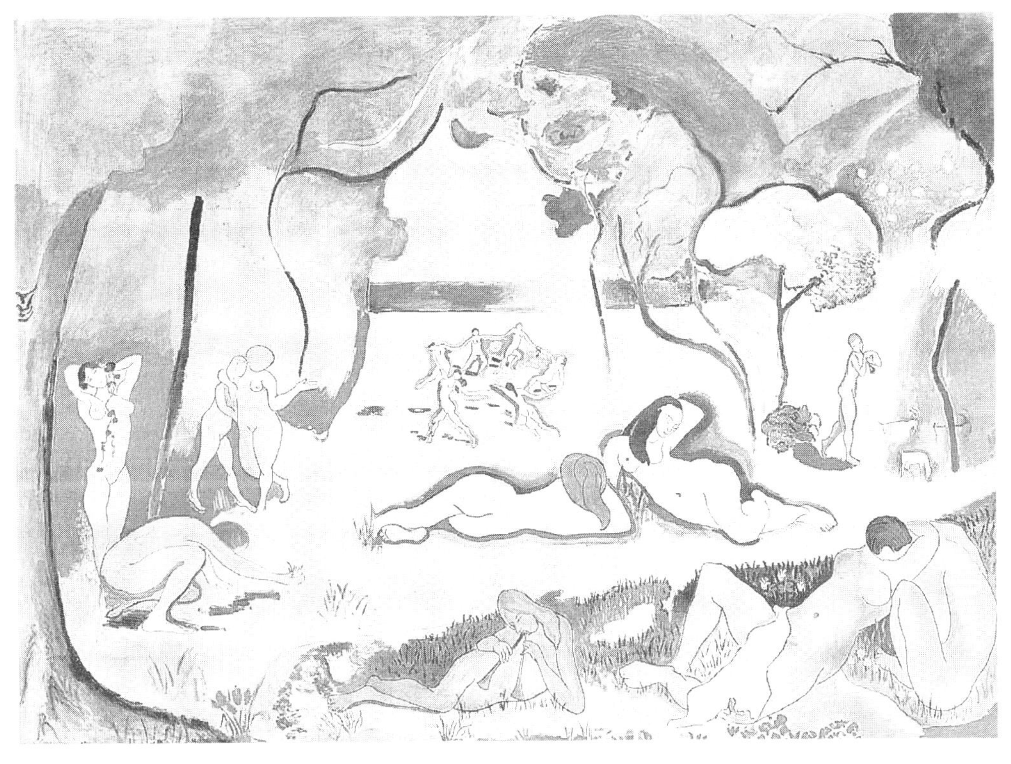

Figure 3.1. Henri Matisse, *The Joy of Life*, 1905–1906. Oil on canvas, 69½ × 94¾ in. Barnes Foundation, Philadelphia. Photo: © 2021 Succession H. Matisse/ARS, NY.

illusion of life and any narrative, transforming each of the figures into a specter. As in de Chirico's works, conflicting scales reify the bodies represented while magnifying their isolation.[23] Finally, all the figures are totally antinaturalistic, more or less distorted, with thick, overflowing, and misaligned outlines, in colors ranging from a flaming pink to the greenish-gray of clay. Matisse's Arcadia seems in the first place to be perfectly artificial: a golden age at the opposite extreme from unspoiled nature.

In the foreground, a couple forms a monstrous assemblage: a man's hairy head seems to be emerging from a woman's neck, signifying both the fusion of lovers and a child's separation from the maternal body.[24] Farther in the distance, a young girl is playing a flute while lying on the ground. In the second row of forms on display, on the left, a female figure is kneeling—her greenish-gray color contrasts with the rose tones of the figures in the foreground. Even farther back, but contiguous with the kneeling figure, the legs of a different female figure are rendered in the same clayey color before they suddenly veer toward flesh tones, probably an allusion to the Pygmalion myth. Emerging from the bright and concave red background between the tree trunks are two interlacing figures whose thin outlines form an arabesque of gestures and featureless faces. In the center of the image are two symmetrical and inverted images of nudes with thick sinuous outlines and massive shadows. Along the same axis, at a greater distance, minuscule figures are dancing. On the right, the convergence of two areas of solid color, white and reddish-orange, forms a slightly recessed wall. The reddish-orange patch is traversed by a diagonal zigzag, a sign suggestive of a tree trunk, which immediately turns into a sign for a fissure. A young shepherd, standing out against the white background, is playing the flute while moving to the right. He is preceded by three goats gliding over the red background: two white goats stand near the shepherd, while the third has gone off ahead of him. This goat's body, barely sketched out, fades away in spots, as if its distance reduces its substantiality so that it belongs less to the real and more to fiction. On the uneven and slightly concave surface, which brings to mind the wall of a cave, the goat's body evokes the copies of parietal art that were beginning to be published at the time in various reviews. In its formal difference from the others, this goat occupies both registers of representation simultaneously: it is both a drawing on a wall and part of an outdoor scene. The pastoral group slowly entering the "cave" is a mise en abyme for the composition as a whole.

There is no known "evidence," iconic or textual, of sources that might have led Matisse to quote prehistory: in his many reported and published remarks, he never referred to that period or to its artifacts.[25] Jack Flam was the first to identify a quotation of parietal art in *The Joy of Life*, noting that such art had only recently come to light at the time. And how can we rule out the possibility that Matisse, an enthusiast of art history in its totality, was attuned to the discoveries of prehistory? Might he have learned of them concretely, courtesy of the review *La Nature*, for example, in which Capitan and Breuil had published their "Origins of Art" in 1902, accompanied by many drawings, including one of a sheep? This is possible. But the quest for sources is not the only means art history has at its disposal to construct its hypotheses. Like the prehistorians Laming-Emperaire and Leroi-Gourhan, whose sources were incomparably sparser than those of art historians of the modern period, we may consider the structural intelligibility of the work itself and wonder whether it encourages, supports, or rules out the reference to prehistory. We might even ponder the specific and irreplaceable role of that reference within the syntax of the image. This question is all the more necessary in that the figures are organized in relation to one another, despite, but also because of their isolation. The passing of time and narrative flow are excluded from the image.

This work articulates the "joy of life." A multitude of quotations from the history of painting, a multitude of ghosts from poetry and myth, are laid out and assembled there: Mantegna, Goya, Ingres, Agostino Carracci, Antonio Pollaiulo, Giorgione, early Greek painting, Watteau, Gauguin, and Cézanne. These are Matisse's more or less explicit references to the plastic arts.[26] Whether in the use of precise elements, such as the poses and gestures of Ingres's odalisques, or of structural devices such as the tree canopy serving as a roof to protect Cézanne's bathers, or of situations such as Giorgione's or Watteau's rural and pastoral compositions, Matisse frenetically engaged in a sort of "eclectic cannibalism."[27] In absorbing all these great painters, he was not seeking to legitimize modernism. His genealogical narrative is more ambiguous; perfectly congruent with the dialectical structure of his work, it enfolds and disconnects at the same time. What Matisse shows is that from cave paintings to *The Joy of Life*, the only Arcadia that has ever existed is that of art, whose exceptionality interrupts the individual's regular life on every occasion. Our eyes, moving from one group to another, are affected by a movement that is more like a leap in time than a spatial transition.[28] Jumping from one field to another, that "peripheral gaze"[29] also brings about a change in the historical era: from prehistory to Ingres's upraised arms, from Cézanne's bathers, to Greek vases, to Gauguin's *cloisons*. For Matisse, art is that leap, that spacing, that disjunction. Prehistoric art, said Leroi-Gourhan, is a matter of repetition and freedom; *The Joy of Life* follows exactly the same path, but in the opposite direction, in the manner of the moderns. This canvas, in its conscious use of history and its critical quest for originality, affirms its difference while repeating certain formulas and gestures.

Nevertheless, the prehistoric moment appears to be necessary in Matisse's system. He goes back to the first available traces of art in order to show its anthropological necessity: to tear apart the continuous weft of the present, to interrupt the repetition of the same with certain fictional gestures that have been performed throughout human history. In that sense, Matisse works in Whistler's antinaturalistic and aesthetic wake. The pastoral is thus *historicized*, keyed to this moment of history, which, because of the absence of written evidence, is called "prehistory." For that reason, it is also very different from the pastoral notion of the first prehistorians, when they sought to account for strange mobiliary artifacts. Placed on equal footing with all the other moments in the painting, prehistory is neither more nor less isolated, neither more nor less somnambulistic.

The Joy of Life is the repetition of a difference: no moment resembles any other, though all have the same suspensive function. Taking our cue from Jacques Derrida, we might say that Matisse sets out to show the historicity of the origin: he refers to a first founding gesture, but a gesture to be reactivated indefinitely, so long as human beings exist.[30] Far from being pure, the originality Matisse claims for modernism is deeply rooted in a long memory of gestures. The universal *and* the particular, the same *and* the different, memory *and* novelty: on the one hand, the theatrical device encompasses all the figures, confirming the suspensive function of art in general, but on the other, that function, like the figures that perform it, always uses particular signs and gaps, because it is always a unique historical manifestation impossible to reiterate.

Why Did Modernity Identify with Prehistory?

A Pathological Regression: Prehistory in the Light of Modernist Evolutionism
Matisse's Arcadia abolishes time, allowing moments of history distant from one another to coexist. Because the viewer's gaze leaps without order from one figure to another, no deterministic view of the progress of human history is possible. Not only did Matisse completely dismantle the evolutionist logic that attributes simplicity, isolation, and disjunction to the origin, but he also made these qualities the universal principle of joy or happiness.

Yet neither modernism nor the avant-garde's artistic practice was monolithic: the reception of prehistoric art attests precisely to the disparity in the temporal notions of artists placed under the wholly inadequate umbrella term "avant-garde." For those steeped in evolutionism, convinced of the growing spiritualization of art and history in general, the naturalistic and rudimentary view of prehistory could be only a negative term of comparison, the irrefutable proof of a radical dissimilarity and a definitive distance between the beginning and the end of time. Any formal or conceptual resemblance to prehistory signified a regression bordering on pathology. It was a sign that progress and the complexity of modern thought had been forgotten in favor of a prior state of crude simplicity.[31] Nevertheless, even in such orthodox evolutionist philosophies, the judgment could change, depending on whether it concerned Paleolithic art, supposedly naturalistic in the extreme, or Neolithic art, more abstract and no doubt more easily assimilable to the complexities of modernist thought.

For detractors of the avant-garde, anxious to dispute its historical legitimacy, prehistory functioned as a metaphor for an irreversible regression similar to degeneration. In 1910, the writer, artist, and cartoonist Gelett Burgess published "The Wild Men of Paris" in the review *Architectural Record*. It was a critique of contemporary art in France, illustrated with many photographs of artists surrounded by their works and their collections of ethnological artifacts. The narrative of "savagery" construed contemporary art as the last link in a genealogy of "ugliness" running from the Gothic and Aztec art to the "Hindu monstrosities" and "other primitive grotesques" and back to prehistory. As Burgess had commented at the time, "men painted and carved grim and obscene things when the world was young. Was this revival a sign of some second childhood of the race, or a true rebirth of art?"[32] It would be pointless to try to identify the "grim and obscene" figures of prehistory to which Burgess referred. He was only displaying his panic in the face of a modernity regressing to early savagery, the childhood of the "race"—which would be confirmed in 1926 by the screenplay he wrote for a film titled *Caveman*. Theodore Roosevelt was better informed for his critique of the Armory Show, where many works by these artists were exhibited in the United States for the first time. He made fun of the futurists, whom he proposed to call "pastists": their contorted figures could be found, strikingly, in remote prehistory, where it was clear that the same men who had painted animals with extraordinary skill proved hopelessly maladroit at painting their own species.[33] Roosevelt was implying that the same contradiction characterized modern works: flawless skill in all areas of culture, but intentional regression in art.

Yet modernism itself was in part an evolutionism. Certain artists and critics, wishing to undermine the legitimacy of the imitation of nature, saw Paleolithic art as a "first stage," now obsolete, in art's development. Thus, Roger Fry wrote in 1910: "The very perfection of vision and presumably of the other senses with which the Bushmen and Paleolithic man were endowed fitted them so perfectly to the surroundings that there was no necessity to develop the mechanical arts beyond the elementary instruments of the chase."[34] In 1917, he would think that this realist form of adaptation was perfectly useless to moderns: the primitive artist "is intensely moved by events and objects; his art is the direct expression of his wonder and his delight in them," while for the "formalist," who "also may be moved deeply by the contemplation of events and objects," "there comes a certain moment when his expression is no longer related to that emotion, but is dominated by passionate feeling about form."[35] It had to be understood that the primitive artist was incapable of establishing any distance between himself and nature, like the academic painter or the child just beginning to draw. In 1915, the painter Kazimir Malevich defended the same viewpoint as Roger Fry, even though he had just asserted, through the abstraction of "suprematism," the greatest distance possible from the "naturalistic" world. "The savage was the first to establish the principle of naturalism."[36] Believing he had transformed himself "in the zero of form" and "through zero" had "reached creation," Malevich declared that with suprematism, "the savage is conquered like the ape."[37] In reality, the same arguments could be found in many other writings of those years.[38]

One of the reasons for the rejection of Paleolithic art was the supposed analogy between it and the impressionism of recent years. Henry van de Velde, a defender of the organic, continuous, and empathetic line as a unifying principle in architecture and in the design of everyday objects, saw an ingenious "Impressionism," an "exhilaration" of life and perception, the "most immediate living, most sensual and perfect form," and the first manifestation of his own "dynamographic" ornament in the lines carved and painted on the "cataclysmic upheavals" of the walls of the caves.[39] He therefore inveighed against Wilhelm Worringer, who devalorized prehistoric art because it supposedly arose from "an inorganic and dead line." That art, van de Velde protested, on the contrary appeared "between these two extreme periods of the history of art—of which Impressionism constitutes the present, and the other, the extreme limit of the past."[40]

But Van de Velde was one of the few to mention in positive terms "the Impressionism of prehistory." Recall de Chirico's pejorative comments on the "impressionist" paintings in the caves. His close friend Guillaume Apollinaire criticized impressionism in order to praise Georges Braque's painting. In the wake of Vico, he wrote that only crazed "primitive men" or "savages terrified by the brilliance of a celestial body" could logically be "impressed" by nature.[41]

Because the European expressionists defined themselves by their opposition to an impressionism judged "passive" vis-à-vis nature, it was not unusual to see an astonishing analogy established between impressionism and Paleolithic art. On the one hand, these artists turned one of the founding aims of impressionism against itself: to strive toward an innocent and fresh vision, untainted by historical traces. On the other, the new art, in its quest for expression, was itself resistant to any "impression," from the most recent to the most ancient of its manifestations. But it was above all in Germany, where the duality between impressionism and expressionism had become highly nationalized, not to say racialized, that virulence toward Paleolithic art was at its height: impressionism, superficial and sensual, was said to be a naturally French art, while expressionism, metaphysical and tormented, was considered naturally German. The best means to devalorize impressionism was to push it back to the most primitive past and root it in the soil of Southern Europe. In Germany, conversely, the discipline of prehistory, by going back to the abstract megaliths of the Neolithic period, would give German art a much more respectable past than that attributed to French art.

Max Verworn, whose dualist interpretation of prehistoric art had deeply marked the reception of prehistory in the German-speaking world, insisted on the "impressionist spirit" of Paleolithic art, which he had previously called "physioplastic." In a collection published by Der Sturm, Verworn argued that the transition from the impressionism of the Paleolithic period to the expressionism of the Neolithic period had been the first "artistic turn" in human history.[42] The hunter's "naïve innocence" had been replaced by a split between body and mind, which led to abstractions and metaphysics. Verworn believed that "reflection and theorization are always characteristic of . . . a stage of human spirituality superior to the reception of sensory impressions," which allowed him to claim that "ideoplastic art constitutes a stage of artistic creation superior to the naïve physioplastic of the primitive hunter."[43] In 1923, in the first book to compare prehistoric and modern art, the mountaineer and geologist Wilhelm Paulcke reiterated the parallel between Paleolithic art and impressionism while granting the latter a greater spirituality.[44] And Herbert Kühn, the inventor of the term "sensorism" in reference to the Paleolithic period, had mentioned two years earlier the individualistic and liberal foundation of that art, whose latest expression, he argued, was modern "impressionism." And since history alternated rhythmically between "sensorism" and "imaginativism," the latter had arisen anew in the form of expressionism and socialism.[45] Eckhart von Sydow, another great defender of expressionism, was sorry not to find the metaphysics of the mystic Franz Marc's *Fate of the Animals* (1913) in monumental prehistoric painting, adding condescendingly: "As the contemporaries of expressionism and abstraction . . . we can imagine the cries of jubilation emitted by the impressionists upon the discovery of these frescoes."[46]

Parietal art, therefore, remained obsolete for these proponents of evolutionism, who saw it as localized and circumscribed within a few remote regions. Paleolithic prehistory, having been fixed at the beginning of history, was a cultural fossil without the temporal plasticity that alone might have made possible its appropriation by late modernity.

Stratified Beings

Whereas evolutionist thought made prehistory a zone that Western humanity — caught up in technological, intellectual, and moral acceleration — had left far behind, other currents of thought shaped a notion of time that was at once regressive, reversible, and polyphonic. The change of scale caused by the shock of parietal art was a first condition for the moderns' appropriation of prehistory. A second condition was the regressive and asynchronous (but not pathological) temporality attributed to Paleolithic prehistory. Since the moderns had internalized the geological scale, with its inert fossils, how could they refuse to identify with the first human symbolic creations, even if they supposed that the beings who made them were as rudimentary as contemporary primitive peoples? Therefore, while Quinet, Nietzsche, and certain linguistic paleontologists such as Pictet invented geological metaphors for human memory, it was decreed that the upper layers of sediment composing that memory were marked by the emotions and symbolic acts of primitive peoples from the past, all ghosts that still haunted subjectivity.

In 1878, for example, Nietzsche described memory as "the function of the brain that sleep encroaches upon most" and by which the modern individual relives the lives of the first humans. The same confusion of perceptions, the same complete embrace of the flow of life, and the same abandonment to hallucinations characterize the eternal present of prehistoric men and the memory of moderns when they sleep: "in sleep and dreams repeat once again the curriculum of early mankind."[47] A few years later, Freud would develop his own theories on the return of prehistoric man in contemporary man. Archaeology provided knowledge of prehistoric man through his monuments, his tools, and his art; folklore brought us closer to him "through the remnants of his ways of thinking that survive in our own manners and customs"; and ethnology allowed us to encounter him individually and socially among the "savage and semi-savage races; their psychic life assumes a peculiar interest for us, for we can recognize in their psychic life a well-preserved, early stage of our own development." Likewise, psychoanalysis was the science that let us rediscover prehistoric man in each of us — in "infantile traces" and in the "psychology of the neurotic."[48] Hence, prehistory survived in the first place in every childhood and then in the antagonistic relations that the adult and society maintain with modern reality. Freud concluded: "The deepest and eternal nature of man . . . lies in those impulses of the mind which have their roots in a childhood that has since become prehistoric."[49] In 1905, the cultural historian Karl Lamprecht set out to write his universal history of the human species, turning to children's drawings to reconstitute its beginnings, convinced that "in order to study the development of a race, it will be necessary to study the development of an individual." In "pedology," he found the materials necessary to reconstitute the childhood of humanity.[50] A few years later, the psychologist Georges-Henri Luquet, studying so-called primitive art in all its manifestations, from childhood to contemporary primitivism to prehistory, would argue that "every child undertakes on his own behalf the reinvention of figural drawing, as if he were the first artist."[51] Clearly, prehistory was a canvas gradually extending to every field of knowledge that took man as its object. Nomadic, partly overlapping concepts—the most important being recapitulation, survival, and regression—ensured the junctures and paths of communication on that canvas.

The law of recapitulation, set forth in 1866 by the Darwinist Ernst Haeckel, legitimized psychoanalysis in its claim to universality by hypothesizing that every individual repeats in brief the biological and psychic evolution of the species.[52] Thanks to that same law, Luquet was able to observe the birth of art in the first scribbles done by a child. But time seemed to store up not only the successive improvements of the species, but also the traces of an imperfect past. When prehistory made an appearance, it often interrupted the linear course of things and obliged time to fold back on itself. In 1881, the psychologist Théodule Ribot formulated his merciless "law of regression or reversion." According to Ribot, the pathologies of memory manifest themselves through the gradual destruction of personal memories: they "vanish in reverse order," "those of childhood being the last to disappear."[53] Regression thus becomes the horizon of human life.

Just as psychology and psychoanalysis universalized regression, folklore and art history universalized the "survival," detecting it in gestures, customs, and proverbial expressions. But the survival had both a primitive face and a modern face: it allowed the homogenization of the singular histories of human societies solely in accordance with the criteria of Western man, and he readily found himself the agent of a series of survivals about which he knew almost nothing. On the one hand, the survival could be used to measure the distance between different civilizations, but also between classes; on the other, when it was perceptible in the gestures of moderns, it measured their distance from their own time and from their own egos.

For the archaeologist and art historian Waldemar Deonna, there were always "connections" between different periods: what he called "survivals" were the "forms and practices that no longer correspond to the ideas or needs of the men of one time, but that have become unconscious and are maintained by habit alone.... The slightest gesture in our lives is thus often only the continuation without reflection of an act that formerly had its importance, but that lost it under new conditions of existence."[54] This meant that a connection between distant eras could act as a rupture between contiguous eras, provided that the survival, tucked away in the automatisms of life, became conscious, thus declaring its difference from the present. Soon, Henri Focillon would come to consider geology, memory, and artistic activity nearly synonymous terms:

> A large number of superimposed, heterogeneous layers, similar to successive alluvial deposits, cover the vestiges of ancient man.... Certain folds that his first experiences were able to impose on his successors and that have become something like permanent aptitudes remain more or less obvious in new acquisitions. But most of these tokens were worn down or dispersed, and even when we believe we grasp them, they sometimes turn out to be unrecognizable, having been, so to speak, "experienced differently." So that we take the most timeworn heritage to be a sign of youth, and it astonishes us as if it were a fresh invention.[55]

In other words, the "survival," a major agent in the workings of the *longue durée*, was now responsible for rupture, change, and the birth of the new, even as it guaranteed the connection to a remote past. And what "worn-down" and "dispersed" survival was more unrecognizable than prehistory? The future was thus understood to be potentially inscribed in a realist, yet unfinished past. It was in that *longue durée*, where the different orders of time permeated one another, that the practices of modern artists were rooted, including the most utopian practices.

"From the Cave Walls to the Factory Walls" was the title Brassaï gave to the first of his texts introducing his photographs in *Graffiti* (1933) (Figure 3.2). Time, he explained, has the capacity to contract to such a degree that it vanishes altogether: "It is all a question of optics. Living analogies establish staggering connections across the ages merely by eliminating the time factor. In the light of ethnography, antiquity becomes youthfulness, the stone age a state of mind, and it is the understanding of childhood that brings the spark of life to flint shards."[56] The camera became an instrument for condensing time: it trained the gaze to see simultaneously, in a few signs furtively carved into a wall, a parietal engraving *and* urban graffiti. In 1958, Brassaï would write that in this work—which he would pursue for a long time yet—he "spanned" the centuries, even millenniums.[57] History, which had fixed antiquity in a bygone time, was itself annihilated by ethnology and child psychology, which were able to revive the past. Time thus slipped away from historical succession or linearity; it became simultaneous, permeable, eminently plastic. The future participated in the past, and the past could become visible in the pure present: "Graffiti," Brassaï continued, "allows us to witness with the voyeur's sensual joy the flower blossoming and being fertilized; the fruit bursts forth, a minuscule and wild fruit still bearing the gold of the pollen among the petals."[58] In a later text, the photographer also wrote that "to engrave on a wall is to rediscover the antique human gesture" (Figure 3.3).[59]

This was an opinion that Brassaï and Picasso shared. In 1943, while photographing the painter's different "stone ages," as Picasso called his sculptural works, Brassaï expressed the emotions he had felt during his visit to Les Eyzies standing before a "cross-section four to five meters high, with layers built up over millennia," which allowed him to "take in thousands of years of history" "in a single glance."[60] The most astonishing thing, he added, was that "every generation, totally unaware of the ones that preceded it, nevertheless organized the cave in the same way, at a distance of thousands of years. . . . You always find the 'kitchen' in the same place."[61] To which Picasso replied, somewhat blasé, "Nothing extraordinary about that. Man doesn't

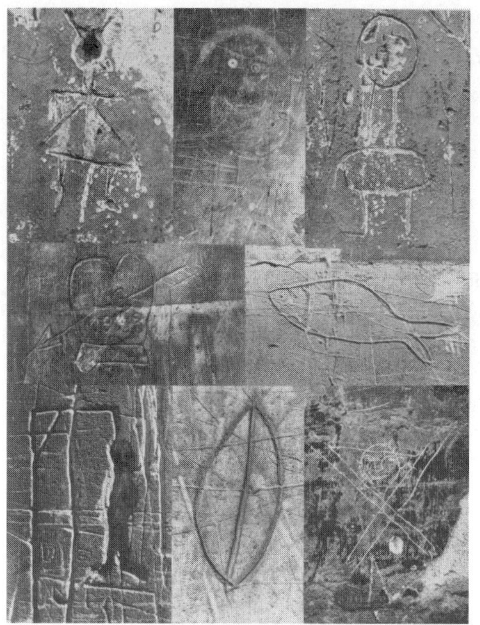

Figure 3.2. Brassaï, *Graffiti parisiens*, *Minotaure* nos. 3–4 (1933). p. 7. © Estate Brassaï-RMN-Grand Palais. © The Museum of Modern Art. Licensed by SCALA/Art Resource, NY.

Figure 3.3. Brassaï, *Graffiti: The Lion*, 1932. Silver gelatin print (NV), 8½ × 10½ in., Centre Pompidou, Paris. © Estate Brassaï-RMN-Grand Palais. Photo: © RMN-Grand Palais/Michèle Bellot.

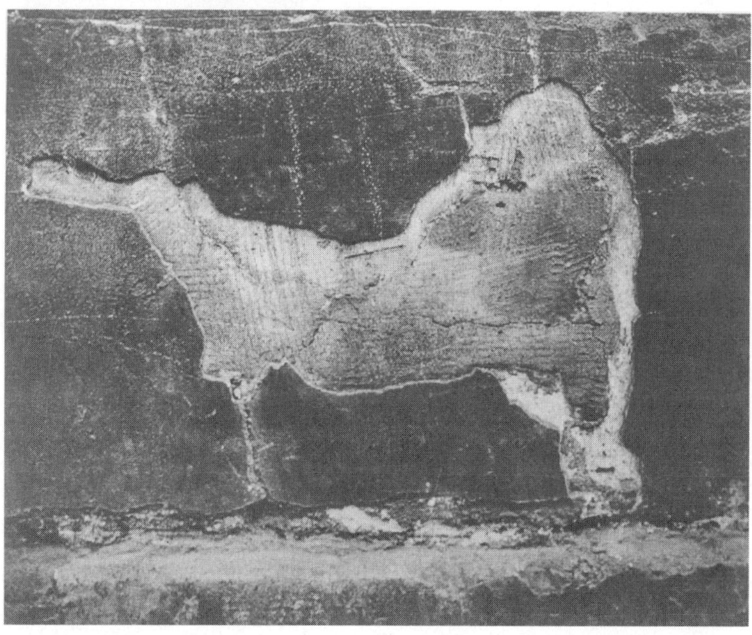

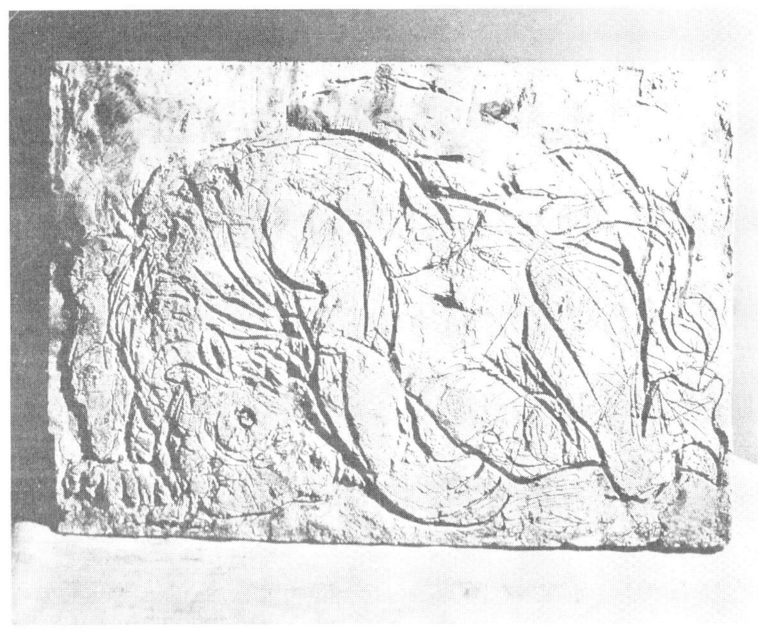

Figure 3.4. Pablo Picasso, *Wounded Minotaur*,
1941. Engraved plaster, 11⅜ × 17 × 1⅜ in. Photographed by Brassaï in 1943–1944. Gelatin silver
print, 9¼ × 11⅜ in. Musée National Picasso,
Paris. Photo: © 2021 ARS, NY / ADAGP, Paris.

change. He keeps his habits." Just as men choose "the same sites" "to
build a city," in the caves, "instinctively, all those people found the
same corner for their kitchen." For Picasso, beliefs could certainly
change, but not the gestures that made them effective: "Venus is
replaced by the Virgin, but the same life goes on," he concluded.[62]
It was undoubtedly this "same life" going on that he represented in
Wounded Minotaur, a sculpted and engraved plaster completed in 1942,
in the midst of World War II (Figure 3.4). With this Minotaur emerging from an inextricable tangle of lines, marks, and incisions, Picasso
was pursuing in his own manner what anonymous generations had

done for centuries. What image and what time dwelt in Picasso's mind when he carved the mythological being? Was it a superimposition of animals engraved on the walls of the caves? Was it the Minotaur of the Greeks, with whom Picasso identified? A bull wounded in the corrida? Or a man wounded in the war taking place far from the painter's studio? Certainly that tangle of meanings, periods, and references inscribed immediately in the jumble of lines was a sort of survival different from the one supposedly stored away in the bodies of the primitive peoples. This was an affirmation, forever to be repeated, of the dialectical struggle of tragedy: the continued struggle of human freedom affirming itself in art against an indifferent *fatum*.[63] And that capacity for struggle and therefore for history was precisely what the primitive peoples of modern times lacked.

Mobile Survivals and Reified Survivals: A Sizable Difference
between Prehistoric Peoples and Primitive Peoples
The difference between the modern uses of prehistory and of primitivism is as great as that between the survival as it existed among moderns and the one they attributed to primitive peoples. Prehistory's universality is without a doubt its most salient trait. By virtue of that universality, prehistory made its way into the interiority of modern man as a survival, a regressive temporality, or a hidden permanence. With its necessarily and definitively lacunary character, universality also opened prehistory to historicization by the present.

By contrast, primitivism, since its inaugural moment in Herder's writings, has been inextricably linked to the "particular," which Herder defended against what he deemed the overwhelming power of the (French) universal. Even later, when the ethnological artifacts of Africa and Oceania were wrested from their context to make them aesthetic, pure, and atemporal objects, their particularism was not set aside.[64] Indeed, these objects were always a reminder that they came from somewhere else and that the artists—anxious to escape their own ancestors and, above all, the norm of the "classical"—had adopted them for that reason. This particularism was directly echoed in artists' limited and intermittent appeal to the primitivist imaginary. It is true that throughout his life, Picasso always remembered and recycled the lessons of African sculpture.[65] But the prehistory that burst forth in Picasso's works was identifiable as such by its universality, its fragmentary nature, and the plurality of its forms, reappearing regularly in its different versions, depending on the artist's needs.

The prehistoric had arisen a first time in his cubist works, with an almost geological compactness and mutism. In *Three Women* (1908), the figures, barely distinct from one another, stand out from this ground as in a diluvian catastrophe. Later on, the prehistoric returned, first in Picasso's dislocation and reassembly of paleontological fossils or megalithic debris (notebooks of Cannes and Paris, drawings at Dinard, series of Dinard *Bathers*) (Figure 3.5), then in his appropriation of formal procedures that prehistoric peoples had used for their symbolic operations in mobiliary or parietal art (Boisgeloup sculpture, engraved stones, even paper sculptures) (Figures 3.6 and 3.7). On the one hand, Picasso used the strangeness of prehistory to maintain a distance from the history of his time, but on the other, the prehistoric allowed him to draw out a different history, more abstract and more mobile, linked neither to a chronology nor to a precise event, but synonymous with *human action*.[66] It is precisely the idea of a prehistory opening up possibilities that distinguished it from primitivism.

Moderns, despite the distrust and sometimes aversion they displayed toward history, could think of themselves only as "historical beings," whereas they thought of the primitive peoples as being outside history, incapable of acting, mere passive documents of time passing unbeknown to them.[67] In 1937, Focillon expounded on this sharp divide between the temporality of the West and that of the spaces bypassed by progress. He described first the accelerated time of the West:

> The urban milieus have an accelerated, extremely mobile notion of time, which is capable even of artificial reversibility (archaism) and anticipation. The multiplicity of tasks to be performed fragments time into a certain

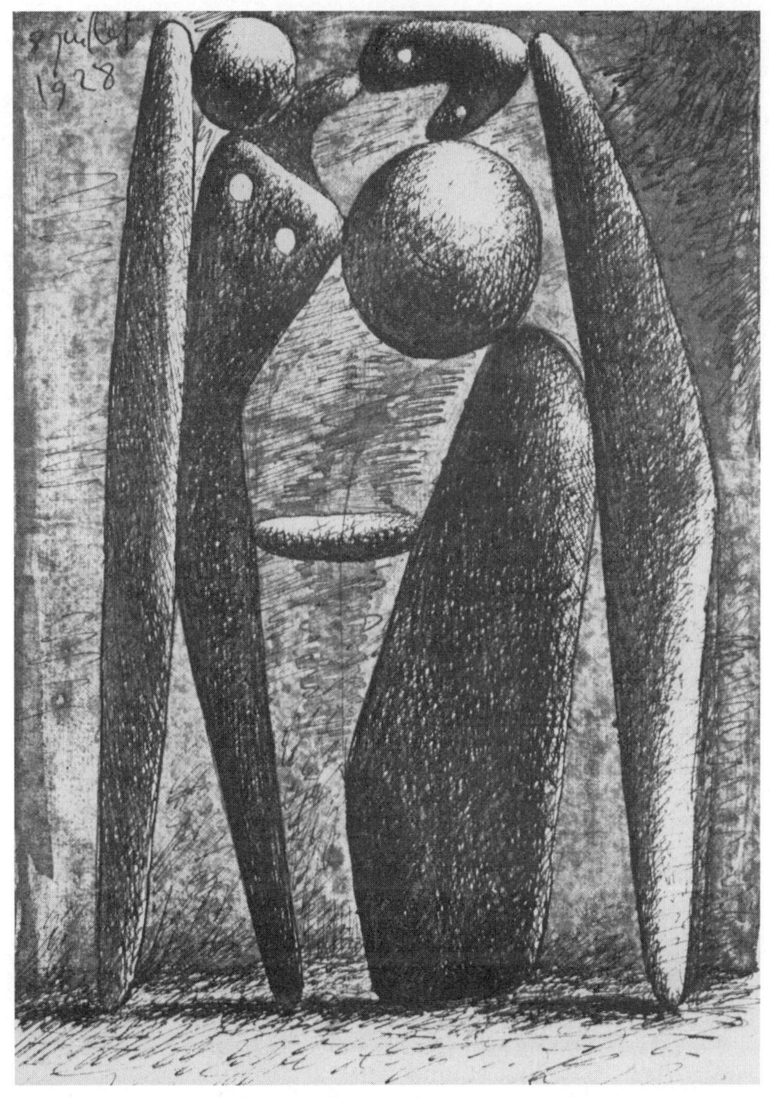

Figure 3.5. Pablo Picasso, *Bathers (Plan for a Monument)*, Dinard, July 8, 1928. Pen, India ink and wash on round-form laid paper, sheet from sketchbook, 11⅞ × 8⅝ in. Musée National Picasso, Paris. Photo: © 2021 ARS, NY / ADAGP, Paris.

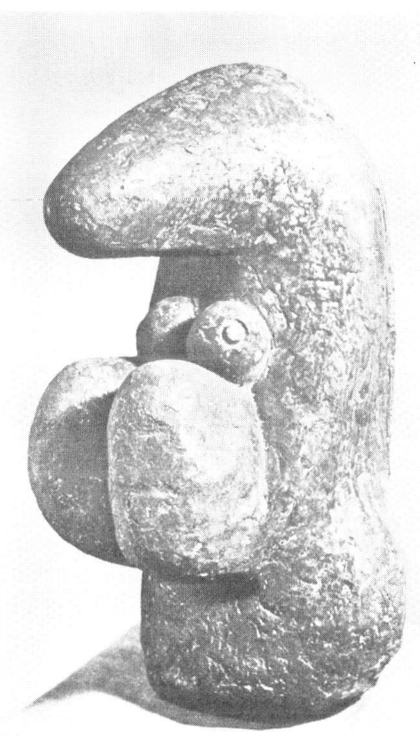

Figure 3.6. Pablo Picasso, bust of woman, Boisgeloup, 1931. Original plaster, 24½ × 11 × 16¼ in. Musée National Picasso, Paris. Photographed by Brassaï. Photo: © 2021 ARS, NY / ADAGP, Paris.

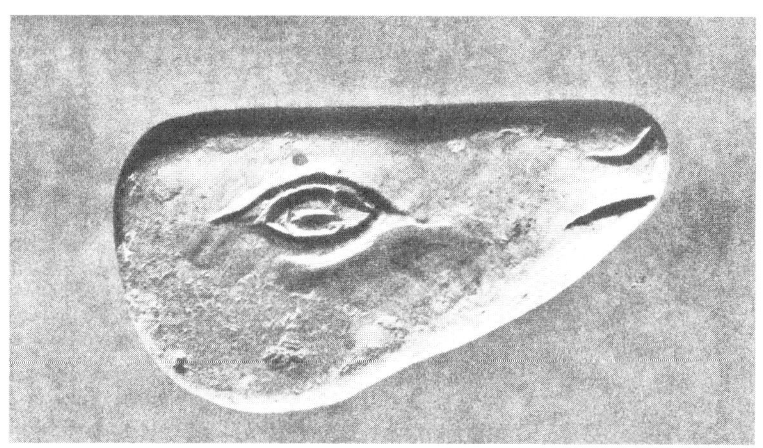

Figure 3.7. Pablo Picasso, engraved pebble (animal head), Paris, 1945. Picasso Administration, Paris, inv. no. 55494. Photo: © 2021 ARS, NY / ADAGP, Paris.

number of short and full periods that crowd out one another and give the actions of ordinary life their jerky and feverish character. It imposes on everyone the impatience to transcend the limits of time and incessantly renew the matter of existence. Thus is born moderns' notion of time, determined by an acute need for synchronism and the fear of being left behind.

He went on to characterize the cultures of slow-motion time:

> In opposition to this accelerated time is a slow-motion or even motionless time, where the past is the contemporary of the present, where the idea of the future eludes the intelligence. In these wastelands of time, in this vast monotony of days, one can do a great deal, but nothing happens. Acts can accumulate without ever giving rise to an event. The cultures of slow-motion time are naturally characterized by survivals, patois, beliefs, folklore, customs, popular art. Invention in the full sense of the term is banished from them.[68]

Even though opposed on principle to the progressive and evolutionist narrative, Focillon nevertheless asserted the West's superiority. In one way or another, historicity remained a Western affair, because evolutionism and antievolutionism were equally mobile, except that evolutionism had opted for a straight line, while anitevolutionism preferred coils, returns, and leaps.

Hence, many theorists of prehistory came to dispute the heuristic value of the analogy between the savage and prehistoric man. The Marxist Max Raphael, a fierce critic of the primitivist orientation of the 1930s, distinguished the "progressive peoples," who had a history, from savages, whose sense of history was nonexistent because they knew nothing of dialectics:

> The Quaternary clans were always better able to master the living conditions imposed on them by nature, as they demonstrated by increasingly perfecting their tools; hence, they transformed the natural conditions of their existence into human existence. Conversely, most of the primitive peoples seek a mode of life that makes the creation of history superfluous: in most cases, they make do with animals that are easy to capture, whereas prehistoric men had to face off against animals that were far superior to them in strength and speed.[69]

At the beginning of history, there was struggle, the will to control living conditions, the transformation and humanization of nature; but among present-day savages, there was only contentment, repetition, stagnation. In fact, according to Raphael, only the progressive peoples had a sedimented (that is, differentiated) memory. The continuity of their actions created "a sort of geology, formed layer by layer, within a country's culture," "so that the most ancient culture goes on living, inasmuch as, on the one hand, it adapts to the new historical conditions, and on the other, exerts its influence."[70] Savages were thus "fossils," he concluded, whereas Westerners displayed an "almost geological continuity, which proves to be elastic, compressive, eruptive." It is for this reason that the ancient traditions "always surge up anew."[71]

Hence, Max Raphael who, in *Minotaure*, harshly criticized the archaism of modern artists, could also extol the paradoxical encounter between prehistory and modernity.[72] Hostile to the idea of an atemporal prehistory, he proposed an approach to art historians and prehistorians based on "two opposing starting points in time": "One is situated in the most ancient art we know of (but which we cannot consider the absolute origin of art); the other, on the contrary, concerns contemporary art. Indeed, only very close contact with contemporary art can prevent us from being caught in the trap of the classification of styles, which takes into account neither art nor history."[73] Modern artists' long-term efforts to undermine aesthetic norms would now work in prehistoric art's favor, helping art historians and prehistorians to observe parietal painting without imposing on it the evolutionist and idealist prejudices characteristic of stylistic analyses. Modern artists provided the tools for seeing the symbolic universe of prehistory, since like it, they worked to destroy atemporality and ideality.

After the discovery of the Lascaux cave and the end of World War II, Georges Bataille, too, would theorize the irreducible difference between prehistoric peoples and savages. Modern man could identify with the Lascaux paintings because they had nothing to do with the art of savages. Bataille conceded that some primitive men were close to prehistoric peoples in terms of their living conditions—the cold, hunting—but these were purely material conditions: "What is missing from these primitives of modern times," he said, "is the outpouring, the fervor, of a creative awakening, by virtue of which Lascaux man is our fellow creature and not that of the Aborigine."[74] And Bataille disputed evolutionism by postulating a complexity and religiosity at the origin of history similar to those of Western cultural production and about which the "primitives of modern times" had not the slightest idea: "Lascaux cave brings to mind those churches where the magic liturgies assemble hundreds of performers, those theaters where we hear in reverence Mozart's most beautiful works. Poetic genius is found in all peoples, it is common to all men, but it manifested itself in Lascaux with the sort of commotion that is unique to birth."[75]

The Possibility of a Different History: Utopia
Prehistory served to strengthen the moderns' historical sense—but only thanks to its irreducibility to historicist history, which threatened to do away with any propensity for action and for evolutionist (linear, causal, cumulative) history. This was one of the most interesting paradoxes of the function prehistory assumed in the modern imaginary. Prehistory guaranteed the viability of history precisely by being irreducible to it because of its lack of chronologies, names, events, and written documents. Even now, we live and write in the wake of that reorganization of historical meaning that occurred in the 1920s to 1950s, when a sort of tenacious and general distrust toward history found expression. As Hayden White has shown, many writers have "implicitly condemned the historical consciousness by suggesting the essential contemporaneity of all significant human experience."[76] Many artists, as well, idealized the simultaneity that stemmed from the means of communication and transportation, a major consequence of technology. As André Malraux's *Museum without Walls* would later do, the English Vorticist movement and the poet T. S. Eliot transformed simultaneity into a sort of compression of history as a whole into the present.

In 1914, the Vorticist sculptor Henri Gaudier-Brzeska expounded his notion of "vortex" in the review *BLAST*. A metaphor for the primordial vital principle, the vortex first manifested itself in "the decoration of the Dordogne caverns": "Early stone-age man disputed the earth with animals. His livelihood depended on the hazards of the hunt—his greatest victory the domestication of a few species. Out of the minds primordially preoccupied with animals Font-de-Gaume gained its procession of horses carved in the rock. The driving power was life in the absolute—the plastic expression the fruitful sphere."[77] In the essay Ezra Pound composed on the sculptor's brief life (he died at the front), we read that Brzeska had a great admiration for cave art, which he understood to be the perfect product of the "intensity of existence," of a "manhood" "strained to the highest potential" and endowed with "brutal" energy. Later, history arrived, with its highs and lows, its periodic variations in the service of deities or of man himself. Its last variation:

> WE the moderns: Epstein, Brancusi, Archipenko, Dunikowski, Modigliani, and myself, through the incessant struggle in the complex city, have likewise to spend much energy. The knowledge of our civilization embraces the world, we have mastered the elements. We have been influenced by what we liked most . . . we have made a combination of all the possible shaped masses—concentrating them to express our abstract thoughts of conscious superiority Will and consciousness are our VORTEX.[78]

History, then, formed a vortex whose motionless center, a sort of eternal present, was occupied by the Vorticist artists. They had finally acquired consciousness of that "vortex," in which prehistoric men had only lived. Just after World War I, with less cannibalistic frenzy, the young T. S. Eliot also affirmed the presence of the past in any art worthy of the name. It was possible to hold onto a certain "historical sense," he conceded, but only on the condition that the connection be made between the more or less remote past and the present. In the work of a poet, Eliot continued, the best and most personal parts "may be those in which the dead poets, his ancestors, assert their immortality most vigorously." But these ancestors had to be far away so as to discourage the servile reproduction of the past and encourage its "presence": "The historical sense involves a perception, not only of the pastness of the past, but of its presence." And he added: "The past should be altered by the present as much as the present is directed by the past." Furthermore, "this change is a development which abandons nothing *en route*, which does not superannuate either Shakespeare, or Homer, or the rock drawing of the Magdelenian draughtsman. . . . The difference between the present and the past is that the conscious present is an awareness of the past in a way and to an extent which the past's awareness of itself cannot show."[79]

In their passionate quest for ancestors other than their own immediate forebears, moderns found an exceptional ally in remote prehistory. As Bataille wrote in various texts about Lascaux, the advantage of that alternative genealogy, which compressed time, rather than space, was to provide respectable "ancestors" with whom it was possible to identify. That identification also involved "race." In addition, the moderns, who had felt the "burden of history," found the least burdensome of ancestors in prehistory: lacunary and enigmatic, that past was indefinitely open to the interpretations of the present. Finally, prehistory, a gap without a referent, reminded modernity of its own genealogical situation: at a time when the moderns were drawing the consequences of the loss of origin and of the original, prehistory itself appeared to be without organic origin or succession. The late nineteenth century was haunted by the famous expression *prolem sine matre creatam*, which Ovid had used in *Metamorphoses* to characterize the birth of the young Erichthonius, generated by the sperm of Hephaestus that had fallen on the ground. Arnauld Pierre reconstituted that genealogy without birth, which linked the mechanomorphic works of the avant-garde to the son of the god of fire and technology.[80] And it was of course when the question urgently arose of the originality of art and of the artist that prehistory added its own enigmas: when Salomon Reinach used the expression *prolem sine matre creatam* to describe that incomprehensible art born of no one and engendering no one, he was echoing Symbolist writers such as Huysmans, who during the same years wrote of a technology that would allow the human species to emancipate itself from the uterus. For a large proportion of modern artists, prehistory was an "origin" precisely because of its lacunae. It was also the most ancient reference to the fundamentally reduced and limited character of the questions preoccupying the species, despite continual changes in historical conditions. That resemblance was thus not rooted in blood and soil at all, but rather in the imaginary of the present seizing on the first traces of human activity, in keeping with every individual's history and biography.

Also during the 1920s to 1950s, years marked by the advent of Fascism and Nazism in Germany, Ernst Bloch conceived the possibility of a history "with multiple tempos and spaces," one that would be able to point out modes of action that neither capitalism nor vulgar Marxism had "extirpated." Nostalgia was not condemned to serve Fascism; it could also foster a "revolutionary" impulse. "Needs and resources of olden times consequently break through the relativism of general lassitude like magma through a thin crust":[81] Bloch hoped to extract these resources from the grip of Fascism and convert them into revolution. He wrote that there were things that have not yet happened and from which it was important to extract the elements that are both stateless and hostile to capitalism. With regard to morbid uses of the past — visible, for example, in Gottfried Benn's "Geology of the Ego" — Bloch had to circumvent two obstacles: historicism and Marxist evolutionism. For Bloch, as for Walter Benjamin, Carl Einstein, and Bataille, the redefinition of the past was generated in large measure by the urgency of defining revolutionary avenues that offered alternatives to Marxism. It was within this framework that the political thought of these authors intersected the philosophy of "regression." Because despite the lightning speed of the evolution of material and technological conditions with which reality could generate archaic psychic and cultural forms, it was necessary to draw from their symbolic resources in order to symbolize reality and change it.

What was true of the individual, namely, the consistently latent character of regression, was thus also true for mass society. This was a further condition indispensable for modernity's appropriation of prehistory: the possibility that society and civilization en masse could project themselves onto it. Modes of production, behaviors, psyches, and modern art itself, despite appearances and despite the great speed of technological evolution, all showed signs of regression toward an archaic, even prehistoric past. Did not mass production bring to mind the serial production of artifacts in protohistoric and prehistoric tribal cultures? Was not the anonymity that artists had pretended to adopt since cubism specific to both primitive cultures and the machine age? And had not automatism, an indubitable sign of backwardness, taken two extreme forms: on the one hand, the gestures of workers, the movement of crowds, and the reception of advertising, and on the other, the unconscious and instinctive attitude attributed to animals and all primitive people, whether in time or space? Everything that was happening to society was akin to what Théodule Ribot had written regarding the individual's psychic and organic life: society devolved from "the unstable to the stable," that is, to the "instinctive sense memory fixed in the organism."[82] For that very reason, as an unexpected dialectical effect, modernity became better and better at generating what was assumed to be its opposite.

Formal Resemblance: The End and the Beginning
Prehistory entered modernist works of art by two paths that would eventually intersect: formal analogy and functional analogy. Some artists, Amédée Ozenfant no doubt being the most eloquent example, emphasized the universalism emanating from prehistoric art, which was also found, with the same purity, in certain forms and practices of modern art.[83]

The theory of a resemblance between the beginning and the end of time was generally based on a psychic and conceptual analogy. The archaeologist Deonna took a particular interest in that view.[84] Invoking the "law of regression," he, too, noted that "nature tends to move backward, to repeat itself indefinitely," and argued that "the same is true for the phenomena of the intelligence: there are mental regressions, and in the presence of modes of activity simple in appearance, we must always wonder whether this is an original simplicity or if there are not vestiges of a past complexity."[85] The idea that history is cyclical would soon become one of the means by which moderns would connect with prehistory, but without giving up their own historicity. Art historians and archaeologists appealed to the idea of the law of regression to explain the evolution of artifacts and styles when amnesia, voluntary or not, about a technique resulted in the return of an archaic style. In response to this simplification in reverse, which blurred the distinction between the elementary and the end, Father Breuil argued that "no art is completely untainted by its more or less complex origins."[86] For Focillon, as well, "the beginning seeks itself out with hesitation, and the decline interrogates itself with anxiety."[87] For Deonna, no "hiatus" separated the Paleolithic from the Neolithic (which was simply a "return" of prehistory's first tentative efforts at abstraction, now definitively lost). That was because "in the entire history of art, there are periods when artists, having grown weary of traditions, return to previous formulas." "Let us distinguish, among these *voluntary regressions*, those that repeat previous forms by *deliberate imitation* from those that rediscover them *unconsciously*."[88] The works of the cubists and the misnamed "Futurists" were excellent examples "of these regressions attributable to an excess of skill, culminating in childish forms from which art had freed itself centuries ago."[89] The same formal expressions that had characterized, first, an origin that was definitively lost, then the Neolithic, then the archaic, and finally the art of late antiquity — marked by the barbarian invasions — also emerged among contemporary artists.[90] In 1914, Deonna again repeated that "the paintings of the cubists, who transform nature into a pile of geometric blocks, and those of the Futurists, who accumulate errors in perspective and want to renounce all traditions," are only "another example of these regressions, which, in eras of advanced technology, lead the artist back to forms long since overtaken by the progress of evolution."[91]

As for Einstein, in 1930, he hailed the salutary simplification he perceived in the art of Miró, who avoided "comparative metamorphosis," that is, the hybridization of eras and styles, "in favor of a simpler ignorance," a "stripping bare": "Prehistoric simplicity. We are becoming increasingly archaic. The end returns to the beginning."[92] A little later, Carola Giedion-Welcker, a critic and historian

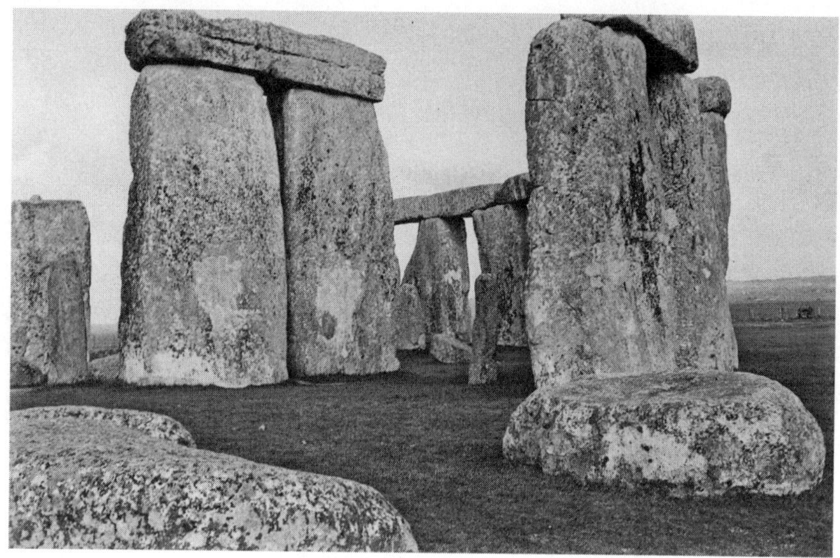

Figure 3.8. Stonehenge, photographs by
Carola Giedion-Welcker and Walter Gropius.
© The gta Archives.

of modern art, related her "visit to Stonehenge and Carnac," made in the company of her husband, the architectural historian Sigfried Giedion, and the architect Walter Gropius (Figure 3.8). Referring to the "artistic perfection" of the rows of stones, she established an analogy with Brancusi's sculptures, quoting this sentence from the sculptor: "Simplicity is not a beginning in art; we arrive at simplicity in spite of ourselves, by moving closer to the real meaning of things."[93] Appealing to Vico's cyclical history in support of her interpretation of the art of her time, she mentioned Joyce's debt to the Italian philosopher, but also his invention, at the beginning of *Finnegans Wake* (then called "Work in Progress"), of an incomprehensible conversation between two stones, obviously inspired by the famous megalithic site. A few years later, the book she devoted to modern sculpture emphasized that the connections between modern art and primitive art (in the broad sense of the term: savage, archaic, and prehistoric) lay neither in "romanticism" nor in "nostalgia": "It may not be immaterial that a century as conscious as our own, with a civilization so complex and highly developed, shows such keen sympathy for the unsophisticated emotions and direct artistic creations of mythic times."[94] The "two poles, opposed chronologically and culturally," had ultimately converged in the "perfection of sculptural forms that highly specialized modern tools have revealed to us but which, in the simplicity of their form, remind us of the dawn of art."[95] In conclusion, linear evolutionism, so incompatible with prehistory, was invalidated by the superior simplicity of the era of technology, which had the capacity to create universal forms anew. It was as if history had finally generated a "first language," by definition exempt from all cultural particularism: modernism itself. The same familiar logic of a cycle returning to the beginning is also found in *The Eternal Present*, a work stemming from the meticulous research on cave art conducted by Sigfried Giedion.[96]

The cyclical regression of moderns discovering prehistory offered a way out of the aporias inherent in evolutionism. The principal advantage of regressive temporality was that it helped modernity escape the ontological impasse to which nineteenth-century evolutionism and historicism condemned it. In the first place, regression stood opposed to the cold and quasi-mechanical history of evolutionism without being arbitrary. On the contrary, regression guaranteed the coherence of a *law* that was supposedly much more impersonal and verifiable. In the second place, in promising a new beginning to the latecomers of modernity, it broke evolutionism's exclusive hold on novelty and difference. In the third place, whereas evolutionism was grounded in the exteriority of nature, regression might be a more human law: evolutionism proved its validity through the rapid transformation of technology, while regression found its way into the most intimate part of human beings: their memory. Finally, if evolutionism was by definition cumulative and capitalizable, compensating for the myriad extinctions of natural species and human inventions by the automatic march of progress, regression bore the

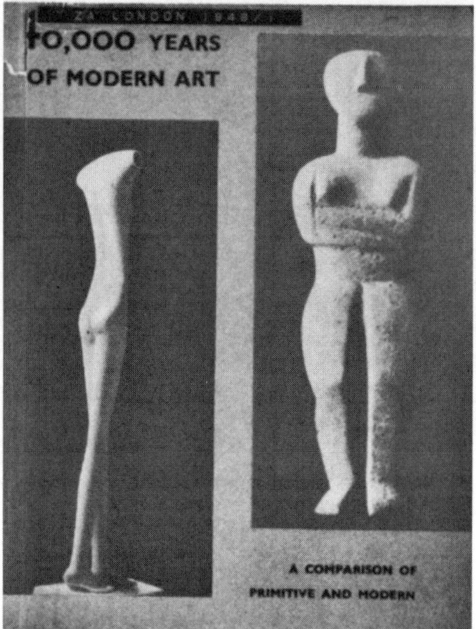

Figure 3.9. W. G. Archer, Robert Melville, and Herbert Read, *40,000 Years of Modern Art: A Comparison of Primitive and Modern*, exhibition catalogue (London: Institute of Contemporary Arts, 1948).

marks of both anxiety and hope: regression absorbed all the material gains of modernity, including obsolescence, but only so that they would be forgotten and then recalled by involuntary memory.

Apprenticeship in the Second Prehistory:
Walter Benjamin, ICA, and Leo Frobenius
In the wake of World War II, the Institute of Contemporary Art (ICA), established in London to inform the general public, held the exhibition *40,000 Years of Modern Art* (Figure 3.9). Its chief organizers, the art historian Herbert Read and the critic, collector, and artist Roland Penrose, emphasized that this title was not meant to be "frivolous"[97] or "paradoxical."[98] Its aim was to show that "modern art discovers that its own interpretation of reality is more akin to the art of forty thousand years ago than to the stylized conventionalism of the late Victorians."[99] Read maintained that "one of the strange facts that emerges is that some of the earliest exhibits, particularly the mammoth ivory Venus

from the caves of the Dordogne," appear to be "the most modern in conception."[100] Read attempted to explain this "modern art," which according to him was "a good forty thousand years old":

> It is not merely that certain modern artists have at certain periods of their development been influenced by primitive art — that is rather something obvious and not requiring an exhibition to demonstrate. What is not obvious is that which we shall call the universality of art, and, more particularly, the eternal recurrence of certain phenomena in art, which, on their appearance are labeled "modern." Modern, in this sense, is not a comparative term — we are not contrasting the modern with the ancient, present with past, or individual talent with tradition. Rather we are suggesting that like conditions produce like effects, and, more specifically, that there are conditions in modern life which have produced effects only to be seen in primitive epochs. To define these conditions would be a vain exercise of dogmatism, for they are archetypal, and buried deep in the unconscious. But generally they can be described as a vague sense of insecurity, a cosmic anxiety (*Angst*, as the Existentialists call it), feelings and intuitions that demand expression in abstract or unnaturalistic forms.[101]

Modernity, having come off its chronological hinges, ceased to be an objective period that had ended, becoming a subjective temporality through and through — an inevitability engraved in the unconscious and reawakened under precise conditions, a universal and eternal recurrence of the most ancient in the present and vice versa. As a result, Read might just as easily have put prehistory in the place of the modern and claimed that it extended into the present.

Read's thinking was, of course, undermined by a contradiction: Was it possible to reconcile the evolutionism that governed nature and civilization with the principle of an eternal recurrence of art forms? Regression and periodic repetition satisfied that dual requirement. It was because modernity was the sophisticated product of a long and complex history that it produced psychic situations similar to those of prehistory: filled with anxiety, worry, and insecurity, technological modernity — the recent war being its grimmest manifestation — called for the same archetypal forms engraved in humankind's memory ever since the first men had begun to confront "first" nature. Read appealed to Worringer to express his vision of prehistory's modernity and of modernity's prehistoricity: "primitive man" reacted to his anxiety in the face of the immensity, indetermination, and mutability of space by reducing it to abstract, inorganic, and immutable forms. Within the context of the exhibition *40,000 Years of Modern Art*, Anton Ehrenzweig—whose *Hidden Order of Art* left its mark on many postwar artists, including Robert Smithson—would give a lecture on "the unconscious meaning of primitive and modern art," identifiable, according to him, in the "distorted" forms they all shared.[102] It hardly mattered, after all, whether modern artists were familiar with prehistoric art, since the similar conditions of the two periods had inevitably impelled them, almost unknowingly, to create forms analogous to those of prehistory. But which forms, exactly? The portrayal of prehistory in *40,000 Years of Modern Art* was utterly skewed. Drawing on the enormous prehistoric archival collection that Leo Frobenius had assembled over the course of his expeditions, the London organizers ignored the copies of works whose naturalism had unsettled those who discovered them. They preferred the rock paintings from the Australian continent, whose character was more fantastical and thus better suited to the spirit of modern art, especially surrealism. Lascaux was the only exception to that rule: recently discovered just as World War II was beginning, the Lascaux cave, depicted in color photographs, conveyed the traumatic aura of the war.

Unlike the ICA group, Walter Benjamin was interested not in pure form, but in the function of art, which he believed to be "mimetic" by definition. The supposed naturalism of parietal art, therefore, was no obstacle to his assertion of its paradoxical affinity with the artistic practices of his time. It was in "The Work of Art in the Age of Mechanical Reproduction" that Benjamin developed his notion of art history as a "working out of the tension" between "two poles": the work's "cult value" and its "exhibition value." The first version of this text (1935) viewed parietal art as a pure manifestation of cult value: "What mattered was their existence, not their being on view." And what sort of art could more strikingly attest to this value than the paintings buried and sealed for millenniums under the earth and suddenly discovered, as if to reveal to moderns what they definitively lacked? Benjamin argued that "the elk portrayed by the man of the Stone Age on the walls of his cave was an instrument of magic. He did expose it to his fellow men, but in the main it was meant for the spirits."[103]

Benjamin began with the observation that the operative mode of art within the realm of reproducibility had undergone a reversal in the modern era. The ubiquity and immediate accessibility of the work of art was now just as absolute as cult value had been in prehistoric times. He noted that the opposite ends of time and the values of art that corresponded to them converged to the point of coinciding:

> This is comparable to the situation of the work of art in prehistoric times when, by the absolute emphasis on its cult value, it was, first and foremost, an instrument of magic. Only later did it come to be recognized as a work of art. In the same way today, by the absolute emphasis on its exhibition value the work of art becomes a creation with entirely new functions, among which the one we are conscious of, the artistic function, later may be recognized as incidental.[104]

Modernity, after long living under the reign of aestheticism, ultimately discovered its "incidental" character and "parasitical" existence.[105] In the same way, prehistory was supposed to have made the work of art obsolete, once it had fulfilled its function. The ages at the two extremes converged in their destruction of aestheticism: externally very dissimilar, the beginning and the end of time dovetailed into each other in accordance with a dialectical reversal in which sophistication of form, over a long process of secularization and thanks to the modern conditions of production, could culminate in an original configuration of art's "cult" value, emancipated from any trace of religion and resolutely political.

The major danger inherent in the material and formal possibilities of the regime of reproducibility was the belief in a possible return to the experience of authenticity inherent in the "cult." Not only did Fascist propaganda provide proof of that misappropriation to the advantage of the "leader," but some major representatives of the film industry were also converting the regime of reproducibility into an aura-producing machine. It does Benjamin's thinking no disservice to detect a similar misappropriation on the part of ICA leaders or the anthropologist Frobenius of the idea of prehistory and of prehistoric artifacts and copies. Even though Frobenius's writings had contributed toward Benjamin's understanding of the prehistoric period, the German philosopher did not believe that prehistory contained the authenticity that his own time had to recapture at all cost. And though, like the London modernists, he set out to articulate a new relationship between art and the masses, his notion of the modalities that would establish that relationship and of the role the idea of prehistory would play in it was different from theirs in every respect.

What interested Benjamin about prehistory was the practical role of art, which he did not for a moment separate from form. For him, as for Leroi-Gourhan later on, the function was served by the form, which was itself imprinted with the function:

> Prehistoric art made use of certain notations in the service of magic practice. In some cases these notations probably comprised the actual performing of magical acts . . . in others, they gave instructions for such procedures . . . and in still others, they provided objects for magic contemplation. . . . The subjects for these notations were humans and their environment, which were depicted according to the requirements of a society whose technology existed only in fusion with ritual.[106]

In other words, parietal representation transmitted the codes of magic rites and those of the relationship men maintained with their environment, including their hunting techniques. Far from being naturalistic, it was a "notation," that is, an arbitrary, but effective transcription—a writing, but one that preserved and transmitted the gestures and techniques of the body. These men, far from confining themselves to the vague animistic evocation of animal spirits, as Read and Ehrenzweig supposed, had fashioned a language that was by definition codified, structured, and social. In a fragment he recorded in 1936, Benjamin made his interpretation of parietal art even more explicit:

We know that the human body is the first material on which mimetic power is exerted, and greater emphasis ought to be placed on taking advantage of it for the prehistory of the arts than we have done so far. We ought to wonder whether the most ancient mimesis of objects in the representation of dances and pictures does not rest in large measure on mimesis of the operations during which primitive man came into contact with these objects. Perhaps Stone Age man's drawings of elk were unsurpassed only because the hand that manipulated the stylus still remembered the bow with which it had shot the animal.[107]

The indistinction between magic, art, and technology was of course at a great remove from modern technology, which, Benjamin hastened to add, was radically opposed to primitive technology by virtue of its "emancipated" character. But that "emancipation" had two different aspects:

> It stands opposed to present-day society as a second nature, no less elementary than the nature available to primitive society, as the economic crises and wars prove. . . . Man, who invented it, but who has not been its master for a long time, needs an apprenticeship similar to the one he needed vis-à-vis first nature. This applies especially to film. *The function of film is to train human beings in the apperceptions and reactions needed to deal with a vast apparatus whose role in their lives is expanding almost daily.* The historical task in whose service film finds its true meaning is to make the vast technological apparatus of our era the object of human innervation.[108]

That lack of control over technology rendered it distant and unmasterable, just as nature itself had formerly been. Directly inspired by Lukács, Benjamin conceived of modern technology as a "second nature." What did he mean by that? He meant that technology, having achieved its most sophisticated form, reverted to the sphere of the irrational and the rudimentary: the economic crisis of 1929, the war that had just ended, and the one on the horizon were concrete historical manifestations of what had previously been blind natural phenomena. The dialectical reversal Benjamin theorized was derived from that transformation of technology into a natural force that moderns had to learn to tame. Whereas Max Ernst had represented an inert world long since deserted by "human innervation," Benjamin assigned art the role of humanly innervating second nature, that is, of making all human beings once again capable of mastering technological operations. And whereas de Chirico had chosen the contemplative conversion of second nature, Benjamin sought to show the dangers of contemplation in the age of technological reproducibility, preferring what he called "distraction"—that is, the human body's conscious and sensory openness to the real world in which it was participating. Art's former function as an "apprenticeship" and its symbolic efficacy became altogether "actual" once again, but this time, the walls of the caves were replaced by movie screens. With technology, the media changed, and with the media, modes of reception. Henceforth, formal cinematographic mechanisms, whose efficacy was increasing, thanks to the technological possibilities, could strike bodies like arrows. "Human innervation," a form of mimetic realization, signified the finality of an art whose "notations" could be transcribed on the bodies of viewers, could shape their reflexes, and could make them experience the wholly unbearable quality of reality, which they would therefore wish to change. Art in the age of revolution was shooting its arrows at viewers, inciting them to begin their "apprenticeship" with second nature.

For Benjamin, the analogy between prehistory and modernity worked in both directions. On the one hand, he was inspired by prehistory to restore the mimetic finality of art to the art of his time. On the other, his knowledge of that art, which fought against the autonomy of the object in favor of a composition conceived as an equilibrium of relationships and a chain of operations, helped him to distance prehistory from a rudimentary animism and a narrow-minded utilitarianism. Benjamin had become too conscious of the mimetic charge of form to neglect its importance for his project of political emancipation. But a dialectic based on visual analogies between forms, such as that developed by Giedion-Welcker and the representatives of British modernism, made no sense to him. Taking no special interest in the final products of these two periods so remote from each other, he focused on their mechanisms and operations, which, moreover, were dissimilar precisely because they were similarly historicized. On the one hand, the prehistoric painter, in close proximity to his art, went so far as to use his breath to paint the cave walls; on the other, the film director carved up reality the way a surgeon transects a patient's organs. In one case, there was the obsessive uniqueness of the painted or engraved figures; in the other, the obsessive multiplicity of the reproducible work of art—on the one hand, the reign of darkness; on the other, a manifold visibility that could turn into tactility. The two periods, though quite dissimilar, were united by the most important thing: they were created and received collectively, and the question of technology and art's function as an "apprenticeship" was for them an urgent matter. Hence, at a moment when Fascism threatened to complete the dehumanization of modern society wrought by capitalism, Benjamin found a privileged accomplice in the era preceding history in his efforts to defend the mere possibility of history—which meant accepting and using the technological, material, and formal possibilities of the present. He based his project on the radical dissimilarity between the two eras, the only guarantee of a mode of thought in and for history, as opposed to the reproduction of the same through myth. Hence, it was Benjamin's preoccupation with historicity that fundamentally distinguished his prehistory from Frobenius's and from that of the British modernists, who strove at all cost to convert exhibition value into cult value.

No one confronted the problem of prehistory's reproducibility in a manner as continuous and complex as Frobenius. In exhaustively archiving the rock and cave art of Africa, Europe, and Australia, he had to make sensitive choices about the nature of his copies, and later, about how they were exhibited in several places, including the Musée d'Ethnographie in Paris in 1933 and the Museum of Modern Art in New York in 1937.[109] Frobenius refused to archive the parietal images by means of photography alone. He formed teams of painters, composed primarily of women, who were given the task of restoring the *authenticity* of the parietal images (Figures 3.10 and 3.11). According to

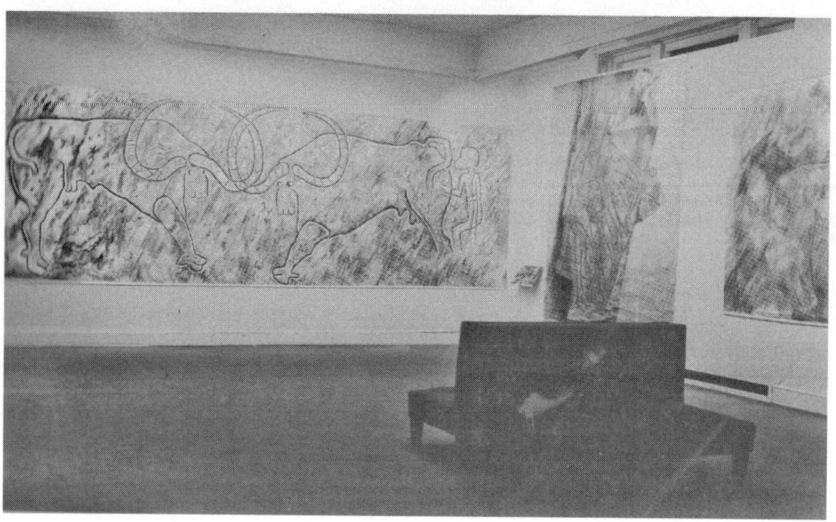

Figure 3.10. Leo Frobenius and Douglas Fox,
Prehistoric Rock Pictures in Europe and Africa.
Museum of Modern Art, New York, Archives,
1937. Photograph of the exhibition, Frobenius-
Institute, Frankfurt. Photo: Soichi Sunami.
Digital image © The Museum of Modern Art/
Licensed by SCALA/Art Resource, NY.

him, the camera, though he used it as a complement to his other practices, did not lend itself to distinguishing between what is essential
and what is not. He undoubtedly believed, like Baudelaire, that photographs flatten and level out objects, making them appear equivalent to one another. As an intrinsically modern instrument, photography seemed ill-suited to the art of prehistory, whereas painting
remained a medium that inspired empathy and an immersion in the
work and that made the artist sensitive to a bygone era. That is why
Frobenius opted without hesitation for copies of parietal and rock art
in their current state, rather than the reconstitution of a hypothetical
original state. The copy, by incorporating the action of time into a
single image, was able to restore its authenticity. Any restoration of

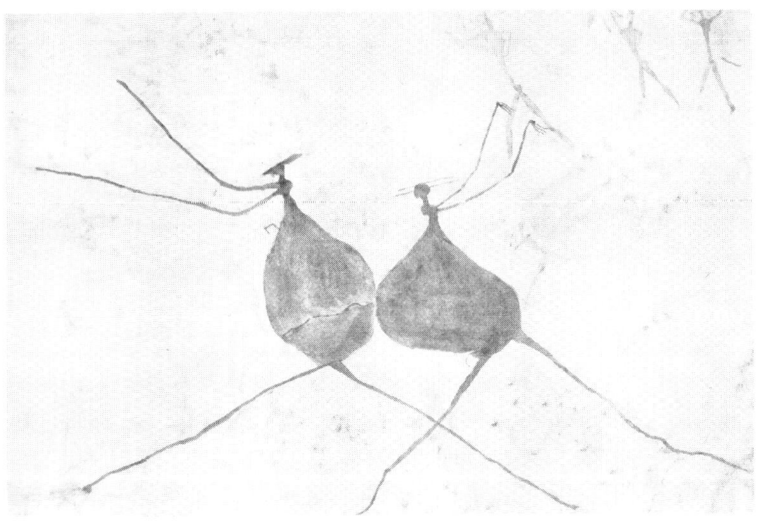

an ideal or conjectural origin would have been artificial; so long as it conveyed the temporal distance that separated it from the present, so long as it was charged with the *capital of time*, which gave it legitimacy, the origin spoke.

The same logic of a return to the cult, as it was imagined to have existed in prehistory and in traditional societies, was at work in the exhibition *40,000 Years of Modern Art*. There, prehistory became a literally *untouchable* sphere, but one ready to welcome an anxious modernity and deliver it from its troubles. Each of the archival photographs from the exhibition shows a single viewer, totally separated from the outside world, contemplating an equally isolated artifact.[110] The body of each viewer—a man or woman of any age—absorbed in the aesthetic experience, appears rigid, as if the object of contemplation had pumped out all its vital force. Around the viewer, the space is immersed in darkness. Penrose explained: "One

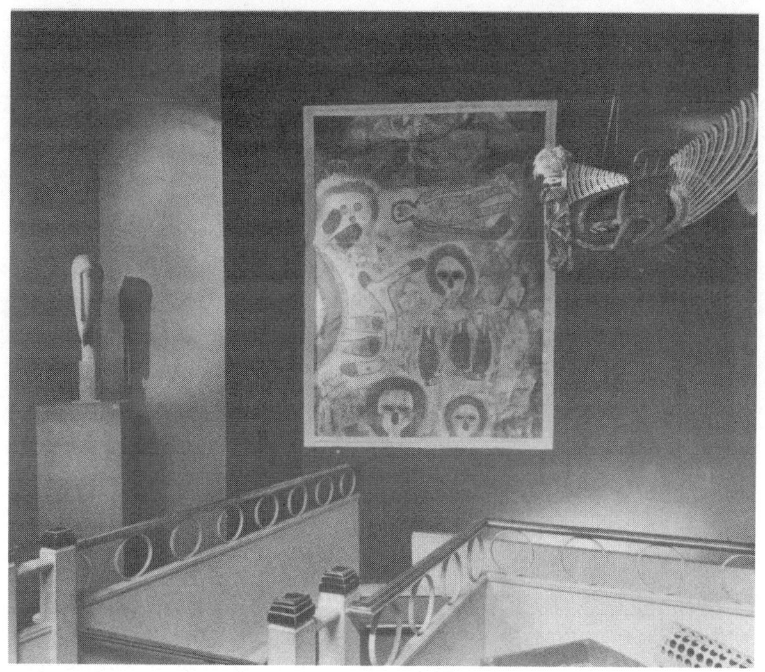

Figure 3.12. Hanging, Frobenius's copies of
parietal art. See W. G. Archer, Robert Melville,
and Herbert Read, *40,000 Years of Modern
Art: A Comparison of Primitive and Modern*,
exhibition catalogue (London: Institute of Contemporary Arts, 1948), p. 38.

thing we had to devise was some means of not putting everything
behind glass and yet making it inaccessible to those fingers that were
going to touch the things otherwise. . . . And so we put great banks
of pebbles in front of them so that anybody trying to get near enough
would be heard at least walking across the pebbles."[111] Because the
objects were not placed behind glass, a sense of immediacy was created in the relation the viewer was supposed to establish with the
object. An aesthetic experience was converted into a cult experience
(Figure 3.12). Unlike the reproducible works of modernity, no one

was supposed to touch the artifacts. That same logic was pursued in a film of the exhibition that George Hoellering made at night, when the exhibition was closed to the public. The preface to the film stated:

> This film is a journey of exploration into the unfamiliar but exciting world of primitive and modern art. The works you will see come from Europe, Africa, Australia, and Oceania. The oldest one among them was carved from the tusk of the now extinct mammoth, in the pre-historic Europe of about 40,000 years ago. The ritual purposes for which many of the pieces were used among primitive tribes are difficult for us to understand to-day. Try, therefore, not to be too puzzled about the exact meaning of what you will see. Enjoy, rather, the strange, yet lovely, shapes of these works, and the way in which their creators have brought out the full beauty of the materials in which they worked. . . . There will be no lecturing to distract your attention. Aided by the music, the camera will be your guide on this journey through an enchanted world, where the human imagination blossoms out luxuriantly in the shapes and forms of art.[112]

Pure form was supposed to act in concert with music (specially written by the Hungarian composer László Lajtha), to the exclusion of speech. Modernity expected to recover, through the magic of the aesthetic experience, the knowledge of rites it had lost. The defamiliarization wrought by prehistory (and "primitivism" in the broad sense) was thus used as a powerful means of resacralization.

Joan Miró and Jean Dubuffet

Active Magic: Joan Miró (with Louis Aragon and Carl Einstein)
During these same years, Joan Miró organized a dazzling encounter between an *exhibited and multiple* modernity and a *unique and remote* prehistory.[113] His *Paintings* series, created in 1933 from a corresponding series, *Collages*, is a plastic reflection on the themes that preoccupied Benjamin during the same period. Miró had taken up the question of prehistory for the first time in the mid-1920s, when he was considering the possibilities that still remained for his medium after cubism, and more generally, the historical boundaries of painting, which had been blurred by mechanization. In summer 1924, he

informed Michel Leiris of his furious destruction of old works and his creation of new ones. Unable to call them "canvases" or "paintings," he designated them with an "X." This phase lasted more than ten years. One sentence, unverifiable, but credible, described the compulsive transformations involved in that work and set out to explain it briefly: "I want to assassinate painting."[114] This assassination was manifested in the intensity, variety, and conflict of his operative modes over the years: he adopted various forms, invented various codes and types of signs, stubbornly mixing media (painting, poetry, sculpture) and establishing contradictory relationships with the history of painting.[115] Between 1930 and 1932, Miró produced many objects meant to be placed on a horizontal surface or hung on a wall. He used timeless materials such as wood, stone, and bone and modern machine-made objects, combining painted and more or less "biomorphic" figures with real objects. Like the "Xs," these, too, were indeterminate objects, straddling natural kingdoms, media, and temporalities. In 1934, Pierre Guéguen wrote: "Having emerged revitalized from the school of the object, a prolific source for his later works," Miró had been able to formulate "active magic in his paintings," in which "the whole modern industrial bazaar will come to prehistoric drawings, with a shared sensuality, a kinship by axis, instinct, and cruelty forming a bridge between them."[116] Guéguen was not mistaken: according to Miró, despite the challenge issued by technical reproducibility and despite the political emergency of the 1930s and 1940s, painting could continue to practice the "active magic" that prehistoric people had attributed to it.

Between January and June 1933, Miró elaborated a series of eighteen pairs of works, each pair consisting of a collage and a painting. They were all humbly titled *Collage* or *Painting*; only the date of the pair's completion was indicated by the painter at the bottom of the collage (Figures 3.13 and 3.14). Miró had obtained a standard sheet of Ingres paper (18 5/8 x 13 7/8 in.), to which he affixed reproductions of objects and very occasionally words, all cut out from newspaper advertisements and sales catalogues. Each object was cut out hastily, usually with a good-sized margin left around it. For the most

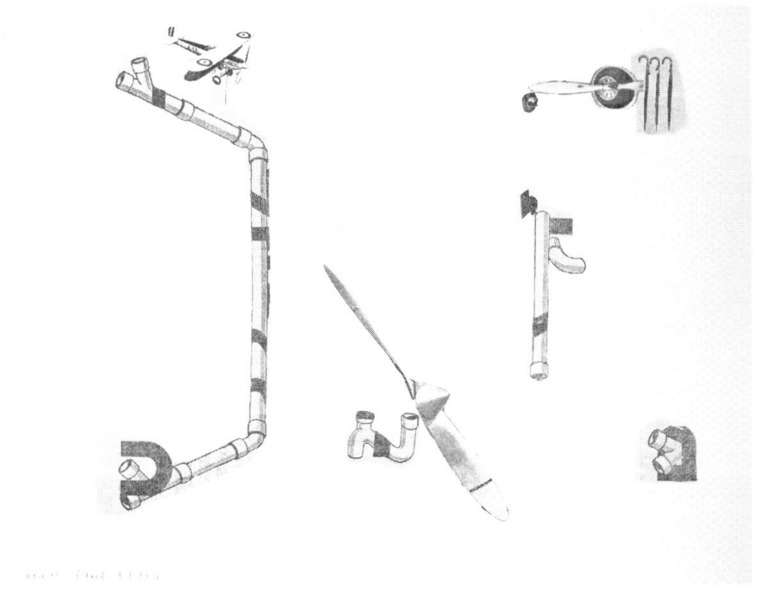

part, these were mechanical products and tools: tubes, propellers, telescopes, various utensils, machines, a hammer and wheelbarrow, but also merchandise such as eyeglasses, stockings, purses, shoes, or a corset being tried on by a woman. A few objects were much less typical: ropes, corners of decorative frames, and other elements, rendered abstract or unidentifiable by decontextualization. In the composition of the pictures, a great deal of space was left between the different elements, and the white surface of the paper was as important as the affixed objects. Miró's attention to the question of scale was very obvious, the objects being in several different, often microscopic formats. They were almost always photogravures, visually similar to drawings. Each collage was completed in a single day,

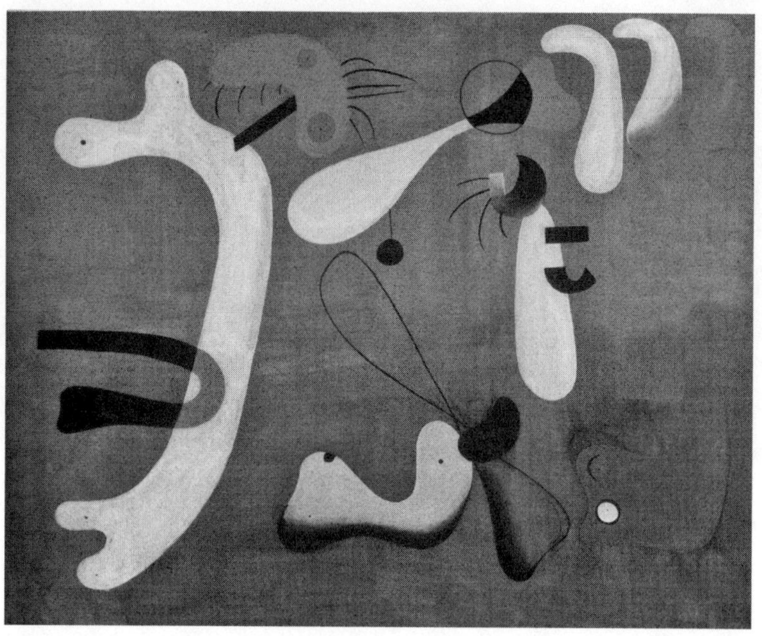

Figure 3.14. Joan Miró, *Painting*, March 8, 1933.
Oil on canvas, 51⅜×64¼ in. Philadelphia
Museum of Art, A. E. Gallatin Collection. Photo:
© Successió Miró/ARS, NY/ADAGP, Paris 2021.

and it was only after the entire series was completed that Miró set out
to transpose it, piece by piece, into a corresponding series of paintings. He worked furiously from March 3 to June 13, 1933, to complete
his eighteen pictures.

Everything about the making of these collages attests to the mechanization of life and painting: the standardization of the medium, the
reproducibility of the images that were cut out and then affixed,
that of the objects represented, the cutting and collaging operation
itself, the daily rhythm of the artist's work, and the protocol of dating
each of the resulting collages and paintings. Finally, the "division" of
labor the painter followed involved rigorous planning of the operational process. As others have noted, the images Miró chose from

Catalan newspapers such as *La Publicitat* and *La Vanguardia* were usually arranged the length of the page in a conspicuously serial manner and organized into vertical columns, as if they were lists of words and objects, which were treated in the same manner.[117] The spirit of these collages is similar to that of Max Ernst's "Overpaintings": there is the same photogravure aesthetic, the same taxonomic seriality, and the same banality. There is an important difference, however: Ernst, to make the reification of these images visible, transformed what had been "knowledge" into inert materials, whereas Miró moved in the opposite direction. The second stage of his work would result in the reenchantment of the fossils of modernity.

Unlike the collages, the canvases did not all have identical dimensions. They were quite large, sometimes nearly six and a half feet wide and five feet tall. In transposing the collages, Miró was especially inspired by the spatial relations between the affixed objects. They would be transformed into more or less biomorphic forms—bones, detached members, unidentifiable single-cell organisms, unknown hybrids. These forms suggest both life and death, the organic and the mineral. The images transposed from the collage to the painting were larger, and their depiction was more frontal. Sometimes saturated with color and sometimes simply drawn, each of them appeared to float separately in an indeterminate, but hermetically closed space, as in a dream. The ground was covered with large zones of colors, often very dark and of irregular density. In some cases, their edges faded away as the objects slipped into one another; in others, the juxtaposition of the various colors was terribly conspicuous, when, for example, the contours of a brown zone crudely spilled over into the green zone. The principal colors for the floating shapes were black and white, interrupted on occasion by the primary colors: red, yellow, and blue. It was a hallucinatory and hermetic world, possessing both the fluidity of a liquid and the irregularity of a rock wall. In addition, the tension between the void silhouettes and the solid painted forms on a dark ground suggests parietal figures. In 1929, the critic Waldemar George pointed out the prehistoric character of the obsessional and spellbinding space of these "vast and empty

paintings, a physical vacuity easily offset by their internal magic."
And he added:

> Spellbound, the viewer/reader submits to the demonic or divine activity of
> the painter, a witch or thaumaturge. Miró defies space. He evokes it, encloses
> it in the frames of his lyrical images. He never manages to make that space
> concrete and material. He confines himself to creating dread and a mental
> image of space-as-depth, of the ideal, intangible, and abstract space. I tend to
> prefer his barbarian works, which resuscitate a rudimentary world and a time
> when men identified the forces of nature with the gods. To them, Miró added
> the troglodytes from the cave of Altamira. He has their strange capacity for
> abstraction, if not their superstitious faith, and at least their cosmic sense and
> ingenious intuition for mystery.[118]

But others have pointed out the obsessiveness of Miró's paintings,
which in fact he did not conceal from himself. In a later interview
(1948), he described the relationship between the collages and paintings of 1933 as an attempt to escape the grip of hallucination by taking
real things as a starting point:

> Little by little I liberated myself from dependence on hallucinations and
> turned toward forms suggested by physical elements, but still fairly different
> from realism. In 1933, for example, I habitually tore crude forms out of newspa-
> pers and affixed them to cardboard. Day after day I accumulated these forms.
> When the collages were finished, they served as my starting point for the
> paintings. I did not copy the collages, I simply let them suggest forms to me.[119]

Rejecting both realism and pure hallucination, Miró chose advertising images, specters of objects: intermediate objects, halfway
between physical reality and hallucination. Once the objects were
cut out, their spectral power increased and formed a disparate, but
potentially meaningful composition. As in de Chirico's or Ernst's
art, the heterogeneity of these forms attracted the eye, obliged it
to linger, even as the ample white space functioned as a screen over
which the gaze could wander and produce its hallucinations. Using
these compositions to support visual latency and suggestions, Miró
resorted to a classic procedure he had already often used, like many

other artists during these years, which achieved its full value among prehistorians speculating on the possible origin of art.

As soon as humankind's antiquity was recognized, Boucher de Perthes made early man an artist. The "stone figures" reproduced by the dozens in his book were "peculiarly abraded pebbles," "fantastic apparitions of fruit, birds, reptiles, saurians, fish, mammals," "inert forms that had never lived, recalling in their oddity life forms," which "must have struck those early peoples as they strike us."[120] Luquet, who had a greater affinity with Miró, attacked theories that made this art a kind of magic, when magic was at best a consequence, a misappropriation, or a reuse of artistic representation and not its origin at all.[121] What might the very first form have been? The first artists found around them and within themselves what had not existed before them, in keeping with a process that Luquet called "self-imitation" and that Miró might also have termed "hallucination": they must have recognized figures in the haphazard shapes of matter or in the traces of the ordinary course of life and then attempted to reproduce them, following the orderly stages of an evolution that has never varied since.

But why, as Guéguen wrote, did "the whole modern industrial bazaar . . . come to prehistoric drawings"? For years, despite the "assassination of painting" Miró perpetrated, painting survived in his hands, though it bore the marks of struggle. Nevertheless, the *Collages* and *Paintings* series of 1933 was undoubtedly a riposte to a specific assault from the outside, Louis Aragon's *In Defiance of Painting*, in particular, a book written for a 1930 exhibition of the same name. In this text, Aragon attributed an extremely ambivalent place to Miró, writing that he could "imagine a time when painters, who even now no longer grind their own colors, will find it childish and undignified to spread the paint themselves," a time when they "won't even have others spread the color for them anymore, won't even draw anymore. Collage gives us a foretaste of that time."[122] For the poet, the Hegelian autosuppression of painting began with the standardization of colors, which led to Marcel Duchamp's ready-mades; it continued with the mechanization of gestures, adopted in multiple ways by the European avant-garde; and it would without a doubt end with the medium's disappearance, pure and simple. Collages, which retained the flatness of the painting surface, but resorted to extrapictorial means to constitute it, attested to that potential self-dissolution. Miró did not hesitate to incorporate collage into his practice in several ways, but he hardly concurred with that deterministic dialectic. He retained the tension and conflict of the dialectic, but not its sublation.

In 1930, shortly before Aragon organized his "defiance of painting" exhibition, Miró had exhibited his recent works twice in succession in the same gallery, dividing them between paintings and collages.[123] His series *Dutch Interiors* (1928) was inspired by Dutch realist painting, whereas according to Carl Einstein, the idea of a return of prehistory could be found in the collages (1929). This was a dialectical conflict: a dialogue with the quintessence of the realist vision versus an extreme minimalism; an explosion of color, versus images produced with the linear apparatus of cubism in its technical version (cardboard, thread, metals); the history of painting, versus an unlearning of that history; and finally, Miró's prolific virtuosity versus his intentional maladroitness and bricolage. The *Collages* and *Paintings* series of 1933 cut short that dialectical conflict while intensifying it: the two practices were no longer parallel, but convergent, so much so that the paintings internalized the collages. When the conflict was over, the painting was transformed by the collage almost as much as the collage was transformed by the painting. At the end of the process, the collage was not discarded, but rather carefully archived and preserved, a stubborn reminder that it was the remote past of the painting, even its origin. But the painting nonetheless embraced its magic efficacy, the very thing that Aragon had so strongly contested in *In Defiance of Painting*: with the collages, Miró wrote, "the new magicians have reinvented incantation."[124]

Surrealism was an attempt to reenchant the world, and its "illuminations"[125] were "of this world," unlike those that Christianity had offered.[126] Aragon was certain that the "collage" and its derivatives were a magic practice capable of transforming the world materially, penetrating to its deepest foundations, that is, its political foundations. And just as Benjamin would soon view the new artistic forms arising from reproducibility and intended for the masses as the dialectical product of an inverted aestheticism, Aragon maintained that the painters who had invented and practiced collage were both the progeny and the murderers of aestheticism and individualism. The "modern collage," he wrote, required attention

> for its concentrated aspect, for what lies at the opposite extreme from paint-
> ing. For … the human possibility it represents … for its restoration of the true
> sense of the old pictorial approach, which prevents the painter from indulging
> in narcissism, in art for art's sake, by returning him to the magic practices
> that are the origin and justification for the plastic representations defended
> by several religions.[127]

Painting had thus hit rock bottom, and the only world possible opened up through practices that reconnected with the magic of the "origin," the justification for any plastic representation. Indeed, "the origin" was truly active, unbeknown to painters grappling with collage: "Yes," continued Aragon, "painters repeat mechanically the magic gestures and ceremonies without attributing them the slightest meaning, having forgotten the reason for them. They are interested only in the beauty of the ceremonial."[128] Painters, though they believed they were practicing art for art's sake, unconsciously reconnected with the magic of the origin. The same gestures that were simply beautiful for some were thus efficacious for others.

Aragon was far from the only one to see aestheticizing art as a weakened and unconscious survival of magic. Examples abound. Folklore studies would support these theories, which postulated that art itself, as operation, is never free of the debt it owes to its origins. The folklorist Andrew Lang, we recall, was the first to dispute the hypothesis that the earliest art was merely a source of pleasure: "It does not seem at all unlikely that we inherit the love, the disinterested love, of imitative art from very remote ancestors, whose habits of imitation had a direct, interested and practical purpose."[129] In formulating this view, Reinach would exclaim: "The idea that art is mere play may be only a modern prejudice; originally, it was a ritual and magic operation. When we speak at present of 'the magic of art,' we do not know how right we are."[130] Not only was art itself a survival of magic, but the widespread expression "magic of art" was a fossil. That was exactly Freud's idea in *Totem and Taboo* when he construed art as the last survival of magic animism in modern society: "We rightly speak of the magic of art and compare the artist with a magician. But this comparison is perhaps more important than it claims to be. Art, which certainly did not begin as art for art's sake, originally served tendencies which to-day have for the greater part ceased to exist. Among these we may suspect various magic intentions."[131] The artists themselves seized on this discourse, as we saw with Picasso in conversation with Brassaï, who would define graffiti, ordinarily considered a playful activity linked to the expression of the unconscious, as follows: "How hard the stone! How rudimentary the instruments! What does it matter! It is no longer a question of playing, but of mastering the frenzy of the unconscious." He added elsewhere that the adjective "charming" acquired a literal meaning in graffiti, because the wall casts a spell and exorcizes simultaneously.[132]

Aragon, too, thought that artists such as Max Ernst effected this return to magic while adapting it to the practices "of this world": impersonal, prosaic, and poor. As for Miró, with his two successive exhibitions of paintings and collages, he seemed incapable of appearing *simultaneously* old and young, prehistoric and modern; he remained torn between the two poles of magic and aestheticism, at the opposite ends of the timeline. "A strange man, that Miró," Aragon exclaimed. Perceiving him and Brancusi as the height of bourgeois aestheticism, a mode of painting "that turns toward the comfortable," he added mildly: "It is difficult to say whether Miró's collages imitate his paintings or whether it was rather his paintings that imitated in advance the collage effect."[133] But the problem raised for Aragon, which kept him from being decisive, was precisely what interested Miró: when he sensed the end of painting, he looked to prehistory for the tension needed to be creative and hence to convince himself that his art was not aestheticizing, but rather terribly efficacious. That crisis was assuredly the source of modern art.

In transferring the tools and products of mechanization to pictorial compositions, Miró, unlike Benjamin and Aragon, affirmed that painting still had a long life ahead of it and that nothing prevented it from continuing to take on the magic function characteristic of it in the age of cave dwellers. Nevertheless, it had to adapt that function to the "cruelty" of the present, no longer the cruelty of wild beasts and raging elements, but that of the rationalization of a technology definitively pervading art and daily life. When Aragon claimed that "painting has not always existed, an origin can be assigned to it,"[134] thereby suggesting above all that it would end, Miró took him at his word: the earliest painting had a richer meaning and could absolutely "irrigate" the most recent painting. And he was not alone in thinking so.[135]

At the dawn of the 1930s, prehistory took on a dual function: it served as a metaphor for terror and menace, but also for an open future. Little remained of the Arcadia of the first prehistorians. Artists and critics took a greater interest in monumental cave art stemming from vanished collectivities whose ghosts still haunted their walls; they advanced interpretations of their techniques, which were transferred willy-nilly from manuals of ethnology to past phenomena and present experiences. Rather than linger on the naturalism of these images, they identified their function, because it involved "action." Rather than take shelter in atemporality, they clung to the possibility and the beginning of history. As René Crevel recalled in "The Childhood of Art," published in the very first issue of the surrealist review *Minotaure* in 1933: "The first drawing by man was an animal silhouette on the wall of a cave. The authoritarian flint with which he engraved it asserted with a truly seismic point the will—stemming from necessity—to metamorphose an object of anxiety into an object of utility."[136] According to Crevel, the surrealists had turned that practice to their own account: their objects had a symbolic function, and though of course they were not intended to be consumed, they "reanimated concretely, without metaphor, the cadavers of things." In an allusion to Dada or expressionism, he added: "After petrifying mirrors and distorting mirrors, surrealist objects became metamorphosing mirrors," because "desire" alone "knows how to give an irradiated, irradiating thickness to time."[137]

For Miró and his contemporaries, what changed with industry and mass consumption was that the objects of utility had now become objects of anxiety. Other artists, such as the Dadaist George Grosz and the Mexican muralist Diego Rivera, adhered to a more orthodox Marxism, turning to parietal art to prove the materialist and tendential character of all art since its origins.[138] Miró, by contrast, in choosing the images in which these objects seemed least useful and hence most exchangeable, underscored their anxiogenic charge. In his paintings, these objects were transformed into intermediate beings, between life and death, between the three natural kingdoms, and they surged up from the "thickness" of time, but they did so as an echo of their intermediate origin as simulacra and products—they were, so to speak, fetishes that began to "dance." There was something both disturbing and hypnotic about his compositions. The gaze that lingered on them attempted to identify their elements: Were they the vestiges or the beginnings of a world? Fossils, or new lives just coming into being? These elements had absorbed what Crevel called "the irradiated, irradiating thickness of time"; they emerged from distant memory and recent memory, but they also opened onto the future. Not without irony, Miró rediscovered the dilemmas that had obsessed archaeologists and art historians for so long: Was art originally "skeuomorphic," a survival of technical processes, as Gottfried Semper and his disciples believed, or was it "biomorphic," an imitation of life, as van de Velde and many others thought? (The terms "biomorphic" and "physicomorphic," which refer to the imitation of animate objects, as opposed to made objects, were coined by Alfred C. Haddon in his *Evolution in Art* and would be found again a few decades later in the writings of the minimalist Carl Andre, who speculated on the differences between his abstract art, inspired by Neolithic works, and pop art, whose origin was "skeumorphic.")[139] Miró reanimated bits of machines, assimilating them to the human experience. His magic, defined as a transformation of matter, consisted of removing the natural inertia of these objects and bringing them to life through the viewer's contemplation of the picture. This idea remained with him for a long time—in 1940, for example, when he vowed to follow this injunction in one of his drawings: "There are too many abstract elements like Sonia Arp [*sic*], eliminate many of them and humanize the others especially / / always think of Iberian prehistoric paintings and those of Las Batuecas, of which there are reproductions in the history of Spain that Alexandre owns."[140]

Miró did not achieve that "humanization" of alienating objects solely through biomorphosis; his composition was also based on "analogy." In 1926, Michel Leiris used an analogy to extol analogy:

> Formerly, the anxious tribes of men would bury their nail peelings and their fallen hairs in fear of sorcery; for they believed that these particles of themselves contained their whole vital spirit. Later, geologists succeeded in reconstructing the enormous skeletons of extinct animals from a piece of bone, buried perhaps for several millennia. Today, there is a new race of men who, from the double world of flesh and spirit, retain only the traces, vestiges of structures which a valueless intelligence can never render form.... There is no question of proving, constructing. The state of mind is a new fetishism which demands nothing but the perfect adhesion of the heart to any sort of object, free of symbol, but reflecting like the tiniest cell the infinite harmony of all the universe.[141]

For Leiris, then, the same absolute synecdoche — the universe within a minuscule cell — was active in the magic practices of primitive societies, in Cuvier's comparative anatomy, and in Miró's art. But whereas Cuvier's simple reconstitution intended to "prove" and "construct," Miró's analogical use of prehistory composed heterogeneous sets that had no established symbolic value, but were capable of forcing the "adherence" of the psyche and of giving rise to free interpretations. Therein lay the difference, precisely, between the reconstitution of prehistory and its fabrication. In the latter case, the first prehistory was definitively lost, and the only remaining possibility was to fabricate a new one from modern ruins.

From Death to Life, from History to the Present: Jean Dubuffet
In 1946, in the aftermath of World War II, Jean Dubuffet held an exhibition titled *Mirobolus, Macadam et Cie, Hautes Pâtes* at the Galerie

René Drouin in Paris. There, the painter exhibited thick, roughly textured paintings obtained by mixing together materials such as gravel, asphalt, and dirt, materials never before used in the practice of painting. Taking inspiration from the heterogeneous reservoir of primitive forms and especially from graffiti, he engraved and immediately covered with paint his compact mix to obtain schematic, flat, and generally frontal figures that filled the entire surface of the canvas. In this work, wall and ground moved considerably closer to each other. Asphalt, gravel, and sand, materials that our feet are forever walking across hastily and mechanically, were here transposed to vertical surfaces, which the eyes were meant to rove over at great length. That conversion of the sense experience specific to horizontality into an aesthetic experience conditioned by the body's vertical posture was the fundamental method Dubuffet used in pursuit of enchantment. In this, he was greatly inspired by both geological and artistic prehistory.[142]

In fact, no painter had ever given such structural and formal importance to the materiality of earth, as the descriptions in the catalogue confirm. They abound in geological metaphors that are usually impossible to untangle from the factual description of the materials used. Metaphor and literal meaning are placed side by side: Dubuffet, for example, describes the "hilly, uneven base," the "layers of sticky lime," and the "bluish ore" that provide a glimpse of a human figure "done in fossil-imprint style" and another "figure" that, "like a large stone in limestone colors flecked with pale ocher and pinkish gray, seemingly iridescent and scratched, shows various colors rising up in a thousand places from the layers underneath."[143] Language itself thus replicates the metamorphosis of matter into form and of ground into wall.[144] Dubuffet's work consisted of a constant *transposition* of words and things. Because it was viscerally material, his painting became all the more analogical, capable of showing at once the *hautes pâtes* and the ground and walls their configurations evoke. In an imaginary interview he wrote in the 1980s, his fictive interlocutor asked him whether he was a "caveman." Dubuffet replied: "The time of the cavemen is very close to us, ten or twenty thousand years ago, it went by fast, nothing changes much in such a short interval. A few hundreds of generations—that's just yesterday. The grandfather might have chosen the wrong path at a crossroads. Let's turn around, it's time, let's explore a different way."[145] In a certain sense, his pictorial use of geology and of prehistoric art pursued to the letter his desire to "turn around," to take a "different way" in space and time.

A few visitors to the 1946 exhibition noted the analogy between the *hautes pâtes* and parietal paintings. In her excellent study of Jean Fautrier and Dubuffet, Rachel Perry reconstituted the series of allusions critics had made to "a return to three thousand years ago" or the "wondrous impression" made on one of them, in 1941, "in Lascaux cave, when Father Breuil discovered these primitive frescoes in front of us."[146] In February 1946, Dubuffet replied to his friend Jean Paulhan: "You are well aware that I subscribe fully to what you say about the rock drawings and paintings. A volume of *Art brut* with a preface you've written would be good. I'll work on putting it together."[147] Although the volume in question never appeared, this statement clearly shows that Dubuffet was interested in parietal art during these decisive years. Above all, it was a symptom of Dubuffet's methodological wager, of that "different way" he would refer to in retrospect forty years later. In his project to transfer painting to ground and aesthetics to geology and archaeology, he must have encountered parietal painting. At issue here, however, is less a positive and deliberate resemblance than a derivative resemblance, the result of an alteration similar to the one Bataille described when he criticized Luquet's theory of the origin of art.[148] Rather than affirming a conceptual or visual resemblance to some object or another, Dubuffet's new object, the pictorial medium itself, affirmed and stabilized itself after a series of destructive acts as important as the product resulting from them.

One way to understand what that derivative resemblance meant is to "turn back," to transpose ourselves from modern painting to prehistory. The intellectual project of the *hautes pâtes* was methodologically opposed to the separation between archaeology and mural painting that still prevailed among prehistorians in 1946. In fact, after long inhibiting the acknowledgment of parietal painting's authenticity in the late nineteenth century, the disjunction between archaeological horizontality and aesthetic verticality persisted in the field of prehistory, but in reverse: that disjunction no longer riveted people's eyes to the ground, it fixed them to the walls. It determined the interpretive grids of parietal painting — including at Lascaux — independently of its geological, paleontological, and archaeological site, going so far as to destroy the latter, to make it as easy as possible to contemplate these now sacrosanct works.[149] Dubuffet, unfamiliar with the questions of prehistorians, encountered them in an objective, chance encounter and without necessarily being conscious of them, simply by stirring up the doxas of his own "discipline" (if that term can be used for this enemy of "asphyxiating culture"). For as it happens, the field of art has a certain coherence, in spite of it all, a priori in its most remote facets. Prehistorians, no less than the art milieu proper, bowed to aestheticism, as we may observe in following the discourses and practices directed at the individualization of the parietal figures. In the late nineteenth century, it had been necessary to lift one's eyes from the ground simply to see the parietal paintings on the wall and, soon after, to recognize their aesthetic value. Fifty years later, Dubuffet, in a challenge to aestheticism, brought contemplation back to the ground.[150] To go back in time ("let's turn back, it's time"), it was necessary above all to change one's position in space.

In his introduction to the exhibition catalogue, the critic Michel Tapié, head of the Foyer de l'Art Brut, was the first to note the analogy between Dubuffet's practice and that of the cave dwellers, even while introducing the "third party" in that relationship, namely, history. Tapié revived the interpretation of both prehistoric and present-day paintings as a form of magic — a theory we have already encountered in the context of the 1930s: "In Dubuffet, we again find, with all the appeal of the current thing, the full magico-incantatory charm of these richly rudimentary signs that a stupidly resigned skepticism had discreetly buried: graffiti in the caves, dolmens, statue menhirs, and mother goddesses with their generous functionality."[151] When art was expelled from aestheticizing museums and official history (written, normative, and connected with the big names), its magic efficacy was enhanced. As Dubuffet wrote to Paulhan, taking up the classic Nietzschean theme of a history that sucks the lifeblood out of life and the present: "I believe history and a taste for history are among the most pernicious things in existence. I find that everywhere, in every domain, people fabricate premeditated history, instead of living and acting.... That is the abominable vice of our age, and it also mucks up everything."[152]

The painter energetically revived the antihistorical discourse of the interwar period, taking it to its extreme limit. This was not unusual in those years and was consistent with his defense of an "oral" art without a "name," without an "object," and rooted in the pure present. Paulhan saw fit to explain "the new beginning of painting originating from the materials, with all the adventures that follow from them (accidents, slides, incidents, magic signs)," in terms of the need to pass through "one's stone age again from time to time" so as not to become calcified in a disembodied formalism. But Dubuffet overstated the case: there was no past, no future, nothing but the most up-to-date, individual, and perishable present. "I am a presentist," he would repeat once again in the introduction to volume 1 of his writings, which Hubert Damisch published in 1967. But for him, the present had lasted several millenniums: compared with the hundreds of millions of years that the earth had existed and the myriads of organisms that had left their traces there, human history was only a fragile present.[153] Technological inventions and events mattered little, periodization even less, consisting only of lines drawn on "shifting soil."[154] All these tools for historical differentiation were destroyed by the observation that human beings are all alike: life on the scale of a single man is equivalent to life on the scale of the entire species, and vice versa. In 1947, he wrote of the anonymous statues he baptized "Barbus Müller":

> What does it matter to us if the artist was bureaucratic or mean, young or old? There are truly no grounds for paying attention to these little circumstances.... And whether he was living or dead and for how long, we don't care. Between a contemporary and someone from the last century, or a companion

of Clovis or of the great fossil saurians, there is only a negligible difference. It is utterly wrong to take an interest in these details. It's a waste of time. One man or another, it comes down to the same thing.[155]

And because human beings are almost alike, their art is nearly so, as well. When Dubuffet's imaginary interlocutor asked him in "Broken Sticks" whether, "in the whole development of our art history," he might be especially fond of certain periods, "archaic or otherwise," he replied that "except for variations in the superficial form, which modify the balance of things very little, art was constantly repetitive, from the origins until the start of our century. It seems to me, in short, to have varied practically not at all since the most ancient times we know of until a recent date."[156]

In 1944, Dubuffet wrote Paulhan that he thought well of his law of a cyclical history and of an era that returned on a regular basis, a history made to the measure of the gods. Who else could have the privilege of contemplating from on high the works and days of men, observing their disappearances and returns? But he countered with a better law, because "made to the measure of men":

> My law is that there are no precedents for anything, every man who comes into the world is the first man who comes into the world, every ball that every girl rushes to attend for the first time is the first ball that has ever taken place. Go tell that little girl that there have been first balls like that since the world has been a world, she won't listen to you, she won't hear you in any case, and then, what difference can that make for her? That observation is not useful for her. Even if that truth, which is not her own, were fully set in her mind, she could no longer dance, she could no longer live a moment longer? It's the law of the gods, you must not eat of that apple.[157]

Then the artist signed his name: "Jean Dubuffet, Actualist."

That actualism was the immediate consequence of his fierce antirealism, based on the primacy of subjectivity: the world barely existed so long as a being could not experience it; man did not live or die as a species, but as an individual; the earth might be curved or flat, depending on the lived experience of the moment; the world was "human" or "froggish" depending on whether the subject who visualized it was a man or a frog; the infinite timescale was reduced to the scale of a single life; and the history of thousands of years was summed up in the present. That radical subjectivism was by definition opposed to any universalist notion of history. But paradoxically, in Dubuffet, subjectivism and universalism converged to the point of coinciding: every being was at once individual and generic; every present was an origin, and the origin present. The painter conceived of one of the most universalistic projects ever in the history of Western art, wishing precisely to eliminate the gap between prehistory and his own art. Here is what he wrote of his musical experiments, which he would soon compare to his painting experiments:

> In my music, I wanted to put myself in the position of a man from fifty thousand years ago, one who knew nothing of Western music and who would invent a music for himself that had no references, no disciplines, nothing that could prevent him from expressing himself in utter freedom for his own pleasure. That is exactly what I was trying to do in my painting, except that I know painting, I studied it — Western painting from the most recent centuries or the most recent millenniums, I know it perfectly well — and I wanted to forget it deliberately, knowingly, whereas I do not know music, and that is what gave me a certain advantage in my musical experiments.[158]

Dubuffet's radical subjectivism and its historical implications were linked to an extreme functionalization of painting, which he aspired to transform into a tool of fascination, first for himself and then for the viewer. That aim to use art as bewitchment was intimately linked to his hatred of history and involved in great part geology and prehistoric art, which were becoming increasingly inextricable in his works, as inextricable as figure and ground in his pictures. In 1950, Dubuffet accentuated the geological nature of his paintings. His "geological landscapes" covered almost the entire surface, allowing only a band of sky to appear in the upper part of the picture (in the manner of *Bibémus Quarries*). These compositions, more formless and with an even thicker impasto than the *hautes pâtes*, though done in oil paint, amplified the perceptual ambiguities by the

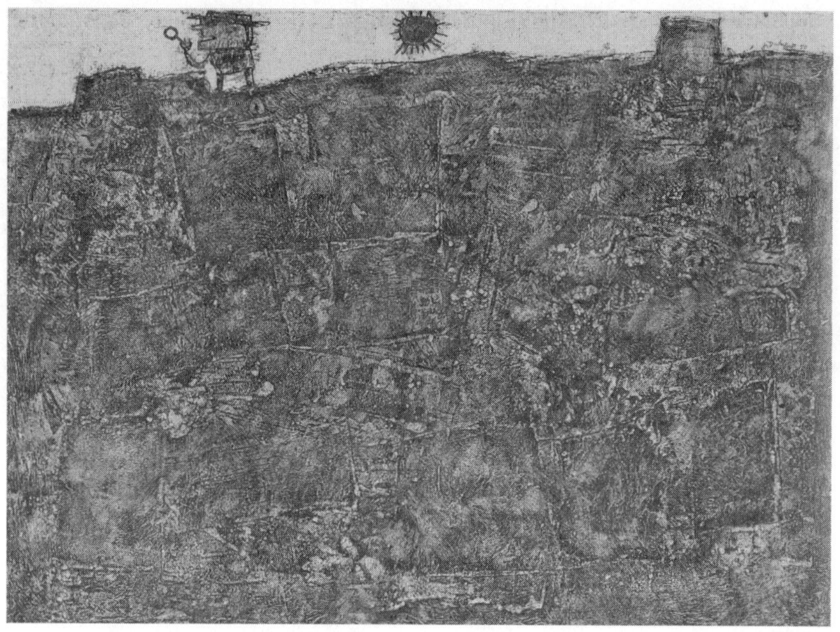

Figure 3.15. Jean Dubuffet, *The Geologist*,
1950. Oil on canvas, 37⅞ × 50⅞ in.
Private collection. Photo: © 2021 ARS,
NY / ADAGP, Paris.

absence of finished forms and the suggestion of at least two spatiotemporal scales. The forms in "fossil-imprint style," exhibited from
1946 on, reduced somewhat more the metaphorical distance from
their signified, since these incomplete and indeterminate forms literally represented fossils. With the geological landscapes, Dubuffet experimented with a scale he set about to "keep uncertain, off-
balance," to evoke simultaneously "a vast expanse" and a "minuscule
ground area," a "dehumanizing" or "metaphysical" direction and an
"interventionist" and "humanizing" direction.[159] *The Geologist* (1950)
could be perceived horizontally or vertically: as a "plot of land" or as a
"vertical cross-section underground," as suggested by the minuscule
walking figure (Figure 3.15).[160] But a man walking on a plot of land

"made to his measure," displaced onto the crest of a geological cross-section, became tragic and grotesque. It was the interplay between these two simultaneous scales, human and geological, domesticated and wild, that ultimately produced Dubuffet's presentist temporality: on the geological scale, the man had not had time to take a step. The French painter, an "applauder" or "celebrator,"[161] in his own words, was diametrically opposed to Smithson, given his melancholic pathos, and he made every fossil observed and recognized into a symbolic form. Obviously, the true geologist in Dubuffet's paintings was the viewer herself: it was up to her to extract the fossils from their mineral shroud in order to "actualize" them as artistic forms. The transition from geology (supremely indifferent to man) to artistic prehistory occurred through that umpteenth act of recognition that Dubuffet asked of the viewer. This was a new reversal and a new "way": whereas the *hautes pâtes* series pulled aesthetics downward, the geological landscapes awaited aesthetic reactivation to be brought back to life. It was recognition that reactivated, on the one hand, the imagined birth of art, when the first man had given a name to some accidental tracing in matter, and on the other, the identification and legitimization of parietal art by moderns, who were finally ready to *see* the figures on the cave walls. But Dubuffet definitively broke with any utilitarian notion of the image. Defining aesthetic vision as a matter of "fascination" between the painter and the viewer, as a "ruse" or even a "hunt,"[162] he cast the viewer into the abyss of the image so that she might lend it her being. In a classic hypnotic process, the painting became a closed circuit that switched off the outside world. The mineral matter was transmuted into an "immaterial world that lives in the human mind: a tumultuous disorder of images, images being born, images fading away, overlapping and intermingling, debris of memories of our spectacles mixed with facts that are purely cerebral and internal — visceral perhaps."[163]

A thing, even a work of art, was nothing without a human being looking at it: just a buried fossil, recognized by no one. Conversely, a picture, despite being fixed in place and framed, was not necessarily a static and well-delimited object; it could become a tool of subjective transformation, even a "posture"[164] adjusted to contradictory and constantly shifting perceptions. A piece of debris could become a sketch, and a fossil, molded automatically by chance, an intentional symbolic form. Death could become life and the past present. Far from being a passive consumer, the viewer performed the magic act of which he was also the object, cerebrally and viscerally. Dubuffet's viewer was both the first viewer and the first artist: "Every man who comes into the world is the first man who comes into the world," he wrote to Paulhan—the first to observe a stone, to recognize it as a form, to detach a singularity from the mineral homogeneity. The viewer dug to the bottom of the picture and discovered the buried figure there in exactly the same way as the artist Antonin Juritzsky, alias Juva, a major forger of prehistoric objects. In Levallois, he said, he had discovered two hundred "figure stones" that he had actually made himself.[165] In 1948, Dubuffet spoke of Juva's activity as a sculptor, which consisted of a fascinated interrogation of matter: "He questions it with a passionate avidity and curiosity, for days and weeks on end, focusing his attention with crystal-gazing tension on the slightest details of its configuration, all its blowholes, its mutilations and cracks, lending an ear to the most muted voices, to the most muffled murmurs that can obscurely be heard. The mineral answers."[166] All in all, Dubuffet did not care very much whether Juva was the creator or merely the discoverer of the "figure stones." He was both at the same time, discoverer and forger, spectator and creator. Paulhan had clearly expressed this equivalence with respect to Juva: "In short, prehistoric man may well have behaved like Juva, since Juva behaves like a prehistoric man."[167]

In the expanded contemporaneity of prehistory, where the disjunction of time is so extreme that time as a whole is encapsulated in a present moment, the different signifiers of prehistoric modernity, as we have followed them thus far, assemble and resemble one another. Fossils, figure stones, and parietal forms are linked by analogical relations of reciprocity. Dubuffet's forms refer to no prehistoric specimens in particular, but to all at once. A century after Boucher de Perthes's "figure stones," Dubuffet transformed them

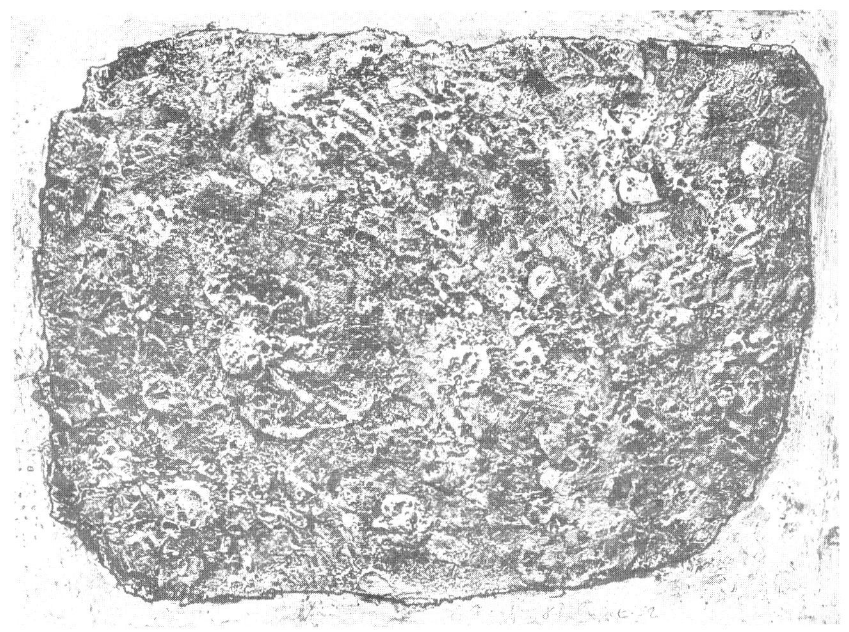

Figure 3.16. Jean Dubuffet, *Stone of Dordogne*,
June 1952. Oil on masonite, 36 × 48 in.
Dubuffet Foundation, Paris. Photo: © 2021
ARS, NY / ADAGP, Paris.

into a painting called *Stones with Figures* (1952). The engraved figure
became a pictorial surface teeming with optical suggestions. *Stone
of Dordogne* (1952) (Figure 3.16) remains forever enigmatic; the capital letter in the first word of the title makes it impossible to decide
whether it is the common noun *pierre* (stone) or the proper noun
"Pierre": Was it a mineral known as the "Dordogne stone," or a man
by the name of Pierre whose remains had been found in Dordogne?
With the suggestive title working in tandem with the visual suggestion, the skeleton stands out almost starkly from the formless.
Finally, the evocation of Dordogne revives the idea of a prehistory
creating forms similar to those the viewer produces in looking at the
picture. And just as prehistoric men brought forth latent forms from

the cave walls, modern men brought into being the latent forms of Dubuffet's paintings.

The fascination of the gaze Dubuffet sought had as its condition, but also as its aim, the effacement of the world. This is the best way to grasp his antihistorical project, both as a desire to leave the conflicts of history behind and as a fierce rejection of any responsibility toward history. In *Contre-histoire*, Kent Mitchell Minturn emphasizes Dubuffet's and Paulhan's opposition to the Sartrean notions of the writer's political engagement and the "purification" of literature.[168] Dubuffet's obsessive defense of Céline was only one of the manifestations of his unconditional need to dissociate art and morality, even in his personal life.[169] It was after the umpteenth protest against the "patriotic" ambience of postwar France that Dubuffet wrote to Paulhan:

> As for me, what terrifies me in our century are not the crematoria and the atomic bomb. Those things seem very normal to me and terrify me not at all; but what frightens me, what gives me horrible anxiety, are the myths, the discovery made in our century of the power of myths and the means to generate them — the discovery that it is possible to invent any myth at all everywhere at every moment, for which no semblance of a foundation serves any purpose, for which no absurdity is a hindrance, so that I can, for example, launch the myth that the Notre-Dame cathedral flew away, and the thousands of Parisians who pass by that church every day will believe that it has flown away and will affirm the myth with me at the very moment they are passing in front of it.[170]

"Crematoria" and "atomic bomb" did not frighten Dubuffet at all: they were historical events he found "normal." What frightened him, by contrast, was the driving force that had generated these events: the fabrication of myths capable of making the masses *see* something entirely different from the reality, capable of creating signifiers that cover or even annihilate the referent. Yet Dubuffet's pictorial project would also consist of making people *see* things that do not exist, if only as suggestions inscribed in paint. Aware that any mechanism of fascination is a mechanism of psychic constraint, he explored the different mechanisms of sensory constraint available to painting, which had the ability to bewitch the viewer and thus transform her.[171]

Clearly, the alternative world he offered up for view had been liberated not only from the harmful power of myth, but also from all the "normal" horrors of history. Why look for a meaning in that history held together entirely by unavowed lies?

That antihistorical approach began soon after the liberation of Paris, with the *Messages* series of June 1944. Dubuffet, using newspapers as a medium or ground, took the names and events that appeared in them — the resistance in London, the labor camps, the dissolution of Vichy's Chantiers de Jeuness (Youth Camps), and so on — and rendered them illegible. In a beautiful text devoted to this series, Perry refutes the antihistorical character of the undertaking; she argues that Dubuffet sought rather to oppose epic history by means of an anonymous history of everyday life as these banal and personal messages delivered it. They would do justice to the "overlooked, trivial, boring nonevents characteristic of banal, everyday life."[172] Nevertheless, there is no trace of historicity in these *Messages* except those Dubuffet has in fact effaced, perforated, and quite simply denied.[173] In soaking, rubbing, and perforating newsprint, Dubuffet silenced the "normal" events in favor of the individual lives that would encapsulate the life of the species: waiting, departing, returning, and so on. Rather than an alternative history of everyday life, the *Messages* series inaugurated the alternative myth, the good myth of painting, the myth that killed no one and constituted a positive denouement of History "with a capital H." Soon after, the gradual geologization of his painting radicalized and completed that process while banishing any medium bearing the trace of history.

In conclusion, the actualization of prehistory provided an escape from fossilized history, but it also provided an escape from history in general. In opting not for clear objects, but for mere suggestions of objects, in choosing forms and often atemporal materials, in championing, finally, a "nameless art," Dubuffet not only opened prehistory to every present moment, he also excluded traumatic and infinitely complex history: the history of events, of names, and of a past that had happened, that had really and truly taken place, and that nothing could change, not even Dubuffet's paintings. Had he given a "name," he would have also recognized the existence of history and endowed it with the contours of an event; he would have halted the course of life and acknowledged death. Nothing had happened in recent years, nothing more, in any case, than what had been happening since the appearance of the species.

The Present

Matisse, Miró, and Dubuffet were three artists who found in prehistory symbolic procedures and forms, legends, and hypotheses that confirmed in their eyes the essential role art continued to play. In a disenchanted world, often experienced as threatening, art came to be accorded the same magic function it was assumed to have had in its first parietal manifestations. Formal resemblance, without disappearing entirely, gradually moved to the background in favor of a functional analogy. It was no longer a question of reviving forms, even less of restoring situations, but of creating syntaxes and artificial orders that alluded to prehistory and that the viewer could seize hold of physically and mentally. The viewer's participation was stimulated by the fragmentary, suggestive, and open character of the compositions. That openness of the form translated directly into an openness to the experience of time. In taking hold of fragments—effaced and indeterminate figures, scraps and fossils of modernity—these artists, like many others, signified what was definitively lost and what still remained open. Indeed, prehistory was not only past, it was also to come: the young shepherd preceded by his goats had disappeared into the cave, but he reappeared farther on in other forms and with other gestures in Matisse's painting. On Miró's surfaces, cheap merchandise had replaced the antediluvian bestiary, but it preserved the same homeopathic magic purpose.

Hence, prehistory is never free from the present: it is fertilized by the present while also fertilizing it. That is the ultimate oxymoron in the dual genetic metaphor of the "child born without a mother" and the "mother who died without a child": prehistory is a matter for the present not only because its origin and progeny remain inexplicable, but because it can exist only in the present, activated by a specific and always fleeting here and now. It is therefore as "disjunctive" as any individuality, any era, any historical narrative.

Realist artists are similar in that respect to actualist prehistorians who seek the literal meaning of the images among "savages"—living fossils of the Stone Age. These artists are concerned with resuscitating life in the present. For the three artists in this chapter, artificiality, as much as natural laws, determines human life. No resurrection is possible in a world touched by artificiality, because ruptures coexist there with the *longue durée* and difference with identity. Every present, wresting itself free from the causal grip of time, discovers in prehistory a dual rupture: the historical rupture of the revelation of an art unknown for centuries and the original and thus entirely fantasized rupture of the "first" art bursting forth. The rupture and the birth of the new join together with the *longue durée*. In a world moving at lightning speed, accelerating as rapidly toward the past as toward the future, the new is always buried under thick sediment—not only as a fossil, melancholic evidence of successive extinctions, but also as proof. So long as there are human beings, they will invent symbolic techniques to negotiate with nature, both second nature and first.

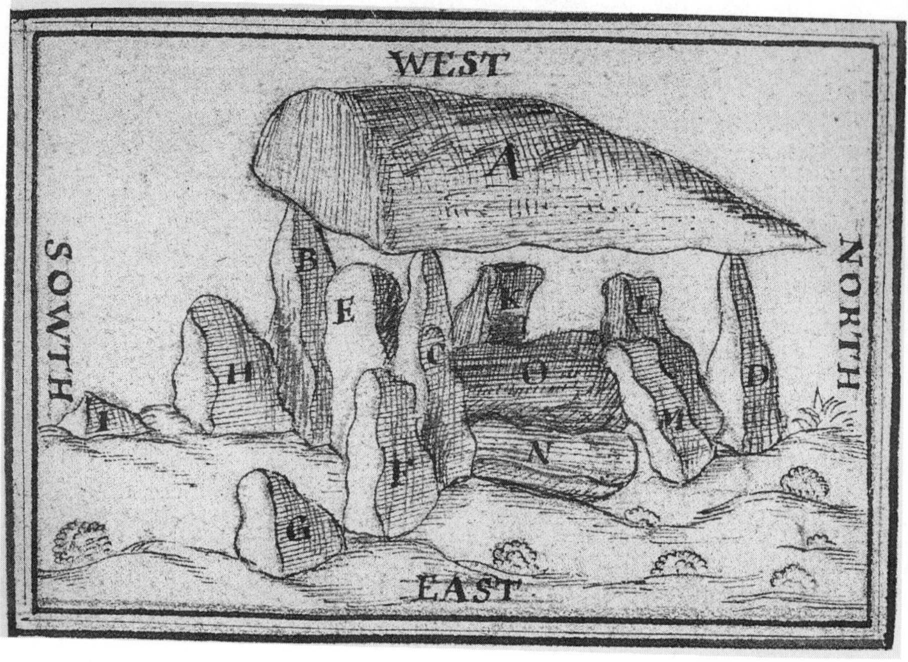

Figure 4.1. Copy of dolmen from Pentre Ifan, Pembrokeshire, Wales, 4500 BP (before the present), in George Owen of Henllys, *The Description of Pembrokeshire* (London, 1603), p. 2.

The Paradox of the Neolithic:

Rupture and Permanence,

Order and Disorder

In his study of Stonehenge in 1663, the British naturalist Walter Charleton addressed head-on the contradiction represented by that enigmatic monument. If the function of a monument is to fight against the forces of forgetfulness by allowing mortals to confer eternity in a moral sense on the men who can "instruct the present and future ages," Stonehenge was one of the monuments that "*themselves are subject to* Forgetfulness, *even while they remain.*" Because "*neither the Writings of men living in the same age, or not long after their erection, nor uncorrupted Tradition hath concurred to give them life,*" these monuments "*stand rather as dead objects of popular wonder, and occasions of Fables, than as certain records of Antiquity.*"[1] Bearing witness to a past about which it said nothing, Stonehenge was the sign of a contradiction commensurate with its extraordinary nature. Charleton expressed it clearly: "*Though this Gigantique Remain be wonderfull as well in respect of the strangeness of its Form, as of the vastness of the stones, of which it is composed,*" it has "*buried as well the Names, as Bones of those Worthies to whose memory it was consecrated.*"[2]

This is one of the key differences between the Paleolithic and the Neolithic as revealed to the imaginary of modernity (Figure 4.1): the caves sealed up their images for millenniums, only to reveal them abruptly, while the megalithic monuments dwelt in long human memory while jealously guarding the truth of their origin. By their formal organization and spatial configuration, the megaliths were mnemotechnical media without a message: Stonehenge's coherence of form implied a meaning that in the absence of any philological source remained undecodable. Its gigantic size also implied a collective subject, but one whose name was forgotten, like bones reduced to dust. Were these structures built by giants? Were they Druid temples built during the time of the Celts or Gauls? Or were they monuments constructed by ancient Danes, as Charleton hypothesized? All these fabulous conjectures filled the space left by the absence of texts and attempted to reconnect the broken thread of memory. A century later, the comte de Caylus deduced from that rupture that the monuments must have belonged to an "antiquity so remote that its traces have been lost since Roman times."[3] In the mid-eighteenth century, the word "prehistory" did not yet exist, but the idea that there might have been an era so remote that it had left few traces became conceivable within a mode of thought rooted in the materiality of objects.

The landscape paintings of the English, German, and Scandinavian Romantics such as Caspar David Friedrich, Carl Gustav Carus, and Johann Christian Dahl depicted dolmens, menhirs, and tumuli as sources of mystery, endowed, moreover, with the full symbolic charge with which the popular imagination had vested them over the years. The megaliths were so ancient and indistinguishable from glacial erratics that they seemed almost to have returned to the natural kingdom. Nevertheless, their configuration, their alignment, and their elevation, which point to a decision made in an immemorial past, made them ruins more suggestive perhaps than those of the ancient temples to the south and the cathedrals to the north. Indeed, these fragments of the past, which no one had been able to link with certainty to any belief, remained as open and uncertain as the future. They became the synecdoche for a nostalgia as tenacious as it was indeterminate, fed by the most varied legends and cultures. They also attested to a desire for the spiritualization of nature that was in perfect harmony with the Romantic project itself. These megaliths seemed to bear witness to the previous existence of a *Volk*, bound to a precise place and irreducible to the universalism of classicism. Finally, the Romantic artists, whose interest in oral culture is well known, were engrossed in these monuments, which, far from having the appearance of "documents," rose up like "occasions of Fables" and "dead objects of popular wonder," as Charleton had written.

The Political Uses of the Neolithic: Revolution and Rootedness (England, ca. 1930; Denmark, ca. 1960)

Revolution, or the Birth of the New

When twentieth-century artists took an interest in these prehistoric vestiges scattered across the landscape, their approach was not very different from that of the Romantics. Artists of the 1930s were similarly attuned to their mystery. Their own formalism, apart from any specific *istoria*, deliberately sought to reproduce the enigmatic effect that emanated from these monuments, whose message had been eroded by time.[4] The formalists of the 1930s were no less sensitive than the Romantics to the *genius loci*, to the idea of a people of builders, and to the legendary, even fairy-tale charge of the immemorial monuments. In the meantime, however, that remote period from the past, which since Lubbock's *Pre-historic Times* had been termed the "Neolithic" (in a reference to its use of polished stone), was now charged with new meanings, the most important being "revolution." The Neolithic, matrix of all the revolutions of human history, was said to have radically cut itself off from the Paleolithic past — slow, long, and as confused in its manifestations as nature itself. As the fierce leftist republican Gabriel de Mortillet had said, whereas the layers of the Paleolithic were superposed slowly and gradually, "that is no longer the case between the Magdalenian, the last of the geological eras, and the Robenhausian, the first of our present-day times. The differences between these two eras are radical: there is a true revolution." He described that revolution as having been "both physical and industrial, natural and social":[5] a total revolution. In 1955, the Marxist art historian Arnold Hauser would argue that the Neolithic was "a general turning-point in culture and civilization which represents perhaps the deepest incision in the history of the human race."[6]

"Revolution" was at issue because what was being postulated was a series of ruptures that—as Hegelianism requires—were interdependent on one another: a rupture between the technology of carved stone and that of polished stone (Figure 4.2); between the naturalistic forms of the Paleolithic and the schematism, even abstraction, of the Neolithic; between a worldview presumed to be monistic and another that was supposedly dualistic; and between the nomadic model and the sedentary model—hence, between a hunting economy and an economy based on the domestication of plants and animals. All these changes broke with immediate nature; the more the Neolithic revolution took hold, the more embedded in nature the Paleolithic became. In the same movement, when the existence of the Neolithic was postulated, the enigma of the megaliths deepened: it no longer concerned only the identity of their collective creator and the function of the monuments, it also extended to how history operated. The word "revolution" itself was a symptom of that enigma, and revolution was the exact secular equivalent of the enigma's metaphysics. Indeed, the inexplicable could occur only all of a sudden, with no one knowing from whence it came or how it came about, like a revolution. The task at hand was to grasp how history had brought about its first great mutation and to understand the modalities of the complex transition from savagery to a social construct so organized that some of its features brought to mind the modern condition. In his book *The Prehistoric*, Mortillet titled the part devoted to the Neolithic "Contemporary Man,"[7] clearly signifying that the moderns had still not left that age behind.

This was therefore another reason for the modernity of jolts and technological and social progress to project its own obsessions onto the *longue durée* of the Neolithic past. For a long time, the vast majority of prehistorians would agree on the hypothesis that there was a total discontinuity between the two ages of prehistory. As the historian Camille Jullian would expound from his lectern at the Collège de France in 1919, the Neolithic period "displays such a prodigious

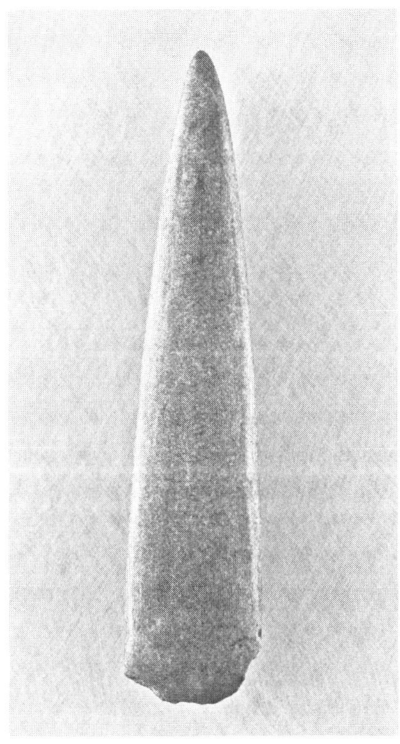

Figure 4.2. Polished ax, Sénart, Yerres, Essonne, Neolithic period. Found in Quiberon. Jadeite. Saint-Germain-en-Laye, France. Musée d'Archéologie Nationale, inv. no. 2151. Discovered 1857, acquired 1865, MAN72459. Photo: Thierry Le Mage. © RMN-Grand Palais / Art Resource, NY.

difference from the Paleolithic times that preceded it that it has sometimes been assumed there is a sort of hiatus between these two periods of the most remote past, an interruption in human life, and, as it were, an abyss in time, similar to the convulsions of nature formerly predicted by the poems of the Gallic Druids or recounted by the Greek poets."[8] "Hiatus"[9] and "abyss"[10] were two terms that, having marked the stupefying discoveries of geology and human paleontology, migrated to the lexical field of cultural history. The "sterile" layers, so called because they were devoid of cultural forms, presupposed the disasters of a cataclysmic event whose only traces were the void. The disappearance of animal species and their migration northward or eastward also suggested the possibility that the races who had until then inhabited these regions had also disappeared. Above all, it was

245

imagined that similar to a few barbarian invasions of late antiquity, there had been an invasion of new, more evolved races—"rugged conquerors, better armed for war,"[11] it was said, who might have known how to prevail against the peaceful reindeer hunters, putting an end to Arcadia. The Neolithic had begun with a cataclysmic event—war or revolution—whose driving force pushed history forward. For some, it pushed history in the right direction, because even while incarnating an ancient era in which collective memory was still steeped, it nevertheless involved a rupture and progress. In seizing on the Neolithic in the 1930s, artists and theorists thus tried to reconcile the revolutionary rupture, progress, and the permanence of a collective past—three modalities of modern times that were contradictory a priori.

The Neolithic was conceived as the first great "mutation" of human history. Whereas the very first forms of the Paleolithic were incredibly slow and inseparable from the fabric of nature, and whereas man's first deliberate gestures were definitively swallowed up by geology, the Neolithic artifacts clearly distinguished themselves from the natural world, and with a certain pride: their polish, their abstract form, and their disposition in space implied a clear distance from nature. One form of modernism, seeking above all to assert the superiority of abstraction over figurative representation, saw Paleolithic art as an original sin, while making the Neolithic the first great leap of the mind. It was in England that this tendency took hold with the greatest force. Roger Fry was not the only British formalist to privilege the Neolithic. The painter Clive Bell, who also belonged to the Bloomsbury group, noted in 1914 that "the quarrel between significance and illusion seems to be as old as art itself," as was proven by most Paleolithic art, which was as bad as it was because of its "preoccupation with exact representation." Evidently, the artisans of the Paleolithic period "had no sense of the significance of form," and that changed completely with "Neolithic art."[12] The following generation, that of Henry Moore, Barbara Hepworth, and Paul Nash, whom Herbert Read defended in writing, would not assess any differently the artistic forms of prehistory. In 1941, Moore, who was attentive enough to Paleolithic art to devote a few drawings to it and to visit many caves in France, wrote a text on the different variations of "primitive art," which he had discovered at the British Museum. But what he accorded to these minuscule figures "made 20,000 years ago" was only a certain grace. He described, for example, "a lovely tender carving of a girl's head, no bigger than one's thumbnail, and beside it female figures of very human but not copyist realism with a full richness of form, in great contrast with the more symbolic two-dimensional and inventive designs of Neolithic art."[13]

Theorists such as Herbert Kühn, Read, Max Raphael, and Hauser, who were not aesthetes to the same degree as Moore, averred that the superiority of Neolithic art was part and parcel of the superiority of Neolithic culture as a whole. An era was conceived as a totality, traversed through and through by a unique and coherent Zeitgeist. Hence, all these authors, who bore witness to an evolutionism inspired by Marxism, valorized the Neolithic for the simple reason that it had put an end to the "state of nature" and its "parasitic" economy favoring individualism and anarchy. Despite their imperfections, these first Neolithic social groups had erected collectivities into the subject of history. The Paleolithic, because it did not constitute a "society," was on the contrary a purely privative state. According to Kühn, it was "without rulers and ruled," "without past and future," fixed in the "present alone," "without religion," "without a cult," "without priests," and with a "negative spiritual life."[14] The same themes were also found in Hauser's analyses three decades later: the art historian added the "consumer-robber economy of the hunters and food gatherers" to the parasitic and anarchist imaginary.[15] Conversely, both of these authors punctuated their analyses of the Neolithic with notions that had collective connotations, writing, for example, of "symbiosis,"[16] an "economic cooperation."[17] All in all, in the face of the anomie of Paleolithic hunter-gatherers, they were quick to idealize the Neolithic, not only because it was assumed to have inaugurated collectivities and the dialectic of history, but also because it could still be perceived as the *juste milieu* that ethnologists, among them Lévi-Strauss, would later declare was shared by the Neolithic period and by some of the primitive societies they studied.[18] Neither excessively natural nor so evolved as to have clearly taken the path of entropy, the "Neolithic" constituted a utopian state of equilibrium.

Emphasis was also placed on the economy's influence on religion. Thanks to the invention of transcendence, religion entered human history by deposing utilitarian magic. Another condition of the "Neolithic revolution" emerged: the *one* — the indistinct, the immediate, the present — had to be divided into two so that the dialectic of revolutionary reason could come into being. For Kühn, the dualism of the here below and the hereafter, of body and soul, was the result of an agrarian economy that personified the earth, anticipated the change of seasons, and was fully integrated into cosmic time. Men, having emerged from the eternal present, began to impose a structure on time, a rhythm, and to invent benevolent or malevolent spirits that arbitrarily determined people's destinies. Following the same division process, magic was dematerialized, taking on the mystic form of spirits that dwelt in animals, plants, the earth, the sun, and the stars. At the same time, the symbiotic economy favored communitarian forms of religion, acts of devotion performed by priests.

Finally, the growing spiritualization of nature and the technological distance taken from it necessarily led to a different artistic vocabulary. The development of a highly intellectualized, even completely abstract language of signs was becoming possible. The historian Camille Jullian established an opposition between an art that was supposedly the direct projection of a living being and a different art, identified instead with minerality. When confronted with the images in caves, he argued, "one senses all the resources of the human being; gaze, intelligence, will, hands, and hopes are extended equally toward the beast he wants and needs."[19] But "let us then turn our eyes to the men and the ruins of Neolithic times":

> What a contrast between these paintings and these stones! . . . I do not deny that the origin of the dolmens lies in the copying of natural things, the imitation of caves and caverns. But what was copied was inanimate nature and not living nature. The force that created them is not the sight of the external thing, but an idea welling up from the depths of the soul.[20]

In his *Icon and Ideal*, Herbert Read also emphasized the evolutionary leap of Neolithic art: "plastic awareness, a unification and classification of sensuous experience."[21] Parietal painting was the automatic and individual product of an immediate vitality, but Neolithic abstraction acceded to the "inventive and comparative" processes of composition and the unity of multiplicity. Read went so far as to contradict his intellectual guide, Wilhelm Worringer, who had seen abstraction as the restrictive and defensive reaction against a vast and threatening world. For the British art historian, abstraction attested not to a withdrawal, but rather to an "extension." It was the result of the subject's openness to the world, which the subject undertook to translate in an abstract, lasting, and regular manner.[22] In sum, the agrarian subject no longer had to sharpen his senses; in breaking down nature to give it a form, he was already obeying "formalist" impulses.

The Neolithic faculty for composition was the expression both of a world that people were beginning to perceive as coherent and of a collective social experiment. The Danish artist Asger Jorn, who in the aftermath of the war would be one of the founders of the CoBrA movement (1948–1951), along with a few Nordic artists, had since the 1930s devoured ethnological and archaeological writings, seeking to identify the archetypal symbolic forces that could foster a new creativity.[23] Having identified in cave art "a consistent *naturalism* or *effect of illusion*" that allowed the hunter to make contact with what was absolutely foreign and unknown to him,[24] he remarked that the rupture between the Paleolithic and the Neolithic had occurred by means of the relation between agriculture and nature. "Culture" in the strict sense was established in the Neolithic period:

> During his evolution, man goes through two different modes of life: that of *collector* and that of *creator*. These two modes produce a notable difference, because they entail a difference between *hunting* and *taking*, *cultivating* and *negotiating*, where it is necessary to give before being able to take. Man cannot create a culture without passing through the latter mode, because to create a culture is to cultivate, and cultivation is nothing other than exploitation, negotiation, and work.[25]

In an unpublished manuscript on "art as magic," he wrote that nature came to belong to the Neolithic farmer in a sense that the hunter did not understand. On the one hand, humanity made the transition to "active, authentic production, active culture, active cultivation of the fertility of animals and of the earth, an activity of giving as a creative activity. This is the real foundation of human culture."[26] On the other, thanks to two practices, the division of labor and social fellowship, art assumed a new role as "the development of a 'communal *language* . . . a real means of communication, a symbolic language among people.'"[27] Even before the war, the so-called Unit One circle, which in the 1930s attracted the British modernists, linked abstraction, collective aspiration, and prehistory. Hence, in the preface to Barbara Hepworth's solo exhibition in London in 1937, the Cambridge University lecturer in crystallography Desmond Bernal pointed out from the start the Neolithic resonance of the sculptures exhibited, whose formalism he declared not at all "primitive," but rather "very sophisticated." Abstract art, he added, could not exist apart from a social utility comparable to that of Neolithic art, directly associated with collective ritual needs.[28] For this Marxist, politics had simply taken the place of the integrative power of religion.

Rootedness in the Landscape

Nevertheless, not all these artists and theories confined themselves to pointing out the universal political, spiritual, and artistic superiority of the Neolithic period. Although they argued that the "Neolithic revolution" had a universal significance for the species, many, including Asger Jorn, emphasized that it had arisen in Northern Europe.[29] The "Scandinavian" heritage of an art predating the Vikings became necessary for all who rejected the tutelage of French modernism. One of the first pages of the review *CoBrA* reproduced a photograph of a rock painting captioned "The Danish Age of Caves," along with two reproductions of murals by Asger Jorn.[30] Elsewhere, Jorn laid claim to a Nordic heritage of the image, not to be confused with the Germanic heritage, which still leaned toward illustration and literature and was tainted by Nazism.[31] In November 1961, Jorn's ideas took an extravagant turn: he designed and partly realized the plan to archive all the Scandinavian monuments, beginning with those of prehistory. Along with the prehistorian Peter V. Glob, with whom he had designed a project in the late 1940s on "ancient Danish art," he cofounded the Scandinavian Institute of Comparative Vandalism. Its principal undertaking, largely inspired by Malraux's "Museum without Walls," was to publish thirty-two volumes on "ten thousand years of Nordic popular art."[32] Gérard Franceschi, accompanied by Jorn, would take twenty-five thousand photographs of monuments in Scandinavia and elsewhere, but in the end, only two volumes would be published (Figures 4.3 and 4.4). Like many other intellectuals on the right and left, Jorn was profoundly suspicious of the social standardization and normalization under way by modern capitalism and Americanism. Wanting to defend and preserve "Scandinavian" values, he laid claim to the creativity of the barbarians, which according to him involved the destructive impulse of graffiti and "spontaneity" and which actively opposed capitalism and the commercialization of modernist art.[33] Jorn's tendency to lay claim to the Nordic heritage of his art grew stronger over time.[34] In his Situationist years, he explained the expressive gesturality of his painting as a "revolution," a "reversal," a departure from "zero," because it gave free rein to the imagination, as "the caveman" had done, but his discourse henceforth became increasingly ethnicized. He even went so far as to defend "work" as the condition for "culture."[35]

As a result, the division between the Paleolithic and the Neolithic was not only temporal, but also spatial, which is to say, national and racial. An art that irrupted suddenly was certainly suggestive of revolution, but it could just as easily signify plant growth. It was in any case an autochthonous art, profoundly rooted in the soil—a theme already encountered with Max Verworn, one of the principal proponents of the idea of prehistoric art in Germany, who laid claim to the Nordic character of so-called ideoplastic art. Following a similar approach and no doubt directly linked to it, Kühn also argued that the megaliths had not migrated from the South to the North, as Oscar Montelius, a major Swedish archaeologist, had assumed, but rather in the

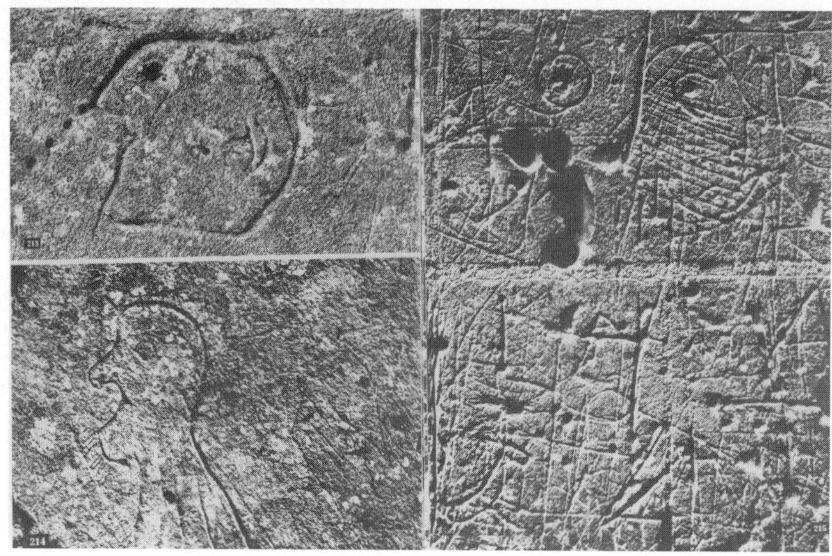

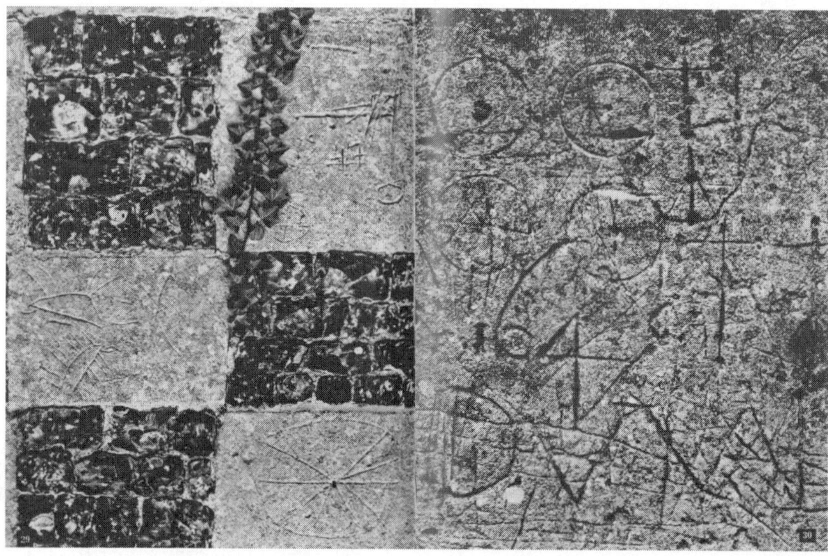

Figures 4.3 and 4.4. Gérard Franceschi, photographs within the framework of Asger Jorn's project, "10,000 ans d'art populaire nordique," in Asger Jorn, ed., *Signes gravés sur les églises de l'Eure et du Calvados* (Copenhagen: Borgen, 1964). Photos: Gérard Franceschi.

opposite direction. The North thus gained prominence as the inventor of a "great culture" and a "strong religious philosophy," which disappeared during certain periods, only to emerge later on. This had been recently demonstrated by expressionism, the latest descendant of the Neolithic.[36] The art historian Frederik Adama von Scheltema, who had also published in the review *Documents*, developed a similar theory, placing the emphasis on the opposition between the "precocious maturity" and "rapid growth" of the Paleolithic South and the "steadfastness" and firmness of the Neolithic North: "It continues steadfastly and, on the whole, it is firmly localized,"[37] he noted, to underscore the astonishing fertility of that more abstract art.

Clearly, Neolithic art maintained a very ambiguous relationship with nature: it was distant and different from it, while at the same time being its consequence. Of course, this was not the same nature, indistinct and immediate, as in the Paleolithic period; it was a nature that had already set off on the path toward the individualization of races. Universalism and particularism, the human race and Germanic, English, Scandinavian or French nations, rupture and continuity, thus coexisted in the imaginary to which the megaliths and menhirs gave rise. If Camille Jullian began his course on the history of the French nation with a lecture on the Neolithic period, it was because that period allowed him to assert the connection to the soil common to the nameless populations of that remote era and to modern French people. After the great cataclysm marking the advent of the Neolithic period, everything had in fact unfolded in accordance with a flawless continuity: "Between us and the first laborers of the Neolithic era, life went by without a cataclysm of matter and without a rupture in thought."[38] The sovereign power of the Neolithic period was "the earth, and no longer the animal." Farmers became "its workers and its masters, its creators and its children," as proven by "these countless fables of European antiquity, which made the Titans and the Gauls the sons of the earth."[39] Woven into the unwavering continuity of the *longue durée* was everything that constituted a "homeland." But much more than towns, roads, and wheat fields were needed for that: also necessary were shared memories, similar habits, a desired understanding, pride in a collective name. But let time do its work, all these things would come at their natural hour. They cannot fail to come to this soil. . . . Our homeland exists as a potentiality, in its materiality, in its earthly foundations. And it is the men who fashioned polished stone, creators and worshipers of the earth, who built these eternal foundations.[40]

Neolithic prehistory, with all its ideological ambiguities, acquired a providential function for one strain of modernism, which in the 1930s sought to reconcile the universalism of industrial technology with the persistent particularisms of cultures and races. In 1935, when Paul Nash, a painter and photographer who sought to combine abstraction and figuration, painted the landscape *Equivalents for the Megaliths* (Figure 4.5), it had been just two years since he had been captivated by his discovery of the megaliths of Avebury. His interest in stones, as he would later tell it, began there:

> The great stones were in their wild state, so to speak. . . . Some were half covered by the grass, others stood up in cornfields or were entangled and overgrown in the copses, some were buried under the turf. But they were wonderful and disquieting, and as I saw them then, I shall always remember them. Very soon afterwards the big work of reinstating the Circles and Avenues began, so that to a great extent that primal magic of the stones' appearance was lost.[41]

Nash had first been struck by the indistinction that time had brought about between nature and these first man-made structures, similar to the indistinction of Romantic paintings. Having long stood on the site, these structures built by humans were literally rooted, intermingling with the copses and buried under the turf. That is why Nash regretted that the restoration of these structures erased the *longue durée* that both separated him from and united him to the men of the Neolithic period. In the essay he wrote for the Unit One collection, he spoke of the "imprisoned spirit" behind the subjects and genres of eighteenth-century English painting. And for him, that spirit was in the first place the spirit of the "land": "Genius loci is indeed almost

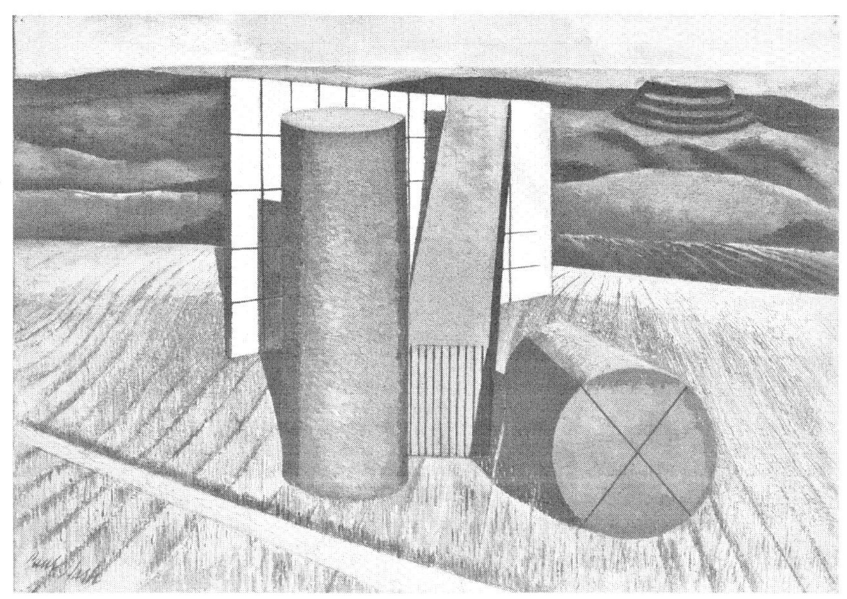

Figure 4.5. Paul Nash, *Equivalents for the Megaliths*, 1935. Oil painting, 17⅞ × 25⅞ in. Tate Gallery, London. Purchased 1970. Photo: © Tate Gallery.

its conception. . . . We, today, must find new symbols to express our reaction to environment."[42]

The megaliths, then, were the answer for those in quest of new forms to express the imprisoned spirit of the *genius loci*, that is, to liberate it. During these years of the Fascist "Third Way," the technological spirit of modernity had to be reconciled with the spirit of the "land" as it was originally embodied in the first human interventions in the landscape. That is why *Equivalents for the Megaliths* had nothing to do with the natural tangle that had struck the artist upon his discovery of the site. It represented rather its opposite: juxtaposed in a landscape that had become geometrical as a result of being molded by human toil were two perfect earth-colored cylinders, one standing, and the other lying on the ground. Between the two, a regular geometrical solid, rectangular in shape and leaning at an angle, was painted bright blue and red. Behind all these forms, a large diagonal white panel appeared on which was drawn an unfinished grid, resembling the regular furrows in the soil. The panel pointed toward a tumulus in the background, amid rolling hills in more or less natural colors. This odd combination of continuity and contrast revealed the artist's singular notion of the Neolithic. Everything began with the furrowed soil, abstract and spiritualized by millennial toil, but everything continued through modern technology, whose formal mastery in itself constituted an evolution of the Neolithic. As the title he chose indicated, Nash sought to restore not the "primal magic" he had experienced in Avebury, but rather its "equivalent." To do so, he drew on the imaginary of a sharp and decisive Neolithic, the exact opposite of Paleolithic indetermination. Instead of the "primal magic" of a humanized site that time had nonetheless almost returned to nature, Nash signified a second magic, produced by the powerful contrasts of pure mental constructions: the contrast between horizontality and verticality, between the flat and the round, and between the straight and the curved. An attentive observer of de Chirico's paintings, he had truly grasped their meaning. Prehistoric incoherence made its return, but this time through human activity.

And in Nash's eyes, that mysterious incoherence constituted the "imprisoned spirit" of his people. In a letter to his wife, he wrote that the megaliths, like Shakespeare, were "a big thing and a complete mystery to everyone," and added: "It's significant of the English that the two biggest works of matter and mind should have a purely speculative history; who knows who wrote 'Shakespeare?'"[43] Thanks to a scrambled, rigged geometry that far from being clear, generated infinite speculations, the artist succeeded in reconciling the universalism of geometrical forms and "English" specificity (Figure 4.6). Nash clarified what he meant by *genius loci* in the tourist guide he composed for the region of Dorset, a region known for its geological landforms and the wealth of fossils in its soil (Figure 4.7).[44] The

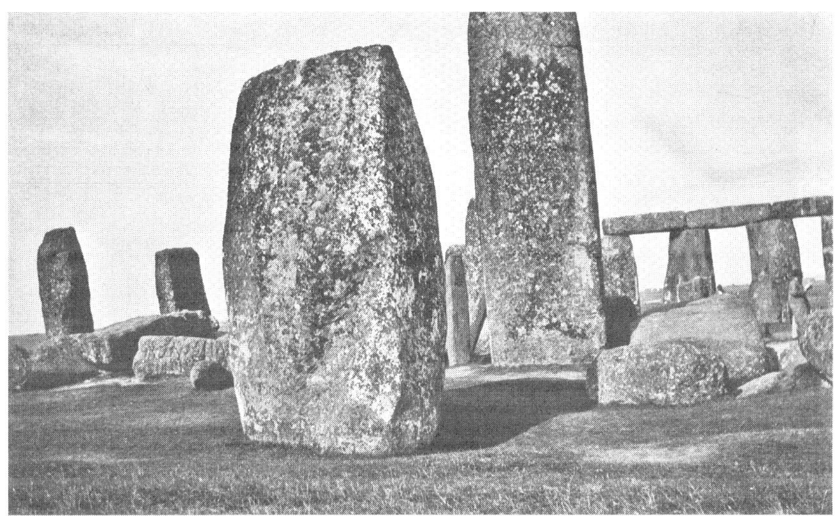

Figure 4.6. Paul Nash, *Stonehenge*, study 2.
Black-and-white negative, 1933. Presented
by the Paul Nash Trust, 1970. Photo:
© Tate Gallery.

cover of this guide, published by the Shell Company and designed
for motorists on sightseeing trips, was a sort of photomontage in
which the rocks at the seaside were barely distinguishable from the
megaliths erected by men. The first pictures in the guide referred to
remote prehistory: fish fossils and a reconstitution of a *Scelidosaurus
harrisonii*, which the artist called a "former native." The following
pages show in succession the geology, flora and fauna, and man-made
structures of Dorset. The only thing absent from that survey span-
ning natural kingdoms and eras is recent modernity—but it is true
the guide was dedicated to the "Landowners of Dorset, the Council
for the Preservation of Rural England, The Society for the Protection
of Ancient Buildings," and, finally, to "All those courageous Enemies
of 'Development' to whom we owe what is left of England."[45] Nash's
appropriation of the Neolithic corresponded to the need to protect

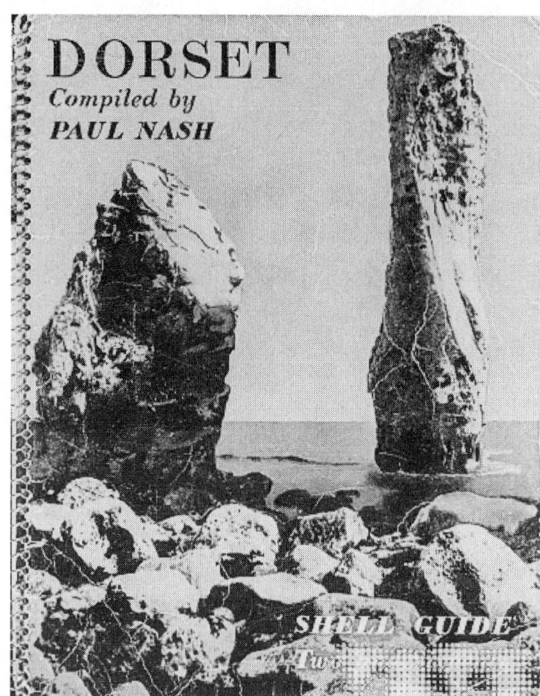

Figure 4.7. Paul Nash, *Dorset* (London: Architectural Press, 1935).

"what is left of England," even if and precisely because that meant sometimes adapting it to a more modern language.

But Nash was not alone in this case. The high priestess of England's spiritual unity, of its inhabitants, and of its words was no doubt Jacquetta Hawkes, an archaeologist and writer very close to such modernist artists as Henry Moore and Barbara Hepworth. Her best-seller, *A Land* (1949), reissued several times, was a remarkable expression of the process by which the modern consciousness internalized geological time.[46] From the outset, Hawkes declared she was interested in "other forms of memory" than that of history, "those recollections of the world and of man that are pursued on behalf of consciousness by geologists and archaeologists."[47] Even though subjective consciousness could not have access to the process of geological formation, of course, the physical relationship to the landscape and the analogy drawn between stratified and buried human memory and the earth's geological strata allowed the author to compose a narrative that wove together the formation of sediment, the evolution of men inhabiting the earth since the glacial period, Neolithic megaliths, and Henry Moore's sculptures. The first chapter, "Recollection," which concerned the stratification of England, ends with these words: "A chapter on method has ended as a narrative, for the subject of study and the study have shown themselves to be one."[48] Although she recognized that her prose ran into difficulty expressing "the extraordinary awareness of the unity of past and present, of mind and matter, of man and man's origin," she pointed out the extent to which Moore's sculptures made that unity "overwhelming."[49] Henry Moore is said to have had "the wisdom" to turn away from marble, which had suited Southern artists such as Michelangelo, and "to have returned to English stones and used them with a subtle sensitiveness for their personal qualities."[50] The transmission of forms occurred both through the biological father and through the race as a whole. Inheriting from his miner father knowledge of the "Carboniferous horizons of Yorkshire," Moore had liberated himself from a "beautiful material" so important for artists from other regions: "Now when our minds are recalling the past and our own origins deep within it, Moore reflects a greater humility in avoiding the white silence of marble and allowing his stone to speak."[51] Just as Rodin had succeeded in extracting the spiritual man from marble, Moore had taken the identification of man with geological matter to the extreme: "Through his visual similes, he identifies women with caverns, caverns with eye-sockets; shells, bones, cell plasm drift into human form."[52] There was no place for the fissures and abysses of history, except, in the end, for "revolution," not that of the Neolithic period, but the revolution that was its ultimate consequence and simultaneously its abolition: the Industrial Revolution, which threatened to put an end to the long history of the English Land. It surged forth sometimes as a telluric force, an "undifferentiated chaos" ready to cover the geological physiognomy of the land, and sometimes as an uncontrollable social force comparable to the barbarian invasions.[53] But Hawkes, hostile to any idea of revolution, whether technological or communist, was in reality defending the synthetic and conservative function of art.[54]

A few years later, the archaeologist had the opportunity to give a visual form to her prose: her screenplay (read in voiceover), *Figures in a Landscape*, directed by Dudley Shaw Ashton in 1953, linked the land of Cornwall, the Neolithic megaliths, and the abstract sculptures of Barbara Hepworth.[55] Hawkes presented these sculptures against a seascape or in her studio, fashioning the stone that "water and wind have shaped before her. Stones cut out from the layered hill." Then, while the camera was filming the dolmens, the voiceover commented: "Yes, they came, these ancient pagans. They entered the landscape, gave it their senses and furnished it with their words. Now it has colour and form; the granite knew the feel of its crystalline surface from the touch of their fingers. They were figures in the landscape."[56] Thus was established the homology between the earth, men, and their works. Nash had the same idea: shaped by men, stones came to life, becoming in turn capable of transmitting the *genius loci* that the barbarians of modernity were threatening. But it was not only the "influences of landscape, natural form and the historically continuous feeling in Cornwall for shape, light and texture, and how these influences have been heightened and turned into a form of visual poetry by Barbara Hepworth,"[57] as the presentation of the film at the Venice Biennale of 1954 noted: it was much rather a circular process in which the stone, brought to life artistically by human beings since prehistory, would in turn instill life in present-day and future artists.[58] And the same circular logic dictated that just as the stones had become megaliths, Hepworth's sculptures had been shaped by impersonal natural forces, such as waves and the wind. In that circular process, where rocks became sculptures and sculptures took root, time was abolished and history eliminated.

The Neolithic of Disorder: Pablo Picasso and Robert Morris

Picasso's Monuments

Picasso seized on the Neolithic period in a series of paintings in which he intermingled other systems of representation. Begun in

Cannes in 1927 and continued in Dinard the next year, these compositions, which for the most part represented monstrous female or hemaphroditic figures, were very remote from the abstractions of British formalism. They were also linked to an intensive production of drawings. In Cannes, the figures in pencil, modeled and rendered in chiaroscuro, were so smooth as to become almost neoclassical in appearance (Figure 4.8). The Dinard drawings, in ink, were more overtly "prehistoric": precarious assemblages of forms partly covered with hatchings, evoking somewhat anthropomorphic stones and bones (see Figure 3.5). The paintings of the years 1929 to 1930 soon affirmed the minerality common to stone and bones. Some canvases represented assemblages, monolithic, to be sure, but anatomical enough to be able to perform a human gesture, such as a kiss. Others represented fossilized bathers, hollow, like skeletons, but at the same time as dense and compact as stone (Figure 4.9). All were isolated figures, standing, seated, or reclining. In 1908, *Three Women* had been made up of almost undifferentiated figures, barely detached from one another and from the rock. but twenty years later, Picasso, placing most of his isolated creatures in an asphyxiating light, gave them a palpable individuality. A temporal inversion took place: *Three Women* marked the transition from geological mutism and its compactness to the symbolic differentiation brought about by man and in particular by the artist; the bathers of the late 1920s, whose forms had incorporated cubist dematerialization, suggested a time after life and after history when fossils and monuments would mingle to the point of indistinction.[59] Even so, there was nothing confused about the provocative mélange of Picasso's compositions, even though natural kingdoms, sexes, and semantic regimes encroached on one another. Far from the vision of Neolithic stones intermingling with plants and turf that would soon transfix Paul Nash, Picasso's figures originated in a unified and paradoxically neoclassical mix, culminating in new forms that were made neither for living nor for dying. Significantly, these paintings had assimilated a sense of mourning, which Picasso transformed, rather than eliminating. In 1930, Michel Leiris wrote that each of these paintings was comparable to a "new organ

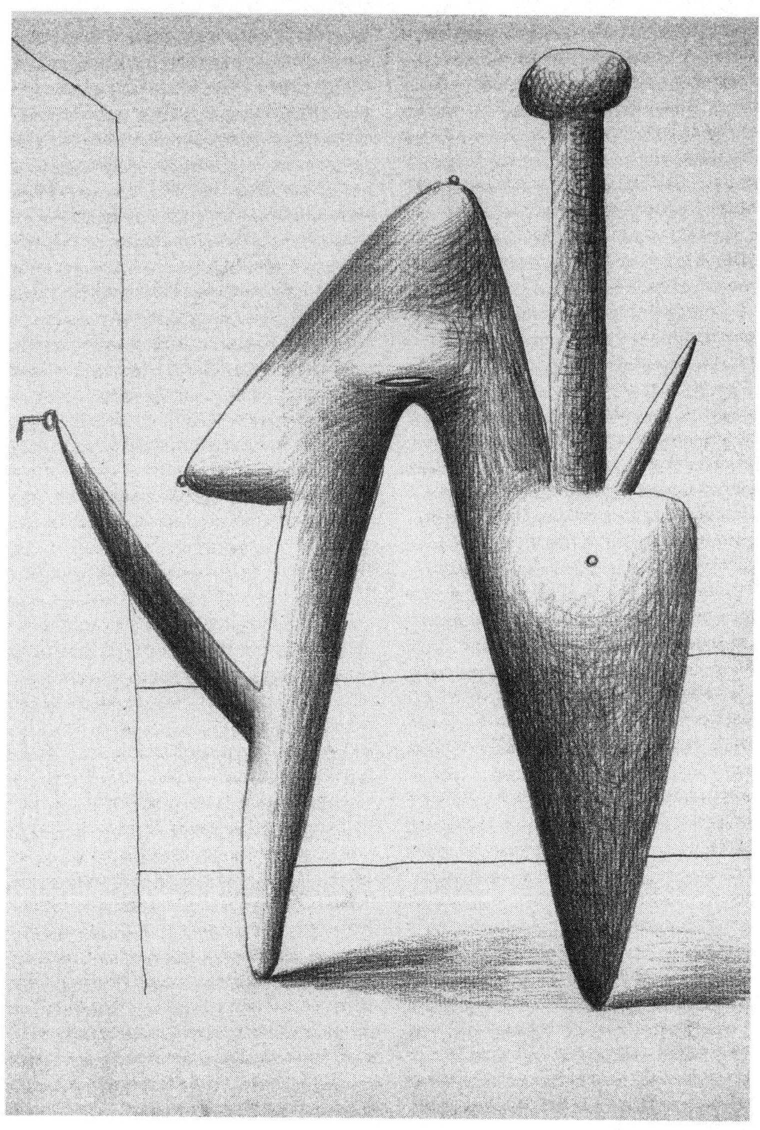

Figure 4.8. Pablo Picasso, Cannes drawings, July 17–September 11, 1927. Pencil on paper, 11⅞ × 9 in. Musée National Picasso, Paris. Photo: © 2021 Estate of Pablo Picasso/ ARS, NY.

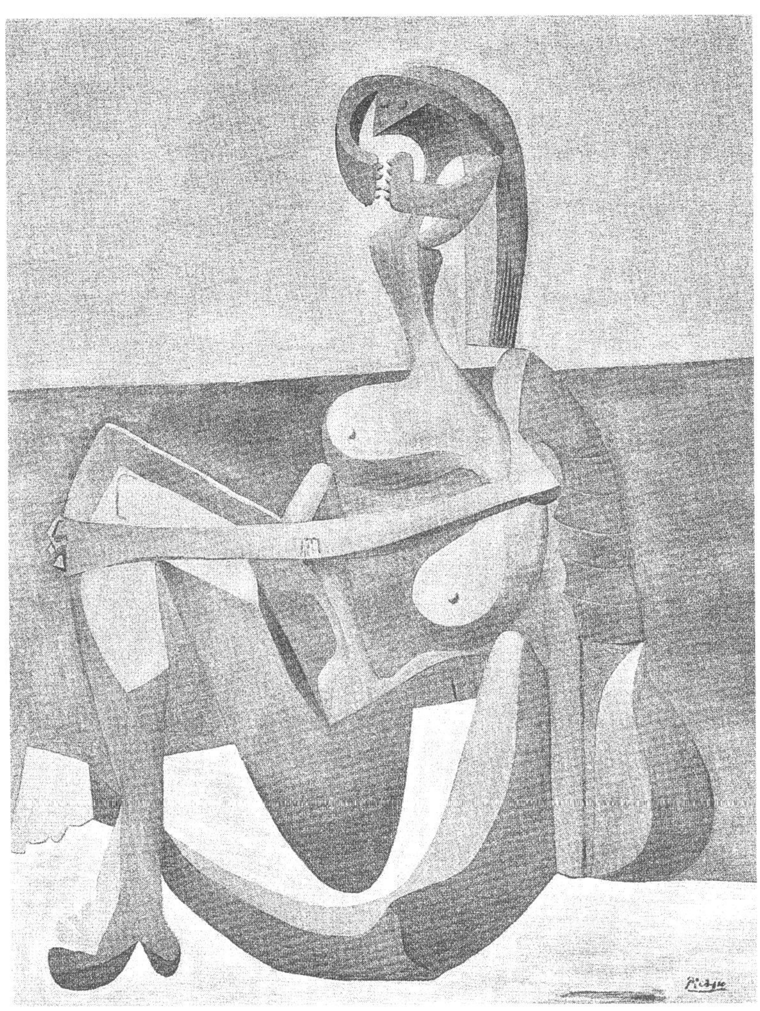

Figure 4.9. Pablo Picasso, *Seated Bather*,
1930. Oil on canvas, 64¼ × 50⅞ in.
Museum of Modern Art, New York. Photo:
© 2021 ARS, NY / ADAGP, Paris.

we add, a new instrument that allows us to insert ourselves more humanly in nature, to become more concrete, more dense, more alive."[60] What for Picasso had begun as a reflection on the monument erected against death culminated here in a study of the provisional, frightening, and intrinsically mythopoetic character of life.

In Cannes during the summer of 1927, the commission Picasso had received for a monument to the memory of his friend the poet Apollinaire, who died in 1918, became increasingly burdensome and no doubt stimulated his interrogation of the status of monuments. According to several accounts, the drawings in the Cannes notebook were sketches of monuments Picasso imagined lined up in a row on La Croisette.[61] There was something both organic and reified about their bodies: resulting from new distributions of organs, some enlarged and others eliminated, they evoked simultaneously an unknown natural world and the world of ordinary objects—like a chair and an easel. Michel Leiris correctly perceived that monstrous dual allegiance to the living world of organisms and the inert world of things. He wrote in spring 1929, after Picasso had shown him his sketchbook of preliminary drawings for a sculpture: "The extremely polished and meticulous drawing, with a very clear bulge made from hatchings, academic as can be. Only the member has almost nothing human about it anymore; it resembles instead a bone instrument from the Neolithic period, fashioned in a very precise manner, in a mysterious aim."[62] If the whole was able to preserve a human appearance, the part became a prehistoric tool. On the stylistic level, however, that prehistoric character was combined with the "academic polish" usually reserved for a completed whole. But the polished tool of the Neolithic period was not the only allusion to prehistory in Picasso's works during these years: the bathers he drew, with their straight and vertical postures, suggested megaliths, even as their physical aberrations recalled the Paleolithic Venuses that fascinated him.[63] He fused all these elements to constitute new organisms, "beings," Leiris also said, "who ignore us and breathe impassively before us, in a world, closed perhaps, but closed only because of our weakness."[64] Picasso anthropomorphized the stones excessively, to the point of making them comical and nonviable, in a closed, autonomous, rootless, and antinatural world, whereas Nash and Hepworth brought the megaliths to life, incorporating them into living nature. Fundamentally, two different notions of art faced off through these two uses of the Neolithic: despite their paean to abstract language, the notion that the two Britons had of art was naturalistic, organic, and continuist, whereas Picasso's position was radically functionalist. Just as chairs and easel were used for precise tasks in everyday life, Picasso's impossible figures, which in fact had assimilated prostheses from everyday life, aspired to a different sort of functionality, which was neither measurable nor an immediate extension of one or another specific organ. They were supposed to act as psychic and cognitive instruments, intended to broaden human thought and desires beyond the known.

The sketches for the monument to Apollinaire belonged to a broader inquiry into the meaning of the modern monument. How to inscribe the individual's life and death into the anonymous public space? How to reconcile the biographical scale with the collective scale? Was there a decent way to evoke for everyone the memory of a departed friend, even if he was an illustrious poet? As Dawn Ades has suggested in a remarkable article, the author of the *Rotting Wizard* (1909) could still inspire the painter's imagination, Apollinaire being himself a "rotting wizard" whose verses remained an active force even beyond his death.[65] Apollinaire identified even more with the figure of Merlin, who was central to his poems, where so many fables, legendary figures, historical eras, and religions coexisted: the Druids spoke with antediluvian figures and the three Magi with fabulous animals. In seizing hold of the megalith, the archetypal monument that was the source of so many survivals, fables, and legends, Picasso transformed it with mixtures as impure as the poet's words: the antediluvian, the neoclassical, and the modern, coexisting in his monuments, were synecdoches for the long term. But these temporalities were not addressed to an insular, imaginary community that had survived prehistory. The impurity of the mixture was similar to that of memory, where fragments and scraps from several eras mingled arbitrarily. What remained common to men, however, and what as a result legitimized a modern study of the monument, was the need for everyone, separately, to think about life and death. The often modest dimensions of the paintings in which Picasso represented these slightly anthropomorphized megaliths can thus be understood as the expression of that tension between the individual and the collective: the painting truly remained the expression of the private passions of the modern era, but Picasso, in carving up and tightly framing the megaliths, making them seem incommensurably large, suggested that these passions were also the most widely shared.

Robert Morris Aligned with Nazca

The Neolithic would reemerge later in American postminimalist art of the 1960s and 1970s. In this "expanded field,"[66] the reified object might be liberated by entering the circuit of museum exhibition and the market. Unlike Robert Morris, in particular, Carl Andre, Richard Long, and Robert Smithson showed no interest in cave art — like the first abstract artists of the twentieth century and generally for the same reasons. They were turning toward British megaliths and the geoglyphic and petroglyphic formations of the New World. Their interpretation of Stonehenge and of a few other sites stripped away the nationalist and racial detritus that the British modernists of the 1930s to 1950s had associated with them. The megalithic structures were imposing in their mysterious syntax, which directly engaged the body, and in their *longue durée*, which defied conventional logic and which, in eluding any certainty offered by shared linguistic codes, encouraged experimentation. From that standpoint, without being formally similar to Picasso's monstrous figures, the Neolithic experiments these artists pursued were analogous conceptual projects. It is simply that their works had in addition the melancholy of late capitalism, which buried the "Neolithic revolution" for good.

In an interview, the gallerist Virginia Dawn, who had collaborated with a number of these artists, stressed their importance for the very *longue durée*. She said that the particular artists with whom she was involved believed that their work was not historical in the sense of having a linear connection. Rather, they wanted to go from 1970 or 1980 — it did not matter much to them — to the year 3000 BCE. They were much more concerned with what had happened a very long time ago than with what had happened in more recent history.[67] The projection of the present onto the past was eminently phenomenological, as Robert Smithson showed by running on his entropic jetty and as we have observed with Robert Morris's phenomenological interpretation of Cézanne's geological landscapes. That total engagement of the body in the experience of the work was the most important and the newest contribution to the modern invention of prehistory by the postminimalist artists. Morris took as his starting point the fact that no linguistic document could explain Stonehenge or the geoglyphs of Nazca: not only did he consider art irreducible to language, because of the part that escaped communication and remained open to the viewer's interpretations, the two Neolithic sites were also located outside linguistic writing. In the Stonehenge era, writing did not yet exist in that region of the world, while in the case of Nazca, the colonial conquest, in exterminating men, destroyed even their oral traditions.[68] Given the absence of writing, Morris decided in 1975 to experience with his body the lines traced in the desert three thousand years earlier. That link established between the body and writing, which was fully inscribed in Morris's dance practice suite at the Judson Gallery, also differentiated his walk through the Nazca Valley from that of Richard Long, taken in 1972.[69] Morris's mediation of phenomenological experience through writing crystallized in his logbook, published in the review *Artforum* in 1975 under the title "Aligned with Nazca": a work of art in itself, the text, which more properly might be called of "Aligned on Nazca,"[70] was the transposition of one system of notation to another, of one cultural system to another, as well as an actualization of Nazca by means of present-day media. "Aligned on Nazca" evokes the sensuous adaptations of Morris's whole body to the lines traced three thousand years ago by unknown men and, metaphorically, the lesson that these lines provided for his own practice. Morris gave the dead writings a body, and in return, they delivered a message to him that he could interpret only in his own way. Morris's practice,

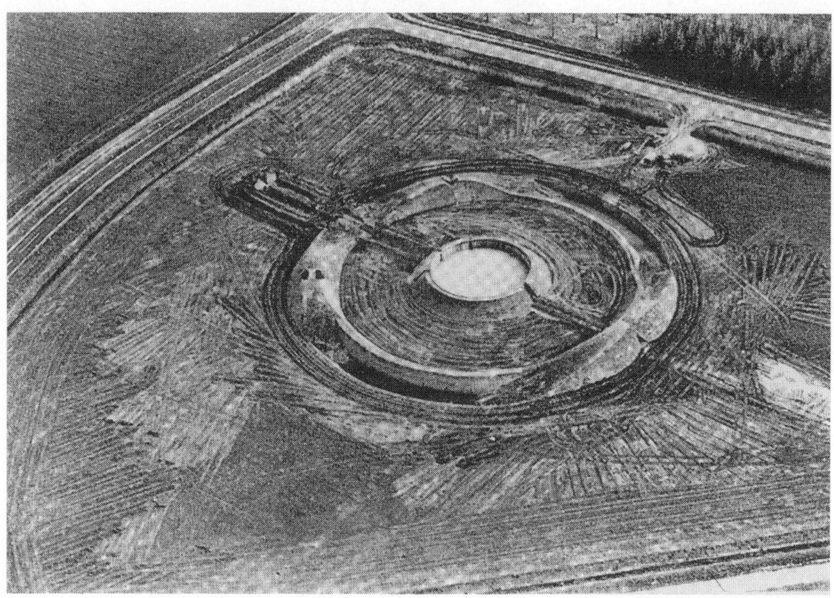

Figure 4.10. Robert Morris, *Observatory*,
1971/1977. Earth, water, wood, granite, steel.
Diameter 298 ft., 6⅞ in. Oostelijk Flevoland.
Photo: © 2021 Estate of Robert Morris/ARS, NY.

as puzzling as the geoglyphs of Nazca, belonged to a loose and vacillating conceptual and corporeal lineage.

Nazca followed *Observatory*, built in 1971 at Santpoort-Velsen, the Netherlands, within the context of the Sonsbeek exhibition (Figure 4.10).[71] The artist called that work "very different from any art being made today," a "para-architectural complex."[72] The graphics of *Observatory* followed the rays of the sun, the four entrances indicating the two solstices and the two equinoxes. Anxious to differentiate his *Observatory* from the earthworks of his contemporaries, which he found formalistic and politically neutral,[73] he laid claim to a much more ancient heritage: that of the "Neolithic and Oriental architectural complexes. Enclosures, courts, ways, sightlines, varying grades, etc.," he wrote, "assert that the work provides a physical experience for the mobile human body." These preoccupations, he added, distinguish this work from other outdoor structures, which exist as monumental works and form a static whole. It is neither a sculpture nor architecture. It is also not an entity that can be taken in with a single glance, nor is it a place to seek shelter. As he explained, the temporal center of the work — the imprint of four sunrises at the moment the seasons are changing — gives it a vaster dimension than that of a mere decorative structure in space.[74] *Observatory* was thus designed to elude the grasp of a subject inclined to reify nature. Simple in appearance, the work's configuration was supposed to suggest the millions of kilometers separating us from the sun, a slightly twisted cosmic impulse that Morris said he found in Yves Klein's work.

But while the earth's trajectory around the sun had not changed since Stonehenge, its rhythm having nothing to do with human history, the lines traced on the ground in the Nazca Valley were charged with history — the kind of history that erases, rather than writes. The Nazca lines, by virtue of their length and shape, were even more resistant than *Observatory* to "constituting an object." At first, Morris found his research on the lines disorienting and unsettling. But once he spotted the first lines in the desert, he became fully engaged with them. It was of course impossible to obtain a gestalt, a total image of the geometric or figurative form drawn over miles and miles. Once located, the line, taken in isolation or in relation to the other lines it crossed, became the only visible datum, and it was always partial. This was no longer an object, therefore, but a form being transformed by the light and by the movement of the walker's body.[75] More precisely, the walker saw it scroll out in front of him at the same time, provided he had adjusted his vision to the right distance — median and far. For what was near remained formless, so that what was low to the ground became disassociated from what was far away. Whereas the line was illegible[76] when Morris lowered his eyes to follow his steps, it became legible when he looked at it from a distance: "The lines become visible only by virtue of the extension of that plain — literally from under one's feet up to the level of one's eyesight." Nevertheless, the visual experience and the kinesthetic experience were not always separated: when he followed with his eyes the horizontal surface until at a certain distance it became "elevation," the lower part slipped imperceptibly into the visual field. The Nazca lines thus established an unexpected kinship with a certain painting by Cézanne that Morris had discovered in Kansas City when he was a child.

All this shows as well the unbridgeable gap separating the Nazca site and contemporary urban spaces, formed by the stark opposition between horizontality and verticality. Not only did this division in the urban space allow a body to walk without getting lost, because its eyes looked always ahead, it taught this body above all to feel surrounded by objects that were always separate, ready to be possessed, even if these objects were skyscrapers. The indetermination between horizontality and verticality characteristic of Nazca also distinguished Morris's experience from all the decisionist gestures and univocal contrasts, such as what had shaped Nash's megalithic landscape.

At Nazca, as in Morris's art, there was the same refusal to constitute an object, the same incapacity to distinguish calmly the low from the high, the same impossibility of classifying forms within a single medium, and the same total adherence of the body to a space he said felt like "a palpable emptiness."[77] In the absence of any knowledge about what the collective rites associated with these lines had been, Morris analyzed his own subjective experience of them. That experience of the phenomenological "self" to which he laid claim and that he recognized in the works of many of his contemporaries posited a self that had ceased to be the seat of the logos in order to experience a discontinuous, changing, but always immanent relationship with a boundless space. The "self" became at once the subject and the object of postminimalist art.[78] Robert Morris had intimate experiences of these ancient monuments whose meaning had been eradicated by men's violence. In his view, these experiences stood in contrast to the efflorescence of American public art in the 1950s and 1960s. He thus contrasted the authoritarian verticality that often characterized such art and that imposed thoughts and feelings to the Nazca lines, which were not at all superhuman, but, according to him, were due to "the maker's care and economy and insight into the nature of a particular landscape."[79]

The inscription of the megaliths in the landscape called for a corporeal response, and it is not by chance that all these artists mentioned the way that bodies (their own, the model's, or the viewer's) brought to life the forms erected or traced in the soil. But the objective of that exchange between human beings and stones was completely different. For the Britons, the stones were supposed to give modern subjects the roots they lacked. Although proud and intrepid, the abstract revolution was in reality a child of the Neolithic revolution. Thanks to the Neolithic, rupture and permanence, mechanical abstraction and organicity, were miraculously reconciled. The political decisionism of these years fabricated its own past, admiring its collective artistic and political constructions. Picasso and Morris perverted the taxonomy of the Neolithic world, beginning with its verticality, which they pulled down to the ground. Picasso reified the figures, and Morris literally aligned himself with lines on the ground. Rather than taking root, the body was invited to let go of its habits, question its perception, its desires, and its finitude. Modernity may have claimed to be jealous of a fantasized collective past, but in fact, it remained personal and intimate. The collective past that interested Morris was that of the others, those struck from the annals by the decisionist force of the West. As for the revolution that had begun in the Neolithic and continued up to modern abstraction, it had given way to doubt, disorder, and randomness. That in fact was why Picasso's and Morris's Neolithic system was not pure, but rather intermingled with many other memories of the art of the most remote past, beginning with the Paleolithic. Whereas Picasso's formal imaginary engendered monsters composed of Venuses and megaliths, Morris would refer increasingly to the caves in the South of France. Obsessed with labyrinths, a form that according to him signified and produced the alogical experience he was searching for, he thought he had found its matrix in the cave, which, consciously or not, had haunted human memory for millenniums.[80]

CHAPTER FIVE

Prehistory in the Atomic Age

The End of History

In 1959, in the preface to *Man before Writing*, the first volume of a universal history in the spirit of the Annales School, the historian Fernand Braudel wrote that it was urgent for the people of his time to project themselves back to the very *longue durée* of the past. Two successive jolts had just turned human history on its head: "The life we have been living since the prodigious shock of World War II, since the even more prodigious revelations of science in the wake of the conflict, this life, our adventure for the time being, raises again and again the whole problem of man, in his past and outside his past."[1] It seemed that the leap into the unknown and an uncertain future would trigger a leap into the forgotten past—a past that in reality was never lived—of an earth without man. Indeed, what was henceforth called "the atomic revolution," a rupture that appeared potentially even more radical than that of the "Neolithic revolution," promised humanity two diametrically opposed destinies: its extinction or the total domestication of the earth—even in its most perilous manifestations, even at its most inhospitable extremes, breaking through what Ernst Jünger called "the time wall" and finally opening onto the colonization of the cosmos.[2]

Clearly, even though the discovery of the earth's vast past and the very long genealogy of the species had since the nineteenth century given rise to the idea of an imminent end to human history, it was only in the aftermath of World War II that this idea crystallized.

This "end" took on multiple aspects, however. Understood as the consequence of the process of the natural extinction of the human species, which had become perfectly credible, it was able to assume the instantaneous form of the explosion of the atomic bomb. Understood as the consequence of the moral extinction of the species, it took the slow form of the capitalist standardization of objects and human beings, the illusion of liberal democracy, and man's enslavement to technology. On these themes, authors as politically different as the French writer Georges Bataille, the American historian Lewis Mumford, the Italian filmmaker and poet Pier Paolo Pasolini, and the German philosopher Arnold Gehlen were in agreement.[3] Conversely, the Italian artists Lucio Fontana and Giuseppe Pinot-Gallizio and the German writer and essayist Ernst Jünger — who also held very different views — celebrated the end of history as the beginning of an unprecedented emancipation. Technology was thus less criticized than glorified, especially in its capacity to free man from the shackles of history and the grip of the past, often by casting him into the expanded present of an everyday messianism.

Man, stripped of any geographical or social sense of belonging, was no longer perceived as a historical being. He was ordinarily invoked as a species finally liberated from the constraints it had inflicted upon itself over the course of its long Neolithic evolution: property, work, and writing. History, made up of names and writing, was the high point of the Neolithic age, to which it was important to put an end. It was becoming possible to think that the end of the Neolithic would trigger a cyclical process leading automatically back to nomadism and the freedom of the Paleolithic age, but in a form developed enough to become compatible with a prodigious technology. Some would even go so far as to celebrate man's liberation from the constraints of his earthly condition: his projection into cosmic space quite naturally freed him from his historical condition, opening onto a space-time so enigmatic and unknown that as in prehistory, he was utterly lacking in names.

Finally, it was in this context of a return to the Paleolithic and a new relationship with nature, a combination of fear and hope, that the space of the cave irrupted for the first time in the works of artists such as Pinot-Gallizio and Fontana, but also those of the architect Frederick Kiesler. Paradoxically, at the same time that man was abandoning the earth and discovering weightlessness in the immensity and darkness of outer space, the cave, a telluric space if ever there was one, "resurfaced" as matrix and shelter. Because human beings now traveled in space beyond the earth, the closed space buried under the earth signified more than ever first nature, inviolate and ready to welcome him. But beyond the "cave," the question raised was that of the global environment. Often formulated was the idea of the earth as a continuous environment shaped by technology and subject to its effects at every instant. According to the architect Roderick Seidenberg, author of *Posthistoric Man* (1950), an unprecedented reversal was taking place in human history: ever since prehistoric times, man had tried to adapt to the earthly environment, but henceforth, the reverse process of expulsion had begun to occur. This suggested that the species had entered "posthistory"—the term irrupted at the time in a multitude of writings.[4] Against such a diagnosis, the architect Richard Neutra attempted to understand "whether by our own design we may attempt and assure our survival."[5] He was convinced that "if design, production, and construction cannot be channeled to serve survival, if we fabricate an environment—of which, after all, we seem an inseparable part—but cannot make it an organically possible extension of ourselves, then the end of the race may well appear in sight."[6]

To summarize, all sorts of ends were decreed: the cultural end of the Bronze Age, or even more decisive, of the Neolithic; the biological or moral end of the species; and finally, the most apocalyptic of all ends, that of the planet as a whole. But the atomic age that was beginning conveyed both the best and the worst. Notions of prehistory, unsurprisingly, adhered to all these narratives proclaiming the end of history. Once again, time miraculously compressed the origin and the end, expressing more exactly the shrinking of planet earth as a result of the expansion of communication and the prodigious development of technology. That *global consciousness* easily gave rise to the memory of earliest humanity, which belonged to no territory, race, or society.

Even more important, for the very first time, man was in a position to understand himself as simultaneously the agent, the witness, and the historian of a change in the geological and cultural era. It was therefore also the very first time that a geological change coincided with a cultural shift. The approximate periodization of human geology and the even more approximate periodization of geology were succeeded by the most precise chronology, that provided by a watch attached to a human wrist. "The Atomic Age began at exactly 5:30 Mountain War Time on the morning of July 16, 1945, on a stretch of semi-desert land about fifty airline miles from Alamogordo, N.M., just a few minutes before the dawn of a new day on the earth," wrote William L. Laurence, one of the witnesses to the first atomic weapons test, in White Sands, New Mexico. Invited by the U.S. Army with the aim of preparing the public for that unheard-of invention and its future uses, he wrote in the *New York Times* on September 26, 1945 (a month after the use of the atomic bomb against Japan, about which he said nothing): "At that great moment in history, ranking with the moment in the long ago when man first put fire to work for him and started on his march to civilization, the vast energy locked within the hearts of the atoms of matter was released . . . in a burst of flame such as had never before been seen on this planet, illuminating earth and sky for a brief span that seemed eternal."[7] Günther Anders's melancholy served as a counterpoint to that Promethean excitement. His diary began in "year 13 of the Atomic Age," that is, in 1958: "August 6, 1945, was day zero, the day it was demonstrated that universal history may not continue, that we are in any case capable of cutting its thread. That day inaugurated a new age in world history."[8] And that "day zero" made all the earlier changes of epoch trivial:[9] "All history is now reduced to prehistory,"[10] Anders also observed.

Georges Bataille: Lascaux-Hiroshima
Before World War II, and more particularly in the two years when he directed the review *Documents* (1929 to 1930), Georges Bataille turned

toward prehistory in search of the tools that would allow him to undermine evolutionism and humanism in favor of a notion of formless and radically contingent history. But after the war, under the influence of Alexandre Kojève, he developed a theory of anthropogenesis that firmly postulated a beginning and an end to history. Between the *Documents* years and the outbreak of the war, when prehistory once again made inroads in his thinking, Bataille ventured a few collective "acephalous" experiments against Fascism. These experiments, because they did not extend beyond the limits of the elective communities, ultimately left a bitter taste in his mouth.[11]

In September 1940, three adolescents discovered the Lascaux cave. (The review *Illustration* devoted a first eight-page report to the discovery on January 4, 1941, accompanied by several breathtaking color photographs.)[12] Five years later, the atomic bomb exploded in a cold light in the skies of Hiroshima and Nagasaki, an event symmetrical with the discovery of Lascaux. The narrative of anthropogenesis to which Bataille would devote himself until the end of his life — his *Lascaux; or, The Birth of Art* (1955) is not the only document concerning it, only the most brilliant — is discontinuous and scattered among several texts. It is nevertheless coherent.[13]

Bataille lived at a remove from the war, having taken refuge in his interiority. On February 3, 1942, he wrote to André Masson, who had emigrated to the United States:

> Europe is obviously closer to Tibet than to Connecticut. Life there is no doubt stranger than people perceive from the outside: we are cast back to the depths of time. Never has the real world seemed more of a dream to me: the air we breathe is dream air, an air of dread. And curiously, I would give up all the clear skies for the mist in which everything is buried here. I have never really understood the few old principles with which one considers history (the history that plays on our desires). History cannot forgo eating up lives. I readily give it mine to eat. I have little doubt that the essential is missing from the imaginary life of a future in which nothing could be eaten any longer, where everything would be free: a tension so true that you yourself become as true as a crab hidden in sand.[14]

Bataille had thus switched off the outside world in order to hide in the "depths of time." Although he did not take an active part or an active stand in immediate history—political history, as he further specified—he nevertheless believed he was sacrificing his life to true History as it was unfolding in its most secret mechanisms. Because he could not sympathize with the clear principles of a formal peace, he preferred to experience the "tension" created by an "idle" negativity. In the midst of history, which he compared to tedious bookkeeping, Bataille thus lived *his* prehistory, his subjective golden age, similar no doubt to the one he had recognized in Frobenius's copies of parietal images when they were exhibited in Paris in 1930.[15] The text he devoted to them shortly thereafter pointed out their "stupefying negation of man," who, "far from seeking to assert himself against nature ... deliberately appears there as a sort of waste product."[16] In them, he added, "the human body appears as a Cartesian diver, like a toy of the wind and the grass, like a cluster of dust charged with an activity that decomposes them."[17] Excrement of nature, a mere plaything, a ball of dust at the mercy of the wind: all these metaphors took away man's sovereign centrality. Of the mythology of the golden age, Bataille preserved only its loss, but he placed that loss at the heart of his approach: far from depicting an Edenic golden age when man would have lived in harmony with the trees and beasts in a state of grace before the fatal separation, he imagined the increased capacity of these men to experience "the blatant heterogeneity of our being in relation to the world." The ontological state of Bataille's golden age was the cheerful consciousness of the tragic: prehistoric men and the Bushmen of Africa, who ate the animals around them, were aware of the "rupture," "heterogeneity beneath all its forms," "the capacity to ever restore that which has been separated by an inconceivable violence."[18] The schema is well known: what had been collective for past golden ages and had manifested itself in great anonymous works remained isolated and hidden among the moderns. In 1942, once the dream of "acephalous" communities was over, prehistory became a golden age buried in the intimate realm, maternal and protective. So it was that during the immediate postwar period, following the same orientation, Bataille maintained the contemplative relationship with prehistoric images — especially those of animals — that their visual sumptuousness allowed. Hence, he found himself at a great distance from the descriptions he had given of them during his time at *Documents*, when he underscored man's simian past and even more, the human figure, altered, sadistically negated by cave paintings. That reversal of his own thinking corresponded to the reversal he detected in long human history: from animal to man — and vice versa.

Before the discovery of Lascaux, during the *Documents* years, Bataille placed the notion of "alteration" at the center of his thinking about prehistory. An alumnus of the École Nationale des Chartes and curator of the Cabinet des Médailles at the Bibliothèque Nationale, he was no doubt inspired by the writings of Sir John Evans, whom we have already encountered at the edge of the quarries of Saint-Acheul confirming the presence of an ax amid antediluvian sediment. Let us recall that Evans was studying the gradual corruption of classical and naturalistic forms that appeared on barbarian coinage, a process he designated by the term "alteration." The linear arrangement of the reproductions of coins in books and museum vitrines was intended to make that degenerative process visible. The discrete differences between contiguous coins in the series ultimately resulted in abysses between the two extremes: what started out as a Medusa's head ended up as a plow, and the horse belonging to Philip, king of Macedon, became a cruciform ornament (Figure 5.1). Bataille extracted *alteration* from this linear and depreciative schema and placed it at the center of creation, of any sort of creation acting "formlessly." Rather than bow to the rhythm of evolution and regression, alteration, according to him, could occur at random, here and there. Moving away from the regressive evolutionism of alteration, Bataille was in a position to contest violently Georges-Henri Luquet's theory of prehistoric art. Rather than see art as a linear process leading to the subject's autonomy and a time capitalizable from the childhood of

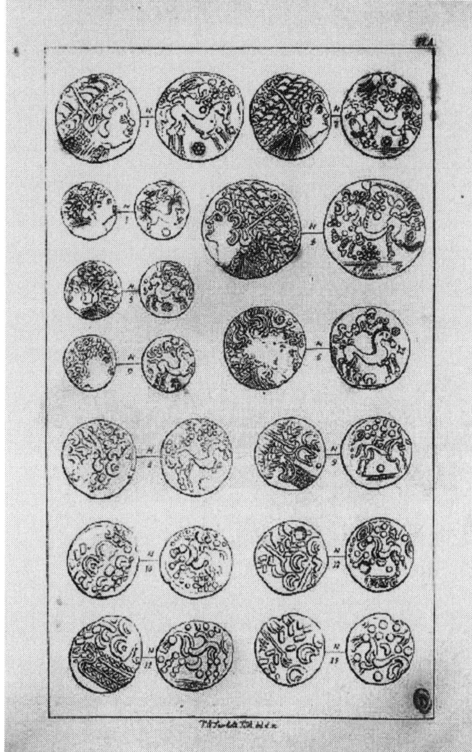

Figure 5.1. Anepigraphic coins of the ancient Bretons, in John Evans, *The Coins of the Ancient Britons* (London: B. Quaritch, 1864), plate A.

humanity to its intellectual and moral maturity, he theorized artistic activity as alteration, an exercise of the sadistic impulse that, in a process contrary to the one Luquet described, *destroys* its object:[19] "The destroyed object (the paper or the wall) is altered to such a point that it is transformed into a new object — a horse, a head, a man. Finally, through repetition, this new object is itself altered through a series of deformations. Art, since undeniably there is art, proceeds in this way by successive destructions. Insofar as it liberates *libidinal* instincts, these instincts are sadistic."[20] According to Bataille, graphic activity, far from constituting a gradual appropriation of the world, was a negation of the world as it is, including and above all a negation of man himself. And far from relying on the partial acknowledgment of the world, to which man had to adapt by imitating it, in order the better to emancipate himself from it subsequently, he negated it little by little as it emerged from the jumble of signs. Furthermore, Bataille differentiated himself as much from Luquet, a defender of art's gratuitousness, as from theories of utilitarian magic. Not only did men not paint the animals they hoped to kill on the hunt, but they also conducted an activity whose aim was to consume itself as a symbolic sacrifice — a sacrifice that would allow them to assert an equally unproductive libidinal instinct: sadism. The unproductivity of art, according to Bataille, extended to history as a whole. Although it is true that children produce scribbles, these are not the legacy of their remote ancestors any more than they are the first stage in an evolutionary process. Children do what they have to do: they find meaning in the negation of the world that preceded them and that was imposed on them. History, without a compass to orient itself in time, is itself also altered, as *formless* as the human face in prehistoric art (Figure 5.2).[21]

Because he detected that same alteration at work in the art of his time, Bataille reproached Luquet for his blindness toward it. Luquet, he said, had "rather abruptly displayed a process of decomposition and destruction that was no less painful to a lot of people than the sight of the decomposition and destruction of a corpse."[22] Immediately after this long text on Luquet, Bataille devoted a very brief text to Miró. The title was neutral and brief: "Joan Miró: Recent Paintings."[23] Hence, he considered the two extremes: the origin and the end of painting, the remote past and the immediate present, two poles that in prodigiously compressing time, produced history — but a history without coherence or a regular rhythm, a history in suspension, a deferred history. All the works by Miró that illustrated Bataille's article were part of a series of compositions on a white ground. Their monumental dimensions (more than six feet wide), the energetic marks, scratched and painted, and the formless spots could have been related to parietal paintings. One of these compositions depicted a human head, suggested by the contour of a profile of uneven thick ness approximately enclosing a red spot covered in part by a black

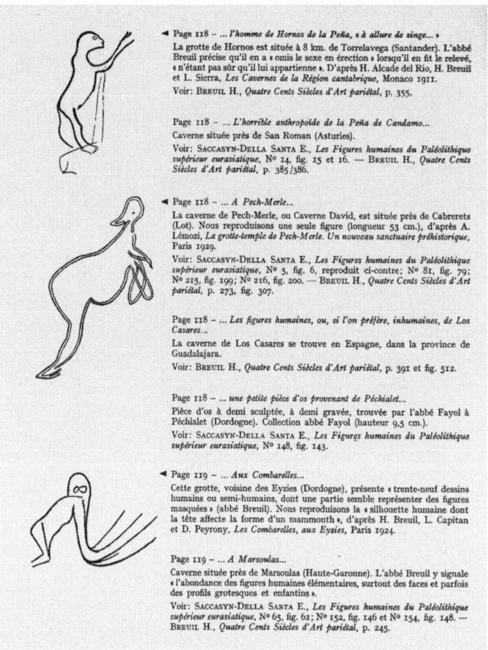

◄ Page 118 – ... *l'homme de Hornos de la Peña, « à allure de singe... »*
La grotte de Hornos est située à 8 km. de Torrelavega (Santander). L'abbé Breuil précise qu'il en a « omis le sexe en érection » lorsqu'il en fit le relevé, « n'étant pas sûr qu'il lui appartienne ». D'après H. Alcade del Rio, H. Breuil et L. Sierra, *Les Cavernes de la Région cantabrique*, Monaco 1911.
Voir: Breuil H., *Quatre Cents Siècles d'Art pariétal*, p. 355.

Page 118 – ... *L'horrible anthropoïde de la Peña de Candamo...*
Caverne située près de San Roman (Asturies).
Voir: Saccasyn-Della Santa E., *Les Figures humaines du Paléolithique supérieur eurasiatique*, Nº 14, fig. 15 et 16. — Breuil H., *Quatre Cents Siècles d'Art pariétal*, p. 385/386.

◄ Page 118 – ... *A Pech-Merle...*
La caverne de Pech-Merle, ou Caverne David, est située près de Cabrerets (Lot). Nous reproduisons une seule figure (longueur 53 cm.), d'après A. Lémozi, *La grotte-temple de Pech-Merle. Un nouveau sanctuaire préhistorique*, Paris 1929.
Voir: Saccasyn-Della Santa E., *Les Figures humaines du Paléolithique supérieur eurasiatique*, Nº 5, fig. 6, reproduit ci-contre; Nº 81, fig. 79; Nº 215, fig. 199; Nº 216, fig. 200. — Breuil H., *Quatre Cents Siècles d'Art pariétal*, p. 273, fig. 307.

Page 118 – ... *Les figures humaines, ou, si l'on préfère, inhumaines, de Los Casares...*
La caverne de Los Casares se trouve en Espagne, dans la province de Guadalajara.
Voir: Breuil H., *Quatre Cents Siècles d'Art pariétal*, p. 391 et fig. 512.

Page 118 – ... *une petite pièce d'os provenant de Péchialet...*
Pièce d'os à demi sculptée, à demi gravée, trouvée par l'abbé Fayol à Péchialet (Dordogne). Collection abbé Fayol (hauteur 9,5 cm.).
Voir: Saccasyn-Della Santa E., *Les Figures humaines du Paléolithique supérieur eurasiatique*, Nº 148, fig. 143.

◄ Page 119 – ... *Aux Combarelles...*
Cette grotte, voisine des Eyzies (Dordogne), présente « trente-neuf dessins humains ou semi-humains, dont une partie semble représenter des figures masquées » (abbé Breuil). Nous reproduisons la « silhouette humaine dont la tête affecte la forme d'un mammouth », d'après H. Breuil, L. Capitan et D. Peyrony, *Les Combarelles, aux Eyzies*, Paris 1924.

Page 119 – ... *A Marsoulas...*
Caverne située près de Marsoulas (Haute-Garonne). L'abbé Breuil y signale « l'abondance des figures humaines élémentaires, surtout des faces et parfois des profils grotesques et enfantins ».
Voir: Saccasyn-Della Santa E., *Les Figures humaines du Paléolithique supérieur eurasiatique*, Nº 65, fig. 62; Nº 152, fig. 146 et Nº 154, fig. 148. — Breuil H., *Quatre Cents Siècles d'Art pariétal*, p. 245.

Figure 5.2. Abbé Henri Breuil, *400 siècles d'art pariétal: Les cavernes ornées de l'âge du renne* (Montignac: Centre d'études et de documentation préhistoriques, 1952), p. 134.

spot (Figure 5.3). Other spots, as well, evoking no known form, were placed around the edges, as if to rival the human face's indisputable centrality. These paintings, according to Bataille, did the same work of alteration of the human figure that he had detected in prehistory and that Luquet had preferred to ignore. Jacques Boucher de Perthes could not imagine any early art other than one resembling the human head: "Of all images, it is his own that gives man the most to think about: it is a mirror in which he sees himself, measures himself, and senses himself" (Figure 5.4).[24] Painting, as soon as it set out to withdraw from man's service, necessarily had to negate that mirror. Visible on the canvas, Miró's brushstrokes, Bataille notes, also spoke in place of a mute prehistory: far from being directed against comestible animals, as the anthropologists thought, the prehistoric arrows were directed against man's sovereignty — man's first prey would thus have been his own image.

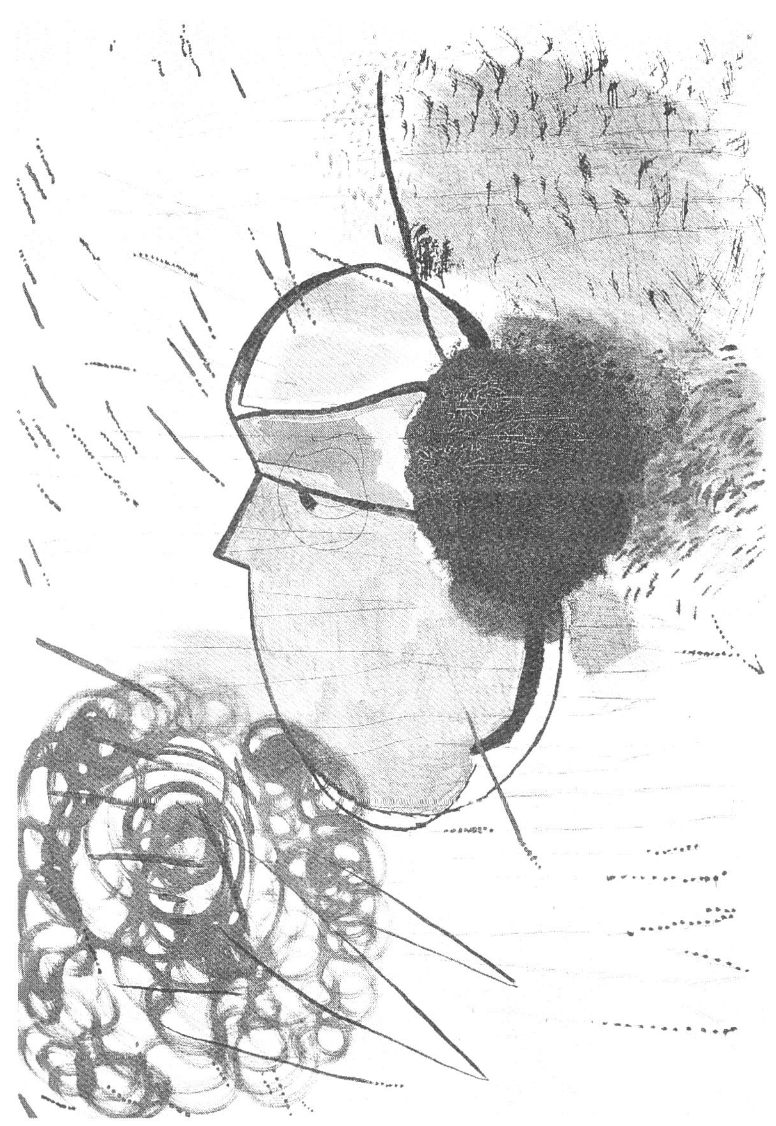

Figure 5.3. Joan Miró, *Painting (Head)*, 1930, 90½ × 65 in. Musée de Grenoble, inv. MG2762. Photo: © 2021 Successió Miró / ARS, NY / ADAGP, Paris.

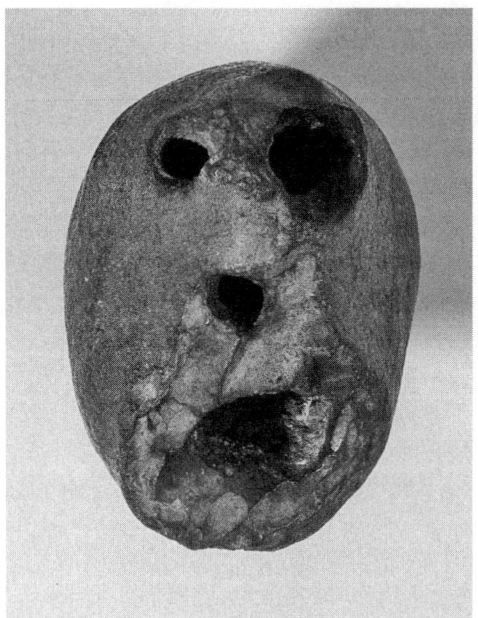

Figure 5.4. Flint known as the "Figure Stone" in the shape of a perforated human head, found in Abbeville, Somme. Paleolithic period? Discovered between 1840 and 1860 by Jacques Boucher de Perthes. Musée d'Archéologie Nationale, national domain of Saint-Germain-en-Laye, MAN7300. Photo: Loïc Hamon. © RMN-Grand Palais/Art Resource, NY.

After Hiroshima, Bataille stopped emphasizing the alteration of the human figure and the sadistic destruction he believed inherent to the sumptuous representation of animals. On the contrary, it was the astonishing material *preservation* of the Lascaux paintings that interested him, because it made the narrative of a "miracle" possible. This miracle did not just *shatter* continuous time, but rather twisted it to the point of actualizing prehistory. It was as if Lascaux had been discovered especially for Bataille: during the war, he had led a life in the "depths of time"; now he could finally confront, in the flesh, prehistory in a "feeling of presence — of clear and burning presence."[25] Lascaux was a challenge issued to anyone who found the courage to confront it — a subjective invention in every respect — and though Bataille readily conceded that many admirable prehistoric works had brought us knowledge of prehistoric art in general, he did so only to remind us immediately that time had distorted their appearance.[26] All the other caves, he added, entailed the work of specialists, who attempted through analysis to restore their integrity and meaning. In reality, what bones were to the altered frescoes, the latter were to Lascaux: fossils without an inner life, dull reflections.[27] At Lascaux, by contrast, "the splendor of the underground halls is incomparable: even when directly before this wealth of animal figures, how is one to avoid a momentary suspicion that it is all a mirage, some deliberate trick? But precisely to that degree we doubt, or, rubbing our eyes, ask whether it could be possible, the truth's evidence makes its simple response to the desire, common to all men, to be wonderstruck" (Figures 5.5 and 5.6).[28] These figures were untruthfully "present": on the one hand, Lascaux revealed the "miracle" of the abolition of time in its pure state; on the other, its phenomenologization of prehistory made possible for everyone the experience of the very first reversal of history: the "transition" from animal to man, which Bataille also called the "decisive" "moment" or "step."[29] Even though here and there he recognized that nothing occurs ex nihilo and that art would have been inconceivable without the experience of work and without the consciousness of death (two earlier acquisitions of the species), he also argued that artistic creation, in spite of everything, constituted an absolute beginning, the tipping point when man ceased to be a beast. He accused the "specialist" Leroi-Gourhan of having forgotten that decisive moment.[30]

Lascaux was so well preserved that it appeared to be fake. Bataille deliberately constructed a dramatic fiction on the basis of that first impression. He drafted a screenplay that was never produced, but a drama emerged from the intertextuality of his many writings: a drama with a beginning, two acts, and an ending.[31] For him, prehistory was the "period about which no narrative left by contemporaries informs us."[32] But that narrative void could then be set in motion and its negative character dynamized by a "dialectical relationship," a system capable of producing historical *difference*, since that prehistoric void gave rise to a fictionalizing mechanism. He believed it important not to seek to fill that gap with bits of oral traditions coming from distant primitive cultures, because it was immaterial to know what the first gesture, the first wall, the first cave were: inasmuch as

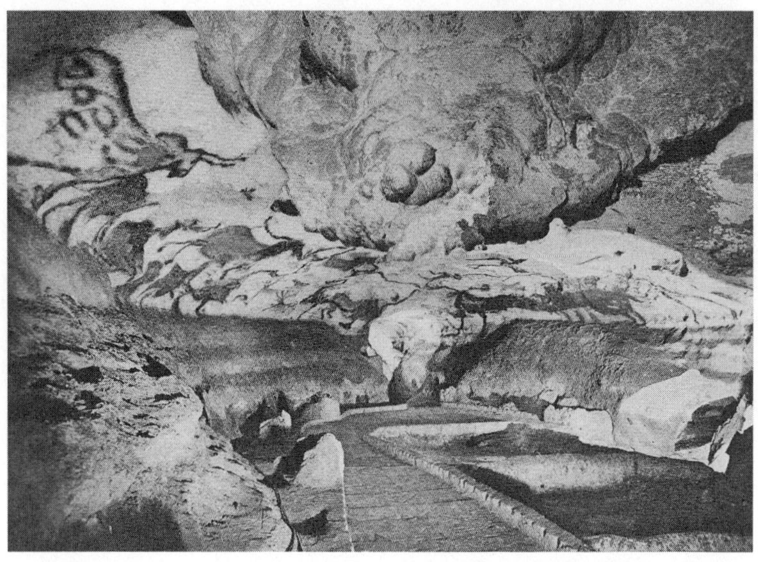

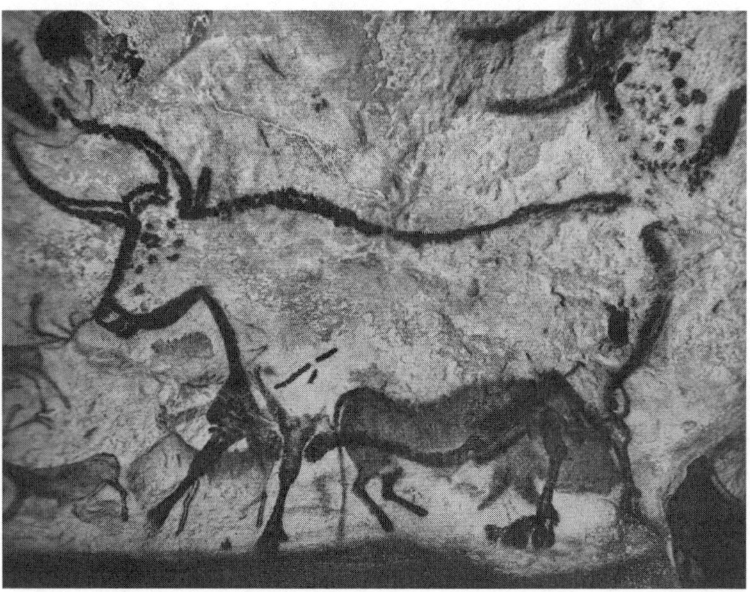

Figure 5.5. Lascaux: entrance of the axial gallery seen from the back. Photograph by Hans Hins in Georges Bataille, *Lascaux ou la naissance de l'art* (Geneva: Skira, 1955), p. 67.

Figure 5.6. Lascaux: first bull, red horse, brown horses, great hall left wall (detail). Photograph by Hans Hins in Georges Bataille, *Lascaux ou la naissance de l'art* (Geneva: Skira, 1955), p. 50.

Lascaux was perfectly well preserved, it became arbitrarily — that is, based purely on a decision on the part of posterity — the beginning of art. Lascaux was thus a history of reception, a response that gave rise to a question, a posterity that invented its ancestry, a repetition that activated an origin. At the very moment when Bataille was weaving the narrative of a universal history, Lascaux was becoming a contemporary history.

The beginning of this narrative corresponds to the nameless duration that no subjectivity has experienced and that, as such, is not time. Before time, according to Bataille, there was a duration of an unrepresentable length, as mute as stones and fossils can be.[33] Then came the beasts and the first representatives of the human species, which barely disturbed that geological inertia. That slowness, stretching out over thousands and thousands of years, was still governed by the law of "stagnation," of the "rut," "repetition," "incubation."[34] Bodies were heavy and movements crude. Through work, the compactness of the environment and of bodies began to fissure imperceptibly. *Homo faber* set out to negate "formless" matter,[35] including his own matter. That was also the first scission, still very discrete, between man and beast. Work delivered two fundamental experiences to *Homo faber*. First, it taught him to *wait*, to defer his desire for the result, to project himself into the future. But that work also caused stupor in the face of death, suddenly interrupting that projection into the future. The suspension and negation of desire also had their erotic side, independent of animal reproduction. That suspension and interruption of *time* through the disjunction of the present and the future was the first subjective fracture in the mute mineral block. But suddenly, time began to accelerate vertiginously, causing a true cataclysm — the first subjective cataclysm. It was the beginning of history, since Bataille, like Kojève, believed there was no history that is not human.

ACT I: APPEARANCE OF THE "SLENDER BEING"

"The Cradle of Humanity: The Vézère Valley" fictionalizes history in the extreme. In it, Bataille recounts the "event" that came to shatter the very *longue durée:* "One day, at the twist of a road, perhaps in a group; perhaps alone, a new kind of man appeared. He was much larger than the inhabitant who for tens of thousands of years occupied these places without contestation. He was much larger, more slender, more human."[36] "Time," said Paul Ricoeur, "becomes human time to the extent that it is organized after the manner of a narrative;."[37] It is that humanization of time that Bataille introduced when he proceeded to "plot" his narrative, as denoted by the traditional, "One day. . . ." It would be beside the point and futile to criticize Bataille's many erroneous claims; it is more productive to understand their utility.

Following Bataille's laudatory critique of *Tristes Tropiques*, Claude Lévi-Strauss, writing to him in 1956, undertook discreetly to correct the theory in *Lascaux*:

> Allow me, finally, to clarify a slight misunderstanding on a minor point (pp. 107–108). I do not ascribe "the beginning of beginnings" to Neolithic times, very much to the contrary. Like Rousseau, whom I am paraphrasing, I consider them an intermediate stage, a "happy medium," says Rousseau, corresponding to a sort of sociological wisdom when man took it upon himself to stand upright. There is, it seems to me, only one "beginning of beginnings" conceivable, and that is the appearance of language. Indeed, for the higher art of the Paleolithic period, it seems to me to attest [*illegible*] to such freedom, I would even say such casualness, that I cannot consider it a beginning, a final term, rather (and with no further consequences) of an evolution about which we know nothing.[38]

Lévi-Strauss corrected Bataille's vision of a founding and fertile miracle with the opposite and no less illusory vision of the Paleolithic as a "child born without a mother" and a "mother who died without a child." The author of "The Archaic Illusion"[39] recalled the futility of the search for the origin and went so far as to locate the "casualness" of the Paleolithic in its exceptionality and its definitive obscurity, due in part to the absence of "further consequences." Bataille, on the contrary, posited a radical break between, on the one hand, geology and natural evolution, slow and gradual in both cases, and on the other, human history, highly conducive to "disasters," both positive and negative. He conceived of Cro-Magnon man as a new man with a "fluid" body.[40] More than "casual," this man was a "slender" being, that is, his "gestures" were free and loose as he drew on the cave walls and at the same time brought man out of his animal lethargy. Far from the continuist notions of artistic production resulting from Gottfried Semper's or Aloïs Riegl's *Kunstgeschichte*, dealing indiscriminately with useful and useless artifacts, Bataille's fiction conformed to the religious model of art, positing at the beginning of human history a creation from "nothing": "In the hands of these men, who created art, who strayed from an empty past, there was a virtue comparable to the most accomplished hands of today. And nearly from the first stroke, art attained the power of evocation, which would thereafter only be found with great difficulty."[41]

The two acts in Bataille's drama thus connected two reversals that lie at the heart of the narrative and take up the aporia of the prehistoric void. Unlike man, the animal does not reverse itself. It is not capable of any dialectic; it cannot deny what it is and cannot affirm what it is not. The animal *is*, and within the long span of Western metaphysics, the animal is not capable of experiencing or of conceiving death.[42] As Bataille wrote in *The Accursed Share*: "Even if he has lost the world in leaving animality behind, man has nonetheless become that *consciousness* of having lost it which we are."[43]

FIRST REVERSAL: THE ANIMAL FELL AND MAN ROSE UP

The "elevation" of man did not come about in the economical and direct manner of modern utilitarianism, but rather in a dialectical and extravagant manner: "What these admirable frescoes proclaim with a youthful vigor is not only that the man who painted them ceased being an animal by painting them but that he stopped being an animal by giving the animal, and not himself, a poetic image that seduces us and seems sovereign."[44] Elsewhere, Bataille explained that Lascaux "forcefully transmitted to us the fact that, being men, they resembled us, but as a means for telling us so they left us innumerable pictures of the animality they were shedding — as though they felt obliged to clothe a nascent marvel with the animal grace they had lost."[45] He accounted for that "chiasmus" in terms of the friendship linking man and beast and the guilt of hunters toward their prey: "While their screams called for its death, they awaited the hunted animal's forgiveness, as in a drama ordered by a tragic fatality."[46] And just as "the first man" extracted the animal from the sphere of being in order to make it a "thing," the "human predator asks forgiveness for treating the animal as a thing so that he will be able to accomplish without any remorse what he has already apologized for doing."[47] But at the very moment when man detached himself from the animal to become its "master," the animal, simultaneously, became a stranger to him, radiating "omnipotence from an impenetrable world."[48]

At the opposite extreme from this drama, a photograph shows a completely different version of the relation between man and animal. Bataille was sufficiently struck by it that he kept it, along with two related articles, in a file dating to 1929. Now held in the Bataille archival collection at the Bibliothèque nationale, these documents are accompanied by this note in Bataille's hand: "On the apes."[49] The photograph in fact depicts an ape called *Ameranthropoides loysi* (Figure 5.7): during the *Documents* years, it undoubtedly symbolized for Bataille the altered figure of man. It was during an expedition undertaken in Venezuela between 1917 and 1920 that the Swiss geologist François de Loys discovered and killed the *Ameranthropoides loysi*. Apart from the members of the expedition, no one had seen it, alive or dead. Yet someone took a striking postmortem snapshot of it. We would probably not know anything about the animal—we do not even know the exact year of its fateful encounter with the geologist's team—if Dr. Georges Montandon (a notorious racist and future collaborator executed by the French Resistance) had not set out to plumb the mysteries of that outrageously anthropoid ape.[50] It was thanks to his publications, two of which appear in the "On the Apes" file, that Bataille learned of the animal. Montandon had recounted how the members of the geologist's team, then in the midst of the forest, "found themselves one day in the presence of a pair of apes of human stature. Filled with fury, [the apes] advanced on them, standing upright, but holding onto the bushes, breaking off branches as if

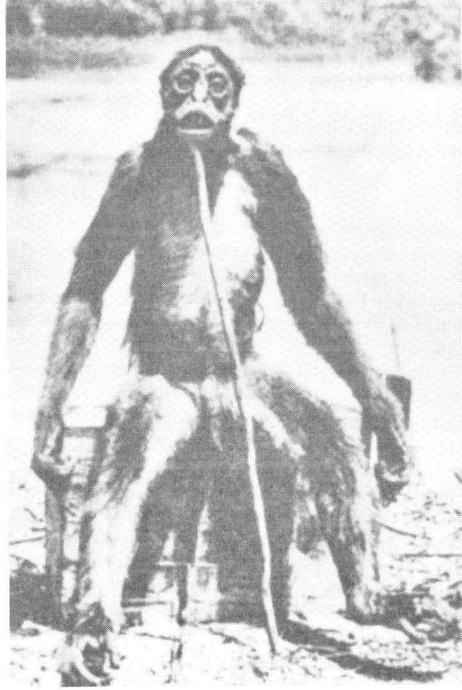

Figure 5.7. *Ameranthropoïdes loysi.* From Georges Montandon, "Découverte d'un singe d'apparence anthropoïde en Amérique du Sud," *Journal de la société des américanistes* 21 (1929), plate 5.

to use them as weapons, discharging excrement into their hands and throwing the excrement at the men."[51]

Once killed, the large ape — it was a female — was seated on a box, her eyes still wide open, a stick placed under her chin to hold her up, her long legs seeming to grip the corners of the box, her legs open to exhibit her genitals. This staging was meant to be disturbing: Was she dead or alive? Was this an animal or a person? A "master" or a "slave"? As for the stick, it served not only to guarantee the inanimate beast's seated position, but also to accentuate her verticality and her resemblance to the human species. A true prosthesis, the stick supporting the ape provided a supplemental human resemblance.[52]

In placing that stick between the ground and the chin, François de Loys's team was appealing to a semiotics instituted by the most canonical naturalistic works.[53] But in transposing that semiotics to the photographic medium, the image became a document whose visual violence was much stronger than that of its graphic anteced-ents: this "document" denied death in order to feign life and imposed an increased anthropomorphism on the animal. Literally and vir-tually supported and steadied, that forced anthropomorphism encapsulated colonial practices.[54] The beast took the place of the "native" — unless it was the image of the Master.

Ape, man, architecture. Here represented by the vertical stick, Bataille made architecture the third link in an evolutionary chain. In his *Critical Dictionary*, he wrote: "In the morphological process, men apparently represent only an intermediate stage between the apes and tall buildings.[55] In Montandon's eyes, *Ameranthropoides loysi* had constituted the missing link between ape and man, but here, Bataille reversed that idea: it was man himself who became the missing link between ape and architecture. The latter coerced man to conform to the ideal. The photograph of *Ameranthropoides loysi*, in spite of itself, condensed that act of undermining the sovereignty of man, transformed into a malleable matter submitted to a norm. It made obvious the function of constraint assumed by the stick/prosthesis. Who was this animal coerced into the semiverticality of a seated man? Who was the architectural ape? What was that "intermediate stage"? Man himself, of course, *anthropos*, the colonial master: notable for his absence, he appeared in negative form in that photographic staging. The stick or the gun — a synecdoche for architecture — and the aggressive ape "flinging excrement" and resolutely resembling the human, constituted for Bataille the unfathomable and formless depths of Western practices. The master coerced the beast to resem-ble him while himself appearing in the image as a subservient beast.

Let us return to Lascaux. A considerable change had occurred in Bataille's thinking since the *Documents* years. *Documents* had emphasized the alteration of the human figure; the Lascaux years only incidentally addressed that alteration in favor of the idea of the fascinating animal. The "drama" of *Documents* had only a single act, repeated indefinitely and unpredictably. That was not the case for Lascaux, whose drama involved an elaborate plot — setting history in motion—and the modicum of duplicity necessary to the plot, with characters who pretended to be something other than what they were. Hence, at a time when a majority of prehistorians explained cave painting as one of the stages in a hunting ritual, Bataille made Lascaux an archirite, a matrix rite, that of the "transition" from beast to man and man's self-generation through art. With his discontinuous, even "miraculous" notion of human history, Bataille had little sympathy for the idea that "primitive" tribes might be "survivals" of the Stone Age: not because he was critical of the racist evolutionism inherent in that idea, but because, as he regularly noted, these "modern primitives lack this outpouring, this upsurge of creative awakening that makes Lascaux man our counterpart and not that of the Aborigine."[56] In the beginning was sovereign art, sacred and unproductive—utilitarianism came only in a second moment. Bataille thus converted the magic theory of the hunt—or the theory of play as education and as man's adaptation to his environment—into a phenomenological interpretation.[57] The cave event consisted of an "apparition," a "nascent image":[58] that of art itself. "Before its use as magic, art appeared," wrote Bataille. The statement could have been written by Luquet, if Bataille had not added: "Specifically, the apparition of the animal was not, to the man who astonished himself by making it appear, the apparition of a definable object, like the apparition in our day of beef at the butcher that we cut up and weigh. That which appeared had at first a significance that was scarcely accessible, *beyond* what could have been defined. Precisely, the equivocal, undefinable meaning was religious."[59] The ambiguity of art was the part of human life that the animal's restricted economy could not provide and that was destined to remain *unsatisfied*. Art was at once the expression of death and the response to it—"a sort of enormous fissure that has continually opened up to us possibilities other than efficacious action."[60] If earlier humanity conveyed the sense of death with prohibitions relating to the corpse—the only inappropriable object—"slender" humanity decided to confront death through the "subterfuge" of the "spectacle" of art.[61] Defined by turns as "apparition," "miracle," and "transition," art was a symbolic sacrifice, the fictive destruction of the object, and as a result, a momentary break in the long history of reification — the other face of anthropogenesis. Hence, far from the theories that made prehistory a peaceful era of abundance and leisure time, far, as well, from the theories of the ruthless struggles for survival in an arid environment, Bataille stipulated the internal wealth that prehistoric men had at their disposal and that they expended at their festivals: it was the vestiges of that expenditure that were discovered on the cave walls. And it was that miracle that those who discovered Lascaux relived.

ACT 2: THE DISCOVERY OF LASCAUX BY THREE ADOLESCENTS ON SEPTEMBER 12, 1940

This discovery was the true reversal, the one that counted most, the mold used to form Bataille's conceptualization of the first reversal of human history. Why did Bataille obsessively use the term "reversal" to account for the experience of the cave's discovery? Primarily for two reasons, one linked to his phenomenological approach, the other to his notion of history and, more precisely, his philosophy of history.

The "discovery" of Lascaux was so "overwhelming" because in the first place, "before us are paintings twenty thousand years old," yet "they have the freshness of youth. . . . Some children found them. Some children scrambled down into the fissure left by an uprooted tree" (Figure 5.8).[62] The geological "fissure" was thus a "fissure" in time, whose most remote beginning suddenly coincided with the present. If the most ancient paintings were to appear as young as the children who had discovered them, a postulate was needed that could trigger a specifically *catastrophist* reversal of time capable of being reproduced ad infinitum. Indeed, the Lascaux cave "unceasingly rewards that expectation of the miraculous which is, in art and passion, the most profound aspiration of life."[63] This, then, is why Lascaux was a posterity before becoming an origin: it provided the miracle that every human life needs. It made possible "communication," even "friendship" between prehistoric man and modern man. In reality, the two "resemble[d] each other" more than one might have thought: just as prehistoric man had left behind the restricted economy of animality, thanks to the sacrificial economy of art, modern man put behind him a restricted — alienated and impoverished — economy in order to accede to the dazzling present of Lascaux.

Bataille remarked that the many visitors who descended the cave's stairs, "similar to those in a Paris subway station," ran the risk that "the present-day world" would follow their exploration, "and only rather indirectly glimpsing from afar the reflection of a world that has vanished, a world which I said had become accessible."[64] He would go even further in an unpublished manuscript: "You should have come in the very days when these secret wonders were revealed. The crowd of tourists, the unceasing, anonymous humanity, the amorphous, vapid crowd of our time will no longer flow ceaselessly under these millennial vaults."[65] He extracted himself from that impoverished and homogeneous present while thinking back

> *to the time when the first of our contemporaries entered the cave*, when they suddenly found themselves in the presence of these marvels that no one had laid eyes on for fifteen thousand years. In this moment, if I had found myself there, it seems to me I could truly have entered this long-lost world, whereas now, as I just said, the present world follows me; it descends into the cave with me.[66]

The three adolescents became the true "mediators" with whom Bataille had to identify if he wanted to escape the mediocrity of his era — an identification that signified the abolition of time, pure and simple. Lascaux was fundamentally an "instant," the only temporality compatible with the much more elusive experience of sovereignty. Just as Lascaux had abolished the "fifteen thousand years" separating the paintings from their discovery, the cave could at any moment crumble with the introduction of *flowing air*. History counted for Lascaux only as "beginning," pure presence, or "decision." That was the reason prehistoric man could not be the fellow creature of present-day primitive peoples, "ruins" of a past time, according to Edward Tylor or James Frazer. Primitive peoples were for Bataille incapable of history, because history happened only to those who were capable of "beginning." But modern man was no more capable of experiencing Lascaux, unless he knew how to wrest himself from his time.

The inverted image of primitive man, the ruin of history, modern man was constantly being projected into the future, absorbed by the dynamic of the "project," becoming ever more the *animal laborans* Hegel had called a "slave." So it was that Bataille denounced the impoverished representation of prehistoric men given by the painter Fernand Cormon, for example. The horde of dry bodies he painted represented only the destitution of his own era dressed up in the garments of prehistory.[67] Bataille contrasted that unconscious, immediate, and passive projection with his own: a willful, active, dialectical projection — all in all, a *determined* projection.

In an original and captivating book devoted to Bataille's writings on prehistory, the anthropologist Daniel Fabre underscored their Christian system: within that discipline obsessed with the denial of the existence of God, but practiced by an army of priests, the apparition of Lascaux to "children" was built on the model of the apparition of the Virgin.[68] Fabre's anthropological approach shows that prehistory came to occupy the void of a world without God. It is altogether true that Bataille's Christianity, though "atheological," remained predominant in his notion of prehistory. His contemplative approach, in fact, preserved a series of themes essential to Christianity: the image that mediates the divine in its "presence," its "clear and burning presence"; the figures of mediators — here, the children Fabre insistently and extensively focused on; the temporality of the "miracle," which delivered a revelation and a cure; and finally, reversal as such. Every man who succeeds in extracting himself from the time of the Fall — the alienated present — is knocked off his horse like Saint Paul and becomes a man transfigured, a "new man."[69] That Christianity was no longer in harmony with the sadistic negation of the figure of man that Bataille had defended before the war, but it was perfectly compatible with the dazzling images of animals. It would therefore be justifiable to address the same grievance to Bataille that he addressed to Luquet: Why did he privilege the positive representations of animals, rather than the negative ones of man? Of course, Bataille did not disavow his initial hypothesis of a formless and sadistically denied human figure, but what now mattered most to him was the miraculous images of animals, capable of providing the experience of reversal by being the object of contemplation.

ENDING/SECOND REVERSAL: HIROSHIMA

Although Lascaux was the apparition of the sacred that allowed contemporary man to extricate himself from the mediocrity of the present, it remained a private and highly elitist experience. In that respect, Lascaux was an experience symmetrical with that of modern art. As has already been pointed out, Bataille wrote a book on Lascaux simultaneously with one on Manet. For him, Manet had altered the body of art, because unlike the anonymous artists of Lascaux, he had no animal at his disposal from which to make the radiant image. The only sovereignty left to him was thus that of his painting, convinced as he was that that autonomous art was still pursuing, in spite of everything, "through research and appearances confined to the plastic realm . . . the quest for a lost world, the sacred world. Does it not often seem to us that, beyond its powerlessness, modern art pursues the end that our utilitarian disasters no longer achieve?"[70] Hence modern art was a stunning, though limited, expression of the exercise of the "idle negativity" that remained the only field conducive to the sacred in the *satisfied* world of modernity. As it happened, what the artists were doing within the "subterfuge" of representation, a chief of state, Harry Truman, made the *decision* to do on a grand scale in real life by ordering that the atomic bomb be dropped on Hiroshima and Nagasaki. When the need to leave the restricted economy and expend its internal wealth remains unsatisfied, that need becomes a "destructive impulse." Roger Caillois had spoken of the modern war as the expression of the sacred. Bataille went further: because it was still assimilated to the restricted economy,[71] war was no longer in a position to fulfill that function. The only objective apparition of the sacred in the homogeneous world was the atomic bomb because of its indisputable annihilating effect. "We in the middle of the twentieth century," wrote Bataille, "are poor, we are very poor, we are incapable of undertaking an important job if it has no return. Everything we undertake is submitted to the control

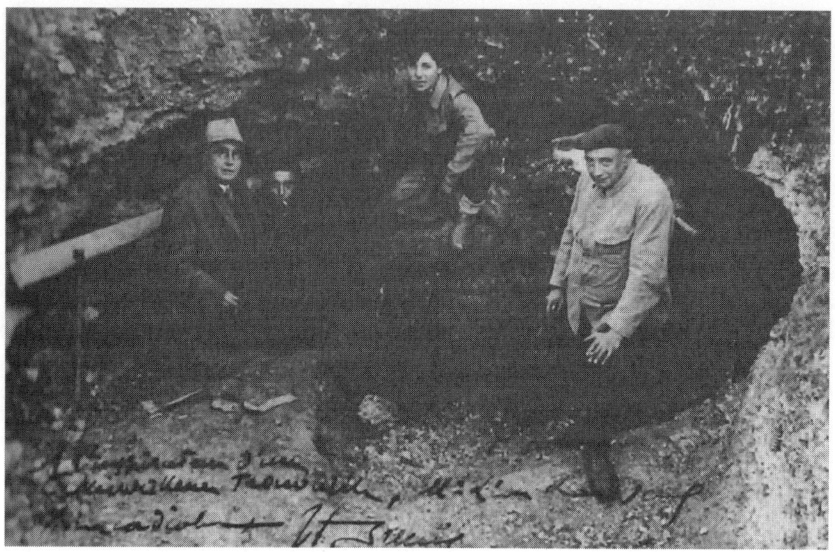

Figure 5.8. Photograph of Leon Laval (teacher), Marcel Ravidat and Jacques Marsal ("inventors" of the cave), and Henri Breuil in front of the entrance to Lascaux, 1940. Conservation Régionale des Monuments Historiques, Périgueux.

of profitability. One sole exception: the engineering and materials of destruction, works that today threaten to exterminate the species, and even to end terrestrial life."[72] The potlatch henceforth included the end of the species and of all life on earth.

It is now easy to understand why the first Lascaux moment was the discovery of the cave, rather than its creation proper. On the one hand, the discovery roughly coincided with the disaster of Hiroshima; on the other, the opposition between the two was so perfect that it made them ipso facto interdependent.[73] One of Bataille's texts on prehistory begins with these lines:

It has become commonplace today to talk about the eventual extinction of human life. The latest atomic experiments made tangible the notion of radiation invading the atmosphere and creating conditions in which life in general could no longer thrive. . . . I do not intend to talk to you about our eventual demise today. I would like, on the contrary, to talk to you about our birth. *I am simply struck by the fact that light is being shed on our birth at the very moment when the notion of our death appears to us.* In fact, only recently have we begun to discern with a kind of clarity the earthly event that was the birth of man.[74]

An implacable symmetry: Lascaux had made the internal experience of prehistoric man "perceptible," and the nuclear bombs had "made tangible the perception of the radiation invading the atmosphere." Lascaux was the *beginning* of a universal history, of which Hiroshima might well constitute the *ending*. "A Message in a Bottle, or, from the Universal History of Origins to the Coming of a Potential Disaster," was the title of one of Bataille's projects that remained unfinished at his death. It contained the following: "The material. Abstract of universal history. (From the first man to man as material)."[75]

The second reversal of universal history was the moment when man found himself reduced to the rank of material or slave, even though he thought he was an acknowledged and satisfied Master. That reversal, celebrated at Hiroshima, continued slowly, gradually, imperceptibly. But Bataille's dramatic fiction needed an event capable of fostering the dramatization of history to the end.[76] Hiroshima was that event, the "One day . . . " It had constituted another great rite, making perceptible the master's reversal into a slave and man's reversal into an animal. It had been the return to animality and the beginning of the return — drawn out again at an incredibly slow pace — to mute geology.

Bataille's analysis was based on eyewitness accounts collected by the American journalist John Hersey: his *Hiroshima*, published in 1946 and translated into French in 1947, was reviewed by Bataille in his journal *Critique*.[77] In 1948, Bataille visited Lascaux for the first time. His reflection on the ending — Hiroshima — thus preceded his experience of the beginning. Hersey had opted to reduce his reporting "to the succession of multiple aspects recorded in the memories of the witnesses,"[78] with no thread weaving them into a continuous narrative. That fraying of the narrative was essential to Bataille. The six principal witnesses in the book were ordinary individuals, like those "we meet every day, to whom we give familiar names."[79] Suddenly, the unique event: "It is after the end of an alert (the city, still intact, was living in the expectation of 'conventional' bombs) and in a clear sky, that the bolt of lightning fell."[80] That event — bolt of lightning — was symmetrical to the arrival of the "slender being" in the Vézère Valley. When the bolt of lightning fell, Bataille recounts, "an avaricious, staggering, interminable revelation began for everyone, within the solitude and ignorance of the unheard-of thing to come. It was in fact the opposite of a revelation; those on both sides were misled by derisory suppositions."[81] In other words, the residents of Hiroshima had suffered an experience in the manner of animals, one that eluded them in every respect. The only thing belonging to them was "the compartmentalized animal view, mistakenly deprived of an opening on the future, of an event whose essence is to decide man's fate."[82] The residents of Hiroshima were plunged into a Cartesian stupor that turned into stupidity, and the bolt of lightning that fell from the sky closed the metaphysical cycle described by Vico, because it no longer caused religious "astonishment," but instead reduced humanity to bestiality.

Before and during the event, only one man knew the meaning of what was happening, only one man had an overall and continuous vision of history: President Truman. Just after the event, everyone knew what had happened except those who had been through it:

> The whole world learned before the residents of Hiroshima that the city had for the first time been subjected to the invention that would turn the world upside down and leave its inventors themselves staggered. To those in the streets of Hiroshima who were dazzled by an enormous bolt of lightning, which had the intensity of the sun and was not followed by a bang, the colossal explosion taught nothing. They suffered it like an animal, they did not even know its enormous scope.[83]

The revelation of Lascaux was thus invalidated by the unintelligible experience of Hiroshima, and the dazzlement of Lascaux was negated by that of the atomic bomb. Bataille had stressed the interlacings and tangles of lines that, though fortuitous and independent of one another, formed as if "miraculously" and "instinctively" an "inextricable totality" in Lascaux; he now insisted likewise on the compartmentalized and confused character of the experience of the atomic bomb. Granted, he had excluded a single man from the total ignorance of the ending, to whom the role of "decider" fell, in the *exceptional* choice of the bomb (a political decisionism in Carl Schmitt's sense), but he attributed nearly the same role to himself—Truman had the monopoly on action, Bataille on contemplation.[84] How can one deny that history for Bataille now had a clear meaning? Its tangles, far from being formless and random, as in the time of *Documents*, now formed an "inextricable totality" for anyone looking at them from above. Several times, however, Bataille had criticized the Hegelian "end of history," whose objectification in the philosopher's thought constituted in Bataille's eyes a sort of return to the inorganic spirit of the beginnings. "Upon reading *The Phenomenology of Spirit* or upon looking at the portrait of the old Hegel," he wrote, "one cannot fail to be struck by an icy impression of completion in which all the possibilities come together."[85]

The course that Kojève devoted to Hegel's *Phenomenology of Spirit* between 1933 and 1939 had a notorious influence on many Parisian intellectuals, from Lacan to Bataille to Queneau. Since these courses were edited and published by Queneau in 1947, it is possible that their impact on Bataille's thought was revived and reinforced.[86] Hegel's universal history became in Kojève an anthropogenesis from the beginning to the end of history: man is distinguished from the "passive quietude" of the animal by his "disquieted desire," which manifests itself in a negative action, the destruction of the desired object. In a hostile world that ignores him, man desires the "recognition" that the negativity of his action brings: both his action on matter through work and his action on other men, who recognize the prestige of the "Master" and turn out to be his "slaves." As long as there are masters and slaves, there will be history. The end of history, according to Kojève, would correspond to the end of negative action, the moment when all slaves would find "satisfaction" in becoming masters. Men would become "posthistorical animals," confining themselves to reflexes.[87] It is exactly this slow animal quietude that Bataille also described, though his dramatic account required an event marking the beginning of the end.

Posthistory (1950–1960): Human History as Natural History
Bataille, it has been said, was far from the only one to envision that regression to a state of quietude that nothing or almost nothing besides natural cataclysms could ever again disturb. Across the Atlantic, in 1950 Roderick Seidenberg wrote his *Posthistoric Man* with the conviction that history was finally becoming a science at the very moment when it was reaching its end. However extraordinary the events might be, the ineluctable laws that governed the course of history differed only very little from implacable natural laws: evolution, extinction, entropy. With the deceleration and the disorder of human history, which was becoming increasingly uniform on the global scale, it was becoming possible to perceive that human history was fundamentally a natural history. The human species had begun in the shadow of prehistory and would end in moral extinction and the return to the inorganic state — such "crystallization" was the lot of all species. All the more so in that humanity was characterized by the production of an artificial world — symbols, thoughts, technology. Its return to the inorganic state would thus not necessarily be natural. It could happen simply through the total organization of life in the slightest of its aspects; through collectivization, which was gaining the upper hand in capitalist and communist societies; and through statistics and social mimetism, which produced average men at the expense of individualities. In short, it could happen through all the manifestations of a disproportionate "intelligence" at the expense of instinct. Between prehistory and posthistory, there had been a "drama," a transition, brief, but sumptuous, commonly called "history." It was the product of a tension between intelligence and instinct that was being resolved in favor of the former. The different episodes of that history — "animism," "Ptolemaic astronomy," "faith in a hereafter," "isolate dignity in an otherwise meaningless

and impersonal world," "even perhaps . . . faith in a God"—all that was disappearing: "The shedding of these inestimable illusions may be merely stages in his diminishing stature before he himself vanishes from the scene—lost in the icy fixity of his final state in a prehistoric age."[88]

It was after reading this book, with its predictive tone, that Lewis Mumford, who until that time had devoted himself to studying the history of the city and of technology over the *longue durée*, would also look pessimistically toward the future. He readily borrowed the expression "posthistoric man" to describe the path taken by his contemporaries, whom he saw as inverted figures of prehistoric man.[89] The risk, then, was that history was coming full circle. Originally, man was distinguished from the animals by the invention of symbols as "expressions of inner states" and as "an externalization and projection of attitudes and desires" that helped him to detach himself "from the pressing suggestions of his immediate environment, from a limited here and now."[90] But "posthistoric" man had become so abstract that emptied of all capacity to create symbols, reduced to a technicity that was beginning to turn against him, he was at the mercy of planetary crises with an intensity comparable to that of the climate of the last glacial period: "But the menace that then came from nature," Mumford added, "now comes from the busy minds and hands of men."[91]

Let us keep in mind the theme of a posthistory that would be the flip side of prehistory: it was central to the most politically incompatible modes of thought. The liberals Seidenberg and Mumford embraced it alongside Heidegger's disciple Jan Patočka, writing his *Heretical Essays in the Philosophy of History* under conditions of extreme distress in Czechoslovakia, as did Arnold Gehlen and Henri de Man, followers of Fascism, alongside the leftist revolutionary Pier Paolo Pasolini in his film *La Rabbia* (1962).[92] But that reversal did not concern human prehistory, henceforth envied for its enormous symbolic potential and its openness to history, but rather natural prehistory—slow, deterministic, and known solely by its fossilized forms. For Patočka, man was becoming a "biological organism," "a part of the material world," seen "in the perspective of a meaningless, basically natural scientific theory," "an organism maintaining a metabolic exchange with its context." Warning against those who would hasten to point out the "paradox of a history resulting in a prehistoricity," he emphasized,

> prehistoricity is not characterized by a deprivation of meaning, it is not nihilistic like our times. Prehistoric meaning may be modest, but it is not relativistic. It is a meaning which is not centered on humans but rather relates primordially to other beings and powers.... They can live at peace with what there is, not in a devastating struggle with it that sacrifices life's possibilities stored up over countless eons, to what is most mundane and utterly meaningless about human existence.[93]

Prior to "prehistory," then, there was the vast and indeterminate time that Patočka called "ahistorical," and without which men diligently seek self-preservation, "the poverty of ... living only to live."[94]

The total naturalization of the history of human societies and their entry into "posthistory" implied that man was no longer either an individual or a society, but rather a species, and that this biological generality was both complemented and confirmed by the globalism prevailing with a necessity and a power equal to those of the climate ages. In essence, posthistory came to absorb the naturalization of history practiced by Fascism, and that was the reason this notion was rapidly adopted by such authors as de Man and Gehlen.[95] We will find not a word, and for good reason, about the recent political past in their writings. In "Theories of German Fascism," Benjamin wrote of another German defeat, that of World War I: he noted that many intellectuals in the country had perverted "the German defeat into an inner victory by means of confessions of guilt which were hysterically elevated to the universally human."[96] And yet, after the disaster of Fascism, a further step was taken: the Fascists were among the first to acknowledge the defeat, not of their ideology and morality, but of humanity as a whole. In order the better to legitimize that admission, it was necessary to adopt the perspective of the very *longue durée*, observing the human species in its evolution. In passing, that allowed them to pulverize recent history, transforming it into a grain of sand in an implacable biologico-historical process running from prehistory to posthistory. The profound meaning of posthistory rests on the transformation of human history into a form of matter appropriate for the procedures of technoscience: man began as nature and will end as nature. It is by this means, in fact — stemming from what Foucault called "biopolitics" — that "posthistory" continues even today to be a notion useful to such thinkers as Giorgio Agamben and Peter Sloterdijk.[97] As for de Man, who remained silent about the Nazi camps and the technoscientific extermination of the Jewish "race" and other inferior "species," he approached the naturalization of history not through its crimes, but through the moral angle of a so-called universal decline. This diluted the guilt, even while making the ego a detached agency that contemplates the history of the human species from above. Describing the evolution of technology from the first biface stone tools to the atomic bomb, Gehlen pointed out technology's tendency to move from specialized forms — designed to extend, even substitute, for human limbs — to a total inorganic form that could substitute for the living thing in general. He observed that that mineralization, which reached all human beings through the diffusion of technology, ruled out freedom and favored automatic reflexes similar to those of primitive peoples and termites.[98] The animal metaphor became increasingly prominent in the descriptions of human societies. "Posthistorical animals," Kojève's term to describe the generalized automatic contentment of capitalist and communist societies, was an image about which many different thinkers were in agreement.

Nevertheless, the "end of history" gave rise not only to posthistorical lamentations, but also to earnest celebrators. In his essay "At the Time Wall," Ernst Jünger adopted an "Archimedean point"[99] that allowed him to consider the evolution of the species on a cosmic scale. What had begun with Herodotus and culminated with the humanistic illusions of progress had slowly, but irrevocably ended with the rise of technology. And in his eyes, among the many symptoms of that end, none had an importance equal to the invention of prehistory in the nineteenth century. "Why now, precisely?" That question, continued Jünger,

> leads us to the crack. On the side of the fissure known to us, we might perhaps say that our historical being has at present reached the highest degree of concentration, the highest degree of passion both rash and conscious, which pushes us to the frontiers of time and space, to caves, to graves, to the bowels of the earth, and to grottoes in the depths of the sea, in the upper reaches and abysses of the cosmos."[100]

The spirit of inquiry specific to history, in exerting itself in a panicked and compulsive manner, ultimately obliterated and pulverized itself, colliding with "the time wall."

Prehistory spoke of the ontological condition of modern men, since the enigmatic and subterranean character of its paintings fundamentally expressed the enigmatic condition of moderns: "Do we not find ourselves in a state of change analogous to that in which Herodotus found himself, or even greater?" wondered Jünger. "Have not the events that arise lost the relationships with one another that we are accustomed to call History, establishing another that we do not yet know how to name?"[101] What changed, then, in so "disconcerting" a manner that no "name" or "historical example" can account for it? Man himself, said Jünger: very simply and very confusedly at the same time, he "began to change in his being, as being. Something new and strange manifested itself in him, and universally so, beyond nations, races, levels of civilization, globally."[102] At a time when "History," and "perhaps even human existence on this earth," were exhausting themselves, Jünger's "Archimedean point" became sidereal, telluric, and cosmic, all at once. If geology and paleontology provided terms of comparison with which to think of man as a natural species, the art of prehistory provided clues to the "magic spirit" with which the species was endowed, allowing a glimpse of its future evolution. Hence, man was analyzed both as a fossil and as a new Antaeus, who, having extracted the power of the earth, was ready to project himself into outer space.

What Jünger called "magic spirit," "earthly spirit," and sometimes even "first foundation" was an idealist postulate with its roots in

Romanticism according to which a common creative force linked earth and man. A first proof of that magic spirit was the universal and transhistorical belief in a "golden age," which implied an abundance and unity between man and earth. The Stone Age, by virtue of its remoteness in time, belonged to that golden age, but was separate from it, inasmuch as the Stone Age had really existed. The first "time wall" was built out of man's obligation to provide for his needs, which obliged him to act within nature. Jünger sensed, at the other end of time, that man's very capacity to destroy the earth and to become extinct lay in the return of the "magic spirit" and the realization of the golden age: "It is not unreasonable to think that the magic forces can gain ground to an unpredictable degree when catastrophes threaten man as a being who participates not only in world history, but in the earth's history, that is, as a species. They can also burst forth in technology. In terms of magic, matter and *bios* are one."[103]

For the first time in the evolution of the species, Jünger remarked, technology ceased to be a mere prosthesis that imitated man's organic body and became abstract, taking the form of "the power stations that receive and give orders,"[104] imitating the nervous system and the organization of the mind. Mediated by his technology, man himself changed form, becoming increasingly less organic and potentially ever more "indestructible." Conversely, spiritualization through technology made the earth a strange planet that had

> acquired a new skin, an aura, which is woven from images and thoughts, melodies, signals and messages. . . . The astonishment that this planet imposes on us at present, having become so small and yet shining with a new light, has nothing to do with the optimism of progress or with the pessimism that covers it in shadow. It is metahistorical, it opens perspectives on a world located beyond History.[105]

Beyond optimism and pessimism, beyond infinite progress and the end, there was another metaphysical "astonishment": that of the discovery of outer space. Thanks to "interplanetary flight,"[106] it was possible to contemplate a planet so evolved that it was becoming an aesthetic object, vibrating and sparkling because it was made by man. And man now took the place of God, who until then had held in his hands the "decision" to end the world. Indeed, when man went outside "historical space,"[107] he realized human sovereignty: only he could now decide on the destruction of the totality — and especially, of himself — by setting down "the human as a worn-out mask."[108] Jünger drew not so much the figure of an ultimate Sardanapalus as the completion of the process of Christian Incarnation: in keeping with an implacable Hegelian logic, human nature was becoming disincarnate (history and feelings were going extinct) in favor of a technological nature that, if it did not destroy itself, would rule the world.

In a language that brings furiously to mind contemporary discourses on what is called "the Anthropocene," Jünger clearly formulated the transformation of the *anthropos* (a subject that was already classless, sexless, and deterritorialized) into a geological agent. "Is it possible to include in geology the changes brought about on the human level?" the writer wondered: "A large capital city, under whose paving stones accumulate the catacombs, tombs, ruins, and domestic and architectural debris of fifty generations, reminds us of a coral reef."[109] He observed especially that the impact of human interventions such as the deforestation of the Amazon had produced a change in scale: though the excavations of a site where fifty generations of men had passed in succession still belonged to history, that was not the case for man from a "paleontological" point of view.[110] Jünger in fact pointed out the dual nature, both passive and active, of that paleontological man: from now on, he wrote, "one does not just find man in one layer; rather, he is a formative being, he determines the layer"[111] — thus sadly echoing the photograph of the worker pointing his finger at an ax found in the antediluvian sediment of Saint-Acheul. That "formative activity of layers" proved that the earth's "magic spirit" had been conveyed through man. Having formed myriads of organisms now extinct, the magic spirit was reflected in man's hands: "No doubt man can be considered a characteristic fossil, typical of a determinate layer and perhaps only beginning to form, but he is at the same time the first living being to undertake excavations, prehistorical and historical. He not only forms a layer, he also penetrates it intellectually."[112]

Caves of the Atomic Age (1949–1959):
Fontana, Kiesler, Pinot-Gallizio

The atomic age created its own shelters and sacred spaces. The artistic environment took root while the planet was becoming more than ever a continuous space, a *second nature.*

The first artistic environment of this type was exhibited by Lucio Fontana in a Milan gallery in February 1949. It was a closed space, dark and empty, where only a few papier mâché sculptures in glitzy colors were visible, one suspended from the ceiling, the others hanging at the corners, all lit by florescent light (Figure 5.9).[113] In a review, the public was introduced to this environment as "the first graffiti of the atomic age."[114] The work aspired to be a response adapted to the radical change in the relationship between Western man and nature. Above all, although the cave had long dominated the popular imagination, it remained curiously overlooked by artists. But after Hiroshima, the cavernous environments done by Fontana, Pinot-Gallizio, Kiesler, and even Claes Oldenburg in *Store*[115] shaped a new use of prehistory that interrupted the recurrence of motifs and formal techniques used until that time.

For a century, prehistory had been so widely metaphorized and internalized by Western thought that it returned whenever the relationship between man and the world was called into question. This time, the "first man" walked on the lunar surface: "Fontana has touched the moon [Fontana ha toccato la luna]," exclaimed the critic Raffaele Carrieri, adding:

> We enter a sort of cabalistic cave covered with black panels. Is it the first or the last night of our planet? Under a spectral sky, between dances of larvae, a large sprawling and unfinished form rises up. Is it a burnt dinosaur? The backbone of a large mammoth? I don't want to make comparisons. The environment created by Fontana on via Manzoni brought us closer to the moon, like looking through astronomical telescopes.[116]

Fontana's carved forms represented nothing. Open and expansive configurations, they were situated between the plant kingdom, the

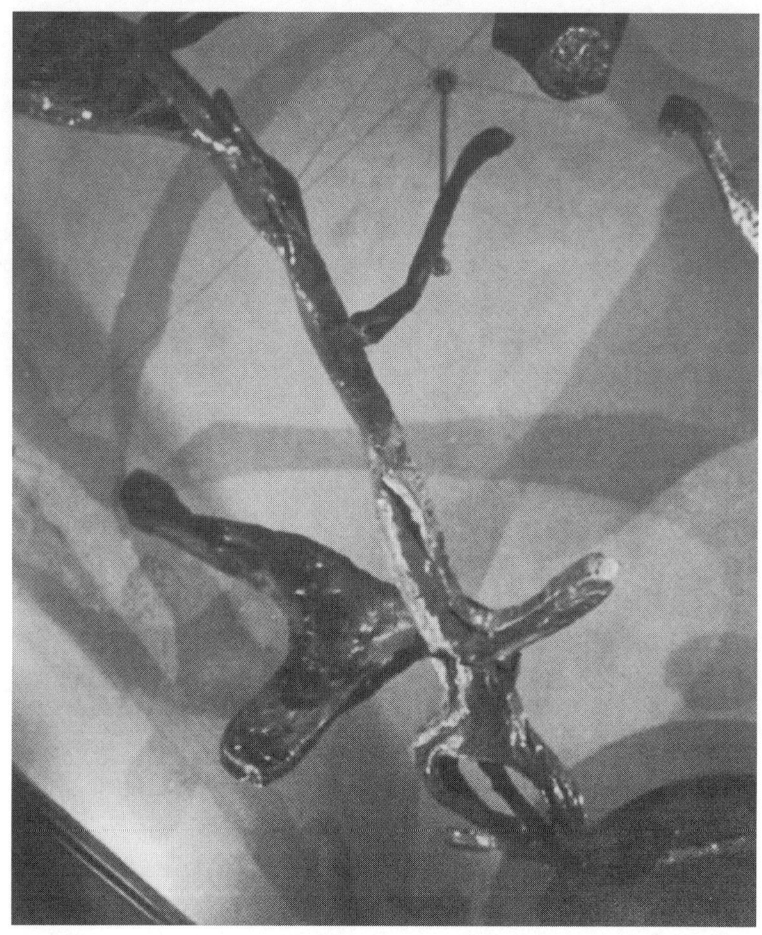

Figure 5.9. Lucio Fontana, *Spatial Environment with Black Light*, 1948–49. Papier mâché, phosphorescent veneer, and blacklight. Galleria del Naviglio, Milan. Fontana Foundation, Milan, C. 48–49 A 2. Photo: © 2021 ARS, NY/ ADAGP, Paris.

animal kingdom, and the mineral kingdom. In calling these forms "grotesque,"[117] the critic expressed his perplexity in the first place, even while suggesting their continuity with Fontana's early baroque-style body of work, their evocation of some hybrid and unclassifiable species, and above all, their temporal indetermination. Indeed, these forms brought to mind the "grotesque" paintings discovered during the Renaissance as much as baroque and prehistoric grottoes, protozoan formations as much as the remains of extinct organisms (mammoths or dinosaurs), fossils as much as graffiti carved by a human being.

The aim was to create an "ambience" that transfixed the visitor and obliged her to experience a disorientation resonant with the upheaval in her fundamental relationship to the world: "Upon entering, you found yourself all by yourself. Every viewer reacted in a way that precisely fit his mood of the moment. I did not influence him with objects and forms assaulting him as objects for sale. Man was alone, with his consciousness, his ignorance, his matter, etc., etc."[118] In enveloping the viewer, *Ambiente spaziale* did not decompose or distract the gaze as individual and portable works of art customarily do: on the contrary, its aim was to bring her back to herself within the cavernous space of his subjectivity, where she could dive down to seek a meaning in the world that surrounded her. Remembering how that environment had struck him "by its lunar effect" and its "liquifying and hallucinatory atmosphere," one viewer recounted:

> You entered a kind of grotto where the violet light rendered the elements spectral. Suspended forms, floating like prehistoric beings or underwater elements, enveloped you as if you were entering one of his large ceramics in dim light. There were no limits, it all referred to the zones of the unconscious where space has no center and the surface no longer exists. More than a fourth dimension, that of space-time, to which Fontana often alluded in his texts, it was another dimension, beyond time, in a sort of inner journey.[119]

The indetermination specific to any *ambience* was above all that of art itself, which at the time was going through an interregnum. Some media were becoming extinct, while others were forming, engendered by the spirit of the time. Fontana wrote: "The first

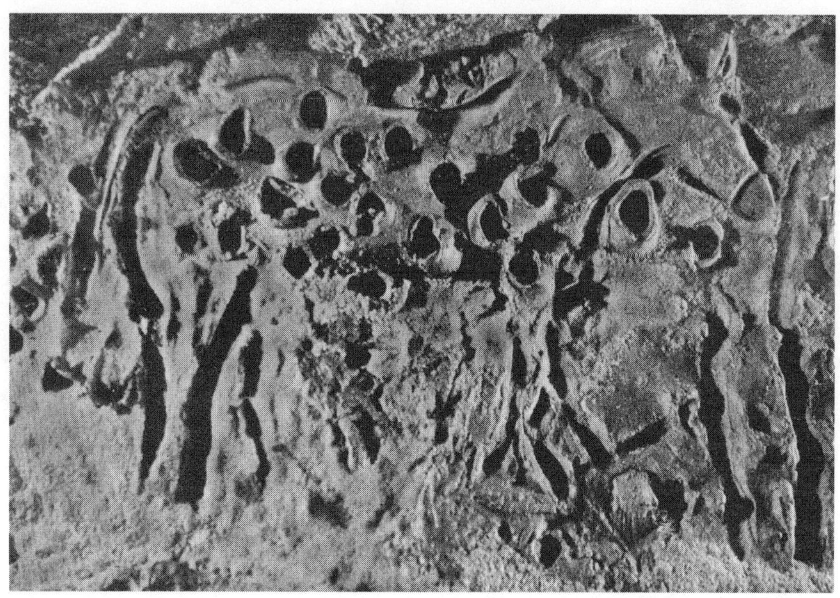

Figure 5.10. Horse incised in the clay of a wall
and riddled with holes, cave of Montespan,
Magdalenian IV, in Christian Zervos, *L'art
de l'époque du renne en France* (Paris: Cahiers
d'art, 1959), p. 313.

spatial environment in the world, neither painting nor sculpture.
Immediate art, free and immediate suggestion to the beholder, in an
environment created by the artist, preparations for concepts of an
art of the future based on the evolution of the medium in art, light,
neon, television, radar."[120] He added: "The gesture remains eternal,
but matter will die" (Figures 5.10 and 5.11).[121] The raw materials for
the new reality had changed once again, but they remained just as
perishable. Light, neon, television, and radar were all means for making immediate nature artificial and for projecting man farther and
farther — even to the stars. Fontana thus developed a very Hegelian
view of art history: if "graffiti" were to return periodically, so long as

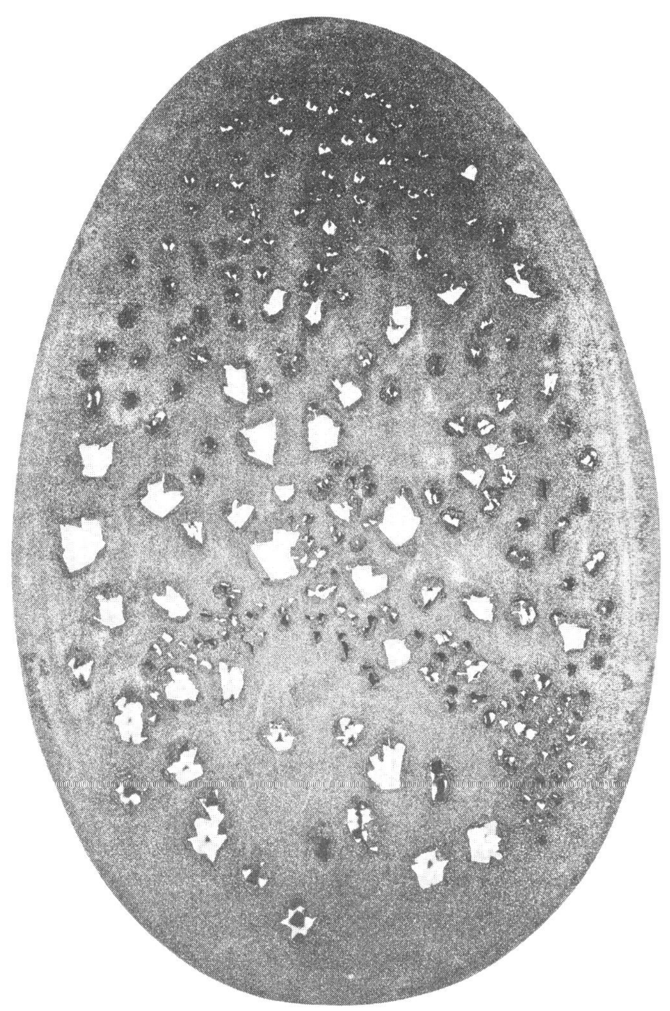

Figure 5.11. Lucio Fontana, *Spatial Concept/ The End of God*, 1963. Oil on canvas, glitter, 70 × 48⅜ in. Fontana Foundation, Milan, FD 29. Photo: © 2021 ARS, NY/ ADAGP, Paris.

man remained unchanged as a species, his materials, his media, and the sensory mechanisms he enlisted had to change constantly. Since his *Manifesto blanco*, composed with his disciples in 1946, Fontana had called that new art, which defied post-Kantian media, "spatial art" or "aerial art," like the "lines" that "do not delimit space" and the space itself, which "passes through matter."[122] Like so many others before him, Fontana was impelled by the historicist spirit to posit a profound analogy between ages and media: "From graffiti to painting, from the Paleolithic to the skyscraper, from painting to neon to television to radar, from here to beyond, pursuing in art as well man's creative path, everything rests on the very simple problem of being in our space age."[123] And like many others before him, he was impelled by that same spirit to predict the end of art itself, destined to disappear the day human evolution had made it obsolete and as indecipherable for the men of the future as the very first gestures of prehistoric man were for those of the present:

> I don't think the artist will always exist, that's not possible, don't you see that the artist is not like before? We were born into a world where people were talking about art, but in five hundred years no one will be talking about art anymore, they'll be talking about other things, and art will be like going today to see two stones put together by the first caveman. We talk about things that man has done while he was on earth, but do you think man will still have time to make art while he is traveling in outer space?[124]

At the beginning of the atomic age, which buried many things before fully revealing its utopian potential, one "gesture" remained for Fontana: the gashes and holes he made in his monochrome canvases and his bronze balls. It was both the first gesture, since the gashes revived the alterations (cupules, incisions, perforations) that men had inflicted on matter since time immemorial, and the last gesture, in that he broke with the earthly conception of space-time. The gash was the Hegelian sublation of historicist thought, a suppression of all the particular figures and ages of history, which culminated in turn in the "Nothingness" of the atomic age. That age would end the periodization that had divided time into parts in order to project human consciousness onto a world where it could have a taste of divine infinity, knowing no bounds, no measure, no beginning, and no end. Fontana was openly inspired by the Nothingness of negative theology:

> Man goes into space and he sees there is no paradise.... When I showed *La fine di Dio* [The end of God], I was told: "Put the end of gods instead." I said no. The gods is one thing. That's the end of gods on earth, which means the end of these gods — but the presence of a god, what's that? Nothing! Who knows what God is like? So I made these holes ... so I made a gesture, I believe in God and I perform an act of faith.... So God is nothing, but that's Everything, no?... And if I have faith, then I can only perform an act of faith, the way another would make a dark blot.[125]

The imaginary of negative theology, of nuclear fission, but also of weightlessness, the void, and the incommensurability of outer space, in their syncretic fusion, broke with the invention of an "incarnate" God and the last vestiges of the classical regime of representation. If God were everything, what particular form could contain him? The "hole" and the "gash" were scrupulous expressions of *Entformung* (deformation), that process of subtraction, of a withdrawal from appearances, recommended by Meister Eckhart in order to experience God's infinity. Hence, the blow dealt to the painted canvas was not only the deliberate destruction of a moribund religion and history, but also an act and a sign: both the process and the product of deformation in pursuit of Nothingness. Before the war, Fontana had developed an ambivalent relationship with the past, both respect and an attitude of parody. After the war, his environment engaged in a historical *purge*, which took the hybrid form of a prehistory of late modernity and would culminate in the gashes of Nothingness.[126]

In Fontana's imagination, the space of the cave was a matrix: in it, man connected with the strangeness common to the primordial world and the world to come. The caves of Frederick Kiesler and Pinot-Gallizio, by contrast, had a defensive and protective function. The *Endless House*, designed, drawn, and modeled by Kiesler beginning in 1950 (Figure 5.12), and Pinot-Gallizio's *Cavern of Antimatter*, exhibited in 1959 (Figure 5.13), reflected their magic notion of art.

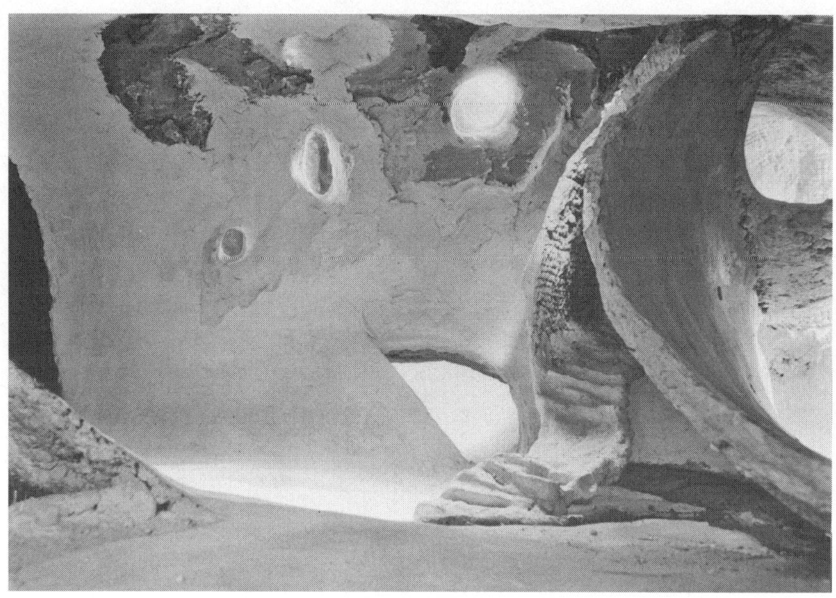

Figure 5.12. Frederick Kiesler, *Endless House.* New York, 1958–60. Black-and-white photograph, interior view. Photo: George Barrows. © 2021 Austrian Frederick and Lillian Kiesler Private Foundation, Vienna, PHO 774/1.

In *Magic Architecture*, a labyrinthine manuscript that was never published, Kiesler wrote that his cave was "endless" not because of its temporal properties as a progressive work, but by virtue of its spatial property (Figure 5.14): a continuous form not interrupted by any angle or straight line. That space, where "all ends converge and converge continuously," was "inevitable in a world coming to an end." It was, he added, "the last refuge for man as man."[127] In stark contrast to Fontana, who breached the totality with a gash, Kiesler's house was an enveloping and indivisible whole. Even as the possible end of the world was being evoked, Kiesler formed a space that, having no fissures, was not vulnerable to the outside and whose interior was completely

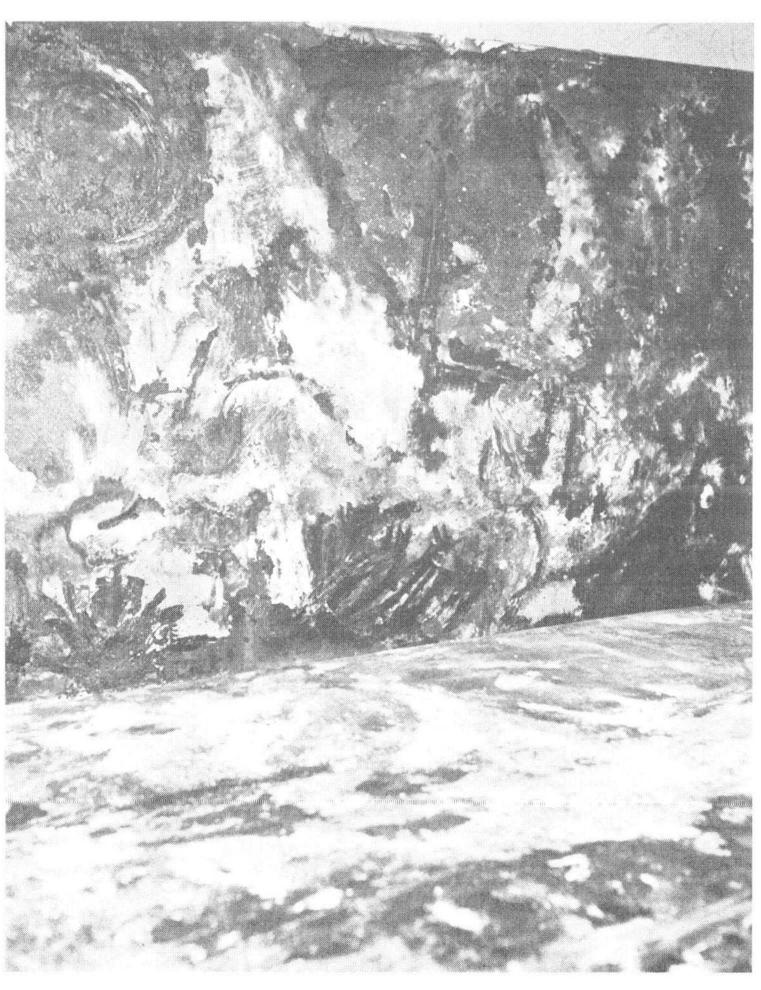

Figure 5.13. Pinot Gallizio, photograph of the *Cavern of Antimatter*, Galerie René Drouin, Paris, 1959. Archives Pinot Gallizio, Turin.

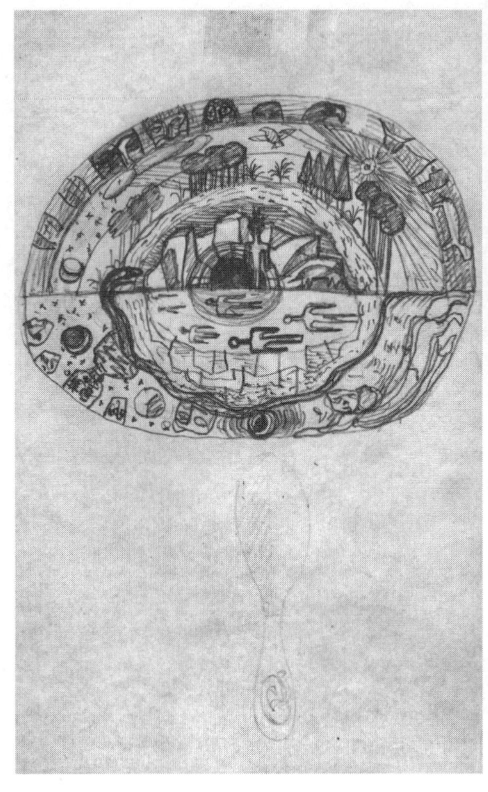

undivided, like the intrauterine environment and the caves of prehistory:

> Timid man and most powerful primates have one fear in common, namely the spontaneous savagery of climatic conditions; wind-storms, rain-squalls, lightning-fires, heat-draught cold and ice. That these onslaughts might mean death is not so frightening as the fact that the blows are delivered from a distance and are struck by an unseen enemy. Man and primate alike, flee; they make for caves above and below the ground; they look for thickets, for rich tropical foliage; they hide in hollow trees.[128]

In an era when reason penetrated every last particle of matter, it seemed to him that men's affects were moving closer to those of the primitive peoples. As Spyros Papapetros has shown, Kiesler, a great reader of ethnology books on magic, saw the effects of the atomic age as a paradoxical return of animism — except that as Benjamin pointed out in the 1930s, animism functioned in reverse, because it was now the wholly domesticated forces whose causes, forms, and effects escaped all control.

The *Endless House* was closed on itself, centripetal, and self-sufficient. Like that second golden age conceived by the Romantics, it was not the fruit of innocence, but of a reason that having completed its analytical-critical phase, achieved its unity. Kiesler, confusing the Paleolithic with the Eolithic (which, strangely, also appeared in his writings some decades later, after Mortillet invented it, only once again to sink into oblivion), spoke of the unity that "Eolithic man" experienced in the caves, which were for him both a magic space and a shelter, spiritual and physical protection. Just as the first tools were a transformation of stone or bones allowing man to survive in a natural world infinitely stronger than he, and just as magic was "the mother of invention" and increased his "power," the *Endless House* was a sophisticated tool and a work of magic. Far from being a simple shelter protecting from the effects of atomic energy, it was conceived as an irenic conversion of the nuclear, what the apostles of technoscience and the political decider in America often called "the good atom."[129] But above all, in what had become the menacing macrocosm, that unified and nevertheless infinite space was a self-sufficient microcosm.

That same magic transmutation of danger into protection and of atomic dissolution into unity was also the source of Pinot-Gallizio's *Cavern*, which differs from the *Endless House* by its anticapitalist content and its very clear mistrust of technology.[130] Created at the Galerie Drouin in Paris in spring 1959 at the initiative of Guy Debord and Michèle Bernstein, this cave was formed by covering a relatively small space from floor to ceiling with dozens of yards of canvas rolls bearing a very gestural painting. During his previous exhibitions, the artist had tried to sell such rolls by the yard, cutting them up with scissors like any ordinary fabric, but he did not meet with the expected success, given that the public was accustomed to formally autonomous works.[131] The quantitative inflation of the product of his labor and the devaluation that resulted were two properties of what the ironic inventor had patented under the name "industrial painting." If art is differentiated from other fabricated objects primarily by its resistance to being measured in any way, this canvas cut up and sold by the yard was a stark reminder that exchange value constituted a measurement that art could not avoid. Pinot-Gallizio, a member of the Internationale Situationniste from the moment it was founded, had a background as a chemist, an herbal pharmacist and inventor of perfumes, an amateur archaeologist excavating the Neolithic sites of his region (Figure 5.15), a resister of Fascism, and a defender of the Gypsies. All his former lives converged in his activity as a gestural painter who combined durable and ephemeral materials, devoted himself to a form of improvisation that included decorative motifs many centuries old, and frequently embarked on joint projects. In an era when patents of every kind were multiplying, his "industrial painting"—a collective enterprise, difficult to repeat, and a waste of matter and energy—represented the antipatent par excellence.

Because of his political views, which he himself characterized as anarchist, and also because of the advent of the atomic age and the anxiety to which it gave rise, Pinot-Gallizio came to have an ambivalent image of prehistory: sometimes paradisal and sometimes harrowing, but always magic. He extended the notion of the potlatch (as polysemic in Situationist circles as "mana" was in certain traditional societies) to the Paleolithic period. He made the system of exchanges of that economy, which operated without money and did not stockpile goods, a model for the exchange of the "poetic experiences" he was hoping for.[132] In classic primitivism, he called for the masses to rediscover the elementary things in life and the new languages that would correspond to them. That elementarism found expression in an apologia for the present: the primitive collective subject did not receive a greater heritage than he transmitted; freed from both the past and the future, he would live fully and without mediation the passing of time. This time was filled, notably, with aesthetic

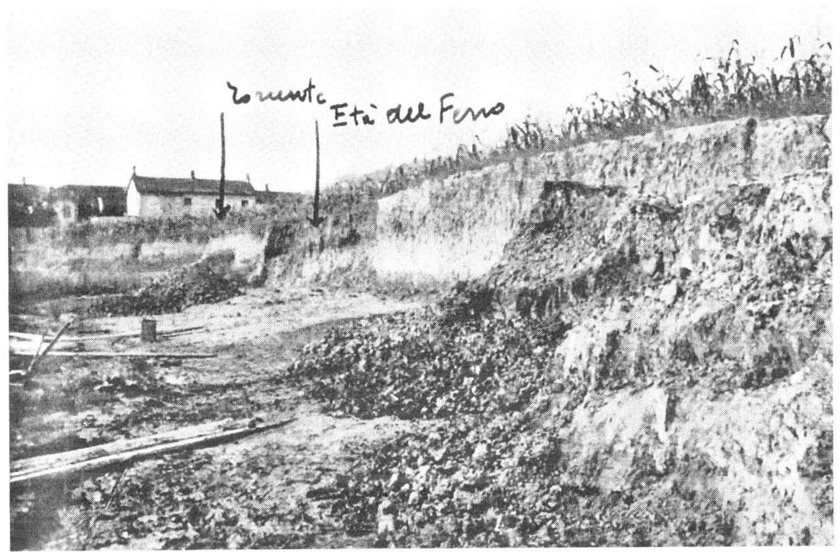

Figure 5.15. Photograph of an excavation
by Pinot-Gallizio in the region of Alba, 1947.
Archives Pinot-Gallizio, Turin.

experiences, which had become an exchange of nonreifiable experiences. One of the magic operations in *Cavern*, conceived as the space of an immersive and collective experience, consisted of transforming the site of the commodification of art (the gallery) into a place of play and exchange.

Like Fontana, Pinot-Gallizio used the cave — total, enveloping, and unique — as an antimercantile model. But the vocation of his *Cavern*, close in that respect to the *Endless House*, was to protect and soothe. As the Italian Situationist explained to the gallery owner Drouin, "the times in which we are living are nothing other than the prehistory of what is called the atomic age"; "modern men have found themselves in the same conditions of terror in the face of material things as men of the Paleolithic age, those cavemen who, because of their great fear, drew and painted in their caves with the acute magic feeling of solving the enigma."[133] More than a discharge of anxiety, painting was in and of itself the magic transmutation of the maleficent atom. Painting, now "atomized," "literally disintegrated," "effectively bombarded, not verbally," according to him, generated "variations in smooth and dark tones on backgrounds, superimposed on erupting materials like moldy-green lava, rimmed, or rather frayed at the edges in yellow-sulphur, the color of an unstable reaction, shifting perpetually like glaciers."[134] At a time when humanity had become "nature within nature," when it had proved capable of "accelerating geological times,"[135] pictorial matter was subject to the cataclysms and earthquakes of subjectivity. Painting was becoming the "prehistoric caprice of a (mechanical) atomic age" because it was reactivating the most ancient gestures and replaying the creation of the cosmos. At a time, therefore, when "humanity [was] fighting geologically to survive," when it was rediscovering "the adversity" of prehistory, its art, having once again become "magico-functional," managed this time to convert destruction into creation: "Thus began the long days of atomic creation. Now it is up to us artists, scientists, poets to create the lands, the oceans, the animals, the sun and other stars, the air, the water, and all things anew. And it will be up to us to breathe life into the clay to create the new-man suited to rest on the seventh day."[136]

The analogy Pinot-Gallizio established between his era and the Paleolithic age implied a dual interpretation of the Neolithic. From a historical and universal point of view, he condemned the age that had introduced sedentism, labor, property, and writing, but he respected it for its specific and regional value, as indicated by his excavations of Neolithic sites, his collections and artifacts, and his writings. He rejected the Neolithic as an "idea," but respected it as a symbolic form guaranteeing the persistence of the *genius loci*. On the one hand, Pinot-Gallizio readily concurred with all the critiques of the spirit of constraint and hierarchy that characterized that age: "The time of the Scribes is over. New expressions worthy of the new instruments will snap the useless pens, and will cancel all the bitter ink that has mortified the world, down to the last trace."[137] It was as if atomic fire spread the same conflagration that had formerly burned down the library of

Alexandria. Significantly, "Library of Alexandria" was the name Jorn gave to the publishing house of his "Scandinavian Institute of Comparative Vandalism," which in 1960 put out a book on Pinot-Gallizio edited by Bernstein and Jorn himself. A symbol of the future abolition of all book-based culture in favor of orality and the pure experience of the present, for Pinot-Gallizio, the library of Alexandria represented the "latest fuel for the new magic," the "synthesis of the Neolithic revolution . . . which in our time burns the remains of Sumerian urban civilizations, and Phoenician nomadism, fueling the hopes of man."[138] But on the other hand, when Pinot-Gallizio presented his Neolithic pottery to the critic Carla Lonzi, he described the spirals that an anonymous artisan had traced as stemming from the same playful activity and the same act of formation he himself was pursuing a few millenniums later.[139] It was fundamentally the same contradiction at work among the Britons in the 1930s when they extolled both the abstract universal spirit of Neolithic forms and their rootedness in English nature. The same tension arose as well when Pinot-Gallizio, a Situationist and defender of the Gypsies, extolled both nomadism and an anticapitalistic anchorage in the *longue durée* of a region.[140]

Yet what could the place of history be in a mental universe where the only valorized past was buried in the unconscious of man and the earth, when time was experienced as a continuous flow with its source in prehistory? Pinot-Gallizio's antihistorical and profoundly presentist view was similar to that of Dubuffet, Jorn, and many other figures from the 1950s. It was possible to connect the present and the past, provided that the latter, well before any writing, would survive only in buried artifacts and afterimages in the mind. Embracing what, paraphrasing Dalí, he called "a critical ignorance," Pinot-Gallizio added:

> Mine is a soft dementia, the state of grace of a *critical ignorance . . .* an ignorance of the recent past up to the Sumerians, keeping the *present* and the *future* in my unconscious: in casting myself into the *remote past*, into the first links of man's evolution — the great age of the carved stones, the Magdalenians and the Aurignacians, who lived on French soil 300,000 years ago; to revive and imagine with them the great ignorance and the great poetry that were nothing other than their magic.[141]

One thread linked prehistory to the present and the future — the thread of the eternal present, without beginning or end: "There is neither time nor end — not today, yesterday, tomorrow; there is only the forever, the endless forever."[142] After the war, Sigfried Giedion, too, had sought in the caves the "eternal present" that could make him forget the contemporary world. Pinot-Gallizio's *Cavern of Anti-matter* aspired to transform commodities magically into a shared experience, novelties into a "perpetual new," the end of history into the "endless forever." The *Endless House* and the *Cavern of Antimatter* were two microcosms that reduced the infinite to human scale, exorcizing the fear of the end and converting the dreary present into a messianic present that gathered together all the orders of time.

Terra Incognita

On December 18, 1994, beyond the narrow fissure of a cliff, three speleologists discovered a decorated cave that would soon become known as "Chauvet Cave."[1] Upon entering the first large room, one of the three speleologists noticed, along the edge of a wall, a few red lines tracing a little mammoth, partly covered in limestone. "They were here!" she shouted. Her exclamation suddenly turned that mineral place, scattered with bear remains—its silence broken only by the sound of dripping water—into a space human beings had chosen, experienced, and transformed. Far from discovering a place untouched by culture, these speleologists were thus only *revenants*, that is, they had come back to a previously inhabited place, almost like ghosts. They were not reenacting Redon's "first creature"; rather, they were repeating the encounter of moderns with the prehistoric peoples Bataille had described. But perhaps these two experiences were linked by a common thread, namely, stupor, and perhaps we are now living that convergence with even greater force.

Upon examining the walls, the three "inventors" found images of animals—horses, lions, mammoths, rhinoceroses, an owl, and others—that stupefied them by their number, the energy of their strokes, their freshness, the preparation of the support, their structural complexity, the way they highlighted the wall's morphology and the mineral matter (Figure c.1). A few months later, Jean Clottes, head of the scientific team, declared before the Académie des Inscriptions et Belles Lettres: "From the outset, this discovery fired

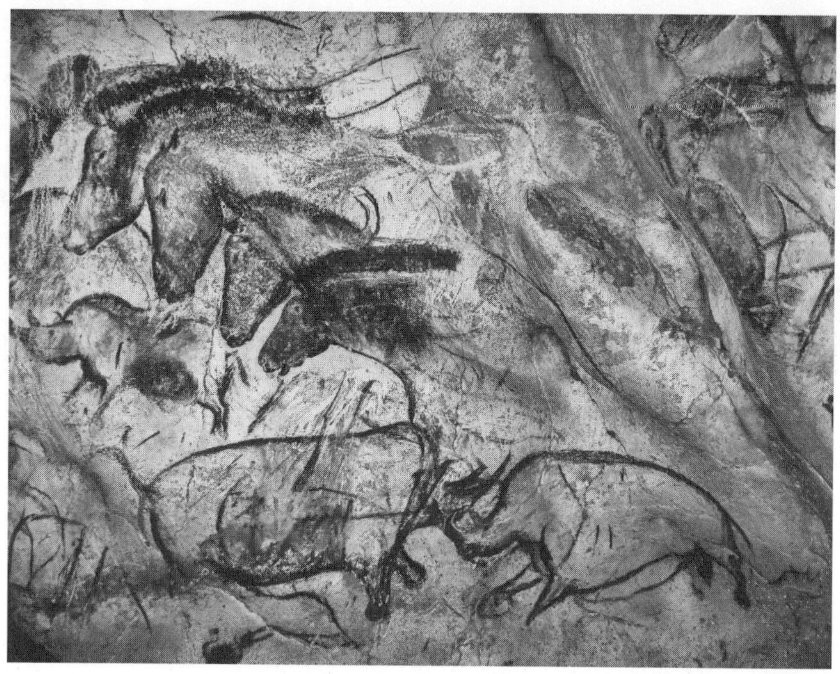

Figure C.1. *The Ride.* Detail of horses and rhinoceroses facing each other. Grotte de Chauvet-Pont-d'Arc (Ardèche), Panneau des Chevaux, Salle Hillaire. ©J. Clottes/MC.

the imagination and excited not only specialists, but also a worldwide audience. What made it an event [*créé l'événement*, literally "created the event"] was the aesthetic quality of the images, their profusion, and the surprising revelation, in the heart of Ardèche, of a major sanctuary unknown for millenniums. Everyone has more or less consciously perceived that this discovery was not like the others."[2]

Chauvet shattered what remained of evolutionism according to Leroi-Gourhan, who had linked the earliest days to crude forms or abstraction. In the early twentieth century, the invention of parietal art had been the indispensable condition for the collective appropriation of prehistory by moderns. But in the late twentieth century, Chauvet, strangely enough, brought back to life the aesthetic speculations of the painter Whistler: everything suggested that a single person, a unique individual, had created the most stunning paintings in the cave. An individual or a structure? Event or repetition? Exception or seriality? Prehistory opened a breach in the debates that had marked the human sciences since Durkheim.

The images of Chauvet, said Clottes, "created the event." "The event is the realm of the marvelous in democratic societies," Pierre Nora wrote in 1972, to combat the supremacy of "structures" defended by the Annales School.[3] The successive inventions of prehistory, sudden eruptions of a forgotten past, created a mythopoetic memory in both specialists and the masses. Hence the "invention" of Chauvet repeated that of Lascaux, which itself repeated that of Altamira—the latter so staggering it had been repressed.

Here, repetition and novelty, structure and event, are no longer incompatible. The "invention" breaks through the inertia of the mineral, and the narrative begins (one day . . . three adolescents . . . a seven-year old girl . . . three speleologists . . . they were here! . . .); the impersonality of the structures fissures; the established theories are undermined and acceleration toward the future suspended. By means of prehistory, moderns, far from being mere conquerors limited by space, time, and things, experienced the suspension of their knowledge and the relinquishment of the world and of things.

Michel Serres wondered whether revolution and rupture might be temporal figures too burdensome for our modernity:

> What if, — behind them or beneath these schisms, flowed (or percolated) slow and viscous fluxes? . . . But underneath, continuous and extraordinarily slow movements explain these sudden breaks where the quakes occur. And even further below these continuous movements that pull, tranquilly but inexorably, is a core of heat that maintains or propels the moving crust. And what is the inner sun of these mechanisms? Our old hot planet, which is cooling. Earth is that very sun.[4]

Were we, then, so ignorant of that tranquil, but inexorable "pull"? Or of that anti-Promethean sun, the earth? Cézanne's dense stratifications, the Nazca lines along which Morris aligned his body, and Smithson's "ruins in reverse" are forceful evidence to the contrary. All these artists had glimpsed Serres's "inner sun," and all may have understood — each in his own way, of course — his evocation of a rocket launched into space: "Yet before our eyes and around our ears, the flash of a storm has been transformed, by thunder and lightning, into a planet. We have now suddenly become again what we had never ceased to be: primitives. Through its propulsive energy, the highly sophisticated performance rediscovers archaism within us."[5]

We must now once again seize on this somewhat forgotten history of modernity. To do so, we must renounce the habitus of novelty, just as we must rid ourselves of the reflex to think in terms of the "first time," which so often triggers the "last time." We must think about what happens to us within a longer, more continuous, more complex framework, inasmuch as the long term and what is known as the "Anthropocene" have always been conceived together. Dipesh Chakrabarty, the active representative of subaltern history, who has devoted himself to an epistemological reflection on the "Anthropocene," overlooks precisely that rootedness in geology, that geological horizon of Enlightenment Humanity.[6] Giving precedence to Vico, Croce, and Collingwood, philosophers of the great divide between human history and natural history, rather than to Buffon,

Nietzsche, or Quinet, who set out to blur the boundaries between them, Chakrabarty maintains that it was the "Great Acceleration" since World War II that made this divide obsolete. But in reality, that obsolescence was understood much earlier, when the West instituted the great divide between culture and nature, between us and the others — and also began to undo that divide by placing the Subject over an abyss. That is why, when Chakrabarty laments the fact that our methods, our tools, and even more our ontological postures prevent us from apprehending the geological scale on which man acts, he sounds a very strange note:

> We cannot ever experience ourselves as a geophysical force — though we now *know* this is one of the modes of our collective existence. We cannot send somebody out to experience in an unmediated manner this "force" on our behalf.... This nonhuman, forcelike mode of existence of the human tells us that we are no longer simply a form of life that is endowed with a sense of ontology.[7]

And the historian then insists on the necessary decentering of man's place within living things, on the importance of a philosophy that combines several timescales.

Throughout this book, however, we have seen many interplays of scales that undermined the sovereignty of human thought: we have lived the nightmare of a bourgeois man dreaming of the extinction of his species after his visit to the Crystal Palace in London; the survival of a human technology of the body in an ichthyosaur of the future; the "antianthropic remedies" prescribed by de Chirico; and even Smithson's spiral dive under the red waters of a lake in Utah. Clearly, we are not the first to experience the difficulties of grasping the geological scale or of projecting ourselves onto it, as individuals and as species. It is true that since the invention of the atomic bomb, the specter of our extinction has never been so present. (Let us remember Jünger and other thinkers of posthistory.) It is also true that the debates about the Anthropocene have an unprecedented impact on epistemology, in the media, in political discourse, and even on governance. Nevertheless, all the ingredients of a supposedly new discourse are perfectly familiar to us: the human species, the earth, capitalism, technology, second nature, extinction. Also familiar is the only technology at our disposal for appropriating the other and making the dissimilar similar: the invention of incongruous, even absolutely monstrous metaphors, fictions, and plastic forms that can help us think of our world differently. In other words, because we are faced with the impossibility of sending "somebody out," as Chakrabarty says, to see on our behalf that much more elusive "force," we ought to begin by looking within ourselves: "deficient" beings (Gehlen) supplemented by fiction, we are woven from the *longue durée* in its multiple forms: language, psychology, anthropology.

A few contemporary artists reveal the potential of fiction inherent in the *longue durée*, immersing themselves anew in prehistory with remarkable insistence. In 2016, the designer Andrea Branzi, along with Kenya Hara, organized the Milan exhibition *Neo-Prehistory—100 Verbs*.[8] A hundred gestures and a hundred words—"strike," "spin," "boil," and so on—were juxtaposed with a hundred objects, from primordial flints to the silicon of microtechnologies, through a dark and boundless space where dolmens and highly sophisticated tools can be found, witnesses to a human history that develops with no precise direction.[9] The metaphor for an age of obscurity, where humanity gropes in the dark, incapable of seeing the slightest light in any future whatever,[10] this space highlights, by its very darkness and the random pathways it favors, the fact that we do not have the monopoly on groping and that with a few exceptions—modernism being the latest one—human beings have not moved forward in any other way since prehistory.[11] Hence the universality that prehistory takes on ("What happened in the stone age is happening again today"),[12] not only as a common origin, but also as an anthropological elaboration of the practices of survival and the technologies of symbolization and power.

That same universality interests Thomas Hirschhorn when he connects the mythic cave "Lascaux II" to the caves of the Taliban in Afghanistan or the cave improvised in Central Park by a homeless man known as the "Caveman of Manhattan." Prehistory is always self-reflexive, that is, it can be taken to the second power:

> With Cavemanman, I wanted to give concrete form to my interest in caves as places that human beings used in the old days but that they continue to use today. In 2001 and 2002, existing caves and caverns, dug into the rock, were used in Afghanistan as hiding places for the Taliban and their allies. . . . Their use as a refuge or hiding place became news in itself.[13]

Nevertheless, the refuge of *Cavemanman* (2002) does not separate friend from foe, nor does it provide protection from the cataclysms of history (Figure c.2). On the contrary, it is ambiguous: it expels as much as it protects, transcending the opposition between repetition and novelty, anthropology and history. Defining prehistory as what escapes all judgment, Hirschhorn adds: "I wanted to make something fragile, uncertain, something unstable, something that could be destroyed, something that could even self-destruct. I wanted to make something that could collapse on itself, the way a thought can collapse, a rickety thought you can't grasp."[14]

We are transfixed by prehistory, in its grasp, because we feel its irreducible ambiguity, likely to signify the fear of the end as much as the hope of the beginning. When the strangeness of dinosaur fossils revealed to us a past reality even more stupefying than that imagined in the craziest tales and legends, it not only prophesied the end of the human species, it equally suggested that life can generate the unimaginable in the future, as it did in the past. It was that improbable creation of the past that J. M. W. Turner imitated when he substituted a real dinosaur for a poor dragon in his picture; it was that operative mode of an extension of life beyond the known that Picasso experimented with in his notebooks when he developed his infinite variations on monolithic monuments, female bodies, and ordinary objects. Finally, it is the same shattering of taxonomies, the same expansion of the world, that Pierre Huyghe is now attempting when he expels man from the situations he creates to make him the contingent witness to a host of microevents produced by encounters with other living creatures (Figure c.3).[15]

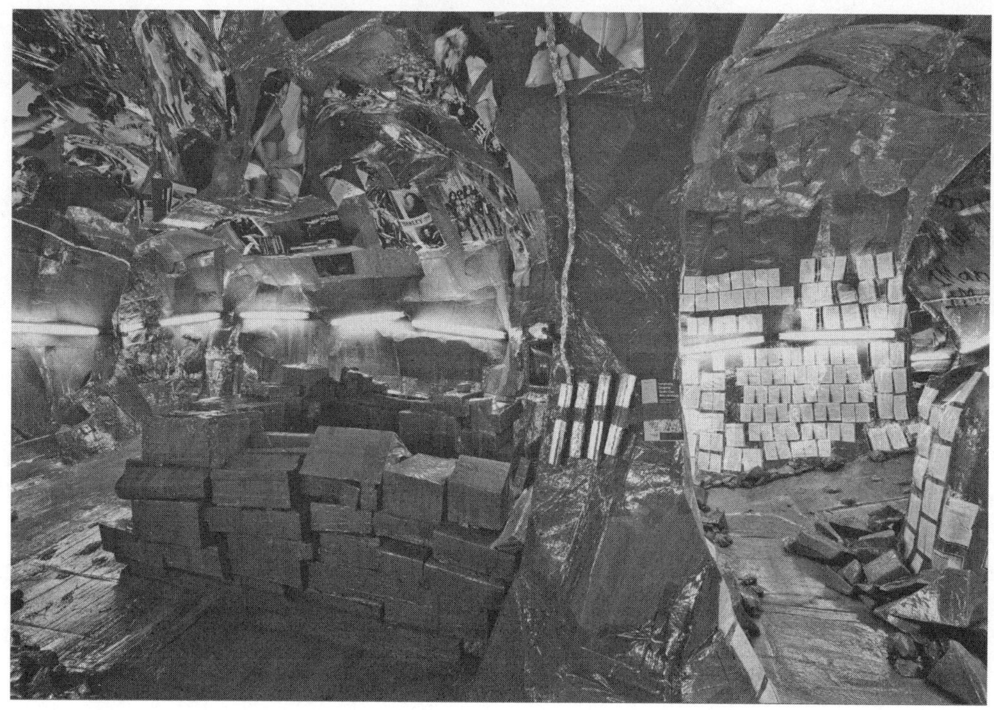

Figure C.2. Thomas Hirschhorn, *Cavemanman*, 2002. Installation: wood, cardboard, tape, aluminum foil, books, posters, videos of Lascaux 2, dolls, cans, shelves, and fluorescent light fixtures; variable dimensions. *Life on Mars*, the 2008 Carnegie International, Pittsburgh. Courtesy of the D. Daskalopoulos Collection.

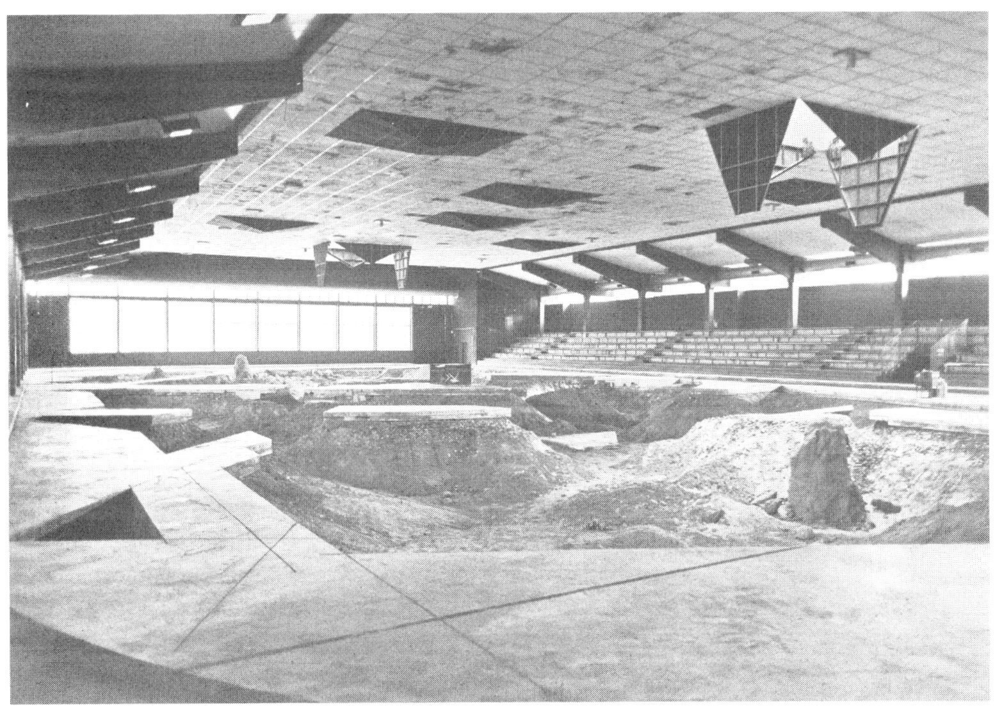

Figure C.3. Pierre Huyghe, *Human Mask. After A Life Ahead*, 2017. Ice rink, concrete, logic game; sand, clay, water tables; bacteria, algae, bees, chimeric peacock; aquarium, black blackout glass, Conus textile; incubator, human cancer cells; genetic algorithm; augmented reality, automated ceiling structure, rain. Courtesy of the artist. Skulptur Projekte 2017. Photo: Ola Rindal.

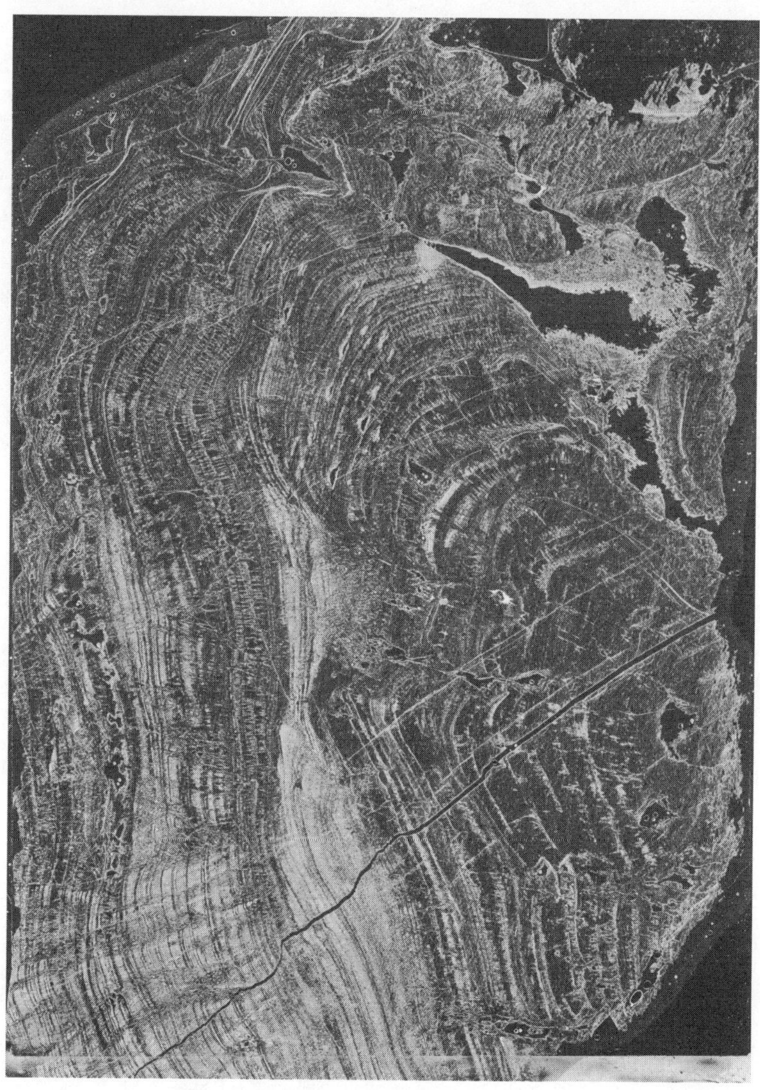

Figure C.4. Dove Allouche, *Pétrographie RSM_3*, 2015. Silver print based on a thin slab of stalagmite mounted on aluminum, 70⅛ × 46½ in. Courtesy Dove Allouche, gb agency, Paris, and Peter Freeman, Inc., New York.

In 1924, Paul Klee said of the artist, "the more deeply he looks, the more readily he can extend his view from the present to the past." The present thus appears to him as "the present state of outward appearances in his own world as accidentally fixed in time and space," "a simple stage in an evolution, fortuitously suspended, accidentally frozen in space and in time." "The world at one time looked different and, in the future, it will look different again," he concluded.[16] A century later, Huyghe, using different media and different materials, found in prehistory the means to "situate oneself outside history, outside the world, beyond knowledge, to make explicit the limits or snip the constructed sutures and imagine other possible worlds."[17] In fact, it is as if the three prehistories—geological, paleontological, and symbolic (artistic)—were now converging to the point of becoming indistinguishable. The images obtained from the artist Dove Allouche, based on mineral samples, are seemingly innervated by life. Not allowing himself to adopt an analogical approach to parietal images, which are absolute enigmas, he makes his appropriation of the long term and its traces the very object of his art (Figure c.4).

Prehistory is no doubt the only land that remains for us to discover. Since the ecumene now extends to the Terra Australis—Antarctica crisscrossed by cruise ships—we are left with the terra incognita of time, a boundless, uncharted, interior land. Cautious as ever, prehistorians have made the ground of the Chauvet Cave into a sanctuary: they do not allow themselves to touch the scattered and buried vestiges. Because they know that "the earth is a book whose pages we destroy as we turn them,"[18] as Leroi-Gourhan wrote, they secure from the start a land that will remain unknown and enigmas that will remain without an answer.

Acknowledgments

My first encounter with the discipline of prehistory occurred during a brief stay at the Institute for Advanced Study at Princeton in spring 2010. When I returned there for a semester in January 2012, I was able to take advantage of the marvelous resources available to me and to move forward with this project. My thanks to Yve-Alain Bois for having welcomed me and for having shared my enthusiasm. Other stays in the United States allowed me to pursue my research and to finish writing this book: at the Clark Art Institute in 2014 and at the Italian Academy at Columbia University in New York in 2018. In the meantime, the Paul Mellon Centre for Studies in British Art had supported my research at the Tate Gallery, London, on the relations between British modernism and prehistory, and the Terra Foundation for American Art supported my work on Robert Smithson at the Archives of American Art, Washington, DC. Without the support of these institutions, this book would not have been the same.

Jean-Pierre Criqui (*Les Cahiers du Musée national d'art moderne*) and Francesco Pellizzi (*RES: Anthropology and Aesthetics*) offered me the opportunity to coedit three special issues at different stages of this project. My thanks to them, as well as to all the contributors whose texts allowed me to refine my own ideas.

For the exchanges I was able to have over the past few years on the inventions of prehistory by moderns and for their invitations to events where I was able to present my research underway, I would like to thank friends and colleagues: Nina Athanassoglou-Kallmyer, Emmelyn Butterfield-Rosen, François Bon, Camille Bourdier,

Sophie de Beaune, Larisa Dryansky, Céline Flécheux, Hal Foster, Anselm Franke, David Freedberg, Peter Geimer, Jean-Louis Georget, Stefanos Geroulanos, Marc Groenen, Emmanuel Guy, Daniel Heller-Roazen, Tom Holert, David Joselit, Hélène Ivanoff, Albrecht Koschorke, Richard Kuba, Angela Lampe, Simon Leung, Sabina Loriga, Philippe-Alain Michaud, Pierre Monet, Alexander Nagel, Jean Nayrolles, Spyros Papapetros, Catherine Perret, Christine Poggi, Yann Potin, Jacques Revel, Julia Robinson, Nicolaas Rupke, Antonio Somaini, Ricardo Venturi, and Gregor Wedekind. I cherish the artists who, between 2016 and 2019, discussed with me their appropriations of the idea of prehistory: Dove Allouche, Gennifer Allora, Guillermo Calzadilla, Tacita Dean, Thomas Hirschhorn, and Pierre Huyghe.

For the publication of this book in English, I am indebted to several people: first, to the three editors at Zone Books, who welcomed *Transfixed by Prehistory* into a world of books that for many long years has enriched my thinking and inspired my admiration; second, to my translator, Jane Marie Todd, whose work was not simply faithful to the original, but improved on it; and finally, to Hal Foster and Daniel Heller-Roazen, who were partners in this publication.

A visit to the Chauvet Cave, made possible by Carole Fritz and Dominique Genty, will undoubtedly mark my life forever.

Finally, this book is informed by my discussions with Éric Michaud, my best reader.

Notes

INTRODUCTION

1. See Paolo Rossi, *The Dark Abyss of Time: The History of the Earth and the History of Nations from Hooke to Vico* (Chicago: University of Chicago Press, 1987).

2. In his manuscript for the new edition of *Les époques de la nature*, Buffon, who had initially given the earth's age as 75,000 years, hesitated between a few hundreds of thousands and a few millions of years. Was it easy, he wrote, or even possible "to form an idea of the whole or of the parts of such a long series of centuries?" His response was no. In the definitive version of *Les époques de la nature*, he returned to his first hypothesis of 75,000 years, which he justified in his introduction: "Is it not, one might ask, 'adding a new cause of obscurity to the difficult things that you claim to explain, when such large numbers and inappropriate lengths of duration are used?'" Quoted in Jacques Roger, *Buffon: A Life in Natural History*, ed. L. Pearce Williams, trans. Sarah Lucille Bonnefoi (Ithaca: Cornell University Press, 1997), p. 412.

3. See Claude Blanckaert, "Nommer le préhistorique au XIXe siècle: Linguistique et transferts lexicaux," *Organon* 49 (2017), pp. 57–103.

4. Michel Foucault, *The Order of Things: An Archaeology of the Human Sciences* (London: Routledge, 2005), p. 347.

5. Immanuel Kant, *Anthropology from a Pragmatic Point of View*, ed. and trans. Robert B. Loudon (Cambridge: Cambridge University Press, 2006), p. 120. [The distinction between "discovery" and "invention," *découverte* and *invention*, is less clear-cut in French than it is in English — trans.]

6. Édouard Lartet, "Nouvelles recherches sur la coexistence de l'homme et des grands mammifères fossiles," *Annales des sciences naturelles*, 4th series, 15, *Zoologie* (Paris: Victor Masson et Fils, 1861), pp. 177–253.

7. Patrick Paillet, "Le mammouth de la Madeleine (Tursac, Dordogne)," *PALEO* 22 (2011), pp. 223–70. But Paillet's consideration of the first discovery of Paleolithic art is treated with the same axiomatic neutrality that characterizes the writings of the first prehistorians, with no analysis of its epistemological, much less ontological, meanings.

8. Édouard Lartet and Henri Christy, *Cavernes du Périgord: Objets gravés et sculptés des temps pré-historiques dans l'Europe occidentale* (1864; Whitefish: Kessinger Legacy Reprints, 2010).

9. Jean-François de Nadaillac, *Les premiers hommes et les temps préhistoriques*, 2 vols. (Paris: Éditions G. Masson, 1881), vol. 1, p. 6.

10. John Lubbock, *Pre-Historic Times as Illustrated by Ancient Remains and the Manners and Customs of Modern Savages*, 6th rev. ed. (New York: D. Appleton, 1900), p. 319.

11. Marcelino Sanz de Sautuola, *Breves apuntes sobre algunos objectos prehistóricos de la Provincia de Santander* (Santander: Telesforo Martínez, 1880).

12. Vitruvius, *De architectura*, bk. 6, chap. 5 in *Vitruvius: The Ten Books on Architecture*, trans. Morris Hicky Morgan (Cambridge, MA: Harvard University Press, 1914), p. 212; André Chastel, *Le grotesque* (Paris: Le Promeneur, 1991); Philippe Morel, *Les grotesques: Les figures de l'imaginaire dans la peinture italienne de la fin de la Renaissance* (Paris: Flammarion, 1997).

13. Leonard Barkan, *Unearthing the Past: Archaeology and Aesthetics in the Making of Renaissance Culture* (New Haven: Yale University Press, 1999), p. 25.

14. *The Theaetetus of Plato*, trans. F. A. Paley (London: George Bell & Sons, 1875), 155d, p. 26.

15. René Descartes, *The Passions of the Soul*, trans. Stephen Voss (1649; Indianapolis: Hackett, 1989), art. 70.

16. Ibid., arts. 76 and 73, translation modified.

17. The mechanism behind this duality and the reasons for it—a duality that allowed modern consciousness to move from denial to appropriation, even obsession—have been neglected in interpretations seeking to explain the hesitancy that marks the reception of parietal art, for example, Ulrich Pfisterer, "Altamira—oder: Die Anfänge von Kunst und Kunstwissenschaft," in Martin Mosebach, ed., *Die Gärten von Capri* (Berlin: Akademie-Verlag, 2007), pp. 13–80.

18. Bruno Latour, *We Have Never Been Modern*, trans. Catherine Porter (Cambridge, MA: Harvard University Press, 1993).

19. Reinhart Koselleck, *Futures Past: On the Semantics of Historical Time*, trans. Keith Tribe (New York: Columbia University Press, 2004).

20. Vladimir Mayakovsky, in his suicide note.

21. Georges Canguilhem provides the broad outlines of this contradictory drive on the part of modernity in an article written late in life, that has great relevance for my argument in this book. The idea of linear progress is linked to the Enlightenment of the eighteenth century, but the nineteenth century abandoned the metaphor of "light" in favor of "heat," linked to machines and the exhaustible energy that sets them in motion. See Georges Canguilhem, "La décadence de l'idée de Progrès," *Revue de Métaphysique et de Morale* 92.4 (1987), pp. 437–54.

22. See Hans Blumenberg, *L'imitation de la nature et autres écrits esthétiques*, trans. Marc Delaunay and Isabelle Kalinowski (Paris: Hermann, 2010).

23. Edgar Quinet, *La création*, 2 vols. (Paris: Librairie internationale, 1870), vol. 1, p. 68.

24. Foucault, *The Order of Things*, p. 356.

25. Ibid., pp. 359–60.

26. Blumenberg, *L'imitation de la nature*, pp. 88–89.

27. Koselleck, *Futures Past*, pp. 33–34.

28. See Sabina Loriga, preface to the second edition of the French translation of Reinhart Koselleck's *Vergangene Zukunft (Futures Past)*, *Le futur passé: Contributions à la sémantique des temps historiques*, trans. Jochen Hoock and Marie-Claire Hoock (Paris: Éditions EHESS, 2016), pp. 1–17.

29. Marcel Proust, *Swann's Way*, trans. C. K. Scott Moncrieff (New York: Vintage, 1970), p. 5.

30. See J. R. McNeill and Peter Engelke, *The Great Acceleration: An Environmental History of the Anthropocene since 1945* (Cambridg, MA: Belknap Press of Harvard University Press, 2016).

31. On the question of the indissociability of form and function in actual prehistoric artifacts, see Horst Bredekamp, "Les sorties de la caverne: Nouvelles découvertes et résultats de la paléontologie," in "Préhistoire/Modernité," ed. Rémi Labrusse and Maria Stavrinaki, special issue, *Cahiers du Musée National d'art moderne* 126 (Winter 2013–2014), pp. 15–23.

32. I made a first attempt to interpret Oldenburg's use of prehistory in my *Saisis par la préhistoire: Enquête sur l'art et le temps des modernes* (Dijon: Les presses du réel, 2019), pp. 296–310. [This section is not included in the present translation of the book — trans.]

33. Nietzsche pointed out this paradox when he commented ironically on modern man's historicization of the entire known world. In his view, the universalization of history was the most narcissistic of enterprises: "The historical imagination has never flown so far,

even in a dream; for now the history of man is merely the continuation of that of animals and plants: the universal historian finds traces of himself even in the utter depths of the sea, in the living slime. He stands astounded in face of the enormous way that man has run, and his gaze quivers before the mightier wonder, the modern man who can see all this way!" Friedrich Nietzsche, *On the Use and Abuse of History*, trans. Adrian Collins, https://en.wikisource.org/wiki/On_the_Use_and_Abuse_of_History_for_Life, section 9, n.p.

34. Lucien Febvre, *Combats pour l'histoire* (1952; Paris: Armand Colin, 1992), pp. 487–89.

35. Leopold von Ranke, *Geschichten der romanischen und germanischen Völker*, in Leopold von Ranke. *Sämmtliche Werke*, 54 vols. in 24 (Leipzig, Duncker und Humblot, 1868–1890), vol. 33, p. vi.

36. I am thinking of the paintings in French caves — with the exception of Lascaux, whose "shaft scene" may have been considered a coherent narrative.

37. Leo Frobenius, *Der Ursprung der afrikanischen Kultur* (Berlin: Borntrager Verlag, 1898). For an analysis of Frobenius's ahistorical reading, I take the liberty of referring the reader to my "Überleben in Afrika: Wiederauferstehung für Europa. Leo Frobenius' Sicht der Vorgeschichte," in Karl-Heinz Kohl, Richard Kuba, and Hélène Ivanoff, eds., *Leo Frobenius* (Berlin: Martin Gropius Bau, 2016), pp. 33–42.

38. Frances Connelly, *The Sleep of Reason: Primitivism in Modern European Art and Aesthetics, 1725–1907* (University Park: Pennsylvania State University Press, 1995), p. 14.

39. Georges Bataille, *Lascaux; or, The Birth of Art: Prehistoric Painting*, trans. Austryn Wainhouse (Lausanne: Skira, 1955).

CHAPTER ONE: "WE SLIP AWAY FROM OURSELVES"

1. "Nous voguons sur un milieu vaste, toujours incertains et flottants, poussés d'un bout vers l'autre." Blaise Pascal, "L'homme dans la nature, les deux infinis," in *Pensées* (Paris: Librairie Générale Française, 1962), p. 54. See *Pascal's Pensées; or, Thoughts on Religion*, ed. and trans. Gertrude Burfurd Rawlings (Mount Vernon: Peter Pauper Press, n.d.), p. 107.

2. "Le silence éternel de ces espaces infinis m'effraie." Pascal, *Pensées*, p. 60. See Blaise Pascal, *Pensées*, trans. A. J. Krailsheimer (New York: Penguin Classics, 1995), p. 66.

3. Edgar Quinet, *La création*, 2 vols. (Paris: Librairie internationale, 1870), vol. 1, p. 33.

4. Charles Lyell, *Principles of Geology: Being an Inquiry How Far the Former Changes of the Earth's Surface Are Referable to Causes Now in Operation*, 3 vols. (London: John Murray, 1830–1833), cited here from the 4th edition, 1835; Georges Cuvier, "Discours préliminaire," in *Recherches sur les ossemens fossiles de quadrupèdes, ou l'on rétablit les caractères de plusieurs*

espèces d'animaux que les révolutions du globe paroissent avoir détruites (Paris: Deterville, 1812), pp. 1–116, published separately in revised form as *Discours sur les révolutions de la surface du globe et sur les changemens qu'elles ont produits dans le règne animal* (Paris: G. Dufour et E. d'Ocagne, 1825).

5. In 1859, Jacques Boucher de Perthes was finally able to prove the age of humankind through his discovery of a flint buried in the same stratum of sediment in Abbeville as vestiges of extinct animals.

6. "L'homme n'est ni ange ni bête." Pascal, *Pensées*, p. 151.

7. "Their being rendered immobile by fear was expressed by the Latins in the heroic phrase *terrore defixi*, and the artists depict them chained band and foot with such links upon the mountains." *The New Science of Giambattista Vico*, trans. Thomas Goddard Bergin and Max Harold Fisch (Ithaca: Cornell University Press, 1948), p. 80.

8. Ibid., pp. 75–76.

9. Georges-Louis Leclerc, le compte de Buffon, *The Epochs of Nature*, ed. and trans Jan Zalasiewicz, Anne-Sophie Milon, and Mateusz Zalasiewicz (Chicago: University of Chicago Press, 2018), p. 119.

10. Immanuel Kant, *Critique of Judgment*, trans. J. H. Bernard (London: Macmillan, 1914), p. 130.

11. See Nasser Zakariya, "Scenes before Grey Antiquity," in "Writing Prehistory," eds. Stephanos Geroulanos and Maria Stavrinaki, special issue, *Res: Anthropology and Aesthetics* 69–70 (2018), pp. 5–19.

12. John Ruskin, letter to Henry Achand of May 24, 1851, in *The Letters of John Ruskin, 1827–1869*, vol. 36 of *The Works of John Ruskin*, ed. E. T. Cook and Alexander Wedderburn, 39 vols. (London: George Allen, 1909), p. 115.

13. A neoclassical term to designate the contraction of time by means of an art of space.

14. Paolo Rossi, *The Dark Abyss of Time: The History of the Earth and the History of Nations from Hooke to Vico* (Chicago: University of Chicago Press, 1987); Wolfhart Langer, "Verzeitlichungs- und Historisierungstendenzen in der frühen Geologie und Paläontologie," *Berichte zur Wissenschaftsgeschichte* 8 (1985), pp. 87–97; Stephen Toulmin and June Goodfield, *The Discovery of Time* (New York: Harper & Row, 1965); Pascal Richet, *L'âge du monde: À la découverte de l'immensité du temps* (Paris: Seuil, 1999).

15. Nicolaus Steno, *De solido intra solidum naturaliter contento dissertationis prodromus* (Florence: Ex typographia sub signo Stellæ, 1699).

16. William Smith, *Strata Identified by Organized Fossils* (London: W. Arding, 1816).

17. Émile Littré, "Études d'histoire primitive," *Revue des deux mondes* (1858), p. 7.

18. Buffon, *The Epochs of Nature*, p. 3.

19. See Nicolaas Rupke, "'The End of History' in the Early Picturing of Geological Time," *History of Science* 36.1 (1998), pp. 61–90.

20. *Routledge's Guide to the Crystal Palace and Park at Sydenham* (London: Routledge, 1854), p. 204.

21. Herman Melville, "Sketch Second: Two Sides of a Tortoise," *The Encantadas*, in *The Piazza Tales* (New York: Dix & Edwards, 1856), n.p., https://www.libertarianism.org/publications/essays/encantadas-two-sides-tortoise.

22. Fernand Braudel, ed., *La Méditerranée*, vol. 1, *L'espace et l'histoire* (Paris: Arts et métiers graphiques, 1977), p. 11.

23. See Paul Ricoeur, *The Rule of Metaphor: The Creation of Meaning in Language*, trans. Robert Czerny with Kathleen McLaughlin and John Costello (London: Routledge, 2003).

24. Robert Hooke, *Discourse of Earthquakes*, in *The Posthumous Works of Robert Hooke* (London: Smith and Walford, 1705). See Martin J. S. Rudwick, *The Meaning of Fossils: Episodes in the History of Paleontology* (London: Macdonald, 1972).

25. Fontenelle, *Histoire de l'Académie Royale des Sciences*, year 1710, pp. 19–21, quoted in Arthur Birembaut, "Fontenelle et la géologie," *Revue d'histoire des sciences et de leurs applications* 10.4 (1957), p. 368.

26. Aristotle, *The "Art" of Rhetoric*, ed. E. Capps, T. E. Page, and W. H. D. Rouse, trans. J. H. Freese (London: William Heinemann, 1926), 1412a5, p. 407.

27. Georges Cuvier, "Discours préliminaire," in Georges Cuvier, *Recherches sur les ossemens fossiles de quadrupèdes, ou l'on rétablit les caractères de plusieurs espèces d'animaux que les révolutions du globe paroissent avoir détruites* (Paris: Deterville, 1812), p. 2.

28. Honoré de Balzac, *The Wild Ass's Skin* (*La peau de chagrin*), trans. Herbert J. Hunt (New York: Penguin Books, 1977), p. 41.

29. This does not mean that geological catastrophism is a myth, only that the flood is a classic theme in human mythic structures.

30. See William Buckland, *Geology and Mineralogy Considered with Reference to Natural Theology*, 2 vols. (London: William Pickering, 1836), vol. 1, p. 21. On this point, see Marianne Sommer, "Earth History and the Order of Society: William Buckland, the French Connection and the Conundrum of Teleology," in Henning Trüper, Dipesh Chakrabarty, and Sanjay Subrahmanyam, eds., *Historical Teleologies in the Modern World* (London: Bloomsbury, 2015), pp. 71–87.

31. Cuvier therefore contrasted physical history and political history. Political history can explain "past events, when we know the passions and intrigues of our time. But we will

see that unfortunately, such is not the case for physical history: the thread of operations is broken; the progress of nature has changed; and none of the objects it uses today would have been sufficient to produce its ancient works." Georges Cuvier, *Discours sur les révolutions de la surface du globe et sur les changemens qu'elles ont produits dans le règne animal* (Paris: G. Dufour et E. d'Ocagne, 1825), p. 18.

32. "These irruptions, these repeated retreats, have not all been slow. They did not all come about by degrees; on the contrary, most of the catastrophes that brought them on were sudden." Ibid., p. 11.

33. James Hutton, *Theory of the Earth, with Proofs and Illustrations* (Edinburgh, 1795), p. 304.

34. According to Gould, however, even Lyell's vision of an eternal present does not avoid the notion of a cycle. See Stephen Jay Gould, *Time's Arrow, Time's Cycle: Myth and Metaphor in the Discovery of Geological Time* (London: Penguin, 1988).

35. Lyell, *Principles of Geology*, vol. 1, p. 75.

36. Gustave Le Bon, *L'homme et les sociétés: Leurs origines et leur histoire* (1881; Paris: Jean Michel Place, 1987), p. 40. On the geologist's temporal ubiquity, see Virginia Zimmerman, *Excavating Victorians* (Albany: State University of New York Press, 2008).

37. Lyell, *Principles of Geology*, vol. 1, p. 87.

38. Dennis Dean has studied in detail a few liminal Romantic figures who absorbed the tension between a divine time that was ending and a geological time that was beginning. See Dennis Dean, *Romantic Landscapes: Geology and Its Critical Influence in Britain, 1765–1835* (Ann Arbor: Scholars' Facsimiles & Reprints, 2000). Byron, for example, referring to Cuvier, outlined in his verse drama *Cain* a boundless hell housing mythical creatures, then extinct species, then current species, and later, no doubt, species of the future, in a catastrophism that indiscriminately and indefinitely subsumed nature and beliefs: "The assertion of Lucifer, that the pre-Adamite world was also peopled by rational beings much more intelligent than man, and proportionably powerful to the mammoth, etc., etc., is, of course, a poetical fiction." Lord Byron, *Cain, a Mystery* (1821; London: William Crofts, 1830), p. viii.

39. Rebecca Bedell, "The History of the Earth: Darwin, Geology and Landscape Art," in Diana Donald and Jane Munro, eds., *Endless Forms: Charles Darwin, Natural Science and Visual Arts* (New Haven: Yale Center for British Art, 2009), pp. 49–79.

40. The American artist Barnett Newman would invert this logic in "The First Man Was an Artist" (1947): the paleontologist believed he was revealing man's unfathomable past for the first time, but the human imagination had already conceived of it in the form

of mythic figures and fables. The divide between metaphysics and physics, the unknowable and the known, remained absolute. See Barnett Newman, "The First Man Was an Artist," *Tiger's Eye* 1 (1947), pp. 57–60.

41. Camille Flammarion, *Le monde avant la création des hommes: Origines de la terre, origines de la vie, origines de l'humanité* (Paris: C. Marpon et E. Flammarion éditeurs, 1886), p. 3.

42. Littré, "Études d'histoire primitive," p. 23.

43. Quinet, *La création*, vol. 1, pp. 37–38.

44. Gillian Beer, *Darwin's Plots: Evolutionary Narrative in Darwin, George Eliot and Nineteenth-Century Fiction* (London: Routledge & Kegan Paul, 1983).

45. Lyell, *Principles of Geology*, vol. 1, p. 110.

46. Ibid., vol. 1, p. 160.

47. Fernand Braudel, preface to the 1st edition of *The Mediterranean and the Mediterranean World in the Age of Philip II*, trans. Siân Reynolds (1949; Berkeley: University of California Press, 1995), p. 17. On the problematic relationship that the Annales School historians maintained with fiction, see Jacques Rancière, *Les mots de l'histoire: Essai de poétique du savoir* (Paris: Seuil, 1992).

48. Lyell, *Principles of Geology*, vol. 1, p. 79.

49. In his "Theory of the Heavens," Kant also wrote that analogy "must always guide us in such cases where understanding lacks the thread of infallible proofs." Immanuel Kant, "Universal Natural History and Theory of the Heavens or Essay on the Constitution and the Mechanical Origin of the Whole Universe according to Newtonian Principles," in Immanuel Kant, *Natural Science*, ed. Eric Watkins, trans. Olaf Reinhardt, Eric Watkins, Jeffrey B. Edwards, Martin Schoenfeld, and Lewis White Beck (Cambridge: Cambridge University Press, 2015), p. 268.

50. Lyell, *Principles of Geology*, vol. 1, p. 165.

51. Ferdinand Braudel, *Memory and the Mediterranean*, ed. Roselyne de Ayala and Paule Braudel, trans. Siân Reynolds (New York: Knopf, 2001), p. 3, translation modified.

52. Hans Blumenberg, *Paradigms for a Metaphorology*, trans. Robert Savage (Ithaca: Cornell University Press, 2010), p. 57.

53. See Jean-Claude Monod, "La patience de l'image: Éléments pour une localisation de la métaphorologie," afterword to *Paradigmes pour une métaphorologie*, trans. Didier Gammelin (Paris: Vrin, 2006), pp. 171–95.

54. Blumenberg, "Terra incognita," in *Paradigms for a Metaphorology*, pp. 52–61.

55. Frédérique Aït-Touati, *Contes de la lune: Essai sur la fiction et la science moderne* (Paris: Gallimard, 2011).

56. Ibid., p. 53.

57. Charles Lyell, journal, May 1832, in *Life, Letters and Journals of Sir Charles, Lyell, Bart.*, 2 vols., ed. Mrs. Lyell (London: John Murray, 1881), vol. 1, p. 381.

58. Charles Lyell, book review of *Memoir on the Geology of Central France*, quoted in Zimmerman, *Excavating Victorians*, p. 33.

59. Quinet, *La création*, vol. 1, p. 3.

60. Ibid., vol. 1, p. 68. My emphasis.

61. Ibid., vol. 1, p. 76.

62. Charles Lyell, letter to Poulett Scrope, June 14, 1830, in *Life, Letters and Journals of Sir Charles Lyell, Bart.*, pp. 269–70.

63. Louis Simond, *Voyage en Angleterre pendant les années 1810–1811*, 2 vols. (Paris: Treuttel et Würz, 1817), vol. 2, pp. 1 and 4.

64. Hans Blumenberg, quoted in Monod, "La patience de l'image," p. 195.

65. Raymond Schwab, "La renaissance de l'archaïque," *Gazette des beaux-arts* (July–August 1936), p. 20.

66. Quinet, *La création*, vol. 1, p. 24.

67. Ibid., vol. 1, p. 98.

68. Ibid., vol. 2, p. 377.

69. Ibid.

70. Ibid., vol. 2, p. 379.

71. John Lubbock, *Pre-Historic Times as Illustrated by Ancient Remains and the Manners and Customs of Modern Savages*, 6th rev. ed. (New York: D. Appleton, 1900), p. 319.

72. I will return to all these themes later on.

73. Flammarion, *Le monde avant la création des hommes*, p. 10. The Deleuzian philosopher Manuel De Landa revived this belief just recently, establishing a continuity between geology, biological organisms, and human language. See Manuel De Landa, *A Thousand Years of Nonlinear History* (New York: Zone Books, 2000).

74. Théodule Ribot formulated the "law of regression" with respect to the pathologies of memory. In opposition to a geological conception of memory, he formulated a synchronic and contiguous conception: "It is extremely plausible that memories occupy the same anatomical site as original impressions." Théodule Ribot, *Les maladies de la mémoire* (1881; Paris: Félix Alcan, 1906), p. 100.

75. Friedrich Nietzsche, *Human, All Too Human*, trans. Alexander Harvey (Chicago: Charles H. Kerr, 1908), § 43, p. 80.

76. Ibid.

77. Quinet, *La création*, vol. 1, p. 347.

78. Claude Blanckaert, "Chrono-logiques: Le tournant historiciste des sciences humaines," in Arnaud Hurel and Noël Coye, eds., *Dans l'épaisseur du temps: Archéologues et géologues inventent la préhistoire* (Paris: Publications scientifiques du Muséum national d'histoire naturelle, 2011), pp. 53–95.

79. William Whewell, *History of the Inductive Sciences from the Earliest Times to the Present*, 3 vols. (London: J. W. Parker, 1837).

80. Adolphe Pictet, *Les origines indo-européennes ou les Aryas primitifs: Essai de paléontologie linguistique* (Paris: Joël Cherbuliez, 1859), pp. vi–vii.

81. Pictet wrote: "Indeed, words last just as much as bones; and, even as a tooth implicitly contains a part of an animal's history, an isolated word can set you on the path toward a whole series of ideas that were attached to it upon its formation." Ibid., p. 14.

82. Max Müller, *Lectures on the Science of Language* (New York: Charles Scribner, 1862), pp. 358 and 328.

83. Ernest Renan, *The Future of Science: Ideas of 1848*, trans. Albert D. Vandam and C. B. Pitman (1848; London: Chapman and Hall, 1891), p. 155.

84. Lubbock, *Pre-Historic Times*, pp. 407–408.

85. James Frazer, *The Golden Bough* (New York: Macmillan, 1894), p. 66.

86. Stephen Jay Gould, *Ontogeny and Phylogeny* (Cambridge, MA: Belknap Press Harvard University Press, 1985).

87. Sándor Ferenczi, *Thalassa: A Theory of Genitality*, trans. Henry Alden Bunker (Albany: Psychoanalytic Quarterly, 1938), p. 45.

88. The term "engram" (*Engramm*) was coined by the German zoologist Richard Semon in *Die Mneme als erhaltendes Prinzip im Wechsel des organischen Geschehens* (Leipzig: Engelmann, 1904). Believing that acquired characteristics could be passed on, he maintained that experiences left mnemic traces, which he called "engrams." They were said to be genetically transmissible and could be reactivated indefinitely.

89. Ferenczi, *Thalassa*, p. 52.

90. Daniel Goldman, "Lost Paper Shows Freud's Effort to Link Analysis and Evolution," *New York Times*, February 10, 1987.

91. Sigmund Freud, "Findings, Ideas, Problems" (1938), in vol. 23 of *The Standard Edition of the Complete Psychological Works of Sigmund Freud*, ed. and trans. James Strachey (London: Hogarth, 1964), p. 299.

92. Virginia Woolf, *Between the Acts* (1941), http://gutenberg.net.au/ebooks03/0301171h.html, n.p.

93. Robert Smithson, "A Tour of the Monuments of Passaic, New Jersey" (1967), in Robert Smithson, *The Collected Writings*, ed. Jack Flam (Berkeley: University of California Press, 1996), p. 72.

94. Robert Smithson, "A Sedimentation of the Mind: Earth Projects," in *The Collected Writings*, p. 100.

95. Max Frisch, *Man in the Holocene*, trans. Geoffrey Skelton (Champaign: London Dalkey Archive Press, 2007).

96. "So now I've landed back in the Midi, which perhaps I should never have left, to hurl myself into the chimerical pursuit of Art." Paul Cézanne, letter to Claude Monet, July 6, 1859, in Paul Cézanne, *Cinquante-trois lettres*, ed. Jean-Claude Lebensztejn (Paris: L'Échoppe, 2011), p. 37.

97. Letter to Monet, June 3, 1899, in Paul Cézanne, *The Letters of Paul Cézanne*, ed. and trans. Alex Danchev (Los Angeles: J. Paul Getty Museum, 2013), p. 297.

98. Henri Bergson, *Matter and Memory*, trans. N. M. Paul and W. S. Palmer (New York: Zone Books, 1990), pp. 137–38.

99. Meyer Schapiro, "The Apples of Cézanne: An Essay on the Meaning of Still-Life," *Art News Annual* 34 (1968), pp. 34–53.

100. Meyer Schapiro, *Paul Cézanne* (New York: Harry N. Abrams, 1952), p. 29.

101. Jean-Claude Lebensztejn, "Persistance de la mémoire: Note sur la datation des confidences de Cézanne," in Jean-Claude Lebensztejn, *Les couilles de Cézanne* (Paris: Séguier, 1995), p. 51.

102. André Dombrowski has explored the convergence of cannibalism and violence in the respective works of the two friends. Just as the early Cézanne took inspiration from these themes, Marion interpreted prehistoric tools and other evidence of prehistory as signs of anthropophagic practices. See André Dombrowski, "Modernism and Extremism: The Early Work of Paul Cézanne (1865–1875)," PhD diss., University of California Berkeley, 2006, pp. 145–51, published as *Cézanne, Murder, and Modern Life* (Berkeley: University of California Press, 2012).

103. Nina Athanassoglou-Kallmyer, *Cézanne and Provence: The Painter in His Culture* (Chicago: University of Chicago Press, 2003). My thanks to the author for directing my attention to Cézanne in 2012, when I began to work on this project.

104. Robert Smithson, interview with William Lipke (1969), in *The Collected Writings*, p. 188.

105. Paul Cézanne, letter to Émile Bernard, April 15, 1904, in Cézanne, *The Letters of Paul Cézanne*, p. 334.

106. Lebensztejn thus alludes to a Cézanne who was "essentially . . . a structural impressionist, a painter of the motif, that is, of the present. Nevertheless, this present is geological, it contains the layers — superficial or buried — of Cézanne's memory. Cézanne himself linked his sensations to his recollections." Lebensztejn, "Persistance de la mémoire," p. 52.

107. Émile Bernard, "A Conversation with Cézanne" (*Mercure de France*, 1921), in *Conversations with Cézanne*, ed. Michael Doran, trans. Julie Lawrence Cochran (Berkeley: University of California Press, 2001), p. 162.

108. Letter to Henri Gasquet, December 23, 1898, in *The Letters of Paul Cézanne*, p. 293.

109. Letter to Monet, June 3, 1899, ibid., p. 297.

110. Robert Morris, "Cézanne's Mountains," *Critical Inquiry* 24.3 (Spring 1998), pp. 814–29.

111. Lubbock, *Pre-Historic Times*, p. 575.

112. Alfred R. Wallace, "The Origin of Human Races and the Antiquity of Man Deduced from the Theory of 'Natural Selection,'" *Journal of the Anthropological Society of London* 2 (1864), p. clxviii. Also quoted in Lubbock, *Pre-Historic Times*, p. 567.

113. M. J. S. Rudwick, *Scenes from Deep Time: Early Pictorial Representations of the Prehistoric World* (Chicago: University of Chicago Press, 1992); Rudwick, *Bursting the Limits of Time: The Reconstruction of Geohistory in the Age of Revolution* (Chicago: University of Chicago Press, 2005).

114. H. G. Wells, "The Extinction of Man" (1894), in H. G. Wells, *Certain Personal Matters* (London: Lawrence & Bullen, 1897), pp. 172–79.

115. Nicolas de Condorcet, *Outlines of an Historical View of the Progress of the Human Mind: Being a Posthumous Work of the Late M. de Condorcet, Translated from the French* (London: J. Johnson, 1795), p. 4.

116. Quinet, *La création*, vol. 2, p. 416.

117. Gideon A. Mantell, *The Medals of Creation; or, First Lessons in Geology, and in the Study of Organic Remains* (London: H. G. Bohn, 1844), pp. 875–76.

118. Lyell, *Principles of Geology*, pp. 249–51, emphasis added.

119. Charles Darwin, *On the Origin of Species* (New York: D. Appleton, 1861), p. 424.

120. Samuel Butler, "Darwin among the Machines" [To the Editor of *The Press*, Christchurch, New Zealand, 13 June, 1863], New Zealand Electronic Text Collection, http://nzetc.victoria.ac.nz/tm/scholarly/tei-ButFir-t1-g1-t1-g1-t4-body.html.

121. Samuel Butler, *Erewhon; or, Over the Range* (Northridge CA: Aegypan, 2008)

122. Mantell, *The Medals of Creation*, p. 922; see Zimmerman, *Excavating Victorians*, p. 51.

123. See Wolfgang Schivelbusch, *The Railway Journey: The Industrialization of Time and*

Space in the Nineteenth Century, trans. Anselm Hollo (Berkeley: University of California Press, 2014).

124. Reinhart Koselleck, *Futures Past: On the Semantics of Historical Time*, trans. Keith Tribe (New York: Columbia University Press, 2004), p. 11.

125. See Sommer, "Earth History and the Order of Society."

126. Antoine Augustin Cournot, *Considérations sur la marche des idées et des événements dans les Temps modernes*, 2 vols. (Paris: Librairie Hachette, 1872), vol. 2, p. 240.

127. See Nikolaus Pevsner, *High Victorian Design: A Study of the Exhibits of 1851* (London: Architectural Press, 1951).

128. See Nancy Rose Marshall, *City of Gold and Mud: Painting Victorian London* (New Haven: Yale University Press, 2012), pp. 233–49.

129. "The tradition of all dead generations weighs like a nightmare [*Alp*] on the brains of the living." Karl Marx, *The Eighteenth Brumaire of Louis Bonaparte*, trans. Saul K. Padover, Marx/Engels Internet Archive, 2010, https://www.marxists.org/archive/marx/works/download/pdf/18th-Brumaire.pdf, p. 5.

130. Jules Jamin, "Le daguerréotype," *L'Artiste* (1839), repr. in André Rouillé, *La photographie en France: Textes et controverse. Une anthologie, 1816–1871* (Paris: Macula, 1989), p. 46.

131. For example, Auguste Belloc, "L'avenir de la photographie," *Revue photographique* 3 (August 1858), p. 109.

132. In addition, William Henry Fox Talbot wrote that photographs were "impressed by Nature's hand." "Introductory Remarks," in William Henry Fox Talbot, *The Pencil of Nature* (London: Longman Brown, Green and Longmans, 1844), pp. 1–2.

133. Jamin, "Le daguerréotype," p. 51.

134. Guillaume Apollinaire, *The Cubist Painters*, trans. Peter Read (Berkeley: University of California Press, 2004), p. 9.

135. Giorgio de Chirico, "Art métaphysique et sciences occultes," in Giorgio de Chirico, *L'art métaphysique*, ed. Giovanni Lista (Paris: L'Échoppe, 1994), p. 112.

136. I am thinking here of Leo Steinberg's analysis in "Resisting Cézanne: Picasso's *Three Women* of 1908," *Art in America* 66 (November–December 1978), pp. 114–33. Steinberg argues that Picasso's painting sought to liberate itself from the "geological pressure" of the walls of the Bibémus quarry or the mountainsides of Mont Sainte-Victoire.

137. De Chirico arrived in Paris in 1912 and was an acquaintance of Picasso.

138. For a formal analysis of how de Chirico converted cubism into a disincarnated illusionism, see Ralph Ubl, "Georgio de Chirico: Exkarnation und Filiation der Malerei," in Johannes Endres, Barbara Wittmann, and Gerhard Wolf, eds., *Ikonologie des Zwischenraums:*

Der Schleier als Medium und Metapher (Munich: Wilhelm Fink Verlag, 2005), pp. 385–416.

139. De Chirico, "Art métaphysique et sciences occultes," p. 112.

140. Giorgio de Chirico, "Nous les métaphysiciens" (1919), in *L'art métaphysique*, p. 118.

141. Giorgio De Chirico, "Méditations d'un peintre," in *L'art métaphysique*, p. 84.

142. Carl Einstein, *Georges Braque*, trans. M. E. Zipruth (Paris: Éditions. des Chroniques du jour, 1934), p. 86.

143. Ara H. Merjian comments on the artist's interest in an Etruscan artifact from the second century BCE, the "bronze liver of Piacenza," which served as a model that diviners used to initiate their disciples. See A. H. Merjian, *Giorgio de Chirico and the Metaphysical City: Nietzsche, Modernism, Paris* (New Haven: Yale University Press, 2014), pp. 171–218.

144. Giorgio de Chirico, "Deuxième partie: Le sentiment de la préhistoire," in *L'art métaphysique*, p. 88.

145. In the chapter "Untimely Objects: The Evil Genius of a King," Ara Merjian points out the connection between the antediluvian and the posthistorical in de Chirico, insisting especially on the importance that Louis Figuier's *La terre avant le Déluge* (Earth before the Flood) had for de Chirico and his brother, Alberto Savinio. All in all, this book was not so far from the imaginary of Jules Verne's novels.

146. Viktor Shklovsky, "Art as Technique" (1917), p. 2, https://www.cbpbu.ac.in/userfiles/file/2020/STUDY_MAT/ENGLISH/JS/30-04-20/Art%20as%20Technique%20-%20Shklovsky.pdf.

147. They were part of the Shchukin collection.

148. He would later say, speaking of himself: "It was at that moment [in Munich in 1919] that Max Ernst noticed reproductions of 'metaphysical' canvases by de Chirico in an issue of the Italian review *Valori Plastici*. He would later say: 'I had the impression I was recognizing something that had always been familiar to me, as when an experience of déjà vu reveals a whole realm of our dream world that we refused to see or understand, as a result of a kind of censorship.'" Max Ernst, "Un jour de pluie, à Cologne (1919)," in Max Ernst, *Écritures* (Paris: Gallimard, 1970), pp. 30–31.

149. See William A. Camfield, *Max Ernst: Dada and the Dawn of Surrealism* (Munich: Prestel, 1993), pp. 333–36; Ralph Ubl, *Prehistoric Future: Max Ernst and the Return of Painting between the Wars*, trans. Elizabeth Tucker (Chicago: University of Chicago Press, 2013).

150. See Maria Stavrinaki, *Dada Presentism: An Essay on Art and History*, trans. Daniela Ginsburg (Stanford: Stanford University Press, 2016).

151. See Yann Harlaut, "La Cathédrale de Reims du 4 septembre 1914 au 10 juillet 1938: Idéologies, controverses et pragmatisme," PhD diss., Université de Reims, 2006.

152. Romain Rolland and Frans Masereel, *Liluli, suivi de La révolte des machines* (Montreuil: Le temps des cerises, 2015), p. 169.

153. Ibid., p. 221.

154. Jean Starobinski, *La mélancolie au miroir: Trois lectures de Baudelaire* (Paris: Julliard, 1989), p. 75.

155. Ludger Derenthal, "Mitteilungen über Flugzeuge, Engel und den Weltkrieg: Zu den Photocollagen der Dadazeit von Max Ernst," in Klaus Herding, ed., *Konstruktionen der Moderne: Im Blickfeld. Jahrbuch der Hamburger Kunsthalle* (Hamburg: Christians, 1994), pp. 41–60.

156. There is a vast bibliography on the invention of camouflage during World War I. As a general guide, see Tim Newark, ed., *Camouflage*, exh. cat. (London: Imperial War Museum, 2007).

157. Roger Caillois made mimetism one of the guiding threads of his thinking. See Roger Caillois, *Le mimétisme animal* (Paris: Hachette, 1963).

158. Fernand Braudel, "Histoire et sciences sociales: La longue durée," *Les Annales* 13.4 (October 1958), repr. in *Réseaux* 27, pp. 12 and 15.

159. Sigmund Freud, *Beyond the Pleasure Principle*, ed. and trans. James Strachey (New York: W. W. Norton, 1961), p. 30.

160. Ernst Jünger, "Total Mobilization" (1920), trans. Joel Golb and Richard Wolin, in Richard Wolin, ed., *The Heidegger Controversy: A Critical Reader* (Cambridge, MA: MIT Press, 1993), pp. 119–39.

161. *Physiomythologisches Diluvialbild (Physiomythological Flood-Picture)* is a joint collage by Max Ernst and Hans Arp, to which a subtitle was later added: "Switzerland, Birthplace of Dada." The "birth" of Dada took place during the deluge of World War I, at the Cabaret Voltaire in Zurich (1916). In the collage, two hybrid, anthropomorphic creatures straddling the plant and animal kingdoms (birds of a sort) are emerging from the receding floodwaters. They mark the beginning of a new natural history, which has left human civilization behind.

162. Ubl, *Prehistoric Future.*

163. Walter Benjamin, "[On the Theory of Knowledge, Theory of Progress]," in *The Arcades Project*, trans. Howard Eiland and Kevin McLaughlin (Cambridge, MA: Belknap Press of Harvard University Press, 1999), pp. 461–62, translation modified.

164. Georg Lukács, *History and Class Consciousness* (1923), trans. Rodney Livingstone (Cambridge, MA: MIT Press, 1971).

165. Ibid., p. 89.

166. Karl Marx, *The Poverty of Philosophy* (1847), trans. Institute of Marxism Leninism (Moscow: Progress Publishers, 1955), https://www.marxists.org/archive/marx/works/1847/poverty-philosophy/cho1b.htm, n.p.

167. Karl Marx, *Capital: A Critique of Political Economy*, vol. 1 (Moscow: Progress Publishers, 1887), https://www.marxists.org/archive/marx/works/download/pdf/Capital-Volume-I.pdf, pp. 47–60.

168. Georg Lukács, *Theory of the Novel*, trans. Anna Bostock (London: Merlin Press, 1971), p. 63.

169. Robert Smithson was very interested in the concept of "dedifferentiation," which appeared in Anton Ehrenzweig's *L'ordre caché de l'art* (Paris: Gallimard, 1982). See Anton Ehrenzweig, *The Hidden Order of Art: A Study in the Psychology of Artistic Imagination* (Berkeley: University of California Press, 1976).

170. J. R. McNeill and Peter Engelke, *The Great Acceleration: An Environmental History of the Anthropocene since 1945* (Cambridge, MA: Belknap Press of Harvard University Press, 2016).

171. Claude Lévi-Strauss, *Tristes Tropiques*, trans. John Weightman and Doreen Weightman (New York: Athaneum, 1975), p. 413.

172. Ibid., translation modified.

173. Jennifer L. Roberts, *Mirror-Travels: Robert Smithson and History* (New Haven: Yale University Press, 2004), pp. 13–35.

174. See the beginning of this chapter.

175. Robert Smithson, interview with Moira Roth (1973), in Eugenie Tsai, ed., with Cornelia Butler, *Robert Smithson*, exh. cat. (Los Angeles: Museum of Contemporary Art, 2004), p. 90.

176. Robert Smithson, "Some Void Thoughts on Museums" (1967), in *The Collected Writings*, p. 41.

177. Jean-Paul Sartre, *Existentialism and Humanism*, trans. Philip Mairet (1946; London: Eyre Methuen, 1973).

178. Smithson, "Some Void Thoughts on Museum," p. 41.

179. Undated letter from Smithson to George Lester, Robert Smithson and Nancy Holt Papers, Archives of American Art, Smithsonian Institution, reel 5438, frame 128.

180. Smithson called his work during this period "iconic." It tended toward "a kind of Byzantine relationship," which coincided, as he immediately added, with his interest "in the theories of T. E. Hulme." Interview with Paul Cummings, in Smithson, *The Collected Writings*, p. 283.

181. Thomas Ernest Hulme, *Essays on Humanism and the Philosophy of Art*, ed. Herbert Read (London: Routledge & Kegan Paul, 1924).

182. James Joyce's well-known metaphor was used several times by Smithson. See, for example, the interview with Cummings, p. 288.

183. Robert Smithson, "A Sedimentation of the Mind," in *The Collected Writings*, p. 105.

184. Smithson, interview with Cummings, p. 288.

185. Robert Smithson, in an interview with Michael Heizer and Dennis Oppenheim, New York, December 1968–January 1969, in *The Collected Writings*, p. 248.

186. Smithson's notion did not differ on that point from the notion of "zaum" in Russian cubo-futurism — painting, poetry, and music combined.

187. Such was the case for Tacita Dean, who, in a first visit had to turn back, an experience that was the occasion for her audio work *Trying to Find the Spiral Jetty* (1997).

188. Robert Smithson, "The Spiral Jetty" (1972), in *The Collected Writings*, p. 147.

189. It should be recalled that Smithson, after Merleau-Ponty and Schapiro, had understood Cézanne's geological positioning.

190. Smithson, "The Spiral Jetty," p. 147.

191. Robert Smithson, "Four Conversations between Dennis Wheeler and Robert Smithson" (1969–1970), in *The Collected Writings*, p. 211.

192. Ibid., p. 207.

193. Robert Smithson, "A Tour of the Monuments of Passaic, New Jersey" (1967), in *The Collected Writings*, p. 74.

194. Robert Smithson, "Fragments of an Interview with P. A. Norvell" (1969), in *The Collected Writings*, p. 194.

195. Robert Smithson, "A Museum of Language in the Vicinity of Art" (1968), in *The Collected Writings*, p. 85.

196. Smithson, "The Spiral Jetty," p. 146.

197. Marshall McLuhan, *Understanding Media: The Extensions of Man* (1964; Cambridge, MA: MIT Press, 1994), p. 16.

198. Robert Smithson, "Entropy and the New Monuments" (1966), in *The Collected Writings*, p. 15.

199. Claude Lévi-Strauss, *Tristes Tropiques*, trans. John Weightman and Doreen Weightman (New York: Atheneum, 1974), p. 413.

200. J. G. Ballard, *The Terminal Beach*, in J. G. Ballard, *The Complete Stories* (New York: Norton, 2009), p. 595.

201. Robert Smithson, interview with Gianni Pettena (1972), in *The Collected Writings*,

p. 298.

202. Smithson, "A Tour of the Monuments of Passaic, New Jersey," p. 71.

203. Ibid.

204. Roland Barthes, "Sémantique de l'objet," in *Oeuvres complètes*, ed. Eric Marty, 5 vols. (Paris: Seuil, 2002), vol. 2, p. 817.

205. Robert Smithson, "Incidents of Mirror-Travel in the Yucatan," in *The Collected Writings*, p. 122.

206. Smithson, "A Tour of the Monuments of Passaic, New Jersey," p. 74.

207. On the notion of the tragic, see Peter Szondi, *An Essay on the Tragic*, trans. Paul Fleming (Stanford: Stanford University Press, 2002).

208. Smithson, interview with Michael Heizer and Dennis Oppenheim, in *The Collected Writings*, p. 251.

209. Robert Smithson and Allan Kaprow, interview, "What Is a Museum?," in *The Collected Writings*, p. 44.

210. Robert Smithson, "A Refutation of Historical Humanism" (1966–1967), in *The Collected Writings*, p. 336.

211. Ibid., p. 337.

212. Jorge Luis Borges, "Pascal's Sphere," in Jorge Luis Borges, *Selected Non-Fictions*, ed. Eliot Weinberger, trans. Esther Allen, Suzanne Jill Levine, and Eliot Weinberger (New York: Viking, 1999), pp. 351–53.

213. Francis Ponge, "Notes toward a Shell," in *Dreaming the Miracle, Three French Prose Poets: Jacob, Ponge, Follain*, trans. Beth Archer Brombert, Mary Feeney, Louise Guiney, William T. Kulik, and William Matthews (Buffalo: White Pine Press, 2003), p. 102.

214. Ibid., translation modified.

215. Jean-Paul Sartre, "L'homme et les choses," in *Critiques littéraires (Situations I)* (Paris: Gallimard, 1947), p. 342.

216. Ibid., p. 352.

CHAPTER TWO: RECONSTITUTING THE ANTIQUITY OF HUMANKIND AND OF ART

1. Recent attempts have been made to identify the two figures: they are said to be Mary Anning (1799–1847), a serious fossil hunter, and Henry de la Beche. See Michael A. Taylor, "Mary Anning (1799–1847) and the Photograph *The Geologists* Ascribed to William Henry Fox Talbot (1800–1877)," *Geoscience in South-West England* 13.4 (2015), pp. 419–27.

2. John Evans, *The Coins of the Ancient Britons* (London: B. Quaritch, 1864).

3. See C. J. Pinsard, "Préhistorique — origine d'Amiens: La première hache en pierre authentiquement découverte à Saint-Acheul," album of photos and sketches, texts, and handwritten notes, in Étienne Jules Adolphe Desmier, vicomte d'Archiac, et al., *1859: Naissance de la préhistoire. Récits des premiers témoins* (Paris: Paléo, 1999), pp. 252–54. For an analysis of two photographs, see Clive Gamble and Robert Kruszynski, "John Evans, Joseph Prestwich and the Stone That Shattered the Time Barrier," *Antiquity* 83 (2009), pp. 461–75.

4. See Donald Grayson, *The Establishment of Human Antiquity* (New York: Academic Press, 1983).

5. See Wiktor Stoczkowski, *Anthropologie naïve, anthropologie savante* (Paris: CNRS Éditions, 1995).

6. Lucretius, *On the Nature of Things*, trans. Martin Ferguson Smith (Indianapolis: Hackett, 2001), bk. 5, introduction; Jean-Jacques Rousseau, *A Discourse on Inequality*, trans. Maurice Cranston (New York: Penguin Classics, 1985); Nicolas de Condorcet, *Outlines of an Historical View of the Progress of the Human Mind: Being a Posthumous Work of the Late M. de Condorcet, Translated from the French* (London: J. Johnson, 1795). For an excellent anthology of discourses on prehistory before the invention of prehistory, see Wiktor Stoczkowski, ed., *Aux origines de l'humanité* (Paris: Pocket, 1996).

7. Rousseau, *A Discourse on Inequality*, p. 90. The luminous pages on the question of the "origin" and of "history" in Rousseau must be read and reread. See Jean Starobinski, *Jean-Jacques Rousseau: Transparency and Obstruction*, trans. Arthur Goldhammer (Chicago: University of Chicago Press, 1988).

8. Ernest-Théodore Hamy, *Précis de la paléontologie humaine* (Paris: J.-B. Ballière et Fils, 1870), p. 3.

9. Claude Blanckaert, "Nommer le préhistorique au XIXe siècle: Linguistique et transferts lexicaux," *Organon* 49 (2017), pp. 57–103.

10. On the term "prehistory," see Christopher Chippindale, "The Invention of Words for the Idea of 'Prehistory,'" *Proceedings of the Prehistoric Society* 54 (1988), pp. 303–14; Alice B. Kehoe, "The Invention of Prehistory," *Current Anthropology* 32.4 (August–October 1991), pp. 467–76; Stig Welinder, "The Word *Förhistorisk*, 'Prehistoric,' in Swedish," *Antiquity* 65 (1991), pp. 295–96. Finally, see Blanckaert's "Nommer le préhistorique au XIXe siècle."

11. Antoine de Jussieu, *De l'origine et des usages de la pierre de foudre* (Paris: Mémoires de l'Académie Royale des Sciences, 1725), pp. 6–9.

12. Auguste Laugel, "L'homme primitif d'après les travaux de MM. Lyell et Huxley," *Revue des deux mondes*, 2nd series, 45 (May 1863), pp. 204–31.

13. See J. E. Gilibert, *Abrégé du système de la nature de Linné ou Des quadrupèdes et cétacés*

(Lyon: Materon, 1802), pp. 55–57.

14. I borrow the term "thickness" (*épaisseur*) from the excellent catalogue on man's antiquity, Arnaud Hurel and Noël Coye, eds., *Dans l'épaisseur du temps: Archéologues et géologues inventent la préhistoire* (Paris: Museum National d'Histoire Naturelle, 2011).

15. John Evans's diary, quoted in Glyn Daniel, *The Idea of Prehistory* (Cleveland: World Publishing, 1963), p. 54.

16. Paul Tournal, "Lettre écrite aux administrateurs du Muséum d'histoire naturelle de Paris" (1829), quoted in Arnaud Hurel, "Paul Tournal, les grottes de Bize et la question de la haute antiquité de l'homme," in *Dans l'*épaisseur du temps, p. 170.

17. Paul Tournal, "Considérations théoriques sur les cavernes à ossements de Bize," quoted in Wictor Stoczkowski, "La préhistoire: Les origines du concept," *Bulletin de la société préhistorique française* 90.1 (1993), p. 17.

18. See Laurent Goulven, "Edouard Lartet (1801–1871) et la paléontologie humaine," *Bulletin de la Société préhistorique française* 90.1 (1993), pp. 22–30.

19. See Claudine Cohen and Jean-Jacques Hublin, *Boucher de Perthes: Les origines romantiques de la préhistoire* (Paris: Belin, 2017); Jean-Yves Pautrat, "L'homme antédiluvien: Les vestiges de l'homme et l'avenir des commencements," in *Dans l'*épaisseur du temps, pp. 97–149.

20. Jacques Boucher de Perthes, *Antiquités celtiques et antédiluviennes: Mémoire sur l'industrie primitive et les arts à leur origine*, 3 vols. (Paris: Treuttel et Wurtz, Derchen Dumoulin et Didron, 1847), vol. 1, p. 34.

21. For an excellent overview of the questions raised by the discovery of man's Paleolithic prehistory, see Marc Groenen, *Pour une histoire de la préhistoire: Le paléolithique* (Grenoble: Jérôme Million, 1994).

22. Boucher de Perthes, *Antiquités celtiques et antédiluviennes*, vol. 1, p. 4.

23. Ibid., vol. 1, p. 5.

24. Here I follow Gabriel de Mortillet's periodization table in *Le préhistorique: Antiquité de l'homme* (Paris: C. Reinwald, 1883), p. 21.

25. Élie Faure, *Histoire de l'art*, vol. 1, *L'esprit des formes* (Paris: Denoël, 1992), p. 25.

26. See Émile Cartailhac, *L'âge de pierre dans les souvenirs et les superstitions populaires* (Paris: C. Reinwald, 1877). Flints were also commonly called "thunderstones" and "glossopetrae." For a history of archaeology before archaeology, see Alain Schnapp's now-classic *La conquête du passé: Aux origines de l'archéologie* (Paris: Le Livre de poche, 1993).

27. John Locke, *Second Treatise on Civil Government*, in *John Locke's Two Treatises of Government*, ed. Peter Laslett (Cambridge: Cambridge University Press, 1963), chap. 5, §49, "Of

Property," p. 343.

28. Antoine de Jussieu, *De l'origine et des usages de la pierre de foudre*, p. 8. The first person to have glimpsed the historicity of the flints was Michele Mercati, director of the botanical garden at the Vatican, who wrote that in the late sixteenth century, "the most ancient men used flint shards for knives." His book, *Metallotheca* would be published posthumously, in 1717. Michele Mercati, *Michaelis Mercati Samminiatensis Metallotheca*, ed. Giovanni Maria Lancisi (Rome: Salvioni, 1717).

29. Boucher de Perthes, *Antiquités celtiques et antédiluviennes*, vol. 1, p. 5.

30. Jean-François de Nadaillac, *Les premiers hommes et les temps préhistoriques*, 2 vols. (Paris: Éditions G. Masson, 1881), vol. 1, p. 6.

31. Augustus Lane-Fox Pitt Rivers, "Principles of Classification" (1875), in Augustus Lane-Fox Pitt Rivers, *The Evolution of Culture and Other Essays* (Oxford: Clarendon Press of Oxford University Press, 1906), p. 24.

32. Pitt Rivers, "Primitive Warfare" (1867), in *The Evolution of Culture and Other Essays*, p. 45.

33. I develop the theme of simplicity and complexity in prehistoric discourses in "Beyond Simplicity: The Late Prehistory of the Moderns," in Albrecht Koschorke, ed., *Komplexität und Einfachheit: DFG-Symposion 2015.* (Stuttgart: J. B. Metzler, 2017), pp. 573–601.

34. Charles Lyell, *The Geological Evidences of the Antiquity of Man* (1863; Charleston: BiblioBazaar, 2008), pp. 495–506.

35. Thomas H. Huxley, introduction to *La place de l'homme dans la nature*, trans. Eugène Dally and Henry de Varigny (Paris: J.-B. Baillière et Fils, 1891), pp. VII–VIII.

36. John Lubbock, *Pre-Historic Times as Illustrated by Ancient Remains and the Manners and Customs of Modern Savages*, 6th rev. ed. (New York: D. Appleton, 1900).

37. Mortillet, *Le préhistorique*, p. 91.

38. Ibid., p. 106. On Gabriel von Max's monkey paintings, and on his relationship to Ernst Haeckel, see Gaëlle Rosendahl, "Die Urgeschichtliche Abteilung," and Wilfried Rosendahl, "Zufall, Vorhersage und Glück: Die Stammesgeschichte des Menschen und die stetige Suche nach dem Missing Link," in Karin Althaus and Helmut Friedel, eds., *Gabriel von Max: Malerstar, Darwinist, Spiritist*, Städtische Galerie im Lenbachhaus und Kunstbau, exh. cat. (Munich: Hirmer, 2010), pp. 272–76 and 277–81, respectively.

39. Salomon Reinach, "Une lettre de Longpérier sur l'art des cavernes," *Anthropologie* 15 (1904), pp. 247–48. The first study devoted to art historians' lukewarm reception of prehistory is Ulrich Pfisterer, "Altamira — oder: Die Anfänge von Kunst und Kunstwissenschaft," in Martin Mosebach, ed., *Die Gärten von Capri* (Berlin: Akademie-Verlag, 2007),

pp. 13–80. See Oscar Moro Abadía, "The Reception of Paleolithic Art at the Turn of the Twentieth Century: Between Archaeology and Art History," *Journal of Art Historiography* 12 (June 2015), https://arthistoriography.files.wordpress.com/2015/06/moro-abadia.pdf. For a study of the periodization of prehistoric art, see François Bon, *Préhistoire: La fabrique de l'homme* (Paris: Seuil, 2009).

40. On the genetic transmission of art, see Éric Michaud, *The Barbarian Invasions: A Genealogy of the History of Art*, trans. Nicholas Huckle (Cambridge, MA: MIT Press, 2019).

41. Reinach, "Une lettre de Longpérier sur l'art des cavernes," p. 248.

42. For an analysis of the impact that the disciplines of ethnology, psychology, and prehistory have had on art history, which suddenly became more liberated from the "text," more objective, and less normative, see Ulrich Pfisterer, "Origins and Principles of World Art History: 1900 (and 2000)," in Kitty Zijlmans and Wilfried Van Damme, eds., *World Art Studies: Exploring Concepts and Approaches* (Amsterdam: Valiz, 2008), pp. 69–89; Ingeborg Reichle, "Vom Ursprung der Bilder und den Anfang der Kunst: Zur Logik des interkulturellen Bildvergleichs um 1900," in Martina Baleva, Ingeborg Reichle, and Oliver Lerone Schultz, eds., *IMAGE MATCH: Visueller Transfer, "Imagescapes" und Intervisualität in globalen Bild-Kulturen* (Munich: Wilhelm Fink, 2012), pp. 131–50.

43. Édouard Piette, *Notes pour servir à l'histoire de l'art primitif* (Paris: G. Masson, 1894), p. 1.

44. According to Eugène Véron, man "manifests himself even in that still-dark period preceding history proper. It is by means of art that man distinguishes himself from the animals." Eugène Véron, *L'esthétique: Origine des arts, le goût et le génie* (Paris: C. Reinwald, 1878), p. 3. Many other examples are analyzed in Susanne Leeb's *Die Kunst der Anderen: "Weltkunst" und die anthropologische Konfiguration der Moderne* (Berlin: Polypen, 2015), pp. 35–66.

45. Édouard Lartet, "Nouvelles recherches sur la coexistence de l'homme et des grands mammifères fossiles," *Annales des sciences naturelles*, 4th series, 15, *Zoologie* (Paris: Victor Masson et Fils, 1861), pp. 177–253.

46. Ibid., pp. 210–11.

47. Ibid., p. 211.

48. Édouard Lartet and Henri Christy, *Cavernes du Périgord: Objets gravés et sculptés des temps pré-historiques dans l'Europe occidentale* (1864; Whitefish: Kessinger Legacy Reprints, 2010), pp. 13 and 19.

49. Ibid., pp. 28–29.

50. Ibid., p. 31.

51. Ibid., p. 33.

52. Ibid., p. 34.

53. Louis Figuier, *L'homme primitif*, illustrated by Émile Bayard and Delahaye (Paris: L. Hachette, 1870); see Claude Blanckaert, "Les bases de la civilisation: Lectures de *L'Homme primitif* de Louis Figuier (1870)," *Bulletin de la société préhistorique française* 90.1 (1990), pp. 31–49.

54. A few months after the events of May 1968, the anthropologist Marshall Sahlins published a first excerpt from his forthcoming book, *Stone Age Economics*, in *Les temps modernes*. In it, he denounced the popular idea of a violent, difficult, and impoverished prehistory, putting forward instead the notion of a society of abundance where material and psychological needs were easily satisfied. It was an inverted image of capitalist modernity, whose abundance was productivist and consumerist. Marshall Sahlins, "La première société d'abondance," *Les temps modernes* 24.268 (October 1968), pp. 641–80; Marshall Sahlins, *Stone Age Economics* (Chicago: Aldine-Atherton, 1972).

55. Salomon Reinach, *Antiquités nationales: Description raisonnée, Musée de Saint-Germain-en-Laye, I. Époque des alluvions et des cavernes* (Paris: Librarie de Firmin-Didot, 1889), pp. 170–71.

56. Aloïs Riegl, *Questions de style* (Paris: Hazan, 1992), p. 25.

57. Ibid., p. 28. On art as "act" as revealed by prehistory, see Horst Bredekamp's works, including "Der Muschelmensch: Vom endlosen Anfang der Bilder," in Wolfgang Hogrebe, ed., *Transzendenzen des Realen* (Göttingen: V. & R. Unipress), pp. 13–74.

58. Émile Cartailhac, *La France préhistorique d'après les sépultures et les monuments* (Paris: Alcan, 1889), p. 61.

59. Rousseau, *Discourse on Inequality*.

60. Condorcet, *Outlines of an Historical View of the Progress of the Human Mind*, p. 6.

61. Cartailhac, *La France préhistorique d'après les sépultures et les monuments*, p. 81.

62. Ibid., p. 40.

63. See Édouard Piette, *Hiatus et lacune: Vestiges de la période de transition dans la grotte du Mas-d'Azil* (Beaugency: Laffray, 1895).

64. Reinach, *Antiquités nationales*, pp. 168–69.

65. See Maria Stavrinaki, "Enfant né sans mère, mère morte sans enfant: Les historiens de l'art face à la préhistoire," in "Préhistoire/Modernité," ed. Rémi Labrusse and Maria Stavrinaki, special issue, *Cahiers du Mnam* 126 (Autumn–Winter 2013), pp. 4–13.

66. Joseph-François Laffitau, *Moeurs des sauvages américains comparées aux moeurs des premiers temps* (Paris: Saugrain l'aîné, 1724), pp. 104–105.

67. Cartailhac, *La France préhistorique d'après les sépultures et les monuments*, p. 61.

68. Maine de Biran, "Ancillon: Notes sur l'essai sur le scepticisme," in *Oeuvres XI–3: Commentaires sur les philosophies du XIXe siecle* (Paris: Vrin, 1990), p. 163.

69. Ernest Renan, *De l'origine du langage* (Paris, Joubert, 1848), p. 14, in which he explicitly refers to Maine de Biran, excerpted from *Liberté de penser* 2 (September 1848), pp. 368–80, and 3 (December 1848), pp. 66–83.

70. Lubbock, *Pre-Historic Times*, pp. 313–14.

71. Henry Balfour, *The Evolution of Decorative Art: An Essay upon Its Origin and Development as Illustrated by the Art of Modern Races of Mankind* (New York: Macmillan,1893), p. 21.

72. Béatrice Fraenkel, "L'invention de l'art pariétal préhistorique: Histoire d'une expérience visuelle," *Gradhiva* 6 (2007), pp. 18–31.

73. Félix Garrigou, quoted in Frankel, "L'invention de l'art pariétal préhistorique," p. 27.

74. Émile Cartailhac and Henri Breuil, "Dessins préhistoriques de la caverne de Niaux, dans les Pyrénées de l'Ariège," *Comptes rendus des séances de l'Academie des inscriptions et belles-lettres* 50.8 (1906), pp. 533 and 534.

75. François Daleau, quoted in Fraenkel, "L'invention de l'art pariétal préhistorique," p. 30.

76. Marcelino Sanz de Sautuola, *Breves apuntes sobre algunos objetos históricos de la provincia de Santander* (Santander: Telesforo Martínez, 1880). The text was translated, but rather badly, into English, French, and Portuguese (Santander: Fondation Botin, 2004), with an introduction by José A. Lashera and Carmen de las Heras.

77. De Sautuola, *Breves apuntes sobre algunos objetos históricos de la provincia de Santande* (1880), pp. 15–16.

78. Ibid.

79. Ibid., p. 21.

80. Émile Cartailhac and Henri Breuil, "Les peintures et gravures murales des cavernes pyrénéennes: I, Altamira à Santillana (Espagne)," *L'Anthropologie* 15 (1904), p. 644.

81. Léopold Chiron, "La grotte Chabot, commune d'Alguèze," *Publications de la Société linnéenne de Lyon* 8 (1889), pp. 96–97.

82. Paul Raymond, "Gravures de la grotte magdalénienne de Jean-Louis à Alguèze (Gard)," *Bulletins et mémoires de la Société d'anthropologie de Paris* 7 (1889), p. 644.

83. "Hurray! For a discovery, this is a big one for Capitan and me together: an enormous cave with engravings. . . . It's like a dream. To come across it just like that, the way you find a stone on the road, it's unbelievable." Henri Breuil to Jean Bouyssonie, quoted in Arnaud

Hurel, *L'Abbé Breuil: Un préhistorien dans le siècle* (Paris: CNRS *Éditions*, 2011), p. 87.

84. Louis Capitan and Henri Breuil, "Les grottes à parois gravées ou peintes à l'époque paléolithique," *Revue de l'école d'anthropologie de Paris* 10 (1901), p. 325.

85. On the "naturalism" attributed to prehistoric art, and more particularly to parietal art, see Oscar Moro Abadía, Manuel R. Gonzalez Morales, and Eduardo Palacio Pérez, "'Naturalism' and the Interpretation of Cave Art," *World Art* 2.2 (2012), pp. 219–40.

86. Louis Capitan and Henri Breuil, "Origines de l'art: Les gravures sur les parois des grottes préhistoriques anciennes," *La Nature* 30.1503 (March 1902), p. 227.

87. Ibid., p. 229.

88. Ibid., p. 227.

89. Ibid.

90. Ibid., p. 229.

91. Émile Cartailhac and Henri Breuil, letter to Salomon Reinach, October 7, 1902, Émile Cartailhac collection, Musée d'archéologie nationale, Saint-Germain-en-Laye, quoted in Arnaud Hurel, *L'Abbé Breuil*, pp. 116–17.

92. Andrew Lang, "The Art of Savages," in Andrew Lang, *Custom and Myth* (New York: Harper and Brothers, 1885), p. 276.

93. Ibid., p. 291.

94. Salomon Reinach, "L'art et la magie" (1903), in Salomon Reinach, *Cultes, mythes et religions*, 5 vols. (Paris: Ernest Leroux, 1905–1923), vol. 1, p. 126.

95. Ibid., vol. 1, p. 127.

96. Ibid., vol. 1, p. 129.

97. Cartailhac, *La France préhistorique d'après les sépultures et les monuments*, p. 536.

98. Henri Begouën, "Les bases magiques de l'art préhistorique," *Scientia* 65.4 (1939), p. 214.

99. Ibid., p. 215.

100. Adolf Stiegelmann, *Altamira: Ein Kunsttempel des Urmenschen* (Godesberg-Bonn: Kulturwissenschaftliche Zeitfragen, 1910).

101. Friedrich Behn, *Der Mensch der Urzeit: Seine Kultur und seine Kunst* (Leipzig: Sachmeister & Thal, 1921); Salomon Reinach, review of Gustave Chauvet, *Notes sur l'art primitif* (1903), *La chronique des arts et de la curiosité* 6 (1903), p. 47.

102. Salomon Reinach, *Apollo: Histoire générale des arts plastiques* (Paris: Hachette, 1904), p. 8.

103. Salomon Reinach, "Totémisme et exogamie" (1902), in *Cultes, mythes et religions*, vol. 1, p. 85.

104. Edward Tylor, *Primitive Culture: Researches into the Development of Mythology, Philosophy, Religion, Language, Art, and Custom* (1871; New York: Henry Holt, 1889).

105. Ibid., p. 16.

106. Johannes Fabian, *Time and the Other: How Anthropology Makes Its Object* (New York: Columbia University Press, 1983).

107. Salomon Reinach, "La théorie du sacrifice" (1902), in *Cultes, mythes et religions*, p. 100.

108. Ernst Bloch, *Heritage of Our Times*, trans. Neville Plaice and Stephen Plaice (1935; Cambridge: Polity, 1991).

109. Renan, *De l'origine du langage*, p. 1.

110. Daniel Wilson, *The Archaeology and Prehistoric Annals of Scotland* (Edinburgh: Sutherland and Knox, 1851); Daniel Wilson, *Prehistoric Man* (London: Macmillan, 1862). On "prehistory" according to Wilson, see Alice B. Kehoe, "The Invention of Prehistory," *Current Anthropology* 32.4 (August–October 1991), pp. 467–76.

111. Lubbock, *Pre-Historic Times*, p. 408.

112. Armand de Quatrefages, *Hommes fossiles et hommes sauvages: Études d'anthropologie* (Paris: J.-B. Baillière, 1884), p. 297.

113. Ibid., p. 298.

114. Leo Frobenius, *La civilisation africaine* (Paris: Le Rocher, 1952).

115. On Frobenius's work on prehistory, see Karl-Heinz Kohl, Richard Kuba, and Hélène Ivanoff, eds., *Kunst der Vorzeit: Felsbilder aus der Sammlung Leo Frobenius* (Berlin: Martin Gropius Bau, 2016) and *Kunst der Vorzeit: Texte zu den Felsbildern der Sammlung Leo Frobenius* (Frankfurt: Frobenius-Institut, 2016).

116. Herbert Read, *Icon and Idea* (Cambridge, MA: Harvard University Press, 1955), pp. 26–27.

117. Theodor Adorno, "Paralipomena" and "Theories on the Origins of Art," in Theodor Adorno, *Aesthetic Theory*, ed. Gretel Adorno and Rolf Tiedemann, trans. Robert Hullot-Kentor (Minneapolis: University of Minnesota Press, 1997).

118. Cartailhac, *La France préhistorique*, p. 288.

119. Tylor, *Researches into the Early History of Mankind*, p. 378.

120. Henri Breuil, "Les origines de l'art," *Journal de psychologe normale et pathologique* 22.4 (1925), pp. 289–96; Breuil, "Les origines de l'art décoratif," *Journal de psychologie normale et pathologique* 23.1–3 (1926), pp. 364–75. On Catlin, see "Du Far West au Louvre: Le Musée indien de George Catlin, "ed. Claude Macherel and Daniel Fabre, special issue of *Gradhiva* 3 (2006).

121. Begouën, "Les bases magiques de l'art préhistorique," p. 205.

122. Henri Focillon, *Les pierres de France* (Paris: Laurens, 1919), p. 3.

123. Friedrich Behn, "Das Tierbild in der Kunst des diluvialen Menschen," *Kosmos (Gesellschaft der Naturfreunde)* 9 (1912), p. 271.

124. Ernst Grosse, *The Beginnings of Art* (New York: D. Appleton, 1897).

125. Max Verworn, *Zur Psychologie der primitiven Kunst: Ein Vortrag* (Munich: Gustav Fischer, 1907), pp. 28–30.

126. Herbert Kühn, *Die Malerei der Eiszeit* (Munich: Delphin, 1921), p. 8.

127. Herbert Kühn, *Die Kunst der Primitiven* (Munich: Delphin, 1923), pp. 14–22.

128. Rousseau, *A Discourse on Inequality*, p. 94.

129. Wilhelm Wundt, *Völkerpsychologie: Eine Untersuchung der Entwicklungsgesetze von Sprache, Mythus und Sitte*, 10 vols. (Leipzig: Wilhelm Engelmann, 1911–1912), vol. 2, pp. 98–100.

130. Moritz Hoernes, *Urgeschichte der bildenden Kunst in Europe von den Anfängen bis um 500 vor Christi* (Vienna: A. Schroll, 1925).

131. Karl von den Steinen, *Unter den Naturvölkern Zentral-Brasiliens: Reiseschilderung und Ergebnisse der Zweiten Schingu-Expedition (1887–1888)* (Berlin: Dietrich Reimer, 2004). The archaeologist Alexander Conze had already made use of von den Steinen in speculating about the "origin of art." See Alexander Conze, "On the Origin of the Visual Arts," lecture on July 30, 1896, trans. Karl Johns, in *Journal of Art Historiography* 7 (December 2012), pp. 3–11.

132. Wundt, Völkerpsychologie, vol. 2, Mythus und Religion, part 1 (Leipzig: Wilhelm Engelmann, 1905), p. 98.

133. Max Raphaël, "Les fondements de l'art pariétal," in Patrick Brault, ed., *Trois essais sur la signification de l'art pariétal paléolithique* (Paris: Le couteau dans la plaie / Kronos, 1986), pp. 21–50.

134. Annette Laming-Emperaire, *La signification de l'art rupestre paléolithique: Méthodes et applications* (1957; Paris: A. et J. Picard, 1962); André Leroi-Gourhan, "La fonction des signes dans les sanctuaires paléolithiques," *Bulletin de la Société préhistorique de France* 55.5–6 (1958), pp. 307–21.

135. On the realist representation of prehistory, see Karia Bush, Philippe Dagen, and Anne Hauzer, eds., *Vénus et Caïn: Figures de la préhistoire 1830–1930* (Paris: Réunion des musées nationaux; Bordeaux: Musée d'Aquitaine, 2003); Kai Artinger, "Der beobachtete Mensch," *Münchner Jahrbuch der bildenden Kunst* 46 (1995), pp. 163–74.

136. Édouard Piette, quoted in Henri Delporte, *Piette: Pionnier de la préhistoire* (Paris: Picard, 1987), p. 126.

137. Ibid., p. 127.

138. Michaud, *Les invasions barbares*, chap. 2.

139. Paul Richer, "L'art préhistorique à propos de la statue: Le premier artiste," *L'Artiste*, 61 n.s. 1 (June 1891), p. 456.

140. Ibid.

141. Ibid., p. 456.

142. Ibid.

143. Ibid., p. 460.

144. Ibid., p. 474.

145. Louis Capitan, "Notice sur Paul Jamin," *Bulletins et mémoires de la Société d'anthropologie de Paris* 4, July 16, 1903, p. 490.

146. See Martha Lucy, "Cormon's Cain and the Problem of the Prehistoric Body," *Oxford Art Journal* 25.2 (2002), pp. 107–26; Maria Gindhart, "Fleshing Out the Museum: Fernand Cormon's Painting Cycle for the New Galleries of Comparative Anatomy, Paleontology, and Anthropology," *Nineteenth Century Art World-Wide* 7.2 (Autumn 2008), https://www.19thc-artworldwide.org/autumn08/38-autumn08/autumn08article/92-fleshing-out-the-museum-fernand-cormons-painting-cycle-for-the-new-galleries-of-comparative-anatomy-paleontology-and-anthropology; Gindhart, "Allegorizing Aryanism: Fernand Cormon's *The Human Races*," *Aurora: The Journal of the History of Art* 9 (2008), pp. 74–100.

147. Charles Clément, "Exposition de 1880," *Journal des débats*, May 1, 1880, quoted in Lucy, "Cormon's Cain and the Problem of the Prehistoric Body," p. 111.

CHAPTER THREE: THE ARTIFICIALITY OF PREHISTORY

1. J. A. M. Whistler, "Ten o'Clock" (Boston: Houghton, Mifflin, 1899), n.p., https://www.google.com/books/edition/TEN_O_CLOCK/uo_eRSoSYiAC?hl=en&gbpv=1&bsq=first%20artist.

2. Ibid.

3. Oscar Wilde, "The Decay of Lying," in Oscar Wilde, *Intentions* (New York: Brentano's 1905), p. 9. My emphasis.

4. Ibid.

5. Roger Marx, *L'art social* (Paris: E. Fasquelle, 1913), pp. 3–4.

6. Barnett Newman, "The First Man Was an Artist," *Tiger's Eye* 1 (1947), p. 52.

7. Ibid., p. 53.

8. See Jacques Derrida, *Of Grammatology*, trans. Gayatri Chakravorty Spivak, corrected edition (Baltimore: Johns Hopkins University Press, 1998), esp. " . . . That Dangerous

Supplement . . . ," pp. 141–64.

9. Henri Bergson, *The Two Sources of Morality and Religion*, trans. R. Ashley Audra and Cloudesley Brereton, with W. Horsfall Carter (London: Macmillan, 1935), pp. 159 and 83, translation modified.

10. Ibid., pp. 195 and 89.

11. Ibid., p. 16.

12. Arnold Gehlen, *Man: His Nature and Place in the World*, trans. Clare McMillan and Karl Pillemer (New York: Columbia University Press, 1988), pp. 13, 71, 222.

13. Hans Blumenberg, quoted in Jean-Claude Monod, "La patience de l'image: Éléments pour une localisation de la métaphorologie," afterword to *Paradigmes pour une métaphorologie*, trans. Didier Gammelin (Paris: Vrin, 2006), p. 195.

14. See Bernard Stiegler, *Technics and Time, 1: The Fault of Epimethus*, trans. Richard Beardsworth and George Collins (Stanford: Stanford University Press, 1998), based on Plato, *Protagoras*, 320d–322c.

15. Clifford Geertz, "The Impact of the Concept of Culture on the Concept of Man," in Clifford Geertz, *The Interpretation of Cultures: Selected Essays* (New York: Basic Books, 1973), pp. 33–54; Tim Ingold, "'People Like Us': The Concept of the Anatomically Modern Human," in Tim Ingold, *The Perception of the Environment: Essays on Livelihood, Dwelling and Skill* (London: Routledge, 2013), pp. 373–90; Ingold, "Beyond Biology and Culture: The Meaning of Evolution in a Relational World," *Social Anthropology* 12.2 (2004), pp. 209–21.

16. For a good study of the different facets of Leroi-Gourhan's thinking, see Marc Groenen, *Leroi-Gourhan: Essence et contingence dans la destinée humaine* (Louvain: Le Boeck Supérieur, 1996); Françoise Audouze and Nathan Schlanger, *Autour de l'homme: Contexte et actualité d'André Leroi-Gourhan* (Antibes: Association pour la promotion et la diffusion des connaissances archéologiques, 2004).

17. André Leroi-Gourhan, *Gesture and Speech*, trans. Anna Bostock Berger (Cambridge, MA: MIT University Press, 1993), p. 235.

18. Ibid., pp. 271, 274–75, 364.

19. Ibid., p. 364.

20. Ibid.

21. Jack Flam, *Matisse: The Man and His Art, 1869–1918* (Ithaca: Cornell University Press, 1986), pp. 151–90.

22. Gustave Moreau (speaking of Michelangelo), in *Théorie et critique d'art*, vol. 2 of Gustave Moreau, *Écrits sur l'art*, ed. Peter Cooke, 2 vols. (Fontfroide: Fata Morgana, 2002), p. 305.

23. Yve-Alain Bois, "L'aveuglement," in Isabelle Monod-Fontaine and Dominique Fourcade, eds., *Henri Matisse, 1904–1917,* exh. cat. (Paris: Centre Georges Pompidou, 1993), p. 41.

24. See Margaret Werth's analysis in *The Joy of Life: The Idyllic in French Art, circa 1900* (Berkeley: University of California Press, 2002), pp. 145–238.

25. See Henri Matisse, *Écrits et propos,* ed. Dominique Fourcade (Paris: Hermann, 1972).

26. Flam, *Matisse,* pp. 151–67.

27. Yve-Alain Bois, "On Matisse: The Blinding. For Leo Steinberg," trans. Greg Sims *October* 68 (Spring 1994), p. 104.

28. Werth, *The Joy of Life,* p. 166.

29. Bois, "The Blinding," p. 113.

30. Jacques Derrida, *Edmund Husserl's "Origin of Geometry": An Introduction,* trans. John P. Leavy, Jr. (Lincoln: University of Nebraska Press, 1989).

31. On the ideologeme of simplicity in the idea of prehistory, see Maria Stavrinaki, "Beyond Simplicity: The Late Prehistory of the Moderns," in Albrecht Koschorke, ed., *Komplexität und Einfachheit: DFG-Symposion 2015* (Stuttgart: J. B. Metzler, 2017), pp. 573–601.

32. Gelett Burgess, "The Wild Men of Paris," *Architectural Record,* May 5, 1910, p. 402.

33. Theodore Roosevelt, "A Layman's View of an Art Exhibition," *Outlook* 103, March 29, 1913, p. 719.

34. Roger Fry, "Bushman Paintings," *Burlington Magazine for Connoisseurs* 16.84 (1910), p. 337.

35. Roger Fry, "Children's Drawings" (1917), in Christopher Reed, ed., *A Roger Fry Reader* (Chicago: University of Chicago Press, 1996), p. 267.

36. Kazimir Malevich, "From Cubism and Futurism to Suprematism: The New Painterly Realism" (1915), in John E. Bowlt, ed. and trans., *Russian Art of the Avant-Garde* (New York: Thames and Hudson, 2017), p. 119.

37. Ibid., p. 133.

38. See Maurice Raynal, "Les arts: Conception et vision," *Gil Blas,* August 29, 1912, p. 4.

39. Henry van de Velde, "Manuscript on Ornament. Chapter 1: 'The Historic Survey of Linear Ornament and Its Development,'" trans. Ellie G. Haddad and Rosemary Anderson, *Journal of Design History* 16.2 (2003), p. 142.

40. Ibid.

41. Guillaume Apollinaire, "Georges Braque" (1908), in Guillaume Apollinaire, *Chroniques d'art, 1902–1918* (Paris: Gallimard, 1960), p. 75.

42. Max Verworn, *Expressionismus: Die Kunstwende,* ed. Herwarth Walden (Berlin: Der Sturm, 1918), reprinted as an article under the title "Die Entwicklung der ideoplastischen

Kunst," in the review *Der Sturm* 10 (January 1919), pp. 126–28.

43. Ibid., p. 128.

44. Wilhelm Paulcke, *Steinzeitkunst und Moderne Kunst: Ein Vergleich* (Stuttgart: Schweizerbartsche, 1923).

45. Herbert Kühn, *Die Malerei der Eiszeit* (Munich: Delphin, 1921), pp. 11–12.

46. Eckhart von Sydow, *Die Kunst der Naturvölker und der Vorzeit* (Berlin: Propuläen, 1923), p. 76.

47. Friedrich Nietzsche, "Dream and Culture," §12 of "Of First and Last Things," in *Human, All Too Human: A Book for Free Spirits*, trans. R. J. Hollingdale (Cambridge: Cambridge University Press, 1986), pp. 16–17.

48. Sigmund Freud, *Totem and Taboo* (1913), trans. A. A. Brill (New York: Vintage, 1946), p. 3.

49. Sigmund Freud, *The Interpretation of Dreams* (1900), trans. James Strachey (New York: Basic Books, 1965), p. 280.

50. Karl Lamprecht, appendices to Siegfried Otto Levinstein, *Kinderzeichnungen bis zum 14. Lebensjahr, mit parallelen aus der Urgeschichte, Kulturgeschichte und Völkerkunde* (Leipzig: R. Voigtländer, 1905), pp. x–xii.

51. Georges-Henri Luquet, *L'art primitif* (Paris: Gaston Doin, 1930), p. 11.

52. See Ernst Haeckel, *Generelle Morphologie der Organismen* (Berlin: Reimer, 1866). For an in-depth study of this question, see Stephen Jay Gould, *Ontogeny and Phylogeny* (Cambridge, MA: Belknap Press Harvard University Press, 1985).

53. Théodule Ribot, *Les maladies de la mémoire* (1881; Paris: Félix Alcan, 1906), p. 100.

54. Waldemar Deonna, *L'archéologie, sa valeur, ses méthodes*, vol. 2, *Les lois de l'art* (Paris: Librairie Renouard-Laurens, 1912), pp. 111–12.

55. Henri Focillon, "Préhistoire et Moyen Âge," *Dumbarton Oaks Papers* 1 (November 1940), p. 3.

56. Brassaï [Gyula Halász], "Du mur des cavernes au mur d'usine," *Minotaure* 3–4 (December 1933), pp. 6–7.

57. Brassaï, "Graffiti parisiens" (1958), in Brassaï, *Graffiti* (Paris: Flammarion, 2016), p. 140.

58. Brassaï, "Du mur des cavernes au mur d'usine," p. 7.

59. Brassaï, *Graffiti*, p. 25.

60. Brassaï, *Conversations with Picasso*, trans. Jane Marie Todd (Chicago: University of Chicago Press, 1999), entry of November 26, 1946, p. 96.

61. Ibid., p. 95.

62. Ibid., p. 96.

63. I refer to the notion of tragedy initially developed by the German idealists, Schelling and Hegel, in particular. For a good study of this question, see Pierre Judet de la Combe, *Les tragédies grecques sont-elles tragiques?: Théâtre et théorie* (Paris: Bayard, 2012).

64. See Wendy A. Grossman, *Man Ray, African Art, and the Modernist Lens* (Washington, DC: International Art and Artists, 2009).

65. Daniel-Henry Kahnweiler, "L'art nègre et le cubisme" (1948), in Daniel-Henry Kahnweiler, *Confessions esthétiques* (Paris: Gallimard, 1963), pp. 222–36; Yve-Alain Bois, "Kahnweiler's Lesson," *Representations* 18 (1987), pp. 33–68.

66. I have developed a synthetic view of Picasso's uses of prehistory in "La puissance diluvienne de l'art: Esquisse des usages de la préhistoire par Picasso," *Actes du colloque international Revoir Picasso* (Paris: Musée Picasso, 2015), https://revoirpicasso.fr/face-a-loeuvre/la-puissance-diluvienne-de-lart-esquisse-des-usages-de-la-prehistoire-par-picasso-•-m-stavrinaki.

67. Emblematic in this regard is Lévi-Strauss's criticism of Jean-Paul Sartre's *Critique of Dialectical Reason*, in the chapter "History and Dialectic of *The Savage Mind*. Claude Lévi-Strauss, *The Savage Mind* (Chicago: University of Chicago Press, 1966), pp. 245–69.

68. Henri Focillon, introduction to *Art populaire: Travaux artistiques et scientifiques du 1er congrès international des arts populaires (Prague, MDCCCCXXVIII)*, vol. 1 (Paris: Éditions Duchartre, 1931), pp. xii–xiii.

69. Max Raphael, "Réflexions méthodologiques sur l'interprétation de l'art quaternaire," in Patrick Brault, ed., *Trois essais sur la signification de l'art pariétal paléolithique* (Paris: Le couteau dans la plaie / Kronos, 1986), p. 163.

70. Ibid.

71. Ibid.

72. Max Raphael, "À propos du fronton de Corfou," *Minotaure* 1 (June 1933), pp. 6–7.

73. Raphael, "Réflexions méthodologiques sur l'interprétation," pp. 113–14.

74. Georges Bataille, "The Cradle of Humanity: The Vezere Valley," in *The Cradle of Humanity: Prehistoric Art and Culture*, ed. Stuart Kendall, trans. Michelle Kendall and Stuart Kendall (New York: Zone Books, 2009), p. 159. I will return at length to Bataille in Chapter 5.

75. Ibid.

76. Hayden V. White, "The Burden of History," *History and Theory* 5.2 (1966), pp. 111–34.

77. Henri Gaudier-Brzeska, "Vortex. Gaudier Brzeska," *Blast* 1 (1914), p. 155. Ezra Pound would also write in his essay on Gaudier Brzeska, who died young at the front, that he was "enthused" by the drawings of Font-de-Gaume and that in his drawings and sculptures

of animals, "the only possible influence upon him was archaic. Fonts de Gaume [*sic*] and Chou bronzes, plus life itself and his genius, which was in this case an abnormal sympathy with, and intelligence for, all moving animal life, its swiftness and softness." Ezra Pound, *Gaudier-Brzeska: A Memoir* (London: John Lane, 1916), pp. 164 and 91.

78. Gaudier-Brzeska, "Vortex. Gaudier Brzeska Vortex," p. 157.

79. T. S. Eliot, "Tradition and the Individual Talent" (1919), in T. S. Eliot, *Selected Essays, New Edition* (New York: Harcourt, Brace & World, 1964), pp. 4, 5, 6.

80. On the question of mechanical genealogy in Symbolism and the avant-garde, see Arnauld Pierre, "Udnie mécanique: Un théâtre d'automates à l'ère de Dada / Mechanical Udnie: A Theater of Automata in the Days of Dada," in William A. Camfield, Beverley Calté, Candace Clements, and Arnauld Pierre, eds., *Francis Picabia: Catalogue raisonné, vol. 2 (1915–1927)* (Brussels: Fonds Mercator, 2016), pp. 146–81.

81. Ernst Bloch, *Heritage of Our Times*, trans. Neville Plaice and Stephen Plaice (1935; Cambridge: Polity, 1991) p. 107.

82. Ribot, *Les maladies de la mémoire*, p. 94.

83. Amédée Ozenfant, *Art. I. Bilan des arts modernes en France. Littérature — peinture — sculpture — architecture — musique — science — religion — philosophie. II. Structure d'un nouvel esprit*, 5th revised and corrected ed. (Paris: Jean Budry 1929), pp. 5–6.

84. Deonna, *L'archéologie, sa valeur, ses méthodes*, vol. 2, *Les lois de l'art*.

85. Deonna, *L'archéologie, sa valeur, ses méthodes*, vol. 3, *Les rythmes artistiques*, pp. 31–32.

86. Henri Breuil, "Les origines de l'art," *Journal de psychologie normale et pathologique* 22.4 (1925), p. 296.

87. Henri Focillon, "Romantisme et déclin," in Matthias Waschek, ed., *Relire Focillon* (Paris: Editions du Louvre / Ecole nationale supérieure des beaux-arts, 1995), p. 141.

88. Waldemar Deonna, "Futuristes d'autrefois," *Revue d'ethnographie et de sociologie* (1912), p. 301.

89. Ibid.

90. Deonna, *L'archéologie, sa valeur, ses méthodes*, vol. 3: *Les rythmes artistiques*.

91. Deonna, *Les lois et les rythmes dans l'art* (Paris: Ernest Flammarion, 1914), p. 180.

92. Carl Einstein, "Joan Miró (papiers collés à la galerie Pierre)," *Documents* 2.4 (1930), pp. 241–43.

93. Carola Giedion-Welcker, "Besuch in Carnac" (1934), in Carola Giedion-Welcker, *Schriften 1926–1971: Stationen zu einem Zeitbild*, ed. Reinhold Hohl (Schauberg: M. DuMont, 1973), pp. 12–13.

94. Carola Giedion-Welcker, *Modern Plastic Art: Elements of Reality, Volume and*

Disintegration, trans. P. Morton Shand (Zurich: Girsberger, 1937), p. 17.

95. Ibid.

96. Sigfried Giedion, *The Eternal Present: The Beginnings of Art* (Washington, DC: National Gallery of Art, 1962). On Giedion's work on prehistory, see Reto Geiser, "Höhlenexpeditionen mit Hugo Paul Herdeg," in Werner Oechslin and Herbor Harbusch, eds., *Sigfried Giedion und Bildinszenierungen der Moderne: Die Fotografie* (Zurich: ZTA, 2010), pp. 278–81; Bruno Maurer, *"The Eternal Present I: The Beginnings of Art* — Grenzen der Fotografie," in ibid., pp. 288–91; Spyros Papapetros, "Retracing the Eternal Present (Sigfried Giedion and André Leroi-Gourhan)," *RES: Journal of Anthropology and Aesthetics* 63–64 (Spring–Autumn 2013), pp. 173–89.

97. Herbert Read, inaugural speech, December 1948, Tate Gallery, London, Institute of Contemporary Arts Archives, TGA, 955/1/12/12, p. 1.

98. Herbert Read, preface, in W. G. Archer, Roberrt Melville, and Herbert Read, *40, 000 Years of Modern Art: A Comparison of Primitive and Modern*, exh. cat. (London: Institute of Contemporary Arts, 1948), p. 6.

99. "ICA: 40, 000 Years of Modern Art Exhibition," Tate Gallery, London, Institute of Contemporary Arts Archives, TGA 955/1/12/10.

100. Herbert Read, inaugural speech, p. 2.

101. Herbert Read, foreword to *40, 000 Years of Modern Art*, p. 6.

102. Anton Ehrenzweig, "The Unconscious Meaning of Primitive and Modern Art," lecture, September 1949, Tate Gallery, Institute of Contemporary Arts Archives, TGA 955/1/7/12.

103. Walter Benjamin, "The Work of Art in the Age of Mechanical Reproduction," in Benjamin, *Illuminations*, ed. Hannah Arendt, trans. Harry Zohn (New York: Schocken Books, 1969), pp. 224–25.

104. Ibid.

105. Ibid., pp. 225 and 224.

106. Walter Benjamin, "The Work of Art in the Age of Its Technological Reproducibility," in *The Work of Art in the Age of Its Technological Reproducibility and Other Writings on Media*, eds. Michael W. Jennings, Brigid Doherty, and Thomas Y. Levin, trans. Edmund Jephcott, Rodney Livingstone, Howard Eiland, et al. (Cambridge, MA: Belknap Press of Harvard University Press, 2008), p. 26. [The French version of Benjamin's text cited by the author does not correspond to any of the versions translated into English. This passage appears in the second German version, dating to 1936 — trans.]

107. Walter Benjamin, "Zur Ästhetik," fr 98 (1936), "Die Erkenntnis, daß die erste

Materie . . . ," in *Fragmente vermischten Inhalts: Autobiographische Schriften*, vol. 6 of Walter Benjamin, *Gesammelte Schriften*, ed. Rolf Tiedemann and Hermann Schweppenhaüser, 7 vols. in 14 (Frankfurt am Main: Suhrkamp, 1972–1989), p. 127.

108. Benjamin, "The Work of Art in the Age of Its Technological Reproducibility," p. 26, emphasis in the original. [The first two sentences and the last sentence of this quotation do not appear in any English version of Benjamin's article. They are my translation from the French version. — trans.]

109. The first exhibition of Frobenius's copies in a space devoted to modern art was at the Museum of Modern Art. See Leo Frobenius and Douglas Claughton Fox, eds., *Prehistoric Rock Pictures in Europe and Africa*, exh. cat. (New York: The Museum of Modern Art, 1937; reissued, Arno Press, 1972). In contrast to the ICA, with its mystical exhibition, Alfred Barr remained faithful to his formalist principle of optical clarity and distinctness. An exhibition of a few modern works belonging to the MoMa collection (Klee, Masson, Larionov, etc.), took place in a separate space, on a different floor of the museum. Aware of the vagueness of the formal analogy between the two sets of works, Barr decided to separate them physically. There is extensive documentation of the prehistoric part in the Museum of Modern Art archives, but not of the modern part, though we have a little information thanks to reviews written at the time. See Richard Meyer, *What Was Contemporary Art?* (Cambridge, MA: MIT Press, 2013), pp. 115–89; Elke Seibert, "Prähistorische Malerei im Museum of Modern Art in New York (1937)," *Kunsttexte.de* 2 (2014); Karl-Heinz Kohl, Richard Kuba, and Hélène Ivanoff, eds., *Kunst der Vorzeit: Felsbilder aus der Sammlung LeoFrobenius* (Berlin: Martin Gropius Bau, 2016); Karl-Heinz Kohl, Richard Kuba, and Hélène Ivanoff, eds., *Kunst der Vorzeit: Texte zu den Felsbildern der Sammlung Leo Frobenius* (Frankfurt: Frobenius-Institut, 2016).

110. Roland Penrose, speaking of ICA, October 1976, Institute of Contemporary Arts Archives typescript (3 pp.), TGA 955/1/12/3. The photos from the display are located in the archives, TGA 955/1/12/12.

111. Penrose, October 1976, typescript, p. 2.

112. George Hoellering, "Preface," Institute of Contemporary Arts Archives TGA 955/1/12/40.

113. The first author to explore the presence of prehistory in the artist's works was Sidra Stich, *Joan Miró: The Development of a Sign Language* (Saint Louis: Washington University Press, 1980), but her analysis confuses primitivism and prehistory and often remains very literal. For an analysis of the uses of prehistory in the Spanish avant-garde generally, see César Calzada, *Arte prehistórico en la vanguardia artística de España* (Madrid: Catedra

Ediciones, 2006).

114. Joan Miró, quoted in Maurice Raynal, *Anthologie de la peinture française de 1906 à nos jours* (Paris: Montagne, 1927), p. 34.

115. On this theme, see Anne Umland, ed., *Joan Miró: Painting and Anti-Painting, 1927–1937* (New York: Museum of Modern Art, 2008).

116. Pierre Guéguen, untitled text in *Cahiers d'art* 9.1–4 (1934), p. 46, issue devoted to the works of Joan Miró.

117. Fèlix Fanés, *Pintura, collage, cultura de masas: Joan Miró* (Madrid: Alianza Editorial, 2007), pp. 196–223.

118. Waldemar George, "Miró et le miracle ressuscité," *Centaure* 8 (May 1929), p. 204.

119. Joan Miró, *Écrits et entretiens*, ed. Margit Rowell (Paris: Daniel Lelong, 1995), p. 231.

120. Jacques Boucher de Perthes, *Antiquités celtiques et antédiluviennes: Mémoire sur l'industrie primitive et les arts à leur origine*, 3 vols. (Paris: Treuttel et Wurtz, Derchen Dumoulin et Didron, 1847), vol. 3, p. 476.

121. See esp. Georges-Henri Luquet, *L'art et la religion des hommes fossiles* (Paris: Masson, 1926), pp. 131–226.

122. Louis Aragon, "La peinture au défi" (1930), in *Les collages* (Paris: Hermann, 1993), pp. 41–42.

123. Anne Umland, "Joan Miró and Collage in the 1920s: The Dialectic of Painting and Anti-Painting," PhD diss., Institute of Fine Arts, New York, 1997.

124. Miró, *Écrits et entretiens*, p. 43.

125. I am thinking here, of course, of Walter Benjamin, "Surrealism: The Last Snapshot of the European Intelligentsia" (1929), trans. Edmond Jephcott, in *Walter Benjamin: Selected Writings, Volume 2: 1927–1934*, ed. Michael W. Jennings, Howard Eiland, and Gary Smith, trans. Rodney Livingstone et al. (Cambridge, MA: Belknap Press of Harvard University Press, 1999), pp. 207–21.

126. Aragon, "La peinture au défi," p. 44.

127. Ibid., pp. 47–48.

128. Ibid., p. 49.

129. Andrew Lang, "The Art of Savages," in his *Custom and Myth* (New York: Harper and Brothers, 1885), pp. 290–91.

130. Salomon Reinach, review of Gustave Chauvet, *Notes sur l'art primitif* (1903), *La Chronique des arts* 6 (February 1903), p. 47.

131. Freud, *Totem and Taboo*, p. 118.

132. Brassaï, "Graffiti parisiens," in *Graffiti*, p. 140.

133. Aragon, "La peinture au défi," pp. 57–58.

134. Ibid., p. 44.

135. Carl Einstein formulated the same theory in a lecture delivered in Berlin during these years. In 1931, he gathered the art of Miró, Masson, and other artists under the rubric "romantic generation," seeing it as a very marked return to magic art as prehistoric man had fashioned it in negotiating his anxieties, because of the importance these artists granted to the expression of unconscious hallucinations. Carl Einstein, "Wir wollen heute Abend über . . . die Grieche der Latinate," lecture, Carl Einstein Archiv, Akademie der Künste, Berlin, no. 315. On Einstein's interpretation of prehistory, see Maria Stavrinaki, *Contraindre à la liberté: Carl Einstein, les avant-gardes, l'histoire* (Paris: Centre allemand d'histoire de l'art / Les presses du réel, 2018), pp. 155–65; and Stavrinaki, "Why Did the 1930s Identify with Prehistory?," in Anselm Franke and Tom Holert, eds., *Neolithische Kindheit / Neolithic Childhood: Art in a False Present, c. 1930*, exh. cat. (Berlin: Haus der Kulturen der Welt / Diaphanes, 2018), pp. 84–92.

136. René Crevel, "L'enfance de l'art," *Minotaure* 1 (1933), p. 4.

137. Ibid.

138. George Grosz and Wieland Herzfelde, *Die Kunst ist im Gefahr* (Berlin: Malik, 1925), trans. as *Art Is in Danger*, in Lucy Lippard, ed., *Dadas on Art* (Englewood Cliffs: Prentice-Hall, 1971), p. 82; Diego Rivera, "Del arte" (1947), in Diego Rivera, *Obras*, 3 vols., in 4, ed. Esther Acevedo, Leticia Torres Carmona, and Alicia Sánchez Mejorada (Mexico City: El Colegio Nacional, 1996–1999), vol. 2, pt. 1, *Textos polémicos (1921–1949)*, p. 348.

139. Alfred C. Haddon, *Evolution in Art: As Illustrated by the Life-Histories of Designs* (New York: Walter Scott Publishing, 1914), pp. 125–26; Carl Andre, "Paleolithic/Neolithic," in James Meyer, ed., *Cuts: Texts 1959–2004* (Cambridge, MA: MIT Press, 2004), pp. 171–72. On Haddon's distinction and its uses by artists of the 1930s, see Guitemie Maldonado, *Le cercle et l'amibe: Le biomorphisme dans l'art des années 1930* (Paris: CTHS / Institut national d'histoire de l'art, 2006).

140. Joan Miró, "Grand cahier de Palma (1940–1941)," in Joan Miró, *Carnets catalans*, ed. Gaëtan Picon, 2 vols. (Geneva: Albert Skira, 1976), vol. 2, p. 33.

141. Michel Leiris, "Joan Miró," (1926), *The Little Review* 12.1 (1926), included in English and in French in Michel Leiris, *Écrits sur l'art* (Paris: CNRS Éditions, 2011), pp. 171–72.

142. Dubuffet's horizontality was an important element in the construction of anti-Greenbergian narratives, such as Leo Steinberg's "flatbed picture plane" and Yve-Alain Bois and Rosalind Krauss's formlessness: *Formless: A User's Guide* (New York: Zone Books, 1997).

143. Michel Tapié, *Mirobolus, Macadam et Cie Hautes Pâtes de J. Dubuffet*, exh. cat. (Paris: René Drouin, 1946), pp. 40, 35, 37.

144. Hubert Damisch, "Dubuffet, un mémoire, 1985–2014," in Hubert Damisch and Jean Dubuffet, *Entrée en matière: Correspondance 1961–1985, Textes 1961–2014*, ed. Sophie Berrebi (Zurich: JRP / Ringier; Paris: Lectures Maison Rouge, 2016), pp. 17–69.

145. Jean Dubuffet, "Réponses à vingt-quatre questions de Valère Novarina" (1982), in Jean Dubuffet, *Prospectus et tous écrits suivants*, ed. Hubert Damisch, 4 vols. (Paris: Gallimard, 1967–95) (Paris: Gallimard, 1995), vol. 4, p. 68.

146. Quoted in Rachel Perry, "*Retour à l'ordure:* Defilement in the Postwar Work of Jean Dubuffet and Jean Fautrier," PhD diss., Harvard University, 2000.

147. Jean Dubuffet to Jean Paulhan, February 1946, in Jean Dubuffet and Jean Paulhan, *Correspondance 1944–1968*, ed. Julien Dieudonné and Marianne Jacobi (Paris: Gallimard, 2003), p. 282.

148. See Georges Bataille, "L'art primitif," *Documents* 2.7 (1930), pp. 389–97.

149. Until the studies of Annette Laming-Emperaire and André Leroi-Gourhan, prehistorians did not establish relationships between the images and the artifacts found underground. Lascaux, discovered in 1940, is exemplary in this respect: the ground, with the traces of the past it contained, was immediately compromised by the installation of walkways, pipes, and so on.

150. In fact, several of Dubuffet's works were physically attacked during the exhibition, after which a guard was hired to protect them.

151. Tapié, *Mirobolus, Macadam et Cie Hautes Pâtes de J. Dubuffet*, pp. 8–11.

152. Dubuffet to Paulhan, September 22, 1947, in Dubuffet and Paulhan, *Correspondance, 1944–1968*, p. 466.

153. Jean Dubuffet, *Prospectus et tous écrits suivants,* vol. 1, p. 45.

154. Jean Dubuffet, *L'homme du commun à l'ouvrage* (Paris: Gallimard, 1991), p. 368.

155. Jean Dubuffet, "Les Barbus Müller et autres pièces de la statuaire provinciale" (1847), in *Prospectus et tous écrits suivants*, vol. 1, p. 498.

156. Jean Dubuffet, "Bâtons rompus," in *Prospectus et tous écrits suivants*, vol. 3, p. 138.

157. Dubuffet to Paulhan, October 31, 1944, in Dubuffet and Paulhan, *Correspondance 1944–1968*, p. 137; also reprinted in *Prospectus et tous écrits suivants*, vol. 2, pp. 230–32.

158. Jean Dubuffet, interview with İlhan Mimaroğlu (June 1966), published in the special issue of *L'Herne* (1973), pp. 340–46; reprinted in *Prospectus et tous écrits suivants*, vol. 4, p. 580.

159. Damisch notes this tension in Dubuffet's oeuvre. See Damisch and Dubuffet,

"Dubuffet, un mémoire, 1985–2014," *Entrée en matière*, p. 41. Without referring to prehistory, Damisch grasped its presence in the pictorial project Dubuffet undertook with his *hautes pâtes*, which consisted of projecting "onto the vertical plane of the canvas the horizonal plane of the ground." "The ground turned upright, and the resulting dissolution of forms, do not have merely a negative meaning: the ground must be wall and the wall must be ground, so that from a surface that no longer offers the eye anything but a layer of confusion or serenity, everything is to be taken up again *by the gesture*. The 'wall of ground' is the obstacle where pictorial doubt is abolished, the original base offered for the gesture, by which man introduces his figurative order into nature. Hasty, elementary graphics, less a line, a *tracé*, than a trace." Damisch and Dubuffet, "Dubuffet ou la lecture du monde" (1962), in *Entrée en matière*, p. 98.

160. Jean Dubuffet, "Tables paysagées, paysages du mental, pierres philosophiques," in *Prospectus et tous écrits suivants*, vol. 1, p. 80.

161. Interview of Dubuffet with Georges Ribemont-Dessaignes, in *Prospectus et tous écrits suivants*, vol. 2, p. 210.

162. Jean Dubuffet, "Avant-propos d'une conférence populaire sur la peinture," in *Prospectus et tous écrits suivants*, vol. 1, p. 61.

163. Jean Dubuffet, "Tables paysagées, paysages du mental," in *Prospectus et tous écrits suivants*, vol. 2, pp. 80–81.

164. Dubuffet, *L'homme du commun à l'ouvrage*, p. 369.

165. See Antonin Juritzky (pseud. Juva), *Prehistoric Man as an Artist* (n.p.: n.p., 1953).

166. Jean Dubuffet, "Les statues de silex de M. Juva," in *Prospectus et tous écrits suivants*, vol, 1, pp. 181–82.

167. Jean Paulhan, "Les silex de Juva ou la sculpture à l'état naissant," *La table ronde* 11 (November 1948), pp. 1885–89.

168. See Kent Mitchell Minturn, "*Contre-histoire*: The Postwar Art and Writings of Jean Dubuffet," PhD diss., Columbia University, New York, 2007.

169. For Dubuffet's anti-Semitism, as well as his choices during World War II, see Minturn, "*Contre-histoire*."

170. Dubuffet to Paulhan, August 3, 1947, in *Correspondance 1944–1968*, pp. 436–37.

171. On the constraint of myth, see Stavrinaki, *Contraindre à la liberté*, pp. 139–92.

172. Rachel Perry, "Les messages de Jean Dubuffet," *Les Cahiers du Mnam* 140 (Summer 2017), pp. 11–12.

173. It is also presumptuous to find "the best description of the *Message* in the writings of Perec," a writer who throughout his life sought only to flush out History with a big

"aitch" (or ax) in the common histories or stories of human beings. For a more extensive analysis of Dubuffet's relation to history, see Maria Stavrinaki, "Circuit fermé: De l'usage de l'histoire et du mythe par Jean Dubuffet," in Baptiste Brun and Isabelle Marquette, eds., *Jean Dubuffet, un Barbare en Europe*, exh. cat. (Paris: Hazan, 2019), pp. 68–75.

CHAPTER FOUR: THE PARADOX OF THE NEOLITHIC

1. Walter Charleton, *Chorea gigantum, or, The Most Famous Antiquity of Great-Britan, Vulgarly Called Stone-Heng, Standing on Salisbury Plain, Restored to the Danes* (London: Henry Herringman, 1663), p. 5, emphasis in the original. See Alain Schnapp, "Aux sources de l'antiquarisme, l'Europe ancienne et l'Amérique du Nord," *Les Nouvelles de l'archéologie* no. 127 (2012), pp. 45–49, as well as Schnapp, *La conquête du passé: Aux origines de l'archéologie* (Paris: Le Livre de poche, 1993).

2. Charleton, *Chorea gigantum*, p. 6.

3. Comte de Caylus, *Recueil d'antiquités égyptiennes, étrusques, grecques, romaines et gauloises* (1752), vol. 6, quoted in Schnapp, *La conquête du passé*, p. 329.

4. Paul Nash, *Comments on His Own Paintings*, Paul Nash Archives, Tate Gallery, London, 769.1.52.

5. Gabriel de Mortillet, *Le préhistorique: Antiquité de l'homme* (Paris: C. Reinwald, 1883), pp. 479–81.

6. Arnold Hauser, *The Social History of Art*, 4 vols. (London: Routledge, 1999), vol. 1, p. 5.

7. Mortillet, *Le préhistorique*, p. 479.

8. Camille Jullian, *Les origines historiques du sol français, leçon d'ouverture du cours d'histoire et d'antiquité nationales, faite au Collège de France, December 8, 1909* (Paris: Éditions de la Revue politique et littéraire et de la Revue scientifique, 1910), p. 5; see also Jullian, "Plaidoyer pour la préhistoire," *Revue bleue* 8.24 (December 1907), pp. 737–44.

9. Édouard Piette, *Hiatus et lacunes: Vestiges de la période de transition dans la grotte du Mas d'Azil* (Beaugency: J. Laffray, 1895).

10. John Evans, *The Ancient Stone Implements, Weapons and Ornaments of Great Britain*, 2nd rev. ed. (London: Longmans, Green, 1898), p. 650.

11. Paul Broca, *Les troglodytes de la Vézère* (1871), lecture quoted in Émile Cartailhac, *La France préhistorique d'après les sépultures et les monuments* (Paris: Alcan, 1889), p. 124.

12. Clive Bell, *Art* (New York, Frederick Stokes, 1914), n. 2.

13. Henry Moore, "Primitive Art" (1941), in Henry Moore, *Writings and Conversations*, ed. Allan Wilkinson (Berkeley: University of California Press, 2002), p. 104.

14. Herbert Kühn, *Die Kunst der Primitiven* (Munich: Delphin, 1923).

15. Hauser, *The Social History of Art*, vol. 1, p. 247.

16. Kühn, *Die Kunst der Primitiven*, pp. 20–22.

17. Hauser, *The Social History of Art*, vol. 1, p. 249.

18. Lévi-Strauss would refer simply to his intellectual guide Rousseau, speaking of the "right balance" between unity and diversity in *Anthropologie structurale: Deux* (Paris: Plon, 1973), p. 300. For Alfred Métraux's "nostalgia for the Neolithic" see Alain Monnier, ed., *Nostalgie du Néolithique de Lausanne à Las Lomitas: Documents sur Alfred Métraux ethnologue* (Geneva: Labor et Fides, 2003).

19. Jullian, *Les origines historiques du sol français*, p. 8.

20. Ibid.

21. Herbert Read, *Icon and Idea* (Cambridge, MA: Harvard University Press, 1955), p. 35.

22. Ibid., p. 37.

23. See Niels Henriksen, "Prehistoric Techniques for Modern Painting: Asger Jorn's Archaeological Picture Books," in "Writing Prehistory," ed. Maria Stavrinaki and Stephanos Geroulanos, special issue, *Res: Anthropology and Aesthetics* 69–70 (Spring–Autumn 2018), pp. 189–204.

24. Asger Jorn, "Art as Magic," unpublished manuscript, quoted in Graham Birtwistle, *Living Art: Asger Jorn's Comprehensive Theory of Art between Helhesten and Cobra, 1946–1949* (Utrecht: Reflex, 1986), p. 115.

25. Asger Jorn, "Yang-yi: Le principe de vie dialectique-matérialiste," in Asger Jorn, *Discours aux pingouins et autres écrits* (Paris: Ensba, 2001), p. 62.

26. Jorn, quoted in Birtwistle, *Living Art*, p. 157.

27. Ibid., p. 115.

28. This information comes from Sam Smiles's "Equivalents for the Megaliths: Prehistory and English Culture, 1920–50," in David Peters Corbett, Ysanne Holt, and Fiona Russell, eds., *The Geographies of Englishness: Landscape and the National Past, 1880–1940* (New Haven: Yale University Press, 2002), pp. 199–223.

29. See Peter Shield, *Comparative Vandalism: Asger Jorn and the Artistic Attitude to Life* (Aldershot: Ashgate, in association with Borgen, 1997).

30. *CoBrA* 2, March 21, 1949, n.p.

31. Asger Jorn, "Gotik kontra germanisme" (1965), quoted in Shield, *Comparative Vandalism*, p. 104.

32. See Shield, *Comparative Vandalism*.

33. Anneli Fuchs, *Asger Jorn and Art History* (Hafnia: Copenhagen Papers in the History of Art / University of Copenhagen, 1985), pp. 128–46.

34. On the tension between internationalism and nationalism in Jorn, see Karen Kurczynski, "Beyond Expressionism: Asger Jorn and the European Avant-Garde, 1941–1961," PhD diss., Institute of Fine Arts, New York University, 2005, p. 514.

35. Asger Jorn, *Concerning Form / Pour la forme* (1957; Silkeborg: Museum Jorn, 2012).

36. Kühn, *Die Kunst der Primitiven*, p. 70.

37. Frederik Adama von Scheltema, *Die altnordische Kunst: Grundprobleme vorhistorischer Kunstentwicklung* (Berlin: Mauritius, 1922), pp. 34–35.

38. Camille Jullian, *Les origines historiques du sol français*, p. 6.

39. Ibid., p. 10.

40. Ibid., p. 27.

41. Paul Nash, "Stones" manuscript, Paul Nash Archives, Tate Gallery, London, 760. 1. 22; Nash, "A Characteristic," *Architectural Record* (March 1937), pp. 39–44, repr. in Paul Nash, *Writings on Art*, ed. Andrew Causey (Oxford: Oxford University Press, 2000), pp. 134–37.

42. Nash, quoted in Andrew Causey, *Paul Nash: Landscape and the Life of Objects* (Farnham: Lund Humphries, 2013), p. 100.

43. Letter from Paul Nash to his wife, Marguerite, Paul Nash Archives, Tate Gallery, London, 8313/1/1/228.

44. Paul Nash, *Dorset* (London: Architectural Press, Shell Guide Collection, 1935).

45. Ibid., p. 6.

46. Jacquetta Hawkes, *A Land* (1949; New York, Random House, 1967), p. 33.

47. Ibid., p. 11.

48. Ibid., p. 33.

49. Ibid., p. 104.

50. Ibid., p. 102.

51. Ibid., p. 103.

52. Ibid., p. 104.

53. Ibid., pp. 216–17.

54. Hawkes in fact criticized the oppressive power of communism, which stifled all individual particularity.

55. Andrew Causey, "Barbara Hepworth, Prehistory and the Cornish Landscape," *Sculpture Journal* 17.2 (2008), pp. 9–22.

56. The screenplay, can be found in the Barbara Hepworth archives at the Tate, as can many other materials linked to the film.

57. British Film Institute, *Figures in a Landscape: Cornwall and the Sculpture of Barbara Hepworth.*

58. On this circular pattern, see Éric Michaud, *The Barbarian Invasions: A Genealogy of the History of Art*, trans. Nicholas Huckle (Cambridge, MA: MIT Press, 2019).

59. On Picasso's transgressive approach in interrogating the earliest art, see Charlie F. B. Miller, "Archéologie de Picasso," in "Préhistoire/Modernité," ed. Rémi Labrusse and Maria Stavrinaki, special issue, *Les Cahiers du Musée national d'art moderne* 126 (Winter 2013–2014), pp. 58–71; I have proposed a synthetic interpretation of Picasso's uses of prehistory in Maria Stavrinaki, "La puissance diluvienne de l'art: Esquisse des usages de la préhistoire par Picasso," *Actes du colloque international Revoir Picasso* (Paris: Musée Picasso, 2015), http://revoirpicasso.fr/face-a-loeuvre/la-puissance-diluvienne-de-lart-esquisse-des-usages-de-la-prehistoire-par-picasso-%E2%80%A2-m-stavrinaki.

60. Michel Leiris, "Toiles récentes de Picasso," *Documents* 2.2 (1930), p. 70.

61. Werner Spies, *Picasso: Das Plastische Werk*, Nationalgalerie Berlin (Stuttgart: Gerd Hatje, 1983); Dawn Ades, "Picasso in Documents," in Yve-Alain Bois, ed., *Picasso Arlequin, 1917–1937*, exh. cat., Palazzo del Vittoriano, Rome, 2009 (Milan: Skira, 2009), pp. 59–69; Elizabeth Cowling, *Picasso: Style and Meaning* (London: Phaidon, 2002), pp. 502–40.

62. Michel Leiris, *Journal 1922–1989*, ed. Jean Jamin (Paris: Gallimard, 1992), p. 155.

63. Picasso kept two casts of the Venus of Lespugue in a cabinet in his studio, one faithful to its current condition (it was severely damaged by a worker's pickaxe), the other a reconstitution of what it had orginally been. See André Malraux, *La tête d'obsidienne* (Paris: Gallimard, 1974), p. 23.

64. Leiris, "Toiles récentes de Picasso," p. 70.

65. Ades, "Picasso in Documents."

66. Rosalind Krauss, "Sculpture in the Expanded Field," in *The Originality of the Avant-Garde and Other Modernist Myths* (Cambridge, MA: MIT Press, 1985), pp. 276–90.

67. Virginia Dawn, interview with Charles Stuckey, oral history, 2010–2011, Archives of American Art, Smithsonian, Washington.

68. Robert Morris, "Spaniards 'Liberated' Nazca Leaving No One to Speak of the 'Lines,'" in Robert Morris, "Aligned with Nazca," *Artforum*, 14.2 (October 1975), pp. 26–39, repr. in Robert Morris, *Continuous Project Altered Daily: The Writings of Robert Morris* (Cambridge, MA: MIT Press, 1993), pp. 143–74.

69. Richard Long, interview with Hamish Fulton, in Richard Long, *Selected Statements and Interviews*, ed. Ben Tufnell (London: Haunch of Venison, 2009), p. 90.

70. "Aligned on Nazca" suggests at once the lines themselves, Morris's attempt to conform his body to the latter, and the idea of a political inversion: an American artist conforming to the lines traced by a people effaced by European colonization.

71. The work was destroyed after the exhibition, but was rebuilt in a larger and more permanent form in 1977.

72. Robert Morris, "Observations on the *Observatory*," in *Robert Morris 1961–1994*, exh. cat. (Arnhem: Sonsbeek, 1971), p. 57, quoted in Catherine Grenier, ed. *Robert Morris 1961–1994: Catalogue du MNAM* (Paris: Centre Pompidou, 1995), pp. 253–54.

73. See Gilles Tiberghien, "The Time of the Earthworks," in Katia Schneller and Noura Wedell, eds., *Investigations: The Expanded Field of Writing in the Works of Robert Morris* (Lyon: ENS Éditions, 2015), http://books.openedition.org/enseditions/3810.

74. Morris, "Observations on the *Observatory*," in Grenier, ed., *Robert Morris 1961–1994*, pp. 253–54.

75. On the phenomenological foundations of Morris's experience, see Anaël Lejeune, "The Subject-Object Problem in 'Aligned with Nazca': On Phenomenological Issues in Robert Morris' Artwork," in Schneller and Wedell, eds., *Investigations*.

76. Robert Morris, "Aligned with Nazca," in *Continuous Project Altered Daily*, p. 154.

77. Ibid., p. 159.

78. Ibid.

79. Ibid., p. 172.

80. Robert Morris, "Five Labyrinths" (1993), in *Robert Morris: From Mnemosyne to Clio, the Mirror to the Labyrinth (1998–1999–2000)* (Lyon, Musée d'Art contemporain; Paris: Seuil; Milan: Skira, 2000), p. 116.

CHAPTER FIVE: PREHISTORY IN THE ATOMIC AGE

1. Fernand Braudel, preface to *L'homme avant l'écriture*, ed. André Varagnac (Paris: A. Collin, 1959), p. ix.

2. See Spencer R. Weart, *Nuclear Fear: A History of Images* (Cambridge, MA: Harvard University Press, 1988); Sebastian Vincent Grevsmühl, *La terre vue d'en haut: L'invention de l'environnement global* (Paris: Seuil, 2014), chap. 1, "Des pôles à l'espace: La géographie à l'heure du monde fini," pp. 13–37.

3. Only Günther Anders saw very early on that the realities of genocide and the atomic bomb were connected.

4. Roderick Seidenberg, *Posthistoric Man: An Inquiry* (Chapel Hill: University of North Carolina Press, 1950).

5. Richard Neutra, *Survival through Design* (New York: Oxford University Press, 1954), pp. 14–15.

6. Ibid., p. 21. On the relation between design and human survival, see Beatriz Colomina

and Mark Wigley, *Are We Human?: Notes on the Archaeology of Design* (Zurich: Lars Müller, 2016).

7. William L. Laurence, "Drama of the Atomic Bomb Found Climax in July 16 Test," *New York Times*, September 26, 1945, p. 1, quoted in Jacob Krell, "Genealogies of Technology and Prehistory in France: The 'Atomic Age,'" *Res: Anthropology and Aesthetics* 69–70 (Spring–Autumn 2018), pp. 158–72. See also Weart's classic *Nuclear Fear*).

8. Günther Anders, *Hiroshima ist überall* (Munich: C. H. Beck, 1995), p. 66.

9. On the notion of "zero" after World War II, see Éric de Chassey and Sylvie Ramond, eds., *1945–1949: Repartir à zéro, comme si la peinture n'avait jamais existé*, exh. cat., Musée des beaux-arts de Lyon (Paris: Hazan, 2008).

10. Günther Anders, "Reflections on the H Bomb," *Dissent* 3.2 (Spring 1956), p. 146.

11. On the years of the "Acéphale" (Acephalous) project, see the rich documentation in Georges Bataille, *L'apprenti sorcier: Du cercle communiste démocratique à Acéphale. Textes, lettres et documents*, ed. Marina Galletti (Paris: Éditions de la Différence, 1999).

12. Pierre Ichac, "La grotte à peintures de Montignac, en Dordogne," *L'Illustration* 5104, January 4, 1941, pp. 9–17.

13. Georges Bataille, *Lascaux; or, The Birth of Art. Prehistoric Painting*, trans. Austryn Wainhouse (Lausanne: Skira, 1955).

14. Georges Bataille, *Choix de lettres* (Paris: Gallimard, 1997), pp. 179–80.

15. On the Frobenius exhibition in Paris, see Hélène Ivanoff, "Exposer l'art préhistorique africain: Le Paris de Léo Frobenius au début des années 1930," in Jean-Louis Georget, Hélène Ivanoff, and Richard Kuba, eds., *Cercles culturels. Léo Frobenius (1873–1938) et ses contemporains / Kulturkreise: Leo Frobenius (1873–1938) und seine Zeitgenossen* (Berlin: Dietrich Reimer, 2015), pp. 267–86.

16. Georges Bataille, "The Frobenius Exhibit at the Salle Pleyel," in Georges Bataille, *The Cradle of Humanity: Prehistoric Art and Culture*, ed. Stuart Kendall, trans. Michelle Kendall and Stuart Kendall (New York: Zone Books, 2005), pp. 45–46.

17. Ibid, p. 46.

18. Ibid.

19. On that altered resemblance, see Georges Didi-Huberman, *La ressemblance informe ou le gai savoir visuel selon Georges Bataille* (Paris: Macula, 1995).

20. Bataille, "Primitive Art," in Bataille, *The Cradle of Humanity*, p. 41.

21. I refer here to the now classic catalog by Yve-Alain Bois and Rosalind Krauss, *Formless: A User's Guide* (New York: Zone Books, 1997).

22. Bataille, "Primitive Art," p. 43.

23. Georges Bataille, "Joan Miró: Peintures récentes," *Documents* 2.7 (1930), p. 399.

24. Jacques Boucher de Perthes, *Antiquités celtiques et antédiluviennes: Mémoire sur l'industrie primitive et les arts à leur origine*, 3 vols. (Paris: Treuttel et Wurtz, Derchen Dumoulin et Didron, 1847), vol. 3, p. 477.

25. Bataille, *Lascaux; or, The Birth of Art*, p. 12.

26. Ibid., p. 14.

27. Ibid., p. 12.

28. Ibid, pp. 14–15.

29. All these terms are found in *Lascaux*, but also in Bataille's other texts on prehistory.

30. For example, in his unfinished project for a universal history, which was in part a response to the section on prehistory in the *Histoire universelle de la Pléiade*, a chapter written by Leroi-Gourhan that Bataille critiqued in "Qu'est-ce que l'histoire universelle?," *Critique* (1956), reprinted in Georges Bataille, *Oeuvres complètes*, ed. Michel Foucault, et al., 12 vols. (Paris: Gallimard, 1970–1988), vol. 12, pp. 414–36. His general reproach to Leroi-Gourhan was that he neglected the "decisive moment" in the evolution of the species (art) and put the emphasis on the technical aspect — an inaccurate interpretation.

31. In "The Cradle of Humanity: The Vezere Valley," Bataille mentions a history in two acts. See *The Cradle of Humanity*, pp. 143–73.

32. Bataille's notes in his archives, NAF, 28086, box 1, I, note 11.

33. "Desert, no birds. / Life has not appeared on earth, the sphere rolls in the immensity of space, opening itself to the light of the sun, the sound of the elements." Georges Bataille, "Notes on a Film" in *The Cradle of Humanity*, p. 181. The manuscript of this screenplay is located in the Bataille archives, Bibliothèque nationale de France, NAF, 28086, envelope 85 bis/a.

34. Bataille, "The Cradle of Humanity," p. 145.

35. Note the pejorative use of the term: "We must never lose sight of the fact that work expanded to consciousness. Above all, work is the intellectual operation that changed the brain of the animal that man initially was into a human brain. This brain took formless flint and separated out by experimentation the actions that changed this rock into a useful object, into a tool." Ibid., p. 150.

36. Ibid., p. 155.

37. Paul Ricoeur, *Time and Narrative, Volume 1*, trans. Kathleen McLaughlin and David Pellauer (Chicago: University of Chicago Press, 1984), p. 3.

38. Claude Lévi-Strauss to Georges Bataille, February 17, 1956, letter no. 62, Georges Bataille Correspondance in the Georges Bataille archive, Bibliothèque nationale de France, NAF, 28086.

39. Claude Lévi-Strauss, "The Archaic Illusion, in *The Elementary Structures of Kinship*, trans. James Harle Bell, John Richard von Sturmer, and Rodney Needham (London: Eyre and Spottiswoode, 1969), pp. 84–97.

40. That is the dominant term in his account in "The Cradle of Humanity."

41. Bataille, "The Cradle of Humanity," p. 158.

42. As Jacques Derrida explained at length in his last seminars, especially *The Animal That Therefore I Am*, ed. Marie-Louise Mallet, trans. David Wills (New York: Fordham Unicversity Press, 2008).

43. Georges Bataille, *The Accursed Share: An Essay on General Economy, Volume I: Consumption*, trans. Robert Hurley (New York: Zone Books, 1988), p. 133.

44. Georges Bataille, "The Passage from Animal to Man and the Birth of Art," in Bataille, *The Cradle of Humanity*, p. 60.

45. Bataille, *Lascaux; or, The Birth of Art*, p. 115.

46. Bataille, "The Cradle of Humanity"; see esp. p. 167.

47. Bataille "The Passage from Animal to Man and the Birth of Art," p. 78.

48. Bataille, *Lascaux; or, The Birth of Art*, p. 121.

49. Georges Bataille archive, Bibliothèque nationale de France, NAF 28086, box X, Qc.

50. On Montandon's study of the anthropoid ape, see Pierre Centlivres and Isabelle Girod, "George Montandon et le grand singe américain: L'invention de l'*Ameranthropoides loysi*," *Gradhiva* 24 (1998), pp. 33–43.

51. Georges Montandon, "Découverte d'un singe d'apparence anthropoïde en Amérique du Sud," *L'Anthropologie* (1929), pp. 137–41 (session of the Institut Français d'Anthropologie, March 20, 1929). In the file "Sur les singes," located in the Bataille archive, there is also an offprint of Georges Montandon's article "Découverte d'un singe d'apparence anthropoïde en Amérique du Sud," *Journal de la société des Américanistes de Paris* 21.1 (1929), pp. 183–95.

52. On the theme of "resemblance" in Bataille, see Didi-Huberman, *La ressemblance informe*.

53. The stick is not only a spontaneously invented device, but an actual code invented in natural history studies at the very end of the eighteenth century. In all likelihood, the first ape with a stick is in the physician Edward Tyson's *Orang-Outang, sive Homo Sylvestris: or, The Anatomy of a Pygmie, Compared with That of a Monkey, an Ape and a Man* (1699). See Silvia Sebastiani, "L'orang-outang, l'esclave et l'humain: Une querelle des corps en régime colonial," *L'Atelier du centre des recherches historiques* 11 (2013), https://acrh.revues.org/5265.

54. For example, Montandon, "Découverte d'un singe d'apparence anthropoïde en Amérique du Sud."

55. Georges Bataille, "Architecture," *Documents* 1.2 (1929), p. 117.

56. Bataille, "The Cradle of Humanity," p. 159.

57. Since the late nineteenth century, in the wake of Darwinism, play has been systematically interpreted as a way of augmenting and making more malleable the inherited instincts, an extension of adaptation. On this point, see, for example, Karl Groos, *The Play of Animals*, trans. James Mark Baldwin (New York: D. Appleton, 1898).

58. Bataille, "The Passage from Animal to Man," p. 77.

59. Georges Bataille, "Prehistoric Religion," in *The Cradle of Humanity*, p. 135.

60. Bataille, *Lascaux; or, The Birth of Art*, p. 29.

61. "That difficulty announces the necessity of the *spectacle*, or generally, *representation*, without whose repetition we could remain a stranger to death, ignorant of it, as beasts apparently are. Nothing in fact is less animalistic than fiction, more or less remote from the real, from death." Georges Bataille, "Hegel, la mort et le sacrifice" (1955), in *Oeuvres complètes*, vol. 12, p. 337.

62. Bataille, *Lascaux; or, The Birth of Art*, p. 14.

63. Ibid, p. 15.

64. Georges Bataille, "Lecture, January 18, 1955," in *The Cradle of Humanity*, p. 94.

65. "Une visite à Lascaux," envelope 85, Georges Bataille archive, Bibliothèque nationale de France, NAF 28086, p. 29.

66. Bataille, "Lecture, January 18, 1955," p. 94.

67. As Marshall Sahlins has clearly seen, the Christian theme of the Fall marked modern ethnology with the seal of destitution: in opposition to a human being condemned to desire, Sahlins proposed the narrative of an age of abundance. See Marshall Sahlins, "The Sadness of Sweetness: The Native Anthropology of Western Cosmology," *Current Anthropology* 37.3 (June 1996), pp. 395–428.

68. Daniel Fabre, *Bataille à Lascaux: Comment l'art préhistorique apparut aux enfants* (Paris: L'Échoppe, 2014).

69. On the Christian determination of the new man, see Éric Michaud, "*Déjà là*, mais encore à *venir*: Le temps de l'homme nouveau en Allemagne, 1918–1945," in Jean Clair, ed., *La fabrique de l'homme nouveau* (Ottawa: Musée National des Beaux-Arts du Canada, 2008), pp. 29–35.

70. Georges Bataille, "L'utilité de l'art" (1952), in *Oeuvres complètes*, vol. 12, pp. 209–12.

71. I refer here to *The Accursed Share*.

72. Bataille, "Lecture, January 18, 1955," p. 99.

73. In his Bataille anthology, *The Cradle of Humanity*, Stuart Kendall points out the

symmetry between Lascaux and Hiroshima, but without inquiring into its polysemic potential.

74. Bataille, "Lecture, January 18, 1955," p. 87, my emphasis.

75. Georges Bataille, "La bouteille à la mer, ou l'histoire universelle des origines à la venue d'un désastre éventuel," Georges Bataille archive, Bibliothèque nationale de France, NAF 28086, box 10H.

76. This is a constant theme in Leroi-Gourhan, *Gesture and Speech*.

77. See John Hersey, *Hiroshima* (Harmondsworth: Penguin, 1946), and Georges Bataille, "À propos de récits d'habitants d'Hiroshima" (1947), in *Oeuvres complètes*, vol. 11, pp. 172–87.

78. Bataille, "À propos de récits d'habitants d'Hiroshima," p. 175.

79. Ibid.

80. Ibid.

81. Ibid., p. 175.

82. Ibid., pp. 182–83.

83. Ibid., p. 175.

84. See the first book in which Carl Schmitt formulated his political decisionism, Schmitt, *Political Theology* (1922), trans. George Schwab (Chicago: University of Chicago Press, 2005).

85. Georges Bataille, "De l'existentialisme au primat de l'économie" (1947), in *Oeuvres complètes*, vol. 11, p. 286.

86. Bataille would later remember emerging that "broke me, crushed me, killed me ten times." Georges Bataille, *On Nietszche*, trans. Stuart Kendall (Albany: State University of New York Press, 2015), p. 281 note.

87. Alexandre Kojève, *Introduction to the Reading of Hegel*, assembled by Raymond Queneau, ed. Allan Bloom, trans. James H. Nichols, Jr. (New York: Basic Books, 1969). There is a vast bibliography on Kojève and Bataille. I will limit myself here to Stefanos Geroulanos, *An Atheism That Is Not Humanist Emerges in French Thought* (Stanford: Stanford University Press, 2010).

88. Seidenberg, *Posthistoric Man: An Inquiry*, p. 238.

89. Lewis Mumford, *The Transformations of Man* (New York: Harper & Bros., 1951).

90. Lewis Mumford, *Art and Technics* (1952; New York: Columbia University Press, 2000), p. 18.

91. Mumford, *The Transformations of Man*, p. 94.

92. In the text he wrote for his documentary *La rabbia* (Rabid), Pasolini went so far as to see "the atomic bomb, with its funereal mushroom cloud expanding in those apocalyptic

skies" as "the result of the division" between the "Master" and the "Slave." Nevertheless, the apocalyptic bomb did not manage to end history, and it was American "democracy" that would slowly and imperceptibly finish it off: "The joy of the American who feels he is identical to another million Americans in his love of democracy: that is the disease of the future world! When the classical world is exhausted—when all the peasants and artisans are dead—when industry has made the cycle of production and consumption unstoppable—then our history will be at an end. In these cries, that racket, these enormous assemblies, these lights, in these mechanisms, in these declarations, these weapons, these armies, in these deserts, in that unrecognizable sun, the new prehistory begins." In Pier Paolo Pasolini, *La rabbia* (Rome: Raro Video, 2011).

93. Jan Patočka, *Heretical Essays in the Philosophy of History*, ed. James Dodd, trans. Erazim Kohák (Chicago: Open Court, 1996), pp. 73–74.

94. Ibid., p. 140.

95. On posthistory in Gehlen, see Lutz Niethammer's classic essay *Posthistoire: Has History Come to an End?* (1989; London: Verso, 1992), as well as Rowan Tepper, "Time and History after Post-Histoire," https://www.academia.edu/31936422/Time_and_History_After_Post-Histoire. According to Gehlen, the concept of "posthistoire" was suggested to him by the Fascist theorist Henri de Man, who wrote a still-unpublished text titled "L'âge de l'ennui" (1950), then, a year later, the book *Vermassung und Kukturverfall* (Munich: Lehnen, 1951), in which the term "posthistory" was used to explain the state in which events occur "outside the framework of history, for there is no significant connection between causes and effects" (pp. 124–25).

96. Walter Benjamin, "Theories of German Fascism: On the Collection of Essays War and Warrior, Edited by Ernst Jünger," trans. Jerolf Wikoff, *New German Critique* 17 (Spring 1979), p. 123.

97. Giorgio Agamben, *The Open: Man and Animal*, trans. Kevin Attell (Stanford: Stanford University Press, 2004); Peter Sloterdijk, *In the World Interior of Capitalism*, trans. Wieland Hoban (Cambridge: Polity, 2015).

98. See Arnold Gehlen, *Die Seele im Technischen Zeitalter und andere sozialpsychologische, soziologische und kulturanalytische Schriften* (Frankfurt: Vittorio Klostermann, 1982), esp. "Über kulturelle Kristallisation" (1961), pp. 298–314.

99. Ernst Jünger, *An der Zeitmauer* (Stuttgart: Klett-Cotta, 2019), translated into French by Henri Thomas as *Le mur du temps* (Paris: Gallimard, 1994). [Cited from the French translation—trans.]

100. Ibid.

101. Ibid., p. 94.

102. Ibid., pp. 95–96.

103. Ibid., p. 131.

104. Ibid., p. 136.

105. Ibid., p. 139.

106. Ibid., p. 177.

107. Ibid., p. 173.

108. Ibid., p. 280.

109. Ibid., pp. 205–206.

110. Ibid., p. 206.

111. Ibid., p. 207.

112. Ibid., p. 209.

113. On Fontana's environment, see Stephen Petersen, *Space-Age Aesthetics: Lucio Fontana, Yves Klein, and the Postwar European Avant-Garde* (University Park: Pennsylvania State University Press, 2009), pp. 47–101; Germano Celant, *Lucio Fontana: Ambienti Spaziali. Architecture, Art, Environments* (Milan: Skira; New York: Gagosian, 2012).

114. Lisa Ponti, "Primo graffito dell'età atomica (Dalla Mostra d'arte spaziale tenuta da Lucio Fontana al Naviglio, a Milano, February 5, 1949," *Domus* 233 (February 1949), p. 44.

115. We read in Oldenburg's diary: "Power of Egyptians, Persian, etc., *grottes sacres* [*sic*, in French in the text]." Claes Oldenburg, "Chapter 3: Guises of Ray Gun. The Store, 1961–1962, Notes," in Achim Hochdörfer, Maartje Oldenburg, Barbara Schröder, and Ann Temkin, eds., *Claes Oldenburg: Writing on the Side, 1956–1969* (New York: Museum of Modern Art, 2013), p. 151.

116. Raffaele Carrieri, "Fontana ha toccato la luna," *Tempo*, February 19–26, 1949, p. 28.

117. Ponti, "Primo graffito dell'età atomica."

118. Lucio Fontana, letter to Enrico Crispolti, 1961, quoted by Valerie da Costa and translated into French in Lucio Fontana, *Écrits de Lucio Fontana (Manifestes, textes, entretiens)*, ed. Valérie Da Costa (Dijon: Les presses du réel, 2013), p. 45.

119. Guido Ballo, quoted by V. da Costa in Fontana, *Écrits*, pp. 44–45.

120. Lucio Fontana, Giorgio Kaisserlian, Beniamino Joppolo, and Milena Milani, "Manifeste, Spatialistes I" (1947) in Fontana, *Écrits*, p. 147.

121. Ibid.

122. All the manifestos associated with spatialism have been translated into French in *Écrits*, pp. 133–64.

123. Lucio Fontana, drafts of letters to Giampiero Giani (1949), in Guido Ballo, ed., *Lucio*

Fontana: Idea per un ritratto (Turin: Ilte, 1970), p. 248.

124. Interview with Tommaso Trini (1968), quoted in Fontana, *Écrits*, p. 102.

125. Lucio Fontana, interview with Carla Lonzi, in *Autoportrait*, ed. Giovanna Zapperi, trans. Marie-Ange Maire-Vigueur (Zurich, JRP Ringier / Lectures Maison rouge, 2013), p. 103; also repr. in Fontana, *Écrits*, pp. 299–300. Ellipses in the original.

126. But the more time passed, the more divine Nothingness lost its impassiveness, to become a source of anxiety, like a terrible shapeless and faceless God. In the 1960s, Fontana's trust in science was weakening, becoming metaphysical anxiety.

127. Frederick Kiesler, *Frederick Kiesler, 1890–1965: Visionary Architecture, Drawings and Models, Galaxies and Paintings, Sculpture*, exh. cat. (New York: André Emmerich Gallery, 1979), n.p.

128. Frederick Kiesler, "The Universe as Architecture," Kiesler Archives, TXT_6686_0_N42-2, quoted in Spyros Papapetros, "Magic Architecture: Caves, Animals, and Tools in the Atomic Era," in Christian Thun-Hohenstein and Dieter Bogner, eds., *Friedrich Kiesler: Lebenswelten / Life Visions: Architektur-Kunst-Designe* (Zurich: Birkhäuser, 2016), p. 62.

129. See Grevsmühl, *La terre vue d'en haut*.

130. On Pinot-Gallizio's *Caverna*, see Frances Stracey, "Pinot Gallizio's 'Industrial Painting': Towards a Surplus of Life," *Oxford Art Journal* 28.3 (2005), pp. 393–405; Stracey, "The Caves of Gallizio and Hirschhorn: Excavations of the Present," *October* 116 (Spring 2006), pp. 87–100; Nicola Pezolet, "The Cavern of Antimatter: Giuseppe 'Pinot' Gallizio and the Technological Imaginary of the Early Situationist International," *Grey Room* 38 (Winter 2010), pp. 62–89.

131. See Sophie Cras, *The Artist as Economist: Art and Capitalism in the 1960s*, trans. Malcolm DeBevoise (New Haven: Yale University Press, 2019).

132. Giuseppe Pinot-Gallizio, untitled notes, ca. 1958 (Fondo Gallizio), in Giuseppe Pinot-Gallizio, *Pinot Gallizio: Il laboratorio della Scrittura / The Laboratory of Writing*, ed. Giorgina Bertolino, Francesca Comisso, and Maria Teresa Roberto (Milan: Charta, 2005), p. 27.

133. Letter from Pinot-Gallizio to René Drouin, December 8, 1958, in *Pinot Gallizio: Il laboratorio della scrittura*, p. 68.

134. Ibid., p. 70.

135. Giuseppe Pinot-Gallizio, "Appunti per il discorso di chiusura di Pinot Gallizio al *I Congresso Mondiale degli Artisti Liberi* / Notes for Pinot-Gallizio's Closing Speech, *I Congress of Free Artists* (September 8, 1956)," in *Pinot Gallizio: Il laboratorio della scrittura*, p. 132.

136. Giuseppe Pinot-Gallizio, "Manifesto of Industrial Painting: For an Applicable Unitary Art" (1959), in *Pinot Gallizio: Il laboratorio della scrittura*, p. 176.

137. Ibid., p. 171.

138. Giuseppe Pinot-Gallizio, notes for the "Manifesto della pittura industriale" (1959), in *Il laboratorio della scrittura*, p. 172.

139. Giuseppe Pinot-Gallizio, interview with Carla Lonzi, partly retranscribed in *Il laboratorio della scrittura*, pp. 42–43.

140. Giuseppe Pinot-Gallizio, "Manifesto della pittura industriale: Per un'arte unitaria applicabile / Manifesto of Industrial Painting: For an Applicable Unitary Art," in *Il laboratorio della scrittura*, pp. 167–68.

141. Giuseppe Pinot-Gallizio, letter of December 8, 1958, to René Drouin, in *Il laboratorio della scrittura*, p. 63.

142. Giuseppe Pinot-Gallizio, untitled notes, 1960, in *Il laboratorio della scrittura*, p. 105.

CONCLUSION: TERRA INCOGNITA

1. The Chauvet-Pont-d'Arc Cave was discovered in December 1994 by Jean-Marie Chauvet, Eliette Brunel-Deschamps, and Christian Hillaire. Immediately convinced of the antiquity of these compositions, the prehistorians were even more struck by the results of the first carbon-14 dating tests, which were later confirmed: estimated to be about thirty-five thousand years old, these images pushed man's symbolic grasp of the world even farther back into the past. They made it necessary to reconsider radically the relations between periods, places, and styles and also between mobiliary art and parietal art.

2. Jean Clottes, "L'originalité de la grotte Chauvet-Pont-d'Arc, à Vallon-Pont-d'Arc (Ardèche)" (background note), *Comptes rendus des séances de l'Académie des Inscriptions et Belles-Lettres* 139.2 (1995), pp. 563–68.

3. Pierre Nora, "L'événement monstre," *Communications* 18 (1972), pp. 162–72.

4. Michel Serres with Bruno Latour, *Conversations on Science, Culture, and Time*, trans. Roxanne Lapidus (Ann Arbor: University of Michigan Press, 1995), p. 139.

5. Michel Serres, *Le contrat naturel* (Paris: Flammarion, 1992), pp. 158–59.

6. The article that initiated these reflections is Dipesh Chakrabarty's "The Climate of History: Four Theses," *Critical Inquiry* 35.9 (Winter 2009), pp. 197–222. For a critique of that approach, see Jean-Baptiste Fressoz and Fabien Locher, "Modernity's Frail Climate: A Climate History of Environmental Reflexivity," *Critical Inquiry* 38.3 (Spring 2012), pp. 589–98, and Fressoz and Locher, "L'agir humain sur le climat et la naissance de la climatologie

historique, XVIIe–XVIIIe siècles," *Revue d'histoire moderne et contemporaine* 62.1 (2015), pp. 48–78.

7. Dipesh Chakrabarty, "Postcolonial Studies and the Challenge of Climate Change," *New Literary History* 43.1 (2012), pp. 12–13. See also Chakrabarty, "Humanities in the Anthropocene: The Crisis of an Enduring Kantian Fable," *New Literary History* 47.2–3 (2016), pp. 377–97.

8. Andrea Branzi and Kenya Hara, eds., introduction to *Neo-Prehistory — 100 Verbs Neo Preistoria — 100 Verbi* / 新先史時代 — *100*の動詞, exh. cat. (Zurich: Lars Müller, 2016), pp. 11–12.

9. Andrea Branzi, interview with Kenya Hara, "Solid Poetry: How to Read the History of Man with Indulgence," in *Neo-Prehistory — 100 Verbs*, p. 243.

10. Ibid., p. 243.

11. See Maria Stavrinaki, "All the Time in the World: Art and Prehistory," *Artforum* (March 2018), pp. 202–14.

12. Branzi, interview with Hara, "Solid Poetry," p. 243.

13. Thomas Hirschhorn, interview with Maria Stavrinaki, February 18, 2016, in "Prehistoire," ed. Chiara Di Stefano, Rémi Labrusse, and Maria Stavrinaki, special issue, *Les Cahiers du musée national d'art moderne* 147 (May 2019), p. 87.

14. Ibid., p. 88.

15. Sheena Wagstaff, "A Conversation with Pierre Huyghe," in Ian Alteveer, Meredith Brown, and Sheena Wagstaff, *The Roof Garden Commission: Pierre Huyghe* (New York: Metropolitan Museum of Art, 2015), pp. 23–34.

16. Paul Klee, *On Modern Art* (1924), trans. Paul Findlay (London: Faber and Faber, 1954), pp. 45–47.

17. Pierre Huyghe, interview with Maria Stavrinaki, January 21, 2019, in "Prehistoire," ed. Chiara Di Stefano, Rémi Labrusse, and Maria Stavrinaki, special issue, *Les Cahiers du musée national d'art moderne* 47 (May 2019), p. 94.

18. André Leroi-Gourhan, *Les chasseurs de la préhistoire* (Paris: Éditions Métailié, 1983), p. 25.

Bibliography

Ades, Dawn. "Picasso in Documents." In Yve-Alain Bois, ed., *Picasso Arlequin, 1917–1937.* Exh. cat., Palazzo del Vittoriano, Rome, 2009. Milan: Skira, 2009, pp. 59–69.

Adorno, Theodor. "Paralipomena" and "Theories on the Origins of Art." In Theodor Adorno, *Aesthetic Theory.* Ed. Gretel Adorno and Rolf Tiedemann. Trans. Robert Hullot-Kentor. Minneapolis: University of Minnesota Press, 1997.

Agamben, Giorgio. *The Open: Man and Animal.* Trans. Kevin Attell. Stanford: Stanford University Press, 2004.

Aït-Touati, Frédérique. *Contes de la lune: Essai sur la fiction et la science modernes.* Paris: Gallimard, 2011.

Aldiss, Brian. *Cryptozoïque* (1967). Paris: Calmann-Lévy, 1977.

Allouche, Dove. Interview with Rémi Labrusse. In "Préhistoire," ed. Chiara Di Stefano, Rémi Labrusse, and Maria Stavrinaki. Special issue, *Les Cahiers du musée national d'art moderne* 147 (May 2019), pp. 73–76.

Althaus, Karin, and Helmut Friedel, eds. *Gabriel von Max: Malerstar, Darwinist, Spiritist.* Städtische Galerie im Lenbachhaus und Kunstbau. Munich: Hirmer, 2010.

Anders, Günther. *Hiroshima ist überall.* Munich: C. H. Beck, 1995.

———. "Reflections on the H Bomb." *Dissent* 3.2 (Spring 1956), pp. 146–55.

Andre, Carl. "Paleolithic/Neolithic." In James Meyer, ed., *Cuts: Texts 1959–2004.* Cambridge: MIT Press, 2004, pp. 171–72.

Apollinaire, Guillaume. "Georges Braque" (1908). In *Chroniques d'art, 1902–1918.* Paris: Gallimard, 1960, pp. 74–77.

———. *The Cubist Painters.* Trans. Peter Read. Berkeley: University of California Press, 2004.

Aragon, Louis, "La peinture au défi" (1930). In *Les collages.* Paris: Hermann, 1993, pp. 31–61.

Archer W. G., Robert Melville, and Herbert Read. *40,000 Years of Modern Art: A Comparison of Primitive and Modern*. Exh. cat. London: Institute of Contemporary Arts, 1948.

Aristotle. *The "Art" of Rhetoric*. Ed. E. Capps, T. E. Page, and W. H. D. Rouse. Trans. J. H. Freese. London: William Heinemann, 1926.

Artinger, Kai. "Der beobachtete Mensch." *Münchner Jahrbuch der bildenden Kunst* 46 (1995), pp. 163–74.

Athaassoglou Kallmyer, Nina. *Cézanne and Provence: The Painter in His Culture*. Chicago: University of Chicago Press, 2003.

Audouze, Françoise, and Nathan Schlanger. *Autour de l'homme: Contexte et actualité d'André Leroi-Gourhan*. Antibes: Association pour la promotion et la diffusion des connaissances archéologiques, 2004.

Balfour, Henry. *The Evolution of Decorative Art: An Essay upon Its Origin and Development as Illustrated by the Art of Modern Races of Mankind*. New York: Macmillan., 1893.

Ballo, Guido, ed. *Lucio Fontana: Idea per un ritratto*. Turin: Ilte, 1970.

Ballard, J. G. *The Terminal Beach*. In J. G. Ballard, *The Complete Stories*. New York: Norton, 2009, pp. 589–604.

Barkan, Leonard. *Unearthing the Past: Archaeology and Aesthetics in the Making of Renaissance Culture*. New Haven: Yale University Press, 1999.

Barthes, Roland. "Sémantique de l'objet." In *Oeuvres complètes*. Ed. Eric Marty. Rev. ed. 5 vols. Paris: Seuil, 2002, pp. 817–27.

Bataille, Georges. *The Accursed Share: An Essay on General Economy, Volume 1: Consumption*. Trans. Robert Hurley. New York: Zone Books, 1988.

———. *L'apprenti sorcier: Du cercle communiste démocratique à Acéphale. Textes, lettres et documents*. Ed. Marina Galletti. Paris: Éditions de la Différence, 1999.

———. "Architecture." *Documents* 1.2 (1929), p. 117.

———. "La bouteille à la mer, ou l'histoire universelle des origines à la venue d'un désastre éventuel." Georges Bataille archive, Bibliothèque nationale de France, NAF 28086, box 10H.s

———. *Choix de lettres*. Paris: Gallimard, 1997.

———. "The Cradle of Humanity: The Vezere Valley." In Georges Bataille, *The Cradle of Humanity: Prehistoric Art and Culture*. Ed. Stuart Kendall. Trans. Michelle Kendall and Stuart Kendall. New York: Zone Books, 2009, pp. 143–73.

———. "De l'existentialisme au primat de l'économie" (1947). In vol 11 of Georges Bataille, *Oeuvres complètes*, ed. Michel Foucault, et al. 12 vols. Paris: Gallimard, 1970–1988, pp. 279–306.

———. "The Frobenius Exhibit at the Salle Pleyel." In *The Cradle of Humanity*, pp. 45–46.

———. "Joan Miró: Peintures récentes." *Documents* 2.7 (1930), p. 399.

———. "Hegel, la mort et le sacrifice" (1955). In *Oeuvres complètes*, vol. 12, pp. 326–45.

———. *Lascaux: or, The Birth of art. Prehistoric Painting*. Trans. Austryn Wainhouse. Lausanne: Skira, 1955.

———. "Lecture, January 18, 1955." In *The Cradle of Humanity*, pp. 87–104.

———. "Notes on a Film." In *The Cradle of Humanity*, pp. 179–85.

———. "The Passage from Animal to Man and the Birth of Art." In *The Cradle of Humanity*, pp. 57–80.

———. "Prehistoric Religion." In *The Cradle of Humanity*, pp. 121–42.

———. "Primitive Art." In *The Cradle of Humanity*, pp. 35–44.

———. "À propos de récits d'habitants d'Hiroshima" (1947). In, *Oeuvres complètes*, vol. 11, pp. 172–87.

———. "Qu'est-ce que l'histoire universelle?" *Critique* (1956). In *Oeuvres complètes*, vol. 12, pp. 414–36.

———. *On Nietszche*. Trans. Stuart Kendall. Albany: State University of New York Press, 2015.

———. "L'utilité de l'art" (1952). In *Oeuvres complètes*, vol. 12, pp. 209–12.

Baubérot, Arnaud. "Les naturiens libertaires ou le retour à l'anarchisme préhistorique." *Revue mille neuf cent: Revue d'histoire intellectuelle* 31 (2013), pp. 117–36.

Baucon, Andrea. "Leonardo da Vinci, the Founding Father of Ichnology." *Palaios* 25.6, pp. 361–67.

Balzac, Honoré de. *The Wild Ass's Skin (La peau de chagrin)*. Trans. Herbert J. Hunt. New York: Penguin Books, 1977.

Baudelaire, Charles. "Salon 1859," including "Le public moderne et la photographie." In vol. 2 of Charles Baudelaire, *Oeuvres complètes*. Ed. Claude Pichois. 2 vols. Paris: Gallimard, 1962, pp. 690–82.

Bedell, Rebecca. "The History of the Earth: Darwin, Geology and Landscape Art." In Diana Donald and Jane Munro, eds., *Endless Forms: Charles Darwin, Natural Science and Visual Arts*. New Haven: Yale Center for British Art, 2009, pp. 49–79.

Beer, Gillian. *Darwin's Plots: Evolutionary Narrative in Darwin, George Eliot and Nineteenth-Century Fiction*. London: Routledge & Kegan Paul, 1983.

Begouën, Henri. "Les bases magiques de l'art préhistorique." *Scientia* 65.4 (1939), pp. 202–16.

Behn, Friedrich. *Der Mensch der Urzeit, seine Kultur und seine Kunst*. Lepizig: Nacmeister & Thal, 1921.

———. "Das Tierbild in der Kunst des diluvialen Menschen." *Kosmos (Gesellaschaft der Naturfreunde)* 9 (1912), pp. 270–74.

Bell, Clive. *Art*. New York: Frederick Stokes, 1914.

Belloc, Auguste. "L'avenir de la photographie," *Revue photographique* 3 (August 1858).

Benjamin, Walter. "Zur Ästhetik," fr 98 (1936), "Die Erkenntnis, daß die erste Materie. . . ." In *Fragmente vermischten Inhalts: Autobiographische Schriften*. Vol. 6 of *Gesammelte Schriften*. Ed. Rolf Tiedemann and Hermann Schweppenhaüser. 7 vols in 14. Frankfurt am Main: Suhrkamp, 1972–1989, pp. 111–29.

———. "N [On the Theory of Knowledge, Theory of Progress]." In *The Arcades Project*. Trans. Howard Eiland and Kevin McLaughlin. Cambridge, MA: Belknap Press of Harvard University Press, 1999, pp. 456–88.

———. "Surrealism: The Last Snapshot of the European Intelligentsia" (1929). Trans. Edmond Jephcott. In *Walter Benjamin: Selected Writings, Volume 2: 1927–1934*. Ed. Michael W. Jennings, Howard Eiland, and Gary Smith. Trans. Rodney Livingstone et al. Cambridge, MA: Belknap Press of Harvard University Press, 1999, pp. 207–21.

———. "Theories of German Fascism: On the Collection of Essays War and Warrior, Edited by Ernst Jünger." Trans. Jerolf Wikoff. *New German Critique* 17 (Spring 1979), pp. 120–28.

———. "The Work of Art in the Age of Its Technological Reproducibility." In *The Work of Art in the Age of Its Technological Reproducibility, and Other Writings on Media*. Ed. Michael W. Jennings, Brigid Doherty, and Thomas Y. Levin. Trans. Edmund Jephcott, et al. Cambridge, MA: Belknap Press of Harvard University Press, 2008.

———. "The Work of Art in the Age of Mechanical Reproduction." In *Illuminations*. Ed. Hannah Arendt. Trans. Harry Zohn. New York: Schocken Books, 1969.

Bergson, Henri. *Matter and Memory*. Trans. N. M. Paul and W. S. Palmer. New York: Zone Books, 1990.

———.*The Two Sources of Morality and Religion*. Trans. R. Ashley Audra and Cloudesley Brereton, with W. Horsfall Carter. London: Macmillan, 1935.

Biran, Maine de. "Ancillon: Notes sur l'essai sur le scepticisme." In *Oeuvres XI–3: Commentaires Sur Les Philosophies Du XIXe Siecle*. Paris, Vrin, 1990.

Birembaut, Arthur. "Fontenelle et la géologie." *Revue d'histoire des sciences et de leurs applications* 10.4 (1957), pp. 360–74.

Birtwistle, Graham. *Living Art: Asger Jorn's Comprehensive Theory of Art between Helhesten and Cobra, 1946–1949*. Utrecht: Reflex, 1986.

Blanckaert, Claude. "Les bases de la civilisation: Lectures de *L'Homme primitif* de Louis Figuier (1870)." *Bulletin de la société préhistorique française* 90.1 (1990), pp. 31–49.

———. "Chrono-logiques: Le tournant historiciste des sciences humaines." In Arnaud Hurel and Noël Coye, eds., *Dans l'épaisseur du temps: Archéologues et géologues inventent la préhistoire*. Paris: Publications scientifiques du Muséum national d'histoire naturelle, 2011, pp. 53–95.

———. "Nommer le *Préhistorique* au XIXe siècle: Linguistique et transferts lexicaux." *Organon* 49 (2017), pp. 57–103.

———. "Pour une paléontologie de l'histoire. L'ethnologie anglaise à l'âge romantique." In "Les sciences des causes passées," ed. Gabriel Gohau and Stéphane Tirard. Special issue, *Cahiers François Viète* 9–10 (2005), pp. 119–34.

Bloch, Ernst. *Heritage of Our Times* (1935). Trans. Neville Plaice and Stephen Plaice. Cambridge: Polity, 1991.

Blumenberg, Hans. *L'imitation de la nature et autres écrits esthétiques*. Trans. Marc Delaunay and Isabelle Kalinowski. Paris: Hermann, 2010.

———. *Paradigms for a Metaphorology*. Trans. Robert Savage. Ithaca: Cornell University Press, 2010.

Bogner, Dieter, and Peter Noever. *Frederick J. Kiesler: Endless Space*. Stuttgart: Hatje Cantz Publishers, 2001.

Bois, Yve-Alain. "L'aveuglement." In Isabelle Monod-Fontaine et Dominique Fourcade, eds., *Henri Matisse, 1904–1917*. Exh. cat. Paris: Centre Georges Pompidou, 1993.

———. "Kahnweiler's Lesson." *Representations* 18 (1987), pp. 33–68.

———. "On Matisse: The Blinding. For Leo Steinberg." Trans. Greg Sims. *October* 68 (Spring 1994), pp. 60–121.

———, and Rosalind Krauss. *L'informe: Mode d'emploi*. Paris: Centre Pompidou, 1996.

Boitard, Pierre. *Paris avant les hommes: L'homme fossile, etc.: Histoire naturelle du globe terrestre*. Paris: Passard, 1861.

Bon, François. *Préhistoire: La fabrique de l'homme*. Paris: Seuil, 2009.

Borges, Jorge Luis. "Pascal's Sphere." In Jorge Luis Borges, *Selected Non-Fictions*. Ed. Eliot Weinberger. Trans. Esther Allen, Suzanne Jill Levine, and Eliot Weinberger. New York: Viking, 1999, pp. 351–53.

Boucher de Perthes, Jacques. *Antiquités celtiques et antédiluviennes: Mémoire sur l'industrie primitive et les arts à leur origine*, 3 vols. Paris: Treuttel et Wurtz, Derchen Dumoulin et Didron, 1847.

———. *De l'homme antédiluvien et de ses oeuvres*. Paris: Jung-Treuttel, Derache, Dumoulin, 1860.

Boulanger, Nicolas-Antoine. S.v. "Déluge." *Encyclopédie, ou dictionnaire raisonné des sciences, des arts et des métiers*. Neuchâtel, 1751–1772.

Branzi, Andrea, and Kenya Hara. *Neo-Prehistory — 100 Verbs Neo Preistoria — 100 Verbi* / 新先史時代—*100*の動詞. Exh. cat. Zurich: Lars Müller, 2016.

Brassaï [Gyula Halász]. *Conversations with Picasso*. Trans. Jane Marie Todd. Chicago: University of Chicago Press, 1999.

——. "Du mur des cavernes au mur d'usine." *Minotaure* 3–4 (December 1933), pp. 6–7.

——. *Graffiti*. Paris: Flammarion, 2016.

Braudel, Fernand, "Histoire et sciences sociales: La longue durée." *Les Annales* 13.4 (October 1958). Reprinted in in *Réseaux* 27 (1987), pp. 7–37.

——. *L'homme avant l'écriture*. Ed. André Varagnac. Paris: A. Collin, 1959.

——. *The Mediterranean and the Mediterranean World in the Age of Philip II*. Trans. Siân Reynolds. Berkeley: University of Califonia Press, 1995.

——, ed. *La Méditerranée*, vol. 1, *L'espace et l'histoire*. Paris: Arts et métiers graphiques, 1977.

——. *Memory and the Mediterranean*. Ed. Roselyne de Ayala and Paule Braudel. Trans. Siân Reynolds. 1968; New York: Knopf, 2001. Bredekamp, Horst. "Höhlenausgänge." In Hermann Parzinger, Stefan Aue, and Günter Stock, eds., *Artefakte: Wissen ist Kunst — Kunst ist Wissen*. Bielefeld: Transcript, 2014, pp. 37–56.

——. "Der Muschelmench: Vom endlosen Anfang der Bilder." In Wolfgang Hogrebe, ed., *Transzendenzen des Realen*. Göttingen: V. & R. Unipress, pp. 13–74.

——. "

——. "Prekäre Vorbilder: Fossilien." In Sandra Abend and Hans Körner, eds. *Vor-bilder: Ikonen der Kulturgeschichte. Vom Faustkeil über Botticellis Venus bis John Wayne*. Munich: Morisel, 2015, pp. 11–25.

——. "Les sorties de la caverne: Nouvelles découvertes et résultats de la paléontologie." In "Préhistoire/Modernité," ed. Rémi Labrusse and Maria Stavrinaki. Special issue, *Cahiers du Musée National d'art moderne* 126 (Winter 2013–2014), pp. 15–23.

Breuil, Henri. "L'évolution de la peinture et de la gravure sur murailles dans les cavernes ornées de l'âge du Renne." In *Congrès préhistorique de France*. Vol. 1, session of Périgueux (1905). Le Mans: Monnoyer, 1906, pp. 107–10.

—— "Lascaux." *Bulletin de la Société préhistorique de France* 47.6–8 (1950), pp. 355–63.

——. "Les origines de l'art." *Journal de psychologie normale et pathologique* 22.4 (1925), pp. 289–96.

——. "Les origines de l'art décoratif." *Journal de psychologie normale et pathologique* 23.1–3 (1926), pp. 364–75.

——. *Les peintures rupestres schématiques de la Péninsule ibérique*. 4 vols. Paris: Imprimerie de Lagny, 1933–1935.

———. "South African Races in the Rock Paintings." In Alex Du Toit, ed., *Robert Broom Commemorative Volume*. Cape Town, Royal Society of South Africa, 1948.

———. *Quatre cents siècles d'art pariétal*. Montignac: Centre d'études et de documentation préhistoriques, 1952.

———. "The White Lady of the Brandberg: Her Companions and Her Guards." *South African Archaeological Bulletin* 3.9 (1948), pp. 1–13.

———, and Émile Cartailhac. *The Cave of Altamira at Santillana del Mar*. Madrid: Tipografia de Archivos, 1935.

———, and Émile Cartailhac. *La caverne d'Altamira à Santillane près Santander (Espagne), planches et figures par l'abbé H. Breuil*. Monaco: Imprimerie de Monaco, 1906.

Buckland, William. *Geology and Mineralogy Considered with Reference to Natural Theology*. 2 vols. London: William Pickering, 1836.

Buffon, Georges Louis Leclerc, comte de. *The Epochs of Nature*. Ed. and trans Jan Zalasiewicz, Anne-Sophie Milon, and Mateusz Zalasiewicz. Chicago: University of Chicago Press, 2018.

Burgess, Gelett. "The Wild Men of Paris." *Architectural Record*, May 5, 1910, pp. 400–414.

Bush, Karia, Philippe Dagen, and Anne Hauzer, eds., *Vénus et Caïn: Figures de la préhistoire 1830–1930*. Paris: Réunion des musées nationaux / Bordeaux: Musée d'Aquitaine, 2003.

Butler, Samuel. "Darwin among the Machines" [To the Editor of *The Press*, Christchurch, New Zealand, 13 June, 1863], New Zealand Electronic Text Collection, http://nzetc.victoria.ac.nz/tm/scholarly/tei-ButFir-t1-g1-t1-g1-t4-body.html.

———. *Erewhon; or, Over the Range*. Northridge, CA: Aegypan, 2008.

Byron, Lord. *Cain, a Mystery* (1821). London: William Crofts, 1830.

Caillois, Roger. *Le mimétisme animal*. Paris: Hachette, 1963.

Calzada, César. *Arte prehistórico en la vanguardia artística de España*. Madrid: Catedra Ediciones, 2006.

Camfield, William A. *Max Ernst: Dada and the Dawn of Surrealism*. Munich: Prestel, 1993.

Canguilhem, Georges. "La décadence de l'idée de Progrès." *Revue de Métaphysique et de Morale* 92.4 (1987), pp. 437–54.

Capitan, Louis. *La caverne de Font-de-Gaume aux Eyzies Dordogne*. Monaco: Imprimerie de Monaco, 1910.

———. "Les figures peintes à l'époque paléolithique sur les parois de la grotte de Font-de-Gaume." *Comptes rendus des séances de l'Académie des inscriptions et belles-lettres* 47.2 (1903), pp. 117–29.

——. "Notice sur Paul Jamin." *Bulletins et mémoires de la Société d'anthropologie de Paris* 4, July 16, 1903, pp. 487–91.

——, and Henri Breuil. "Les grottes à parois gravées ou peintes à l'époque paléolithique." *Revue de l'école d'anthropologie de Paris* 10 (1901), pp. 321–25.

——, and Henri Breuil. "Origines de l'art: Les gravures sur les parois des grottes préhistoriques anciennes." *La Nature* 30.1503 (March 1902), pp. 226–30.

Carrieri, Raffaele. "Fontana ha toccato la luna." *Tempo*, February 19–26, 1949, p. 28.

Cartailhac, Émile. *L'âge de pierre dans les souvenirs et les superstitions populaires.* Paris: C. Reinwald, 1877.

——. "Les cavernes ornées de dessins, la grotte d'Altamira, Espagne, 'Mea culpa' d'un sceptique." *L'Anthropologie* 13 (1902), pp. 348–54.

——. *La France préhistorique d'après les sépultures et les monuments.* Paris: Alcan, 1889.

——, and Henri Breuil. "Dessins préhistoriques de la caverne de Niaux, dans les Pyrénées de l'Ariège." *Comptes rendus des séances de l'Academie des inscriptions et belles-lettres* 50.8 (1906), pp. 533–37.

——, and Henri Breuil. "Les peintures et gravures murales des cavernes pyrénéennes. I, Altamira à Santillana (Espagne)." *L'Anthropologie* 15 (1904), pp. 625–44.

——, and Henri Breuil. "Les peintures et gravures murales des cavernes pyrénéennes: II, Marsoulas, près Salies-du-Salat (Haute-Garonne)." *L'Anthropologie* 16 (1905), pp. 431–44.

Causey, Andrew. "Barbara Hepworth, Prehistory and the Cornish Landscape." *Sculpture Journal* 17.2 (2008), pp. 9–22.

——. *Paul Nash: Landscape and the Life of Objects.* Farnham: Lund Humphries, 2013.

Celant, Germano. *Lucio Fontana: Ambienti Spaziali. Architecture, Art, Environments.* Milan: Skira / New York: Gagosian, 2012.

Centlivres, Pierre, and Isabelle Girod. "George Montandon et le grand singe américain: L'invention de l'*Ameranthropoides loysi.*" *Gradhiva* 24 (1998), pp. 33–43.

Cézanne, Paul. *Cinquante-trois lettres.* Ed. Jean-Claude Lebensztejn. Paris: L'Échoppe, 2011.

——. *Conversations with Cézanne.* Ed. Michael Doran. Trans. Julie Lawrence Cochran. Berkeley: University of California Press, 2001.

——. *The Letters of Paul Cézanne.* Ed. and trans. Alex Danchev. Los Angeles: J. Paul Getty Museum, 2013.

Chakrabarty, Dipesh. "The Climate of History: Four Theses." *Critical Inquiry* 35 (Winter 2009), pp. 197–222.

——. "Humanities in the Anthropocene: The Crisis of an Enduring Kantian Fable." *New Literary History* 47.2–3 (Spring–Summer 2016), pp. 377–97.

———. "Postcolonial Studies and the Challenge of Climate Change." *New Literary History* 43.1 (Winter 2012), pp. 1–18.

Charleton, Walter, *Chorea gigantum, or, The Most Famous Antiquity of Great-Britan, Vulgarly Called Stone-Heng, Standing on Salisbury Plain, Restored to the Danes*. London: Henry Herringman, 1663.

Chastel, André. *Le grotesque*. Paris: Le Promeneur, 1991.

Chippindale, Christopher. "The Invention of Words for the Idea of 'Prehistory.'" *Proceedings of the Prehistoric Society* 54 (1988), pp. 303–14.

Chirico, Giorgio de. *L'art métaphysique*. Ed. Giovanni Lista. Paris: L'Échoppe, 1994. Chiron, Léopold. "La grotte Chabot, commune d'Aiguèze." *Publications de la Société linnéenne de Lyon* no. 8 (1898), pp. 96–97.

Clottes, Jean. "L'originalité de la grotte Chauvet-Pont-d'Arc, à Vallon-Pont-d'Arc (Ardèche)" (background note). *Comptes rendus des séances de l'Académie des Inscriptions et Belles-Lettres* 139.2 (1995), pp. 563–68.

Cohen, Claudine, and Jean-Jacques Hublin. *Boucher de Perthes: Les origines romantiques de la préhistoire*. Paris: Belin, 2017.

Collingwood, Robin G. "Human Nature and Human History." In *The Idea of History*. Oxford: Clarendon Press of Oxford University Press, 1946, pp. 205–31.

Colomina, Beatriz, and Mark Wigley. *Are We Human?: Notes on the Archaeology of Design*. Zurich: Lars Müller, 2016.

Condorcet, Nicolas. *Outlines of an Historical View of the Progress of the Human Mind: Being a Posthumous Work of the Late M. de Condorcet, Translated from the French*. London: J. Johnson, 1795.

Connelly, Frances. *The Sleep of Reason: Primitivism in Modern European Art and Aesthetics, 1725–1907*. University Park: Pennsylvania State University Press, 1995.

Conze, Alexander. "On the Origin of the Visual Arts." Lecture on July 30, 1896. Trans. Karl Johns. *Journal of Art Historiography* 7 (December 2012), pp. 3–11.

Cournot, Antoine Augustin. *Considérations sur la marche des idées et des événements dans les Temps modernes*, 2 vols. Paris: Librairie Hachette, 1872.

Cowling, Elizabeth. *Picasso: Style and Meaning*. London: Phaidon, 2002.

Cras, Sophie. *The Artist as Economist: Art and Capitalism in the 1960s*. Trans. Malcolm DeBevoise. New Haven: Yale University Press, 2019.

Crevel, René. "L'enfance de l'art." *Minotaure* 1 (1933).

Cuvier, Georges. "Discours préliminaire." In *Recherches sur les ossemens fossiles de quadrupèdes, ou l'on rétablit les caractères de plusieurs espèces d'animaux que les révolutions du globe paroissent avoir détruites.* Paris: Deterville, 1812, pp. 1–116. Published separately in revised form as *Discours sur les révolutions de la surface du globe et sur les changemens qu'elles ont produits dans le règne animal.* Paris: G. Dufour et E. d'Ocagne, 1825.

Damisch, Hubert, and Jean Dubuffet. "Dubuffet, un mémoire, 1985–2014." In Hubert Damisch and Jean Dubuffet, *Entrée en matière, Correspondance 1961–1985, Textes 1961–2014.* Ed. Sophie Berrebi. Zurich: JRP / Ringier / Paris:Lectures Maison Rouge, 2016.

Daniel, Glyn. *The Idea of Prehistory.* Cleveland: World Publishing, 1963.

Darwin, Charles. "Darwin Correspondence Project," University of Cambridge: https://www.darwinproject.ac.uk/letter/?docId=letters/DCP-LETT-250.xml.

———. *On the Origin of Species.* New York: D. Appleton, 1861.

Davis, Whitney. "The First Date Painting: On Kawara at Altamira." In Jeffrey Weiss, ed., *On Kawara — Silence.* New York: Guggenheim, 2015, pp. 179–89.

Dawn, Virginia. Interview with Charles Stuckey. Oral history, 2010–2011. Archives of American Art, Smithsonian, Washington, DC.

De Chassey, Éric, and Sylvie Ramond, eds. *1945–1949: Repartir à zéro, comme si la peinture n'avait jamais existé.* Exh. cat., Musée des beaux-arts de Lyon. Paris: Hazan, 2008.

De Landa, Manuel. *A Thousand Years of Nonlinear History.* New York: Swerve, 2000.

De Maistre, Joseph. *Les soirées de Saint-Petersbourg* (second evening). Paris: Éditions du Sandre, 2006.

De Man, Henri. *Vermassung und Kukturverfall.* Munich: Lehnen, 1951.

De Mortillet, Gabriel. *Le préhistorique: Antiquité de l'homme.* Paris: C. Reinwald, 1883.

De Nadaillac, Jean-François. *Les premiers hommes et les temps préhistoriques.* Vol. 1. Paris: Éditions G. Masson, 1881.

De Quatrefages, Jean-Louis Armand. *Hommes fossiles et hommes sauvages: Études d'anthropologie.* Paris: J.-B. Baillière, 1884.

De Sautuola, Marcelino Sanz. *Breves Apuntes sobre algunos objetos prehistóricos de la Provincia de Santander.* Santander: Telesforo Martínez, 1880.

De Simone, Christina. *Proférations! Poésie en action à Paris (1946–1969).* Dijon: Les presses du réel, 2018.

Dean, Dennis. *Romantic Landscapes: Geology and Its Critical Influence in Britain, 1765–1835.* Ann Arbor: Scholars' Facsimiles & Reprints, 2000.

———. "'Through Science to Despair': Geology and the Victorians." *Annals of the New York Academy of Science* (1981), pp. 111–36.

Delporte, Henri. *Piette: Pionnier de la préhistoire.* Paris: Picard, 1987.

Deonna, Waldemar. *L'archéologie, sa valeur, ses méthodes.* 3 vols. Paris: Librairie Renouard-Laurens, 1912.

———. "Futuristes d'autrefois." *Revue d'ethnographie et de sociologie* (1912), pp. 298–301.

———. *Les lois et les rythmes dans l'art.* Paris: Ernest Flammarion, 1914.

Derenthal, Ludger. "Mitteilungen über Flugzeuge, Engel und den Weltkrieg: Zu den Photocollagen der Dadazeit von Max Ernst." *Konstruktionen der Moderne: Im Blickfeld. Jahrbuch der Hamburger Kunsthalle.* Hamburg, 1994, pp. 41–60.

Derrida, Jacques. *The Animal That Therefore I Am.* Ed. Marie-Louise Mallet. Trans. David Wills. New York: Fordham University Press, 2008.

———. *Edmund Husserl's "Origin of Geometry": An Introduction.* Trans. John P. Leavy, Jr. Lincoln: University of Nebraska Press, 1989.

———. *Of Grammatology.* Trans. Gayatri Chakravorty Spivak. Corrected edition. Baltimore: Johns Hopkins University Press, 1998.

———. "Plato's Pharmacy" (1968). In Jacques Derrida, *Dissemination.* Trans. Barbara Johnson. Chicago: University of Chicago Press, 1981, pp. 61–171.

Descartes, René, *The Passions of the Soul* (1649). Trans. Stephen Voss. Indianapolis: Hackett, 1989.

Diderot, Denis. *Pensées sur l'interprétation de la nature* (1754). In vol. 9 of Denis Diderot, *Oeuvres complètes.* Ed. Herbert Dieckmann et al. 25 vols. Paris: Hermann, 1975–2004, pp. 25–112.

———. "Le salon de 1767, à propos d'un tableau de Hubert Robert, aujourd'hui perdu (*Grande galerie éclairée du fond,* 1767)." In *Salon de 1767. Salon de 1769: Beaux-arts III.* Ed. Else Marie Bukdahl, Michel Delon, and Annette Lorenceau. Vol. 16 of *Oeuvres complètes,* pp. 174–237.

Didi-Huberman, Georges. *La ressemblance informe ou le gai savoir visuel selon Georges Bataille.* Paris: Macula, 1995.

Dilthey, Wilhelm. *The Formation of the Historical World in the Human Sciences.* Ed. Rudolf A. Makkreel and Frithjof Rodi. Princeton: Princeton University Press, 2002.

Dombrowski, André. *Cézanne, Murder, and Modern Life.* Berkeley: University of California Press, 2012.

———. "Modernism and Extremism: The Early Work of Paul Cézanne (1865–1875)." PhD diss., University of California Berkeley, 2006.

Dryansky, Larisa. "Paléofuturisme. Robert Smithson entre préhistoire et Posthistoire." In "Préhistoire/Modernité," ed. Rémi Labrusse and Maria Stavrinaki. Special issue, *Les Cahiers du Musée national d'art moderne* 126 (Winter 2013–2014), pp. 72–81.

Dubuffet, Jean. *L'homme du commun à l'ouvrage*. Paris: Gallimard, 1991.

———. *Prospectus et tous écrits suivants*. 4 vols. Ed. Hubert Damisch. Paris: Gallimard, 1967–1995.

———. and Jean Paulhan. *Correspondance 1944–1968*. Eds. Julien Dieudonné and Mairanne Jacobi. Paris: Gallimard, 2003.

Ehrenzweig, Anton. *The Hidden Order of Art: A Study in the Psychology of Artistic Imagination*. Berkeley: University of California Press, 1976.

———. *L'ordre caché de l'art*. Paris: Gallimard, 1982.

———. "The Unconscious Meaning of Primitive and Modern Art." Lecture, September 1949. Tate Gallery, ICA archives, TGA 955/1/7/12.

Einstein, Carl. *Georges Braque*. Trans. M. E. Zipruth. Paris: Éditions. des Chroniques du jour, 1934.

———. "Joan Miró (papiers collés à la galerie Pierre)." *Documents* 2.4 (1930), pp. 241–43.

———. "Wir wollen heute Abend über . . . die Grieche der Latinate." Lecture, Carl Einstein Archiv, Akademie der Künste, Berlin, no. 315.

Eliot, T. S. "Tradition and the Individual Talent" (1919). In *Selected Essays, New Edition*. New York: Harcourt, Brace & World, 1964, pp. 3–11.

Ernst, Max. *Écritures*. Paris: Gallimard, 1970.

Evans, John. *The Ancient Stone Implements, Weapons, and Ornaments of Great Britain*. London: Longmans, Greens, 1897.

———. *The Coins of the Ancient Britons*. London: B. Quaritch, 1864.

Fabian, Johannes. *Bataille à Lascaux: Comment l'art préhistorique apparut aux enfants*. Paris: L'Échoppe, 2014.

———. *Time and the Other: How Anthropology Makes Its Object*. New York: Columbia University Press, 1983.

Fabre, Daniel, ed. "Arts de l'enfance, enfances de l'art." Special issue, *Gradhiva* 9 (2009).

———. *Bataille à Lascaux: Comment l'art préhistorique apparut aux enfants*. Paris: L'Échoppe, 2014.

Fanés, Fèlix. *Pintura, collage, cultura de masas: Joan Miró*. Madrid: Alianza Editorial, 2007.

Faure, Élie. *Histoire de l'art*. Vol. 1. *L'esprit des formes*. Paris: Denoël, 1992.

Febvre, Lucien. *Combats pour l'histoire* (1952). Paris: Armand Colin, 1992.

Ferenczi, Sandor. *Thalassa: A Theory of Genitality*. Trans. Henry Alden Bunker. Albany: Psychoanalytic Quarterly, 1938.

Figuier, Louis. *L'homme primitif*. Illustrated by Émile Bayard and Delahaye. Paris: L. Hachette, 1870.

Fil, Sarah. "Paul Nash, Surrealism and Prehistoric Dorset." In Emma Chambers, ed., *Paul Nash*. London, Tate Gallery, 2016, pp. 46–187.

Flam, Jack. *Matisse: The Man and His Art, 1869–1918*. Ithaca: Cornell University Press, 1986.

Flammarion, Camille. *Le monde avant la création des hommes: Origines de la terre, origines de la vie, origines de l'humanité*. Paris: C. Marpon et E. Flammarion, 1886.

Focillon, Henri. Introduction to *Art populaire: Travaux artistiques et scientifiques du 1er congrès international des arts populaires, Prague, MDCCCCXXVIII*. 2 vols. Paris: Éditions Duchartre, 1931, pp. xii–xiii.

———. *Les pierres de France*. Paris: Laurens, 1919.

———. "Préhistoire et Moyen Âge." *Dumbarton Oaks Papers* 1 (November 1940), pp. 1–23.

Fontana, Lucio. *Écrits de Lucio Fontana (Manifestes, textes, entretiens)*. Ed. Valérie Da Costa. Dijon: Les presses du réel, 2013.

Foucault, Michel. *The Order of Things: An Archaeology of the Human Sciences*. London: Routledge, 2005.

Fraenkel, Béatrice. "L'invention de l'art pariétal préhistorique: Histoire d'une expérience visuelle." *Gradhiva* 6 (2007), pp. 18–31.

Frazer, James. *The Golden Bough*. New York: Macmillan, 1894.

Fressoz, Jean-Baptiste, and Fabien Locher. "L'agir humain sur le climat et la naissance de la climatologie historique, XVIIe–XVIIIe siècles." *Revue d'histoire moderne et contemporaine* 62.1 (2015), pp. 48–78.

———, and Fabien Locher. "Modernity's Frail Climate: A Climate History of Environmental Reflexivity." *Critical Inquiry* 38.3 (Spring 2012), pp. 589–98.

———, and Muriel Louâpre. "L'ère anthropocène: Pour en finir avec la fin de l'histoire. Entretien avec Jean-Baptiste Fressoz." *Écrire l'histoire* 15 (2015), pp. 53–60.

Freud, Sigmund. *Beyond the Pleasure Principle* (1920). Ed. and trans. James Strachey. New York: W. W. Norton, 1961.

———. "Findings, Ideas, Problems" (1938). In vol. 23 of *The Standard Edition of the Complete Psychological Works of Sigmund Freud*. Ed. and trans. James Strachey. London: Hogarth, 1964, pp. 299–300.

———. *The Interpretation of Dreams* (1900). Trans. James Strachey. New York: Basic Books, 1965.

———. "A Note upon the 'Mystic Writing Pad'" (1925). In vol. 19 of *The Standard Edition of the Complete Psychological Works of Sigmund Freud*, pp. 227–32.

———. *Totem and Taboo* (1913). Trans. A. A. Brill. New York: Vintage, 1946.

Frisch, Max. *Man in the Holocene*. Trans. Geoffrey Skelten. Champaign: Dalkey Archive Press, 2007.

Frobenius, Leo. *La civilisation africaine*. Paris: Le Rocher, 1952.

———. *Modern Plastic Art: Elements of Reality, Volume and Disintegration*. Zurich: Girsberger, 1937.

———. *Der Ursprung der afrikanischen Kultur*. Berlin: Borntrager, 1898.

———, and Douglas Claughton Fox, eds. *Prehistoric Rock Pictures in Europe and Africa*. Exh. cat. New York: Museum of Modern Art, 1937; Arno Press, 1972.

Fry, Roger. "Bushman Paintings." *Burlington Magazine for Connoisseurs* 16.84 (1910), pp. 334–38.

———. "Children's Drawings" (1917). In Christopher Reed, ed., *A Roger Fry Reader*. Chicago: University of Chicago Press, 1996, pp. 266–70.

Fuchs, Anneli. *Asger Jorn and Art History*. Hafnia: Copenhagen Papers in the History of Art / University of Copenhagen, 1985.

Gamble, Clive, and Robert Kruszynski. "John Evans, Joseph Prestwich and the Stone That Shattered the Time Barrier." *Antiquity* 83 (2009), pp. 461–75.

Gaudant, Jean. "Aux sources de la Préhistoire: Les céraunies, ces pierres étranges supposées tombées du ciel." *Travaux du Comité français d'histoire de la géologie* 21 (2007), pp. 97–112.

Gaudier-Brzeska, Henri. "Vortex. Gaudier Brzeska." *Blast* 1 (1914), pp. 155–57.

Geertz, Clifford. "The Impact of the Concept of Culture on the Concept of Man." In Clifford Geertz, *The Interpretation of Cultures: Selected Essays*. New York: Basic Books, 1973, pp. 33–54.

Gehlen, Arnold. "Ende der Geschichte?" (1973). In Arnold Gehelen, *Einblicke*. Frankfurt: Klostermann, 1975.

———. *Man: His Nature and Place in the World*. Trans. Clare McMillan and Karl Pillemer. New York: Columbia University Press, 1988.

———. *Der Mensch: Seine Natur und seine Stellung in der Welt*. Berlin: Junker und Dünnhaupt, 1940.

———. *Die Seele im Technischen Zeitalter und andere sozialpsychologische, soziologische und kulturanalytische Schriften*. Frankfurt: Vittorio Klostermann, 1982.

Geiser, Reto. "Höhlenexpeditionen mit Hugo Paul Herdeg." In Werner Oechslin and Herbor Harbusch, eds., *Sigfried Giedion und Bildinszenierungen der Moderne: Die Fotografie*. Zurich: ZTA, 2010, pp. 278–81

George, Waldemar. "Miró et le miracle ressuscité." *Centaure* 8 (May 1929), pp. 201–204.

Geroulanos, Stefanos. *An Atheism That Is Not Humanist Emerges in French Thought*. Stanford: Stanford University Press, 2010.

Giedion, Sigfried. *The Eternal Present: The Beginnings of Art.* Washington, DC: National Gallery of Art, 1962.

Giedion-Welcker, Carola. "Besuch in Carnac" (1934). In Carola Giedion-Welcker, *Schriften 1926–1971: Stationen zu einem Zeitbild.* Ed. Reinhold Hohl. Schauberg: M. DuMont, 1973, pp. 11–13.

———. *Modern Plastic Art: Elements of Reality, Volume and Disintegration.* Trans. P. Morton Shand. Zurich: Girsberger, 1937.

Gilibert, J. E. *Abrégé du système de la nature de Linné ou Des quadrupèdes et cétacés.* Lyon: Materon, 1802.

Gindhart, Maria. "Allegorizing Aryanism: Fernand Cormon's *The Human Races*," *Aurora: The Journal of the History of Art* 9 (2008), pp. 74–100.

———. "Fleshing Out the Museum: Fernand Cormon's Painting Cycle for the New Galleries of Comparative Anatomy, Paleontology, and Anthropology." *Nineteenth Century Art World-Wide* 7.2 (Autumn 2008), http://www.19thc-artworldwide.org/autumn08/92-fleshing-out-the-museum-fernand-cormons-painting-cycle-for-the-new-galleries-of-comparative-anatomy-paleontology-and-anthropology.

Goldman, Daniel. "Lost Paper Shows Freud's Effort to Link Analysis and Evolution." *New York Times*, February 10, 1987.

Gombrich, Ernst. *The Story of Art.* London: Phaidon Press, 1950.

Gould, Stephen Jay. *Ontogeny and Phylogeny.* Cambridge, MA: Belknap Press of Harvard University Press, 1977.

———. *Time's Arrow, Time's Cycle: Myth and Metaphor in the Discovery of Geological Time.* London: Penguin, 1988.

Goulven, Laurent. "Edouard Lartet (1801–1871) et la paléontologie humaine." *Bulletin de la Société préhistorique française* 90.1 (1993), pp. 22–30.

Grayson, Donald. *The Establishment of Human Antiquity.* New York: Academic Press, 1983.

Grenier, Catherine, ed. *Robert Morris 1961–1994: Catalogue du MNAM.* Paris: Centre Pompidou, 1995.

Grevsmühl, Sebastian Vincent. *La Terre vue d'en haut: L'invention de l'environnement global.* Paris: Seuil, 2014.

Groenen, Marc. *Leroi-Gourhan: Essence et contingence dans la destinée humaine.* Louvain: Le Boeck Supérieur, 1996.

———. *Pour une histoire de la préhistoire: Le paléolithique.* Grenoble: Jérôme Million, 1994.

Groos, Karl. *The Play of Animals.* Trans. James Mark Baldwin. New York: D. Appleton, 1898.

Grosse, Ernst. *Beginnings of Art.* New York: D. Appleton, 1897.

Grossman, Wendy A. *Man Ray, African Art, and the Modernist Lens*. Washington, DC: International Art and Artists, 2009.

Grosz, George, and Wieland Herzfelde. *Art Is in Danger*. In Lucy Lippard, ed., *Dadas on Art*. Englewood Cliffs: Prentice-Hall, 1971.

Guéguen, Pierre. Untitled text, *Cahiers d'art* 9.1–4 (1934), p. 46.

Haddon, Alfred Cort. *Evolution in Art as Illustrated by the Life-History of Designs*. London: Walter Scott Publishing, 1895.

Haeckel, Ernst. *Generelle Morphologie der Organismen*. Berlin: Reimer, 1866.

Hamy, Ernest-Théodore. *Précis de la paléontologie humaine*. Paris: J.-B. Ballière et Fils, 1870.

Harlaut, Yann. "La Cathédrale de Reims du 4 septembre 1914 au 10 juillet 1938: Idéologies, controverses et pragmatisme." PhD diss., Université de Reims, 2006.

Hauser, Arnold. *Social History of Art*. 4 vols. London: Routledge, 1999.

Hawkes, Jacquetta. *A Land* (1949). New York: Random House, 1967.

———. *The First Great Civilizations: Life in Mesopotamia, the Indus Valley, and Egypt*. New York: Knopf, 1980.

Henriksen, Niels. "Prehistoric Techniques for Modern Painting: Asger Jorn's Archaeological Picture Books." In "Writing Prehistory," eds. Maria Stavrinaki and Sterfanos Geroulanos. Special issue, *Res: Anthropology and Aesthetics* 69–70 (Spring–Autumn 2018), pp. 189–204.

Hersey, John. *Hiroshima*. New York: Harmondsworth, 1946.

Hirschhorn, Thomas. Interview with Maria Stavrinaki. In "Prehistoire," eds. Chiara Di Stefano, Rémi Labrusse, and Maria Stavrinaki. Special issue, *Les Cahiers du musée national d'art moderne* 147 (May 2019), pp. 85–89.

Hirn, Yrjö. *The Origins of Art: A Psychological and Sociological Inquiry*. London: Macmillan, 1900.

Hitchcock, Edward. *Religion of Geology and Its Connected Sciences*. Boston: Philips Sampson, 1857.

Hoernes, Moritz. *Urgeschichte der bildenden Kunst in Europe von den Anfängen bis um 500 vor Christi*. Vienna: A. Schroll, 1925.

Hollier, Denis. *Les dépossédés*. Paris: Minuit, 1993.

———. *La prise de la concorde: Essais sur Georges Bataille*. Paris: Gallimard, 1974.

Hooke, Robert. *Discourse of Earthquakes*. In *The Posthumous Works of Robert Hooke*. London: Smith and Walford, 1705.

———. *Micrographia: Some Physiological Descriptions of Minute Bodies Made by Magnifying Glasses with Observations and Inquiries Thereupon*. London: John Martyn and James Allestry, 1665.

Hugo, Victor. *Notre-Dame de Paris, vol. 2.* Book 5, chap. 2. In vol. 4 of Victor Hugo, *Oeuvres complètes.* 14 vols. Paris: J. Hetzel, 1880, pp. 136–41.

Hulme, Thomas Ernst. *Essays on Humanism and the Philosophy of Art.* Ed. Herbert Read. London: Routledge & Kegan Paul, 1924.

Hurel, Arnaud. *L'Abbé Breuil: Un préhistorien dans le siècle.* Paris: CNRS Éditions, 2011.

———. "Paul Tournal, les grottes de Bize et la question de la haute antiquité de l'homme." In Arnaud Hurel and Noël Coye, eds, *Dans l'épaisseur du temps: Archéologues et géologues inventent la préhistoire.* Paris: Museum National d'Histoire Naturelle, 2011, pp. 150–211.

Hutton, James. *Theory of the Earth, with Proofs and Illustrations.* Edinburgh, 1795.

Huyghe, Pierre. Interview with Maria Stavrinaki. In "Préhistoire," ed. Chiara Di Stefano, Rémi Labrusse, and Maria Stavrinaki. Special issue, *Les Cahiers du musée national d'art moderne* 147 (May 2019), pp. 93–96.

Huxley, Thomas H. Introduction to *La Place de l'homme dans la nature.* Trans. Eugène Dally and Henry de Varigny. Paris: J.-B. Baillière et Fils, 1891.

———. *Man's Place in Nature: And a Supplementary Essay.* London: Watts, 1921.

ICA. "ICA: 40,000 Years of Modern Art Exhibition." Tate Gallery, London, ICA Archives, TGA 955/1/12/10.

Ichac, Pierre. "La grotte à peintures de Montignac, en Dordogne." *L'Illustration* 5104, January 4, 1941, pp. 9–17.

Ingold, Tim. "Beyond Biology and Culture: The Meaning of Evolution in a Relational World." *Social Anthropology* 12.2 (2004), pp. 209–21.

———. "'People Like Us': The Concept of the Anatomically Modern Human." In Tim Ingold, *The Perception of the Environment: Essays on Livelihood, Dwelling and Skill.* London: Routledge, 2013, pp. 373–90.

Ivanoff, Hélène. "Exposer l'art préhistorique africain: Le Paris de Léo Frobenius au début des années 1930." In Jean-Louis Georget, Hélène Ivanoff, and Richard Kuba, eds., *Cercles culturels: Léo Frobenius (1873–1938) et ses contemporains / Kulturkreise: Leo Frobenius (1873–1938) und seine Zeitgenossen.* Berlin: Dietrich Reimer, 2015, pp. 267–86.

Jacob, Christian, ed. "Lieux de la carte, espace du savoir." Special issue, *Villa Gillet* (1996), pp. 67–94.

Jamin, Jules. "Le daguerréotype" In *L'Artiste* (1839). Reprinted in André Rouillé, *La photographie en France: Textes et controverse. Une anthologie, 1816–1871.* Paris: Macula, 1989, pp. 46–51.

Jaspers, Karl. *The Origin and Goal of History.* New Haven: Yale University Press, 1953.

Jonas, Hans. "*Homo pictor* and the Differentia of Man." *Social Research* 29.2 (Summer 1962), pp. 201–20.

Jorn, Asger. *Concerning Form / Pour la forme* (1957). Silkeborg: Museum Jorn, 2012.

———. *Discours aux pingouins et autres écrits.* Paris: Ensba, 2001.

Judet de La Combe, Pierre. *Les tragédies grecques sont-elles tragiques?: Théâtre et théorie.* Paris: Bayard, 2012.

Jullian, Camille. *Les origines historiques du sol français, leçon d'ouverture du cours d'histoire et d'antiquité nationales, faite au Collège de France, December 8, 1909.* Paris: Éditions de la Revue politique et littéraire et de la Revue scientifique, 1910.

———. "Plaidoyer pour la préhistoire." *Revue bleue* 8.24 (December 1907), pp. 737–44.

Jünger, Ernst. *An der Zeitmauer.* Stuttgart: Klett-Cotta, 2019.

———. *Le mur du temps.* Trans. Henri Thomas. Paris: Gallimard, 1994.

———. "Total Mobilization" (1920). Trans. Joel Golb and Richard Wolin. In Richard Wolin, ed., *The Heidegger Controversy: A Critical Reader.* Cambridge, MA: MIT Press, 1993, pp. 119–39.

Juritzky, Antonin. (Pseud. Juva.) *Prehistoric Man as an Artist.* N.p.: n.p., 1953.

Jussieu, Antoine de. *De l'origine et des usages de la pierre de foudre.* Paris: Mémoires de l'Académie Royale des Sciences, 1725.

Kahnweiler, Daniel-Henry. "L'Art nègre et le cubisme" (1945). In Daniel-Henry Kahnweiler, *Confessions esthétiques.* Paris: Gallimard, 1963, pp. 222–36.

Kandinsky, Wassily. "Réflexions sur l'art abstrait." *Cahiers d'art* 7–8 (1931), pp. 7–8.

Kant, Immanuel. *Anthropology from a Pragmatic Point of View.* Ed. and trans. Robert B. Loudon. Cambridge: Cambridge University Press, 2006.

———. *Critique of Judgment.* Trans. J. H. Bernard. London: Macmillan, 1914.

———. *Natural Science.* Ed. Eric Watkins. Trans. Olaf Reinhardt, Eric Watkins, Jeffrey B. Edwards, Martin Schoenfeld, and Lewis White Beck. Cambridge: Cambridge University Press, 2015.

Kehoe, Alice B. "The Invention of Prehistory." *Current Anthropology* 32.4 (August–October 1991), pp. 467–76.

Kiesler, Frederick. *Frederick Kiesler, 1890–1965: Visionary Architecture, Drawings and Models, Galaxies and Paintings, Sculpture.* Exh. cat. New York, André Emmerich Gallery, 1979.

Klee, Paul. *On Modern Art* (1924). Trans. Paul Findlay. London: Faber and Faber, 1954.

Kohl, Karl-Heinz, Richard Kuba, and Hélène Ivanoff, eds. *Kunst der Vorzeit: Felsbilder aus der Sammlung Leo Frobenius.* Berlin: Martin Gropius Bau, 2016.

———. *Kunst der Vorzeit: Texte zu den Felsbildern der Sammlung Leo Frobenius.* Frankfurt: Frobenius-Institut, 2016.

Kojève, Alexandre. *Introduction to the Reading of Hegel.* Assembled by Raymond Queneau. Ed. Allan Bloom. Trans. James H. Nichols, Jr. New York: Basic Books, 1969.

Koselleck, Reinhart. *Futures Past: On the Semantics of Historical Time.* Trans. Keith Tribe. New York: Columbia University Press, 2004.

Krauss, Rosalind. "Sculpture in the Expanded Field. In *The Originality of the Avant-Garde and Other Modernist Myths.* Cambridge, MA: MIT Press, 1985, pp. 276–90.

Krell, Jacob. "Genealogies of Technology and Prehistory in France: The 'Atomic Age.'" *Res: Anthropology and Aesthetics* 69–70 (Spring–Autumn 2018), pp. 158–71.

Kühn, Herbert. *Die Kunst der Primitiven.* Munich: Delphin, 1923.

———. *Die Malerei der Eiszeit.* Munich: Delphin, 1921.

Kurczynski, Karen. "Beyond Expressionism: Asger Jorn and the European Avant-Garde, 1941–1961." PhD diss., New York, Institute of Fine Arts, 2005.

Lafitau, Joseph-François. *Moeurs des sauvages américains comparées aux moeurs des premiers temps.* Paris: Saugrain l'aîné, 1724.

Lahuerta, Juan José. "Signs of Prehistory in the Artistic Economy of l'*Esprit nouveau.*" In "Writing Prehistory," ed. Maria Stavrinaki and Sterfanos Geroulanos. Special issue, *Res: Anthropology and Aesthetics* 69–70 (Spring–Autumn 2018), pp. 99–117.

Laming-Emperaire, Annette. *La signification de l'art rupestre paléolithique: Méthodes et applications* (1957). Paris: A. et J. Picard, 1962.

Lamprecht, Karl. Appendices to Siegfried Otto Levinstein, *Kinderzeichnungen bis zum 14. Lebensjahr, mit parallelen aus der Urgeschichte, Kulturgeschichte und Völkerkunde.* Leipzig: R. Voigtländer, 1905.

Landa, Manuel. *A Thousand Years of Nonlinear History.* New York: Swerve, 2000.

Lang, Andrew. "The Art of Savages." In Andrew Lang, *Custom and Myth.* New York: Harper & Brothers, 1885, pp. 276–304.

Langer, Wolfhart. "Verzeitlichungs- und Historisierungstendenzen in der frühen Geologie und Paläontologie." *Berichte zur Wissenschaftsgeschichte* 8 (1985), pp. 87–97.

Lartet, Édouard. "Nouvelles recherches sur la coexistence de l'homme et des grands mammifères fossiles." *Annales des sciences naturelles,* 4th series, 15. *Zoologie.* Paris: Victor Masson et Fils, 1861, pp. 177–253.

———, and Henry Christy. *Cavernes du Périgord: Objets gravés et sculptés des temps pré-historiques dans l'Europe occidentale.* Whitefish: Kessinger Legacy Reprints, 2010.

Latour, Bruno. *We Have Never Been Modern.* Trans. Catherine Porter. Cambridge, MA: Harvard University Press, 1993.

Laugel, Auguste. "L'homme primitif d'après les travaux de MM. Lyell et Huxley." *Revue des deux mondes*, 2nd series, no. 45 (May 1863), pp. 204–31.

Le Bon, Gustave. *L'homme et les sociétés: Leurs origines et leur histoire* (1881). Paris: Jean Michel Place, 1987.

Lebensztejn, Jean-Claude. "Persistance de la mémoire: Note sur la datation des confidences de Cézanne." In in Jean-Claude Lebensztejn, *Les couilles de Cézanne*. Paris: Séguier, 1995, pp. 38–96.

Leeb, Susanne. *Die Kunst der Anderen: "Weltkunst" und die anthropologische Konfiguration der Moderne*. Berlin: Polypen, 2015.

Leiris, Michel. "Graffiti abyssins." *Arts et Métiers graphiques* 44 (1934), pp. 56–57.

———. "Joan Miró," (1926), *The Little Review* 12.1 (1926). In Michel Leiris, *Écrits sur l'art*. Paris: CNRS Éditions, 2011, pp. 171–72.

———. *Journal 1922–1989*. Ed. Jean Jamin. Paris: Gallimard, 1992.

———. "Toiles récentes de Picasso." *Documents* 2.2 (1930), pp. 57–70.

Lemaire, Gérard-Georges, ed. *Wyndham Lewis et le vorticisme, Cahiers pour un temps*. Paris: Centre Georges Pompidou, 1982.

Leroi-Gourhan, André. *Les chasseurs de la préhistoire*. Paris: Éditions Métailié, 1983.

———. "La fonction des signes dans les sanctuaires paléolithiques " (pp. 307–21), "Le symbolisme des grands signes dans l'art pariétal paléolithique" (pp. 384–98), "Répartition et groupement des animaux dans l'art pariétal paléolithique" (pp. 515–28), *Bulletin de la société préhistorique française* 58.5–6 (1958).

———. *Les fouilles préhistoriques, techniques et méthodes*. Paris: Picard, 1950.

———. *Gesture and Speech*. Trans. Anna Bostock Berger. Cambridge, MA: MIT University Press, 1993.

———. *Préhistoire de l'art occidental*. Paris: Mazenod, 1965.

———. *Les religions de la préhistoire*. Paris: Presses Universitaires de France, 1964.

Lévi-Strauss, Claude. *Anthropologie structurale: Deux*. Paris: Plon, 1973.

———. "The Archaic Illusion." In Claude Lévi-Strauss, *The Elementary Structures of Kinship*. Trans. James Harle Bell, John Richard von Sturmer, and Rodney Needham. London, Eyre and Spottiswoode, 1969, pp. 84–97.

———. "Introduction à l'oeuvre de Marcel Mauss." In Marcel Mauss, *Sociologie et anthropologie*, 8th ed. Paris: Presses Universitaires de France, 1999, pp. ix–lii.

———. *The Savage Mind*. Chicago: University of Chicago Press, 1966.

———. *Tristes Tropiques*. Trans. John Weightman and Doreen Weightman. New York: Athaneum, 1975.

Levinstein, Siegfried Otto. *Kinderzeichnungen bis zum 14. Lebensjahr, mit parallelen aus der Urgeschichte, Kulturgeschichte und Völkerkunde.* Leipzig: R. Voigtländer, 1905, pp. x–xii.

Littré, Émile. "Études d'histoire primitive." *Revue des deux mondes* (1858), pp. 5–32.

Locke, John. *Second Treatise on Civil Government.* In *John Locke's Two Treatises of Government.* Ed. Peter Laslett. Cambridge: Cambridge University Press, 1963.

Long, Richard. *Selected Statements and Interviews.* Ed. Ben Tufnell. London: Haunch of Venison, 2009.

Lonzi, Carla. *Autoportrait.* Ed. by Giovanna Zapperi. Trans. M.-A. Maire-Vigueur. Zurich, JRP Ringier / Lectures Maison rouge, 2013.

Loriga, Sabina. Preface. In Reinhart Koselleck, *Le futur passé: Contribution à la sémantique des temps historiques.* 2nd. ed. Trans. Jochen Hoock and Marie-Claire Hoock. Paris: Éditions. EHESS, 2016, pp. 1–17.

Lubbock, John. *Pre-Historic Times as Illustrated by Ancient Remains and the Manners and Customs of Modern Savages.* 6th rev. ed. New York: D. Appleton, 1900.

Luquet, Georges-Henri. *L'art primitif.* Paris: Gaston Doin, 1930.

———. *L'art et la religion des hommes fossiles.* Paris: Masson, 1926.

———. *Le dessin d'un enfant: Étude psychologique.* Paris: Félix Alcan, 1913.

———. *Le dessin enfantin.* Paris: Félix Alcan, 1927.

Lucretius. *On the Nature of Things.* Trans. Martin Ferguson Smith. Indianapolis: Hackett, 2001.

Lucy, Martha. "Cormon's Cain and the Problem of the Prehistoric Body." *Oxford Art Journal* 25.2 (2002), pp. 107–26.

Lukács, Georg. *History and Class Consciousness (1923).* Trans. Rodney Livingstone. Cambridge, MA: MIT Press, 1971.

———. *Theory of the Novel.* Trans. Anna Bostock. London: Merlin Press, 1971.

Lütticken, Sven. "Returns of the Stone Age." *Texte zur Kunst* 102 (June 2016), pp. 147–52.

Lyell, Charles. *The Geological Evidences of the Antiquity of Man.* Charleston: BiblioBazaar, 2008.

———. *Life, Letters and Journals of Sir Charles, Lyell, Bart.,* 2 vols. Ed. Mrs. Lyell. London: John Murray, 1881.

———. *Principles of Geology: Being an Inquiry How Far the Former Changes of the Earth's Surface Are Referable to Causes Now in Operation.* 4 vols. London: John Murray, 1830–1833. Quoted from the 4th edition, 1835.

Macherel, Claude, and Daniel Fabre, eds. "Du Far West au Louvre. Le Musée indien de George Catlin." Specisal issue, *Gradhiva* 3, 2006.

Maldonado, Guitemie. *Le cercle et l'amibe: Le biomorphisme dans l'art des années 1930*. Paris: CTHS / Institut national d'histoire de l'art, 2006.

Malevich, Kazimir. "From Cubism and Futurism to Suprematism: The New Painterly Realism." In John E. Bowlt, ed. and trans. *Russian Art of the Avant-Garde*. New York: Thames and Hudson, 2017), pp. 116–35.

Malraux, André. *La tête d'obsidienne*. Paris: Gallimard, 1974.

Mantell, Gideon A. *The Medals of Creation; or, First Lessons in Geology, and in the Study of Organic Remains*. London: H. G. Bohn, 1844.

Marc, Franz. *Écrits et correspondances*. Ed. Maria Stavrinaki. Trans. Thomas De Kayser. Paris: Ecole Nationale Supérieure des Beaux-Arts, 2007.

Marshall, Nancy Rose. *City of Gold and Mud: Painting Victorian London*. New Haven: Yale University Press, 2012.

Marx, Karl. *Capital: A Critique of Political Economy*. Vol. 1. Moscow: Progress Publishers, 1887, https://www.marxists.org/archive/marx/works/download/pdf/Capital-Volume-I.pdf.

———. *The Eighteenth Brumaire of Louis Bonaparte*. Trans. Saul K. Padover. Marx/Engels Internet Archive, 2010, https://www.marxists.org/archive/marx/works/download/pdf/18th-Brumaire.pdf.

———. *The Poverty of Philosophy* (1847). Trans. Institute of Marxism Leninism. Moscow: Progress Publishers, 1955, https://www.marxists.org/archive/marx/works/1847/poverty-philosophy/cho1b.htm.

Marx, Roger. *L'art social*. Paris: E. Fasquelle, 1913.

Matisse, Henri. *Écrits et propos*. Ed. Dominique Fourcade. Paris: Hermann, 1972.

Maurer, Bruno. "*The Eternal Present I: The Beginnings of Art* — Grenzen der Fotografie." In Werner Oechslin and Gregor Harbusch, eds., *Sigfried Giedion und die Fotografie: Bildinszenierungen der Moderne*. Zurich: ZTA, 2010, pp. 288–91.

Mauss, Marcel. *Sociologie et Anthropologie*. Paris: PUF, 1950.

McLuhan, Marshall. Review of László Moholy-Nagy, *Vision in Motion* and of Sigfried Giedion, *Mechanization Takes Command*. *Hudson Review* 1.4 (Winter 1949), pp. 599–602.

———. *Understanding Media: The Extensions of Man*. Cambridge, MA: MIT Press, 1994.

McNeill, J. R., and Peter Engelke. *The Great Acceleration: An Environmental History of the Anthropocene since 1945*. Cambridge, MA: Belknap Press of Harvard University Press, 2016.

Melville, Herman. "Sketch Second: Two Sides of a Tortoise." *The Encantadas*. In *The Piazza Tales*. New York: Dix & Edwards, 1856, https://www.libertarianism.org/publications/essays/encantadas-two-sides-tortoise.

Mercati, Michele. *Michaelis Mercati Samminiatensis Metallotheca*. Ed. Giovanni Maria Lancisi. Rome: Salvioni, 1717.

Merjian, Ara H. *Giorgio de Chirico and the Metaphysical City: Nietzsche, Modernism, Paris*. New Haven: Yale University Press, 2014.

Meyer, Richard. *What Was Contemporary Art?* Cambridge, MA: MIT Press, 2013.

Michaud, Éric. "Autonomie et distraction." In Éric Michaud, *Histoire de l'art: Une discipline à ses frontières*. Paris: Hazan, 2005, pp. 13–47.

———. *The Barbarian Invasions: A Genealogy of the History of Art*. Trans. Nicholas Huckle. Cambridge, MA: MIT Press, 2019.

———. "*Déjà là*, mais encore à *venir*: Le temps de l'homme nouveau en Allemagne, 1918–1945." In Jean Clair, ed., *La fabrique de l'homme nouveau*. Ottawa: Musée National des Beaux-Arts du Canada.

Miller, Charlie F. B. "Archéologie de Picasso." In "Préhistoire/Modernité," ed. Rémi Labrusse and Maria Stavrinaki. Special issue, *Les Cahiers du Musée national d'art moderne* 126 (Winter 2013–2014), pp. 58–71.

Minturn, Kent Mitchell. "*Contre-histoire:* The Postwar Art and Writings of Jean Dubuffet." PhD diss., New York, Columbia University, 2007.

Mircan, Mihnea, and Vincent W. J. van Gerven Oei. *Allegory of the Cave Painting*. Antwerp: Mousse Publishing / Dijon: Les presses du réel, 2015.

Miró, Joan. *Écrits et entretiens*. Ed. Margit Rowell. Paris: Daniel Lelong, 1995.

———. "Grand cahier de Palma (1940–1941)." In vol 2 of Joan Miró, *Carnets catalans*. Ed. Gaëtan Picon. 2 vols. Geneva: Albert Skira, 1976.

Monnier, Alain, ed. *Nostalgie du Néolithique de Lausanne à Las Lomitas: Documents sur Alfred Métraux ethnologue*. Geneva: Labor et Fides, 2003.

Montandon, Georges. "Découverte d'un singe d'apparence anthropoïde en Amérique du Sud." *L'Anthropologie* (1929), pp. 137–41. (Session of the Institut Français d'Anthropologie, March 20, 1929.)

———. "Découverte d'un singe d'apparence anthropoïde en Amérique du Sud." *Journal de la société des Américanistes de Paris* 21 (1929), pp. 183–95.

Monod, Jean-Claude. "La patience de l'image: Éléments pour une localisation de la métaphorologie." Afterword to Hans Blumenberg, *Metaphorology: Paradigmes pour une métaphorologie*. Trans. Didier Gammelin, Paris: Vrin, 2006, pp. 171–95.

Moore, Henry. "Primitive Art" (1941). In Henry Moore, *Writings and Conversations*. Ed. Allan Wilkinson. Berkeley: University of California Press, 2002.

Moreau, Gustave. *Théorie et critique d'art*. Vol. 2 of *Écrits sur l'art*. Ed. Peter Cooke. 2 vols. Fontfroide: Fata Morgana, 2002.

Morel, Philippe. *Les grotesques: Les figures de l'imaginaire dans la peinture italienne de la fin de la Renaissance*. Paris: Flammarion, 1997.

Morgan, Lewis H. *Ancient Society; or, Researches in the Lines of Human Progress from Savagery through Barbarism to Civilization*. Calcutta: Booksellers and Publishers, 1944.

Morris, Robert. "Cézanne's Mountains." *Critical Inquiry* 24.3 (Spring 1998), pp. 814–29.

———. "Cinq Labyrinthes" (1993). In *Robert Morris: From Mnemosyne to Clio, the Mirror to the Labyrinth (1998–1999–2000)*. Exh. cat. Lyon, Musée d'Art Contemporain, Paris: Seuil / Milan: Skira, 2000, pp. 116–17.

———. *Continuous Project Altered Daily: The Writings of Robert Morris*. Cambridge: MIT Press, 1993.

———. "Observations on the *Observatory*." In *Robert Morris 1961–1994*. Exh. cat. Arnhem: Sonsbeek, 1971, p. 57.

Moro Abadía, Oscar. "The Reception of Paleolithic Art at the Turn of the Twentieth Century: Between Archaeology and Art History." *Journal of Art Historiography* 12 (June 2015), https://arthistoriography.files.wordpress.com/2015/06/moro-abadia.pdf.

———, Manuel R. Gonzalez Morales, and Eduardo Palacio Pérez. "'Naturalism' and the Interpretation of Cave Art." *World Art* 2.2 (2012), pp. 219–40.

Müller, Max. *Lectures on the Science of Language*. New York: Charles Scribner, 1862.

Mumford, Lewis. *Art and Technics* (1952). New York: Columbia University Press, 2000.

———. *The Transformations of Man*. New York: Harper & Brothers, 1951.

Nadaillac, Jean-François de. *Les premiers hommes et les temps préhistoriques*. 2 vols. Paris: Éditions G. Masson, 1881.

Nash, Paul. *Comments on His Own Paintings*. Paul Nash Archives, Tate Gallery, London, 769.1.52.

———. *Dorset*. London: Architectural Press, Shell Guide Collection, 1935.

———. *Fertile Image*. London: Faber and Faber, 1951.

———. "Stones." Manuscript. Paul Nash Archives, Tate Gallery, London, 760.1.22

———. *Writings on Art*. Ed. Andrew Causey. Oxford: Oxford University Press, 2000.

Neutra, Richard. *Survival through Design*. New York: Oxford University Press, 1954.

Newark, Tim, ed. *Camouflage*. London: Imperial War Museum, 2007.

Newman, Barnett. "The First Man Was an Artist." *Tiger's Eye* 1 (1947), pp. 57–60.

Niethammer, Lutz. "Afterthoughts on Posthistoire." *History and Memory* 1.1 (Spring–Summer 1989), pp. 27–53.

———. *Posthistoire: Has History Come to an End?* London: Verso, 1992.

Nietzsche, Friedrich. *Human, All Too Human: A Book for Free Spirits.* Trans. R. J. Hollingdale. Cambridge: Cambridge University Press, 1986.

———. *The Gay Science.* Trans. Thomas Common, Paul V. Cohn, and Maude D. Petre. New York: Dover, 2020.

———. *On the Use and Abuse of History.* Trans. Adrian Collins. Wikisource, https://en.wikisource.org/wiki/On_the_Use_and_Abuse_of_History_for_Life.

Nora, Pierre. "L'événement monstre." *Communications* 18 (1972), pp. 162–72.

Oldenburg, Claes. "Chapter 3: Guises of Ray Gun. The Store, 1961–1962, Notes." In Achim Hochdörfer, Maartje Oldenburg, Barbara Schröder, and Ann Temkin, eds., *Claes Oldenburg: Writing on the Side, 1956–1969.* New York: Museum of Modern Art, 2013, pp. 151–62.

Oldroyd, D. R. "Historicism and the Rise of Historical Geology." Parts 1 and 2. *History of Science* 17 (1979), pp. 191–243 and 227–325.

Olivier, Laurent. *Le sombre abîme du temps: Mémoire et archéologie.* Paris: Seuil, 2008.

Ong, Walter J. *Orality and Literacy: The Technologizing of the Word.* London: Routledge, 1982.

Ozenfant, Amédée. *Art. I: Bilan des arts modernes en France. Littérature — peinture — sculpture — architecture — musique — science — religion — philosophie. II: Structure d'un nouvel esprit.* Paris: Jean Budry, 1929.

Paillet, Patrick. "Le mammouth de la Madeline (Tursac, Dordogne)." *PALEO* 22 (2011), pp. 223–70.

Papapetros, Spyros. "Commencements ou origines — commencements et fins: Une (pré) historiographie de Sigfried Giedion." In "Dossier Sigfried Giedion." Special issue, *Les Cahiers du Musée national d'art moderne* (2015), pp. 83–89.

———. "Magic Architecture: Caves, Animals, and Tools in the Atomic Era." In Christian Thun-Hohenstein and Dieter Bogner, eds., *Friedrich Kiesler: Lebenswelten / Life Visions: Architektur-Kunst- Design* Zurich: Birkhäuser, 2016.

———. "Retracing the Eternal Present (Sigfried Giedion and André Leroi-Gourhan)." *Res: Journal of Anthropology and Aesthetics* 63–64 (Spring–Autumn 2013), pp. 173–89.

Pascal, Blaise. *Pensées.* Paris: Librairie Générale Française, 1962.

———. *Pensées.* Trans. A. J. Krailsheimer. New York: Penguin Classics, 1995.

———. *Pascal's Pensées; or, Thoughts on Religion.* Ed. and trans. Gertrude Burfurd Rawlings. Mount Vernon: Peter Pauper Press, n.d.

Pasolini, Pier Paolo. *La rabbia.* Rome: Raro Video, 2011.

Paulcke, Wilhelm. *Steinzeitkunst und Moderne Kunst: Ein Vergleich.* Stuttgart: Schweizerbartsche, 1923.

Paulhan, Jean. "Les silex de Juva ou la sculpture à l'état naissant." *La table ronde* 11 (November 1948), pp. 1885–89.

Pautrat, Jean-Yves. "L'homme antédiluvien: Les vestiges de l'homme et l'avenir des commencements." In Arnaud Hurel and Noël Coye, eds. *Dans l'épaisseur du temps: Archéologues et géologues inventent la préhistoire*. Paris: Museum National d'Histoire Naturelle, 2011, pp. 97–149.

Perry, Rachel. "Les messages de Jean Dubuffet." *Les Cahiers du Mnam* 140 (Summer 2017), pp. 3–33.

———. "*Retour à l'ordure*: Defilement in the Postwar Work of Jean Dubuffet and Jean Fautrier." PhD diss., Harvard University, 2000.

Petersen, Stephen. *Space-Age Aesthetics: Lucio Fontana, Yves Klein, and the Postwar European Avant-Garde*. University Park: Pennsylvania State University Press, 2009.

Pevsner, Nikolaus. *High Victorian Design: A Study of the Exhibits of 1851*. London: Architectural Press, 1951.

Pezolet, Nicola. "The Cavern of Antimatter: Giuseppe 'Pinot' Gallizio and the Technological Imaginary of the Early Situationist International," *Grey Room* 38 (Winter 2010), pp. 62–89.

Pfisterer, Ulrich. "Altamira — oder: Die Anfänge von Kunst und Kunstwissenschaft." In Martin Mosebach, ed., *Die Gärten von Capri*. Berlin: Akademie-Verlag, 2007.

———. "Origins and Principles of World Art History: 1900 (and 2000)." In Kitty Zijlmans and Wilfried Van Damme, eds., *World Art Studies: Exploring Concepts and Approaches*. Amsterdam: Valiz, 2008, pp. 69–89.

Pierre, Arnauld. "Udnie mécanique: Un théâtre d'automates à l'ère de Dada / Mechanical Udnie: A Theater of Automata in the Days of Dada." In William A. Camfield, Beverley Calté, Candace Clements, and Arnauld Pierre, eds., *Francis Picabia: Catalogue raisonné, vol. 2, (1915–1927)*. Brussels: Fonds Mercator, 2016, pp. 146–81.

Piette, Édouard. *Hiatus et lacune: Vestiges de la période de transition dans la grotte du Mas-d'Azil*. Beaugency: J. Laffray, 1895.

———. *Notes pour servir à l'histoire de l'art primitif*. Paris: G. Masson, 1894.

Pitt Rivers, Augustus Lane-Fox. "Primitive Warfare" (1867). In Augustus Lane-Fox Pitt Rivers, *The Evolution of Culture and Other Essays*. Oxford: Clarendon Press of Oxford University Press, 1906.

———. "Principles of Classification" (1875). In *The Evolution of Culture and Other Essays*.

Pinsard, C. J. "Préhistorique — origine d'Amiens: La première hache en pierre authentiquement découverte à Saint-Acheul." Album of photos and sketches, texts, and handwritten notes. In Étienne Jules Adolphe Desmier, vicomte d'Archiac, et al., *1859: Naissance de la préhistoire. Récits des premiers témoins*. Paris: Paléo, 1999, pp. 252–54.

Pictet, Adolphe. *Les origines indo-européennes ou les Aryas primitifs: Essai de paléontologie linguistique*. Paris: Joël Cherbuliez, 1859.

Pinot-Gallizio, Giuseppe. *Pinot Gallizio: Il laboratorio della Scrittura / The Laboratory of Writing*. Ed. Giorgina Bertolino, Francesca Comisso, and Maria Teresa Roberto. Milan: Charta, 2005.

Plato, *The Theaetetus*. Trans. F. A. Paley. London: George Bell & Sons, 1875.

Ponti, Lisa. "Primo graffito dell'età atomica (Dalla Mostra d'arte spaziale tenuta da Lucio Fontana al Naviglio, a Milano, February 5, 1949." *Domus* 233 (February 1949), p. 44.

Pound, Ezra. *Gaudier Brzeska: A Memoir*. London: John Lane, 1916.

Proust, Marcel. *Swann's Way*. Trans. C. K. Scott Moncrieff. New York: Vintage, 1970.

Quinet, Edgar. *La création*. 2 vols. Paris: Librairie internationale, 1870.

Raphaël, Max. "Les fondements de l'art pariétal." In Patrick Brault, ed., *Trois essais sur la signification de l'art pariétal paléolithique*. Paris: Le couteau dans la plaie / Kronos, 1986, pp. 21–50.

———. "À propos du fronton de Corfou." *Minotaure* 1 (June 1933), pp. 6–7.

———. "Réflexions méthodologiques sur l'interprétation de l'art quaternaire." In Patrick Brault, ed., *Trois essais sur la signification de l'art pariétal paléolithique*, pp. 109–84.

Rancière, Jacques. *Les mots de l'histoire: Essai de poétique du savoir*. Paris: Seuil, 1992.

Raymond, Paul. "Gravures de la grotte magdalénienne de Jean-Louis à Alguèze (Gard)." *Bulletins et mémoires de la Société d'anthropologie de Paris* 7 (1889), pp. 643–45.

Raynal, Maurice. *Anthologie de la peinture française de 1906 à nos jours*. Paris: Montagne, 1927.

Read, Herbert. *40, 000 Years of Modern Art: A Comparison of Primitive and Modern*, exh. cat. London: ICA, 1948.

———. *Icon and Idea*. Cambridge, MA: Harvard University Press, 1955.

———. Inaugural speech, December 1948, Tate Gallery, London. ICA Archives, TGA, 955/1/12/12.

Reichle, Ingeborg. "Vom Ursprung der Bilder und den Anfang der Kunst: Zur Logik des interkulturellen Bildvergleichs um 1900." In Martina Baleva, Ingeborg Reichle, and Oliver Lerone Schultz, eds., *IMAGE MATCH: Visueller Transfer, "Imagescapes" und Intervisualität in globalen Bild-Kulturen*. Munich: Wilhelm Fink, 2012, pp. 131–50.

Reinach, Salomon. *Antiquités nationales: Description raisonnée, Musée de Saint-Germain-en-Laye, I. Époque des alluvions et des cavernes*. Paris: Librairie de Firmin-Didot, 1889.

———. *Apollo: Histoire générale des arts plastiques*. Paris: Hachette, 1904.

———. *Cultes, mythes et religions.* 5 vols. Paris: Ernest Leroux, 1905.

———. Review of Gustave Chauvet, *Notes sur l'art primitif: La chronique des arts et de la curiosité* 6 (1903), p. 47.

Renan, Ernest. *The Future of Science: Ideas of 1848* (1848). Trans. Albert D. Vandam and C. B. Pitman. London: Chapman and Hall, 1891.

———. *De l'origine du langage.* Paris: Joubert, 1848.

Raynal, Maurice. "Les arts: Conception et vision," *Gil Blas*, August 29, 1912, p. 4.

Ribot, Théodule. *Les maladies de la mémoire* (1881). Paris: Félix Alcan, 1906.

Richard, Nathalie, ed. *L'invention de la préhistoire.* Paris: Pocket, 1992.

Richer, Paul. "L'art préhistorique à propos de la statue: Le premier artiste," *L'Artiste*, 61 n.s. 1 (June 1891), pp. 453–74.

Richet, Pascal. *L'âge du monde: À la découverte de l'immensité du temps.* Paris: Seuil, 1999.

Ricoeur, Paul. *The Rule of Metaphor: The Creation of Meaning in Language.* Trans. Robert Czerny with Kathleen McLaughlin and John Costello. London: Routledge, 2003.

———. *Time and Narrative, Volume 1.* Trans. Kathleen McLaughlin and David Pellauer. Chicago: University of Chicago Press, 1984.

Riegl, Aloïs. *Questions de style.* Paris: Hazan, 1992.

Rivera, Diego. "Del arte" (1947). In Diego Rivera, *Obras.* 3 vols, in 4. Ed. Esther Acevedo, Leticia Torres Carmona, and Alicia Sánchez Mejorada. Mexico City: El Colegio Nacional, 1996–1999. Vol. 2, pt. 1. *Textos polémicos (1921–1949).*

Robert Smithson and Nancy Holt Papers, Archives of American Art, Smithsonian Institution.

Roberts, Jennifer L. *Mirror-Travels: Robert Smithson and History.* New Haven: Yale University Press, 2004.

Roger, Jacques. *Buffon: A Life in Natural History.* Ed. L. Pearce Williams. Trans. Sarah Lucille Bonnefoi. Ithaca: Cornell University Press. 1997.

Rolland, Romain, and Frans Masereel. *Liluli, suivi de La Révolte des machines.* Montreuil: Le temps des cerises, 2015.

Roosevelt, Theodore. "A Layman's View of an Art Exhibition." *Outlook* 103, March 29, 1913, p. 719.

Rossi, Paolo. *The Dark Abyss of Time: The History of the Earth and the History of Nations from Hooke to Vico.* Chicago: University of Chicago Press, 1987.

Rouillé, André. *La photographie en France: Textes et controverses, une anthologie, 1816–1871.* Paris: Macula, 1989.

Rousseau, Jean-Jacques. *A Discourse on Inequality*. Trans. Maurice Cranston. New York: Penguin Classics, 1985.

Routledge's Guide to the Crystal Palace and Park at Sydenham. London: Routledge, 1854.

Rudwick, Martin J. S. *Bursting the Limits of Time: The Reconstruction of Geohistory in the Age of Revolution*. Chicago: University of Chicago Press, 2005.

———. *Georges Cuvier, Fossil Bones, and Geological Catastrophes*. Chicago: University of Chicago Press, 1997.

———. *The Meaning of Fossils: Episodes in the History of Palaeontology*. London: Macdonald, 1972.

———. *Scenes from Deep Time: Early Pictorial Representations of the Prehistoric World*. Chicago: University of Chicago Press, 1992.

Rupke, Nicolaas. "'The End of History' in the Early Picturing of Geological Time." *History of Science* 36.1 (1998), pp. 61–90.

Ruskin, John. *The Letters of John Ruskin: 1827–1869*. Volume 36 of *The Works of John Ruskin*. Ed. E. T. Cook and Alexander Wedderburn. 39 vols. London: George Allen, 1909.

Sahlins, Marshall. "La première société d'abondance." *Les Temps modernes* 24.268 (October 1968), pp. 641–80.

———. "The Sadness of Sweetness: The Native Anthropology of Western Cosmology." *Current Anthropology* 37.3 (June 1996), pp. 395–428.

———. *Stone Age Economics*. Chicago: Aldine-Atherton, 1972.

Sartre, Jean-Paul. *Existentialism and Humanism*. Trans. Philip Mairet. 1946; London: Eyre Methuen, 1973.

———. "L'homme et les choses." In *Critiques littéraires (Situations I)*. Paris: Gallimard, 1947, pp. 298–358.

———. "Jean-Paul Sartre répond." Interview with Bernard Pingaud. Special issue, "Sartre aujourd'hui," *L'arc* (October 1966), pp. 87–96.

Schapiro, Meyer. "The Apples of Cézanne: An Essay on the Meaning of Still-Life." *Art News Annual* 34 (1968), pp. 34–53.

———. *Paul Cézanne*. New York: Harry N. Abrams, 1952.

Schivelbusch, Wolfgang. *The Railway Journey: The Industrialization of Time and Space in the Nineteenth Century*. Trans. Anselm Hollo. Berkeley: University of California Press, 2014.

Schlanger, Nathan. "Boucher de Perthes au travail. Industrie et préhistoire au XIXe siècle." In Kapil Raj and H. Otto Dibum. eds., *Modernité et globalisation, 1770–1914*. Vol. 2 of Stéphane Van Damme et al., eds., *Histoire des sciences et des savoirs*. 3 vols. Paris: Seuil, 2015, pp. 267–83.

Schmitt, Carl. *Political Theology.* Trans. George Schwab. Chicago: University of Chicago Press, 2005.

Schnapp, Alain. "Aux sources de l'antiquarisme, l'Europe ancienne et l'Amérique du Nord." *Les Nouvelles de l'archéologie,* no. 127 (2012), pp. 45–49.

———. *La conquête du passé: Aux origines de l'archéologie.* Paris: Le Livre de poche, 1993.

Schwab, Raymond. "La renaissance de l'archaïque." *Gazette des beaux-arts* (July–August 1936), pp. 1–28.

Sebastiani, Silvia, "L'orang-outang, l'esclave et l'humain: Une querelle des corps en régime colonial." *L'Atelier du centre des recherches historiques* 11 (2013), https://acrh.revues.org/5265.

Seibert, Elke. "Prähistorische Malerei im Museum of Modern Art in New York (1937)." *Kunsttexte.de* 2 (2014).

Seidenberg, Roderick. *Posthistoric Man: An Inquiry.* Chapel Hill: University of North Carolina Press, 1950.

Semon, Richard. *Die Mneme als erhaltendes Prinzip im Wechsel des organischen Geschehens.* Leipzig: Engelmann, 1904.

Serres, Michel, *Le contrat naturel.* Paris: Flammarion, 1992.

———. *Éclaircissements: Entretiens avec Bruno Latour.* Paris: François Bourin, 1992.

———, with Bruno Latour. *Conversations on Science, Culture, and Time.* Trans. Roxanne Lapidus. Ann Arbor: University of Michigan Press, 1995.

Shield, Peter. *Comparative Vandalism: Asger Jorn and the Artistic Attitude to Life.* Aldershot: Ashgate, in association with Borgen, 1997.

Shklovsky, Viktor. "Art as Technique." https://www.cbpbu.ac.in/userfiles/file/2020/STUDY_MAT/ENGLISH/JS/30-04-20/Art%20as%20Technique%20-%20Shklovsky.pdf.

Simond, Louis. *Voyage en Angleterre pendant les années 1810–1811.* 2 vols. Paris: Treuttel et Würtz, 1817.

Sloterdijk, Peter. *In the World Interior of Capitalism.* Trans. Wieland Hoban. Cambridge: Polity, 2015.

Smiles, Sam. "Equivalents for the Megaliths: Prehistory and English Culture, 1920–50." In David Peters Corbett, Ysanne Holt, and Fiona Russell, eds., *The Geographies of Englishness: Landscape and the National Past, 1880–1940.* New Haven: Yale University Press, 2002, pp. 199–223.

Smith, Rachel. "Barbara Hepworth, Prehistory and the Cornish Landscape." *Sculpture Journal* 17.2 (2008), pp. 9–22.

Smith, William. *Strata Identified by Organized Fossils*. London: W. Arding, 1816.

Smithson, Robert. *The Collected Writings*. Ed. Jack Flam. Berkeley: University of California Press, 1996.

Sommer, Marianne, "Earth History and the Order of Society: William Buckland, the French Connection and the Conundrum of Teleology." In Henning Trüper, Dipesh Chakrabarty, and Sanjay Subrahmanyam, eds, *Historical Teleologies in the Modern World*. London: Bloomsbury, 2015, pp. 71–87.

Spies, Werner. *Picasso: Das Plastische Werk*. Nationalgalerie Berlin, Gerd Hatje, 1983.

Starobinski, Jean. *Jean-Jacques Rousseau: Transparency and Obstruction*. Trans. Arthur Goldhammer. Chicago: University of Chicago Press, 1988.

———. *La mélancolie au miroir: Trois lectures de Baudelaire*. Paris: Julliard, 1989.

Stavrinaki, Maria. "L'âge de l'étonnement: Préhistoire et jeu d'échelles chez Robert Smithson." In Céline Flécheux and Jean-Pierre Criqui, eds. *Robert Smithson: Paysage et entropie*. Dijon: Les presses du réel, 2018, pp. 169–88.

———. "All the Time in the World: Art and Prehistory." *Artforum* (March 2018), pp. 202–14.

———. "Beyond Simplicity: The Late Prehistory of the Moderns." In Albrecht Koschorke, ed., *Komplexität und Einfachheit: DFG-Symposion 2015*. Stuttgart: J. B. Metzler, 2017, pp. 573–601.

———. "Circuit fermé: De l'usage de l'histoire et du mythe par Jean Dubuffet." In Baptiste Brun and Isabelle Marquette, eds., *Jean Dubuffet, un Barbare en Europe*. Exh. cat. Paris: Hazan, 2019, pp. 68–75.

———. *Contraindre à la liberté: Carl Einstein, les avant-gardes, l'histoire*. Paris: Centre allemand d'histoire de l'art / Dijon: Les presses du réel, 2018.

———. *Dada Presentism: An Essay on Art and History*. Trans. Daniela Ginsburg. Stanford: Stanford University Press, 2016.

———. "'Enfant né sans mère, mère morte sans enfant': Les historiens de l'art face à la préhistoire." In "Préhistoire/Modernité," eds. Rémi Labrusse and Maria Stavrinaki. Special issue, *Les Cahiers du Musée national d'art moderne* 126 (Winter 2013–2014), pp. 4–13.

———. "Fossil." In Brooke Holmes and Karen Marta, eds., *Liquid Antiquity*. Athens: DESTE Foundation for Contemporary Art, 2017, pp. 174–77.

———. "L'histoire de l'art à l'épreuve de la préhistoire, 19e–21e siècles: Petite histoire d'une stupeur surmontée." In Pierre Monnet, Thomas Maissen, and Barbara Mittler, eds., *L'usage des temporalités dans les sciences humaines et sociales*. Bochum: Winkler, 2019.

———. "Lascaux-Hiroshima: La préhistoire de Pierre Huyghe à Georges Bataille." *Les Cahiers du musée national d'art moderne* 135 (Spring 2016), pp. 25–63.

——. "Modernité préhistorique: Techniques d'"auto-imitation' et temporalités à rebours dans l'art de Max Ernst et de Joan Miró." *Perspective* 3 (June 2011), pp. 574–79.

——. "Oralité et anonymat: Un nouveau paradigme historique dans la pensée du médium après la Deuxième Guerre mondiale." In Larysa Dryansky and Antonio Somaini, eds., *Actes du colloque international Repenser le médium: Matière technique et transmission dans l'art contemporain et le cinéma*. Dijon: Les presses du réel, 2021.

——. "La puissance diluvienne de l'art: Esquisse des usages de la préhistoire par Picasso." *Actes du colloque international Revoir Picasso*. Paris: Musée Picasso, 2015, http://revoir-picasso.fr/face-a-loeuvre/la-puissance-diluvienne-de-lart-esquisse-des-usages-de-la-prehistoire-par-picasso-%E2%80%A2-m-stavrinaki.

——. *Saisis par la préhistoire: Enquête sur l'art et le temps des modernes*. Dijon: Les presses du réel, 2019.

——. "Überleben in Afrika: Wiederauferstehung für Europa. Leo Frobenius' Sicht der Vorgeschichte." In Karl-Heinz Kohl, Richard Kuba, and Hélène Ivanoff, eds., *Leo Frobenius*. Berlin: Martin Gropius Bau, 2016, pp. 33–42.

——. "Warum haben sich die Dreißigerjahre mit der Steinzeit identifiziert?" / "Why Did the 1930s Identify with Prehistory?" In Anselm Franke and Tom Holert, eds, *Neolithische Kindheit / Neolithic Childhood: Art in a False Present, c. 1930*. Exh. cat. Berlin: Haus der Kulturen der Welt / Diaphanes, 2018, pp. 84–92.

——. "'We Escape Ourselves': The Invention and Interiorization of the Age of the Earth in the Nineteenth Century." *Res: Anthropology and Aesthetics* 69–70 (Spring–Autumn 2018), pp. 20–37.

Steinberg, Leo. "Resisting Cézanne: Picasso's Three Women of 1908." *Art in America* 66 (November–December 1978), pp. 114–33, 2008.

Steno, Nicolaus. *De solido intra solidum naturaliter contento dissertationis prodromus*. Florence: Ex typographia sub signo Stellæ, 1699.

Stiegelmann, Adolf. *Altamira: Ein Kunsttempel des Urmenschen*. Godesberg-Bonn: Kulturwissenschaftliche Zeitfragen, 1910.

Stiegler, Bernard. "Leroi-Gourhan: L'inorganique organisé." *Les Cahiers de médiologie* 2.1 (1998), pp. 187–94.

——. *Technics and Time, 1: The Fault of Epimethus*. Trans. Richard Beardsworth and George Collins. Stanford: Stanford University Press, 1998.

Stich, Sidra. *Joan Miró: The Development of a Sign Language*. Saint Louis: Washington University Press, 1980.

Stoczkowski, Wiktor. *Anthropologie naïve, anthropologie savante*. Paris: CNRS Éditions, 1995.

———, ed. *Aux origines de l'humanité*. Paris: Agora Pocket, 1996.

———. *Explaining Human Origins: Myth, Imagination and Conjecture*. New York: Cambridge University Press, 2002.

———. "La Préhistoire dans les manuels scolaires ou notre mythe des origines." *L'Homme* 30.116 (1990), pp. 111–35.

———. "La préhistoire: Les origines du concept." *Bulletin de la société préhistorique française* 90.1–2 (1993), pp. 13–21.

Stout, Adam. *Creating Prehistory: Druids, Ley Hunters and Archaeologists in Pre-War Britain*. Hoboken: Wiley-Blackwell, 2008.

Stracey, Frances. "The Caves of Gallizio and Hirschhorn: Excavations of the Present." *October* 116 (Spring 2006), pp. 87–100.

———. "Pinot Gallizio's 'Industrial Painting': Towards a Surplus of Life." *Oxford Art Journal* 28.3 (2005), pp. 393–405.

Szondi, Peter. *An Essay on the Tragic*. Trans. Paul Fleming. Stanford: Stanford University Press, 2002.

Tapié, Michel. *Mirobolus, Macadam et Cie Hautes Pâtes*. Exh. cat. Paris: René Drouin, 1946.

Taylor, Michael A. "Mary Anning (1799–1847) and the Photograph *The Geologists* Ascribed to William Henry Fox Talbot (1800–1877)." *Geoscience in South-West England* 13.4 (2015), pp. 419–27.

Tepper, Rowan. "Time and History after Post-Histoire," https://www.academia.edu/31936422/Time_and_History_After_Post-Histoire.

Tiberghien, Gilles. *Land Art*. Paris: Carré, 1993.

Toulmin, Stephen, and June Goodfield. *The Discovery of Time*. New York: Harper & Row, 1965.

Trautmann, Thomas. "The Revolution in Ethnological Time." *Man*, n.s. 27.2 (June 1992), pp. 379–97.

Tsai, Eugenie ed., with Cornelia Butler. *Robert Smithson*. Exh. cat. Los Angeles: Museum of Contemporary Art, 2004.

Tuma, Kathryn A. "Cézanne and Lucretius at the Red Rock." *Representations* 78.1 (Spring 2002), pp. 56–85.

Tylor, Edward. "On the Tasmanians as Representatives of Palaeolithic Man." *Journal of the Anthropological Institute of Great Britain and Ireland* 23 (1894), pp. 141–52.

———. *Primitive Culture: Researches into the Development of Mythology, Philosophy, Religion, Language, Art, and Custom*, 1871; New York: Henry Holt, 1889.

Ubl, Ralph. "Giorgio de Chirico. Exkarnation und Filiation der Malerei." In Johannes

Endres, Barbara Wittmann, and Gerhard Wolf, eds., *Ikonologie des Zwischenraums: Der Schleier als Medium und Metapher*. Munich: Wilhelm Fink Verlag, 2005, pp. 385–416.

———. *Prehistoric Future: Max Ernst and the Return of Painting between the Wars*. Trans. Elizabeth Tucker. Chicago: University of Chicago Press, 2013.

———. "Préhistoire et histoire moderne. *L'Europe après la pluie*, 1933." In Giovanni Careri and Bernhard Rüdiger, eds., *Le temps suspendu*. Lyon: Presses universitaires de Lyon, 2016.

Umland, Anna. "Joan Miró and Collage in the 1920s: The Dialectic of Painting and Anti-Painting." PhD diss., Institute of Fine Arts, New York, 1997.

———, ed. *Joan Miró: Painting and Anti-Painting, 1927–1937*. New York: Museum of Modern Art, 2008.

Valéry, Paul. *Regards sur le monde actuel*. In Paul Valéry, *Regards sur le monde actuel et autres essais*. Paris: Folio Essais, 1990.

Van de Velde, Henry. "Manuscript on Ornament. Chapter 1: 'The Historic Survey of Linear Ornament and Its Development.'" Trans. Ellie G. Haddad and Rosemary Anderson. *Journal of Design History* 16.2 (2003), pp. 139–55.

Véron, Eugène. *L'esthétique: Origine des arts, le goût et le génie*. Paris: C. Reinwald, 1878.

Verworn, Max. *Expressionismus: Die Kunstwende*. Ed Herwarth Walden. Berlin: Der Sturm, 1918. Reprinted as an article under the title "Die Entwicklung der ideoplastischen Kunst," *Der Sturm* 10 (January 1919), pp. 126–28.

———. *Zur Psychologie der primitiven Kunst: Ein Vortrag*. Munich: Gustav Fischer, 1907.

Vico, Giambattista. *The New Science of Giambattista Vico*. Trans. Thomas Goddard Bergin and Max Harold Fisch. Ithaca: Cornell University Press, 1948.

Vitruvius. *The Ten Books on Architecture*. Trans. Morris Hicky Morgan. Cambridge, MA: Harvard University Press, 1914.

Von Ranke, Leopold. *Geschichten der romanischen und germanischen Völker*. Vol. 33 of Leopold Von Ranke, *Sämmtliche Werke*. 54 vols. in 24. Leipzig, Duncker und Humblot, 1868–1890.

Von den Steinen, Karl. *Unter den Naturvölkern Zentral-Brasiliens: Reiseschilderung und Ergebnisse der Zweiten Schingu-Expedition (1887–1888)*. Berlin: Dietrich Reimer, 2004.

Von Scheltema, Frederik Adama. *Die altnordische Kunst: Grundprobleme vorhistorischer Kunstentwicklung*. Berlin: In Mauritius, 1922.

Von Sydow, Eckhart. *Die Kunst der Naturvölker und der Vorzeit*. Berlin: Propuläen, 1923.

Youngblood, Gene. *Expanded Cinema*. Introduction by R. Buckminster Fuller. New York: P. Dutton, 1970.

Wagstaff, Sheena. "A Conversation with Pierre Huyghe." In Ian Alteveer, Meredith

Brown, and Sheena Wagstaff, *The Roof Garden Commission: Pierre Huyghe*. New York: Metropolitan Museum of Art, 2015, pp. 23–34.

Wallace, Alfred R. "The Origin of Human Races and the Antiquity of Man Deduced from the Theory of "Natural Selection." *Journal of the Anthropological Society of London* 2 (1864), pp. clviii–clxxvii.

Wäspe, Roland, ed. *On Kawara 1964 Paris-New York Drawings*. Exh. cat. St. Gallen: Kunstverein St. Gallen Kunstmuseum, 1997.

Weart, Spencer R. *Nuclear Fear: A History of Images*. Cambridge, MA: Harvard University Press, 1988.

Welinder, Stig. "The Word *Förhistorisk*, 'Prehistoric,' in Swedish," *Antiquity* 65 (1991), pp. 295–96.

Wells, H. G. "The Extinction of Man" (1894). In *Certain Personal Matters*. London: Lawrence & Bullen, 1897, pp. 172–79.

Werth, Margaret. *The Joy of Life: The Idyllic in French Art, circa 1900*. Berkeley: University of California Press, 2002.

Whewell, William, *History of the Inductive Sciences from the Earliest Times to the Present*. 3 vols. London: J. W. Parker, 1837.

Whistler, J. A. M. "Ten o'Clock." Boston: Houghton, Mifflin., 1899, n.p., https://www.google.com/books/edition/TEN_O_CLOCK/ uo_eRSoSYiAC?hl=en&gbpv=1&bsq=first%20artist.

White, Hayden V. "The Burden of History." *History and Theory* 5.2 (1966), pp. 111–34.

Whitmann, Barbara. "A Neolithic Childhood: Children's Drawings as Prehistoric Sources." *Res: Anthropology and Aesthetics* 63–64 (Spring–Autumn 2013), pp. 123–42.

Wilde, Oscar. "The Decay of Lying." In Oscar Wilde, *Intentions*. New York: Brentano's 1905, pp. 1–57.

Wilson, Daniel. *The Archaeology and Prehistoric Annals of Scotland*. Edinburgh: Sutherland and Knox, 1851.

———. *Prehistoric Man*. London: Macmillan, 1862.

Woolf, Virginia. *Between the Acts* (1941), http://gutenberg.net.au/ebooks03/0301171h.html, n.p.

Wundt, Wilhelm. *Völkerpsychologie: Eine Untersuchung der Entwicklungsgesetze von Sprache, Mythus und Sitte*. 10 vols. Leipzig: Wilhelm Engelmann, 1911–1912.

Zakariya, Nasser. "Scenes before Grey Antiquity." In "Writing Prehistory," eds. Maria Stavrinaki and Stephanos Geroulanos. Special issue, *Res: Anthropology and Aesthetics* 69–70 (2018), pp. 5–19.

Zervos, Christian. *L'art de l'époque du renne en France, avec une étude sur la formation de la science préhistorique par Henri Breuil.* Paris: Éditions Cahiers d'Art, 1959.

Zimmermann, Virginia. *Excavating Victorians.* Albany: State University of New York Press, 2008.

Index

Picasso, 185–87, 222; *Graffiti*, 185, *186*, 222; photography of Picasso, 185, *187*.

Braudel, Fernand: and the *longue durée*, 25, 45, 38, 91, 273; *Man before Writing*, 273; *Memory and the Mediterranean*, 45.

Breuil, Henri: and Altamira, 139, 144; and Font-de-Gaume and Les Combarelles, 140, *141*, *142*, 362 n.83; in front of Lascaux entrance, *298*; on the origin of art, 153, 155, 199; "Origins of Art," 140–44, *143*, 175; *400 siècles d'art pariétal, 282*.

British modernists, 206, 208–209, 250, 266; formalism, 246, 261.

Brixham Cave, 115.

Brunel-Deschamps, Eliette, 391 n.1.

Bruniquel (Courbet Cave), 122, *123*, 133.

Buckland, Reverend William, 40, 41, 68.

Buffon, Georges, 9–10, 120, 328; *Les époques de la nature*, 33, 35, 89, 339 n.2.

Burgess, Gelett, "The Wild Men of Paris," 178.

Bushmen, 142, 151, 157, 178.

Busts, 156–57. *See also* "Venuses."

Butler, Samuel, *Erewhon*, 71, 89–90.

Byron, Lord, *Cain*, 345 n.38.

CAILLOIS, ROGER, 297.

Camouflage, 90, 153.

Canguilhem, Georges, 341 n.21.

Capitalism, 266, 330; critiques of, 22, 87, 94, 98, 197, 209, 319; and commercialization, 95, 251; and the Industrial Revolution, 73–74; and standardization, 251, 274.

Capitan, Louis, 140, *141*, 161, 362 n.83; "Origins of Art," 140–44, *143*, 175.

"Care," 168–69.

Caro, Anthony, 100, 101.

Carrieri, Raffaele, 309–11.

Cartailhac, Émile, 131–33, 139, 146, 147, 152, 159.

Carus, Carl Gustav, 242.

Catastrophism, 32, 33, 40, 43, 54, 294, 344 n.29, 345 n.38; Cuvier and, 26, 32, 70, 345 n.32; Lyell's critique of, 44–45, 70–71.

Catlin, George, 153.

Cave art: approaches to, 26–27; appropriated by twentieth-century moderns, 15–16, 227, *334*, 335; archaeology and, 227–28; Benjamin on, 204–205; copying of, 142–44, 209–212, *212*; discovery of, 13–15, 134;

engravings, 139–40; and impressionism, 179–80; interpretation of, 140–42, 146–48, 148, 152; and Matisse's *Joy of Life*, 171, 175; naturalism of, 78, 140, 204, 249; purpose of, 144, 146; reception of, 16, 139, 140, 340 n.17; and surrealism, 223; and the Vorticist movement, 194–95. *See also* Mural paintings.

"Caveman of Manhattan," 330–31.

Caves, 275, 330–31; decorated, 139–40. *See also* Altamira; cave art; Chauvet-Pont-d'Arc Cave; Font-de-Gaume; Lascaux.

Caylus, comte de, 242.

Céline, Louis-Ferdinand, 236.

Cézanne, Paul, 10, 42, 328; bathers, 57, 176; *Bibémus Quarries*, 58, 59, 231; *The Eternal Feminine*, 66; geological sketches, 60–61; human figures, 57, 60, 64–66; and impressionism, 61, 350 n.106; *In the Bibémus Quarries*, 64–66, *65*; landscapes of Aix-en-Provence, 57–66, 79, 351 n.136; *The Millstone*, 58; Mont Sainte-Victoire motif, 57–58, 61–62, 66, 351 n.136; Morris on, 66–67, 270; repressed sexuality of, 59, 66; sketchbooks, 60, *62–63*, 349 n.102; Smithson and, 101, 355 n.189; still lifes, 59.

Chabot Cave, 139.

Chakrabarty, Dipesh, 328–29, 330.

Charleton, Walter, 241–42.

Chauvet, Jean-Marie, 391 n.1.

Chauvet-Pont-d'Arc Cave, 325, 335, 391 n.1; *The Ride, 326*.

Chirico, Giorgio de: "antianthropic remedies," 84, 86, 329; comparisons to, 37, 81, 83, 171, 174, 208, 218; defamiliarization in, 86–87; *The Fatal Temple*, 81, *82*; geological metaphors, 83, 85–86, 87, 107; interest in fossils, 78–79; *The Melancholy of Departure, 80*; as observed by Nash, 256; and Picasso, 81, 351 n.137; *pittura metafisica*, 23, 79, 81–84, 94, 352 n.148; *Portrait of Guillaume Apolliniare*, 81; on prehistoric art, 83, 85, 180; on regression to prehistory, 85, 352 n.145; on role of art, 79–81; use of contradictory perspectives, 88.

Chiron, Léopold, 139.

Christianity, 96–99, 296; the Fall, 40, 68, 164, 296, 386 n.67; the flood, 114, 115. *See also* Bible.

Zone Books series design by Bruce Mau

Typesetting by Meighan Gale

Image placement and production by Julie Fry

Printed and bound by Maple Press